THE MINOR PROPHETS

AN
EXPOSITIONAL
COMMENTARY

Volume 1

Hosea-Jonah

Books by Dr. Boice . . .

Witness and Revelation in the Gospel of John
Philippians: An Expositional Commentary
The Sermon on the Mount
How to Live the Christian Life (originally, *How to Really Live It Up*)
Ordinary Men Called by God (originally, *How God Can Use Nobodies*)
The Last and Future World
The Gospel of John: An Expositional Commentary (5 volumes in one)
"Galatians" in the *Expositor's Bible Commentary*
Can You Run Away From God?
Our Sovereign God, editor
Our Savior God: Studies on Man, Christ and the Atonement, editor
Foundations of the Christian Faith (4 volumes in one)
The Foundation of Biblical Authority, editor
The Epistles of John
Does Inerrancy Matter?
Making God's Word Plain, editor
Genesis: An Expositional Commentary (3 volumes)
The Parables of Jesus
The Christ of Christmas
The Christ of the Open Tomb
Standing on the Rock
The Minor Prophets: An Expositional Commentary (2 volumes)
Christ's Call to Discipleship
Daniel: An Expositional Commentary (available in 1989)
Ephesians: An Expositional Commentary (available in 1989)

THE MINOR PROPHETS

AN EXPOSITIONAL COMMENTARY

JAMES MONTGOMERY BOICE

Ministry Resources Library

Zondervan Publishing House • Grand Rapids, MI

THE MINOR PROPHETS
VOLUME 1: HOSEA–JONAH
Copyright © 1983 by The Zondervan Corporation
Grand Rapids, Michigan

Requests for information should be addressed to:
Zondervan Publishing House
Academic and Professional Books
Grand Rapids, Michigan 49530

Library of Congress Cataloging in Publication Data

Boice, James Montgomery, 1938–
   The Minor Prophets.

   Includes index.
   Contents: v. 1. Hosea–Jonah.
   1. Bible. O.T. Minor Prophets—Commentaries.
I. Bible. O.T. Minor Prophets. English. 1983.   II. Title.
BS1560.B57 1983   224′.9077   83-5794

ISBN 0-310-21551-X (v. 1)

Printed in the United States of America

92 93 94 / CH / 12 11 10 9 8

*To the Lord our God,
gracious and compassionate,
slow to anger and abounding
in love*

Contents

Preface

One winter several years after I had begun my ministry at Tenth Presbyterian Church in Philadelphia, which I still serve, I decided to preach on the Minor Prophets. My motives were not noble. I had recently completed a very heavy load of writing, and I was looking for books that were not too long and which I could handle, as I thought, without an unusual amount of difficulty. I was not expecting much, but as I began to preach, the Minor Prophets came alive with such force (even with my little preparation) that I decided to stop the series until I would have time to study them more thoroughly and write the studies for eventual release in book form.

It took me some time to get to them. And when I did, I found that I could not simply rush through them as one might push on through other, better-known books of the Bible. These works were powerful. They spoke to present sins and called for present action. I found that I could not absorb more than one or two at a time, and as a result I spread out the preaching on these books over ten years.

The proper way to describe their impact on me is to say that they dramatize the character of God as few other books do. They emphasize three basic attributes. First, they highlight God's sovereignty. Indeed, they do more than merely highlight it; they breathe it throughout. Nothing is more central to the thinking of these twelve writers than the fact that God is the sovereign Lord of history and that nothing happens, either to Israel or to the gentile nations, that is not the result of His direct determination. The locust plague of Joel was His doing. The destruction of Ninevah was from Him, just as its earlier repentance under the preaching of Jonah was

God-given. When Israel was invaded by Assyria and Judah by Babylon, it was the Lord who did it. Whatever problems the prophets may have with the specific nature of God's actions—Habakkuk is one who had great problems—they never doubt for a second that the almighty God is in charge of history.

The second great attribute of God seen in the Minor Prophets is holiness. An awareness of holiness was the driving force behind their sharp denunciations of sin. It makes no difference where the sin was found, whether in foreign lands (Edom, as in Obadiah; Assyria, as in Nahum) or among God's people—it was still an offense to God and called for judgment. Nowhere in the Bible are there stiffer denunciations of sin and heartier calls for a deep and pervasive repentance than in the Minor Prophets. Apart from repentance, judgment falls.

Third, the prophets speak of God's love. The conjunction of love and justice is sometimes so stark that critical, liberal scholars resort to excluding sections of the books that deal with God's love. They miss a great truth when they do this, for love is not incompatible with justice. On the contrary, it is because of God's great love for His people (even His love for Nineveh) that He sends prophets with the message of judgment and, indeed, eventually sends the judgment itself. God knows that sin is an outrage against Himself, humanity, and even the one pursuing it. He knows that sin is destructive. So He judges sin—in the case of His own people in order to turn them back from sin to Himself.

We need these emphases today. We need them as individuals, for we sin and run away from God just as Israel did. We need them as a nation also, for God will not deal with America or Britain or any other contemporary nation differently in regard to its sin than He dealt with the nations of antiquity. We need to learn— deeply and in a way that changes us— that "righteousness exalts a nation, but sin is a disgrace to any people" (Prov. 14:34).

Over the years portions of these studies have been aired over the Bible Study Hour, on which I am the speaker, and they have been printed in the magazine *Bible Studies*, which is mailed monthly to supporters of the radio program. One segment, the messages on Jonah, has appeared in book form under the title *Can You Run Away from God?* (Victor Books, 1977). That book is now out of print, and the messages are included here by special, prior arrangement with Scripture Press. In preparing these studies I have been indebted to many individuals. Acknowledgment for academic help is usually given in the footnotes and text. My secretary, Miss Caecilie M. Foelster, has rendered invaluable assistance in typing the manuscript and checking points of reference.

As usual in my books, I want to thank the congregation of Tenth Presbyterian Church for allowing me time to pursue this kind of study and write these and other messages for the benefit of many beyond our immediate church fellowship.

JAMES MONTGOMERY BOICE
Philadelphia, PA

HOSEA

1

The Second Greatest Story in the Bible

(Hosea 1:1–2:1)

When the LORD *began to speak through Hosea, the* LORD *said to him, "Go, take to yourself an adulterous wife and children of unfaithfulness, because the land is guilty of the vilest adultery in departing from the* LORD.*" So he married Gomer daughter of Diblaim, and she conceived and bore him a son.*

Then the LORD *said to Hosea, "Call him Jezreel, because I will soon punish the house of Jehu for the massacre at Jezreel, and I will put an end to the kingdom of Israel. In that day I will break Israel's bow in the Valley of Jezreel."*

Gomer conceived again and gave birth to a daughter. Then the LORD *said to Hosea, "Call her Lo-Ruhamah, for I will no longer show love to the house of Israel, that I should at all forgive them. Yet I will show love to the house of Judah; and I will save them—not by bow, sword or battle, or by horses and horsemen, but by the* LORD *their God."*

After she had weaned Lo-Ruhamah, Gomer had another son. Then the LORD *said, "Call him Lo-Ammi, for you are not my people, and I am not your God."*

The prophecy of Hosea comes first in the biblical order of the Minor Prophets. Rightly so. It is not the first of the twelve either to be written or spoken, but it is first in regard to its message, being what I have called "the second greatest story in the Bible." No Christian can doubt that the greatest story in the Bible is the story of the incarnation, life, suffering, death, and resurrection of the Lord Jesus Christ. But the story of Hosea is second precisely because it is an anticipation in pageant form of Christ's story.

Hosea was a preacher during the reigns of four successive kings of Judah, the oldest and most southern of the two Jewish states, and during the reign of Jeroboam, one of the kings of the northern state of Israel—as the introductory caption to the prophecy tells us (v. 1). It must have been a long period of ministry, perhaps fifty or sixty years, but we are told nothing about Hosea's life during those years save the poignant story with which the prophecy begins.

It would seem that on one occasion, no doubt early in his life, God came to Hosea to ask him to do a very difficult thing. God said, "Hosea, I want you to marry a woman who is going to prove unfaithful to you but to whom you are nevertheless going to be faithful. You will love her, but she will disgrace your love. I am asking you to do this because we are to present a pageant to Israel by your marriage. It is going to be symbolic, an object lesson. You are going to play the part of God. The woman is going to play the part of My people. The reason she is going to run away and be unfaithful is that this is the way My people act in the spiritual marriage that I have established with them. You are going to be faithful, because I am faithful to Israel even though she dishonors My name."

Hosea married a woman named Gomer. He tells us about it in the prophecy's opening words: "When the LORD began to speak through Hosea, the LORD said to him, 'Go, take to yourself an

13

adulterous wife and children of unfaithfulness, because the land is guilty of the vilest adultery in departing from the LORD.' So he married Gomer daughter of Diblaim, and she conceived and bore him a son" (1:2, 3).

BEST AND WORST OF TIMES

A beginning like that would probably cause most readers to rush right on to see how the story was going to work out. But we should first pause to see that the age of Hosea was much like our own age and that the lessons of his story are those we also need to hear. Otherwise we are likely to be touched by the story, as we might by any moving play or novel, but dismiss it as having very little to do with ourselves.

Hosea, whose name means "salvation," lived at the same time as Isaiah (who prophesied to Judah in the south) and Amos (who visited the northern kingdom of Israel from the rural area of Tekoa). It is from these three prophets then that we learn what the characteristics of this age were. We might say, as Dickens did of eighteenth-century Europe: it was "the best of times" as well as "the worst of times." To many the period must have appeared to be a good one indeed. It was an age of luxurious materialism, apparent religious devotion and activity, freedom, and even an apparent national security in which politics, law, and religion all seemed to play into the favored people's hands. Amos is particularly clear in diagnosing this spirit. Yet, as Isaiah, Amos, and Hosea also show, it was the worst of times, because the hearts of the people were empty, religion was shallow, and corruption was rampant on every hand.

In particular, law was manipulated to the advantage of the rich, and much if not most of the religious activity was mere show. Hosea's cry is that the people had been unfaithful to God, just as an adulterous wife is unfaithful to her husband. God had blessed His people; prospered them both materially and spiritually. But they had begun to live for pleasure. They had abandoned hard work, morality, and integrity in order to live for themselves.

Can such things be said of our age, the latter quarter of the twentieth century? Some would deny it; they see only the prosperity and the apparent religious activity. But thoughtful people, who probe below the surface, see the parallel.

One person who has seen this very clearly is the brilliant Russian author Aleksandr Solzhenitsyn. He has been harshly critical of his own country, as anyone who has read the *Gulag Archipelago* knows. He cannot be accused of lopsided national pride or particularity. Yet he is also critical of the West, bringing to his remarks that insight which only the perspective of an independent observer provides. It is significant to our study of Hosea that Solzhenitsyn's criticism of the West almost precisely parallels the ancient prophet's harsh critique of Israel. Solzhenitsyn said in an address to the graduates of Harvard University in the spring of 1978, "I hope that no one present will suspect me of offering my personal criticism of the Western system to present socialism as an alternative. Having experienced applied socialism in a country where the alternative has been realised, I certainly will not speak for it. . . . But should someone ask me whether I would indicate the West such as it is today as a model to my country, frankly I would have to answer negatively. No, I could not recommend your society in its present state as an ideal for the transformation of ours. Through intense suffering our country has now achieved a spiritual development of such intensity that the Western system in its present state of spiritual exhaustion does not look attractive. Even those characteristics of your life which I have just mentioned [materialism, manipulation of law, misuses of freedom, fadism] are extremely saddening."

The observer then adds these criticisms: "After the suffering of decades of violence and oppression, the human soul longs for things higher, warmer, and purer than those offered by today's mass living habits, introduced by the revolting invasion of publicity, by TV stupor, and by intolerable music. . . .

"We have turned our backs upon the Spirit and embraced all that is material with excessive and unwarranted zeal. . . .

"Two hundred or even 50 years ago, it would have seemed quite impossible, in America, that an individual could be granted boundless freedom simply for the satisfaction of his instincts or whims. Subsequently, however, all such limitations were discarded everywhere in the West. . . .

"All the glorified technological achievements of progress, including the conquest of outer space, do not redeem the 20th century's moral poverty which no one could imagine even as late as in the 19th century. . . . Only voluntary inspired self-restraint can raise man above the world stream of materialism."[1]

Some may object that while the description that Solzhenitsyn and others have given is true of our culture at large, it is not true of the church, which is, as it has always been, a faithful remnant in the midst of an otherwise corrupt world. But is it? We note that it is precisely to those who considered themselves to be spiritual that Hosea's words were written. Is the church faithless? Does it give lip service to God while actually pursuing its own comfort and "success"? We will have to ask ourselves these questions as Hosea's story unfolds.

A REAL STORY

There is a question often raised in introductions to Hosea that bears upon the application of the story to the church and is therefore worth mentioning here. It has been objected by some—no less a commentator than John Calvin among them—that it is utterly inconceivable that God should ask one of His children, Hosea, to marry a woman who was to prove unfaithful to Him. These believe that the story must not be a real story. Rather it is something more in the nature of an allegory.

Apart from the fact that the story of Hosea's marriage is told as a real story and rings true, we must say that God does sometimes lead His children into situations that are parallel if not identical to this. We live in an age where everything good is interpreted in terms of happiness and success. So when we think of spiritual blessing we think of it in these terms. To be led of God and be blessed by God means that we will be "happy" and "successful." In fact, if a Christian does not appear to be happy or successful, there are scores of people who will be ready (like Job's counselors) to work with him or her to see what is wrong. This is shallow thinking and shallow Christianity, for God does not always lead His people into ways that we would naturally regard as happy or as filled with success. Was Jesus happy? He was undoubtedly filled with joy and all the other fruits of the Spirit. But He was also called "a man of sorrows and acquainted with grief." Was Jesus successful? Not by our standards, nor by any standards that might have been applied to Him by anyone living in that time. Let us put this down as a great principle: God sometimes leads His children to do things that afterward involve them in great distress. But because God does not think as we think or act as we act, it is often in these situations that He accomplishes His greatest victories and brings the greatest blessing to His name.

If God has allowed tragedy to slip into your life, this does not necessarily mean

---

[1]Aleksandr Solzhenitsyn, "A World Split Apart," copyright 1978 Aleksandr Solzhenitsyn, *Harvard University Gazette,* June 8, 1978, pp. 17–19.

that you were out of His will when you married that husband or wife, took that job, or made that commitment. He may be giving you a chance to show the love and character of Christ in your situation.

Again, you may be able to learn something of God's love for you through the difficulty. For what is the story of Hosea if it is not the story of ourselves as members of that body which is the bride of Christ? We are Gomer, and God is Hosea. He married us when we were unclean. He knew that we would prove unfaithful again and again. He knew that we would forsake Him. Still He loved us and purchased us to Himself through Christ's atonement. If Hosea's story cannot be real (because "God could not ask a man to marry an unfaithful woman"), then neither is the story of salvation real, because that is precisely what Christ has done for us. He has purchased us for Himself to be a bride "without stain or wrinkle or any other blemish, but holy and blameless" (Eph. 5:27), and He has done this even though He knew in advance that we would often prove faithless.

Symbolic Names

At the beginning the story is really Gomer's story, however. So we must see what the prophecy teaches about her. It tells us how children were born to Gomer and how these were named to suggest what would happen to her as the result of her unfaithfulness. It was what would happen to Israel whom she symbolizes.

Some commentators have felt that Hosea married one of the temple prostitutes, presumably because the opening command to Hosea seems to suggest that the woman was a prostitute even before the marriage. This is not right, for these words were written in retrospect. Moreover, the text says clearly that the first child at least was *Hosea's,* and not another's. No doubt Hosea married a woman who was pure at the time—though he knew the outcome of God's prediction. Perhaps Hosea and Gomer

even lived together happily for years. In any case, during the early period three children were born into the family: a son, a daughter, and another son. When each was born God intervened to give the children symbolic names.

God named the first child Jezreel (v. 4). Jezreel means "scattered." We can imagine that when Hosea first heard the name he thought that the Lord had made a mistake, for in Hebrew Jezreel is almost identical both in spelling and in sound to Israel, which means "God perseveres." "Surely the Lord means Israel," Hosea must have thought. But God did not mean Israel. He meant Jezreel ("scattered"). This was a word of judgment, and God was revealing that He was soon to scatter Israel throughout the world for her unfaithfulness.

There are three areas to which this prophecy applies. First, there is a political application to the house of Jehu for the massacre at Jezreel. This story goes back a long way. In the days of Ahab, before Jehu, that wicked king had wanted a certain vineyard that belonged to Naboth who came from the valley of Esdraelon south of Mount Carmel, called Jezreel. Ahab first offered Naboth another piece of land for his vineyard. When Naboth refused to give up his vineyard because it was a family inheritance Ahab offered him money for it. But Naboth would not sell. So, on the advice of his wife Jezebel, Ahab had Naboth killed and then took the property. God pronounced doom on Ahab's family because of this, saying that judgment would come on them in the valley of Jezreel, where Naboth had been slain. Ahab himself fell at Ramoth Gilead (1 Kings 22:29–38). Jezebel was slain in Samaria. But hundreds of others were struck down at Jezreel through Jehu, who then assumed the throne. In this judgment Jehu was fulfilling God's prophecy on the house of Ahab. But the terrible massacre of the family, friends, prophets, and hangers-on of wicked Ahab, by which Jehu ascended the throne, was itself a horror and called for judgment too. Thus, although God passed over Jehu himself, because he was God's tool in judging Ahab, He indicates in this prophecy that Jehu's descendants, the "house of Jehu," will be judged.

A second, fuller application of the prophecy is to Israel herself. Jezreel means "scattered." So since Hosea is prophesying not long before the fall of Samaria and the captivity of the people of the northern kingdom in 722 B.C., he is really forecasting the scattering of the Jewish people that began in 722 B.C. and then continued through successive disasters and deportations in the south. Today the people of Israel are scattered all the way from Samaria to San Francisco, from Nazareth to New York.

Third, this is an application to others than the Jewish people. When we read prophecy we have a tendency to apply it only to others, but we need to apply it to ourselves as well. The principle involved here is that when you reject God you get into trouble. Hosea is a story of God's faithfulness and love, but one expression of His love is chastisement, just as the love of a father for a son will cause him to discipline that son when he is disobedient. I think of Jonah in this connection. Jonah ran away from God. But he never got to where he was going, and he did not get a refund on his ticket though he had paid in full for it. When you run away from God you never get to where you are going and you always pay your own bills. But when you go God's way you always get to where you are going and He pays the bills. God is faithful, but one expression of His faithfulness is that when we run away from Him things will not go well. God guarantees that they will not go well. He will scatter our dreams in our faces. You may think that you are going to satisfy yourself by seizing the world and its pleasures, but God will cause them to turn to dust in your mouth, even as you de-

vour them greedily.

When the second child, a daughter, was born we are not told that she was born *to Hosea*, as was the case with the first child (to "him," v. 3). This seems to mean (1:2 and 2:4, 5 reinforce it) that by this time Gomer had already played Hosea false and the daughter was not his child. If this was the case, it is remarkable that Hosea did not chide or take the case to the divorce courts, which was his right. Instead, he continued in the marriage, naming the second child Lo-Ruhamah as the Lord directed (v. 6).

Lo-Ruhamah is composed of two Hebrew words, *lo* meaning "no" or "not" and *ruhamah* meaning "pitied" or "loved." God was saying, "We are going to call this child Not-Loved because the time is coming when the sin of the people will cause Me to have no pity on them." Does this sound strange to you? Throughout the Bible God is repeatedly referred to as a God of great love and constant pity. The Bible says, "As a father has compassion on his children, so the LORD has compassion on ('pitieth,' KJV) those who fear him" (Ps. 103:13). It says, "For the LORD is good and his love endures forever" (Ps. 100:5). In Psalm 136 we are told twenty-six times that the love or mercy of God "endures forever." Is this a contradiction? Not at all! God *is* merciful. He *is* long-suffering. His love *does* endure forever. But when we insist on our own way and persevere in our sin, the time comes when the daily mercies of the Lord are withdrawn from us and we are abandoned to our folly so that we might learn to turn back to Him. During such periods God will not be actively showing mercy, save in the judgment itself, and we will be conscious of great spiritual darkness.

When we think of this prophecy in relation to Israel we cannot forget the great atrocities that have been inflicted on this people down through the centuries. The name Not-Pitied is a perfect description of them. Can we expect less if we turn from the God who has shown great mercy to us through the cross of Christ?

The last child was again a son, and God said, "Call the son Lo-Ammi" (v. 9). Again, this is a compound name composed of the negative *lo*, meaning "not" and the noun *ammi* (with suffix), meaning "my people." God was saying, "The time is coming when the Jews will no longer be my people."

Some may object, "But the Jews are God's chosen people." No, they are not! Not in this day. I know that much is often made of this point by many people, among them some who are particularly interested in Jewish evangelism. They stress that the Jews have a special place in God's dealings, and that evangelistic outreach must be made to them first of all, following the pattern Paul set for himself in his evangelism. But to say that the Jews have had a special place in God's plan in the past and will yet have a special place in God's plan in the future, as prophecy shows, does not prove that they have a special place now. Nor is it right to say that they are now God's people. They *were* God's people. They will yet be again. But in this present age God's people are those who have entered into the family of God by faith in Jesus Christ, that is, the church, composed of both Jews and Gentiles, as is frequently indicated (cf. Eph. 2:11–22).

Such is the course of God's judgments. Such is His way even in this age if those who have profited by God's redemptive acts in Christ prove faithless. Paul writes of this in his letter to the Romans. After having agonized over God's harsh dealings with Israel—showing that God has broken the Jewish nation off like branches off an olive tree, so that the Gentiles might be grafted in—Paul goes on to say, "If some of the branches have been broken off, and you, though a wild olive shoot, have been grafted in among the others and now share in the nourishing sap from the olive root, do not boast over those branches. . . . Do not be arrogant, but be afraid. For if God did not spare the natural branches, he will not spare you either" (Rom. 11:17, 18, 20, 21). Paul's point is not that we may lose our salvation, but rather that we are to make certain that we really are saved—through faith in and obedience to Christ. If we are believers, we are to be certain not to lose that place of blessing that we have by grace and so suffer chastisement.

THE END AT THE BEGINNING

Someone may be saying, "But I thought a moment ago, when you were introducing this story, that it was to be a story of God's faithfulness. Hosea was to represent God, and he was to be faithful in his love for Gomer to show that God is faithful in His love for us. So far, however, the story is only one of judgment. The names are: Scattered, Not-Pitied, Not-My-People. How is this a story of God's faithfulness?"

"Well," says God, "It is just a case of your not yet having heard the end of the story. This is just the beginning, and the beginning of the story *is* a story of disobedience and judgment. But notice that I am going to call Israel back, and I am going to change those names that seem so dreadful when first given. I am going to change Jezreel with the meaning 'scattered' to Jezreel with the meaning 'planted' [the same word in Hebrew]; I am going to take My people and plant them in their land again." This may be happening in our own time. Beginning in 1948, for the first time in almost two thousand years, large portions of the Jewish people are once again settled in their homeland. (Jezreel has these two meanings, because the same gesture with which a person would throw something away—a backward flip of the hand—is the gesture with which a farmer would plant grain.)

"Moreover," says God, "I am going to change the name Lo-Ruhamah to Ruhamah, dropping the negative. Instead of 'not-pitied,' she will be 'pitied'; I will have pity on My people again. Finally, I will change Lo-Ammi to Ammi, 'not-my-people' to 'my people'; they will be My people again in that day."

Here is the way God puts it, "Yet the Israelites will be like the sand on the seashore, which cannot be measured or counted. In the place where it was said to them, 'You are not my people,' they will be called 'sons of the living God.' The people of Judah and the people of Israel will be reunited, and they will appoint one leader and will come up out of the land, for great will be the day of Jezreel [i.e., the day of their 'planting']. Say of your brothers 'My people,' and of your sisters, 'My loved [or "pitied"] one'" (1:10–2:1).

In his valuable commentary on this book Charles Feinberg speaks of five great blessings promised to Israel nationally, each of which may be in the process of fulfillment today: national increases (1:10a), national conversion (1:10b), national reunion (1:11a), national leadership (1:11b), and national restoration (2:1).[2] This is true. But as a pageant of God's dealings with His people in all places and at all times these verses are no less filled with lessons for us, whoever we may be.

There are lessons for Christians, first of all. You may not have run so far from God as Gomer ran from Hosea. You may not have been so unfaithful as to deny Him and seek other gods, committing spiritual adultery with them. But you have certainly flirted with other gods. You have taken the overpowering love of your great bridegroom and lover Jesus Christ with less obedience and respect than He deserves. You have been half-hearted in your love. You have given God a tip in the offering plate on Sunday mornings, and you have allowed His name to pass your lips lightly—"Oh, yes, I'm a Christian"—while actually living for yourself in this materialistic and self-serving age. You have had a chance to show what it really means and what an honor it is to be the bride of Christ. But you have disgraced that name, in small ways if not in large ones, and you know that you are scarcely the stainless, wrinkle-free, holy and blameless bride He merits (Eph. 5:27). If this is the case, learn what it means to be Christ's bride. Learn what a horror spiritual adultery is, and flee from it to Christ. Lie in His arms. Tell Him of your love. Do not continue in disobedience, allowing little infidelities to become those great spiritual adulteries that bring chastisement.

There are also encouragments here for those who are not yet Christians. If you are not a Christian, you have never known a love like this. Because you have not experienced a love like this, you may be wondering if it really exists or, if it does, how you can have a part in it. You may even be wondering if it is possible for one like yourself to be loved by God in this way. If this is your case, you should know that what you feel of your own inadequacies is true of all who are brought into God's spiritual family. We were all in fellowship with God once . . . in Adam. Since then we have gone our own way. We may be described as Scattered, Not-Pitied, Not-God's-People. It is for people like us that Christ died. If you are touched by this story and sense that Christ died for you, then do not let thoughts of your own inadequacies or past sins hold you back. Run to Him. Believe on Him. Know for yourself that Christ's love really is as this story describes it.

The apostle Peter was one who originally understood little of God's love for others, particularly for those who were not Jews, but he came to know of this love through Christ. We see this in the

---

[2]Charles Lee Feinberg, *Hosea: God's Love for Israel* (New York, American Board of Missions to the Jews, 1947), p. 20

first of his two New Testament letters, written, as he says, to "God's elect . . . *scattered* throughout Pontus, Galatia, Cappadocia, Asia and Bithynia" (1 Peter 1:1). These were not special people, but they were called to faith in Christ and now their case was different. Thus, Peter writes in clear reference to the story of Hosea, "Once you were not a people, but now you are the people of God; once you had not received mercy, but now you have received mercy" (1 Peter 2:10).

That is the story of all who have ever been saved: Scattered! Not-Pitied! Not-My-people! But now: Planted! Pitied! The People of God!

2

Hope for the Hopeless

(Hosea 2:2–25)

Their mother has been unfaithful and has conceived them in disgrace. She said, "I will go after my lovers, who give me my food and my water, my wool and my linen, my oil and my drink." . . . She has not acknowledged that I was the one who gave her the grain, the new wine and oil, who lavished on her the silver and gold—which they used for Baal.

It must have been a terrible shock to Hosea that first night when he came home to find Lo-Ammi crying in the corner and Jezreel and Lo-Ruhamah sitting silently at the table unfed. Gomer was gone! Hosea had been told what was coming; God had revealed it to him. He had even known of Gomer's adulteries and had asked the children to plead with their mother after his own cries had proved useless (2:2). But her departure was still a shock, and now—if it had not happened before—Hosea's heart was broken. What was he to do? What could he say to Gomer or do for her that he had not already said and done repeatedly?

This is a pageant, as we have already seen. And since it is, we must ask what the grief of Hosea teaches us about the grief of God. We must be careful how we speak of this, of course. We are warned that God's thoughts are not our thoughts, neither are His ways our ways (Isa. 55:8). We cannot say that God grieves exactly as we grieve, if only because He controls all things and always works them out in accordance with His own good pleasure. Nevertheless, there is a parallel between God's feelings and ours, and in this case the entire story is designed to show the nature of God's love toward those who have proved unfaithful to Him. To the philosophers of Greece God was unfeel-

ing, indeed incapable of any feelings whatever. Their word for this was *apatheia* (apathy). But the Greek god is not the God of the Bible. In the Bible God weeps for His people, yearns for them, works for their deliverance. Moreover, He remembers the past and grieves over it. Jeremiah portrays Him as saying, "I remember the devotion of your youth, how as a bride you loved me and followed me through the desert, through a land not sown" (Jer. 2:2). God grieves because now the people have forsaken Him, "the spring of living water, and have dug their own cisterns, broken cisterns that cannot hold water" (Jer. 2:13).

What would you do in a situation like this? If it were you or I, we might give up. But God does not give up. He works to turn sorrow into joy and the tragedy of unfaithfulness into the triumph of love.

PURSUING LOVE

Gomer must have been a woman of beauty and personal charm. But her desires were shallow, and as she embarked on her path of sin she was soon to see where these shallow ideals would take her. In our culture we tend to glamorize adultery. It is the chief product of Hollywood. But the Word of God tells of life as it is, and Gomer is an example of life in this area. Gomer left Hosea, first (so the text says) for pleasure, and then, second, for the material things she imagined her lovers could provide. Hosea quotes her as saying, "I will go after my lovers, who give me my food and my water, my wool and my linen, my oil and my drink" (2:5).

What a pity that this poor woman had not learned to value the pure and faithful love of Hosea above these mere earthly treasures. For not valuing such love, she was bound to lose it . . . and the material things too. What happens to a woman who lives this kind of life? The answer is that her way of life is downhill. One year she will be living with a man who is able to take care of her fairly well. In contemporary terms we would say that he is able to provide her with a Cadillac and a mink coat. But the year after that, after the first lover has grown tired of her and she is a bit jaded, she will be living with a man who is only able to provide her with an Oldsmobile and an artificial fur coat with a mink collar. The year after that it will be a Toyota and a tweed. Eventually she will be pulling something out of the trash heap. That is what happened to Hosea's wife. She sank lower and lower in the social scale of the city of Samaria until the time came when she was living with a man who was not even able to take care of her. He could not provide her with enough food to eat or clothes to wear. She was hungry and was clothed in rags.

We say at this point, do we not, "I get the idea: when we run away from God things get bad. Here is the point at which God is going to say, 'You ran away from me. Aren't you sorry you ran away? I hope you're miserable.'" That is the way we think. It seems to be logical. But that is not the way God thinks, even though in time sin does lead to such consequences. Later on in the story Gomer will be deprived of things. But the first thing God does—we see it here—is to intervene in order that the child of God might not lack necessities.

Here is how the events must have unfolded in Hosea's story, though I admit that we have to reconstruct it from the incidental things the prophet says. God must have spoken to Hosea to ask, "Hosea, do you know that your wife is living in the poorest area of the city and that she is living with a man who is not even able to take care of her?"

"Yes," said Hosea.

"Well," God said, "I want you to go down to the market place, buy the food and clothing she needs and see that she gets it, because that is the way I deal with My people when they run from Me."

It might have been hard, but Hosea did what God commanded. As we read the story carefully we are struck with the poignancy of the moment. Hosea must have bought the food, gone to the area of the city where his wife was living and then looked up, not his wife, but the lover. "Are you the man who is currently living with Gomer the daughter of Diblaim?"

"What business is it of yours?"

"I'm Hosea, her husband."

The man must have drawn back, thinking that Hosea was there to cause trouble. But Hosea said, "No, I'm not here to cause trouble. I understand that you're not able to take care of her. So I brought these things because I love her. Here, take them and see that she doesn't lack anything."

The lover would have thought, "What a fool this man is!" But he took the groceries—scoundrel that he was—and then went to Gomer and said, "Look what I've brought you!" She, foolish woman, believed him and threw her arms around his neck to thank him and give him the love she should have given Hosea. I think Hosea must have been lingering in the shadows to make sure Gomer got what he provided, for he comments on the nature of her folly. "She said, 'I will go after my lovers, who give me my food and my water, my wool and my linen, my oil and my drink.' . . . She has not acknowledged ['did not know,' KJV] that I was the one who gave her the grain, the new wine and oil, who lavished on her the silver and gold—which they used for Baal" (2:5, 8).

Does love act like that? Does love take valuable money and spend it on a worthless woman? In this life, perhaps not very often. But this is the way God acts constantly. We spurn His love and squander His resources, but still He loves us and provides for us. Donald Grey Barnhouse, who has written well on this story and from whom much of my exposition of this point is taken, asks, "Who can explain the sanity of true love? Love is of God, and it is infinite. Love is sovereign. Love is apart from reason; love exists for its own reasons. Love is not according to logic; love is according to love. Thus it was with Hosea, for he was playing the part that God has played with you, all of your life, and with me."[1]

Does God really act like that? Does He love us and provide for us even while we are running away? The answer of this story and indeed of the entire Bible is that He does.

Barnhouse writes, "The pursuing love of God is the greatest wonder of the spiritual universe. We leave God in the heat of our own self-desire and run from His will because we want so much to have our own way. We get to a crossroads and look back in pride, thinking that we have outdistanced Him. Just as we are about to congratulate ourselves on our achievement of self-enthronement, we feel a touch on our arm and turn in that direction to find Him there. 'My child,' He says in great tenderness, 'I love you; and when I saw you running away from all that is good, I pursued you through a shortcut that love knows well, and awaited you here at the crossroads.' We

have torn ourselves free from His grasp and rushed off again, through deepest woods and farthest swamp, and as we look back again, we are sure, this time, that we have succeeded in escaping from Him. But, once more, the touch of love is on our other sleeve and when we turn quickly we find that He is there, pleading with the eyes of love, and showing Himself once more to be the tender and faithful One, loving to the end. He will always say, 'My child, my name and nature are Love, and I must act according to that which I am. So it is that I have pursued you, to tell you that when you are tired of your running and your wandering, I will be there to draw you to myself once more.'

"When we see this love at work through the heart of Hosea we may wonder if God is really like that. But everything in the Word and in experience shows us that He is. He will give man the trees of the forest and the iron in the ground. Then He will give to man the brains to make an axe from the iron to cut down a tree and fashion it into a cross. He will give man the ability to make a hammer and nails, and when man has the cross and the hammer and the nails, the Lord will allow man to take hold of Him and bring Him to that cross; He will stretch out His hands upon it and allow man to nail Him to that cross, and in so doing will take the sins of man upon Himself and make it possible for those who have despised and rejected Him to come unto Him and know the joy of sins removed and forgiven, to know the assurance of pardon and eternal life, and to enter into the prospect of the hope of glory with Him forever. This is even our God, and there is none like unto Him."[2]

Have you ever run away from God? Of course, you have. And has He not

---

[1]Donald Grey Barnhouse, "Epistle to the Romans," Part 37 (Philadelphia: The Bible Study Hour, 1952), p. 1841. Barnhouse's version of the story appears in *God's Freedom* (Grand Rapids: Eerdmans, 1961), pp. 187-92; *This Man and This Woman* (Philadelphia: Evangelical Foundation, 1958), pp. 21-26; and in parts 37 and 38 of the published radio studies in the *Epistle to the Romans*.

[2]*The Epistle to the Romans*, Part 38, pp. 1843, 1844.

taken you back? Of course, He has. God's love is like this, and He has done this to teach you to know His love and come to Him.

HEDGE OF THORNS

We must not think that this is the end of the story, however. For although it is true that God provides for us and pursues us even when we run away, this does not mean that our way will therefore be smooth, as if God were to say, "I want you to come to Me. But if you don't want to come, I'll still pave the path of your disobedience and aid you in it." It does not work that way. The love of God is a pursuing, faithful love. But it is also a disciplining love. Consequently, when Gomer failed to perceive the hand of Hosea in the provision of her necessities, the next step was for God to begin to withhold even these things from her.

The outline of the second chapter of Hosea is conveyed to us at this point by a threefold repetition of the word "therefore" (in vv. 6, 9, and 14). Each use introduces something that God does when we refuse to come back to Him. First, God says that He will hedge up Gomer's path with thornbushes. "Therefore I will block her path with thornbushes; I will wall her in so that she cannot find her way. She will chase after her lovers but not catch them; she will look for them but not find them. Then she will say, 'I will go back to my husband as at first, for then I was better off than now'" (vv. 6, 7).

I cannot read this passage, particularly in the King James Version (which uses the word "hedge") without thinking of the entirely contrasting but instructive use of the same word in the story of Job. The Book of Job begins with a description of who Job was, followed immediately by a scene in heaven in which Satan came with the angels to present himself before God. God initiated a conversation with Satan in which He called his attention to Job. "Have you considered my servant Job?" God asked. "There is no one on earth like him; he is blameless and upright, a man who fears God and shuns evil" (Job 1:8).

Satan immediately replied, "Does Job fear God for nothing? Have you not put a hedge around him and his household and everything he has? You have blessed the work of his hands, so that his flocks and herds are spread throughout the land. But stretch out your hand and strike everything he has, and he will surely curse you to your face" (vv. 9–11).

The last part of this retort was untrue, of course, as the story shows. Job did not curse God even when his substance was taken from him and his sons and daughters were killed. Nevertheless, we note that the first part was true and that it contains a great admission. Satan imputed wrong motives to Job, to be sure. He implied that Job served God only because God protected him. But the true part—the interesting part in view of the story of Hosea—is that God had been protecting Job by setting up a hedge around him. Satan was admitting that he had been attacking Job—either himself or one of the other fallen angels—but he had been unsuccessful because of the protecting shield that God throws about all who have put their trust in His grace. Later in the story God lowers the hedge a bit to allow Satan to touch Job's property, but not Job himself—to show that Job truly loved God, but not merely for the protection He had been providing. However, the point of the story is that God controlled even the level of these temptations and did not allow Job to be tempted more than he was able to bear (cf. Heb. 2:18).

Contrast this with the case of Gomer. In the case of Job, God set up a hedge against Satan, for Job's protection. In the case of Gomer, the same God who had used a hedge to protect Job erected a hedge to keep one of His children from the evil thing she desired.

Thus it is in the Christian life. If you

take the talents God has given you and then run away from Him to seek whatever it is you want out of this life, God will first come gently to remind you that He is the source of the gifts you squander and that you are doing wrong to squander them. But if you will not come to your senses through such a reminder, God will bring you up short so that you will not attain your desires. If you think you are going to get rich through a job that excludes God and a Christian witness, God will let you get close enough to the wealth to taste it but then keep it just beyond your grasp. If you think you are going to become famous in show business and are willing to leave the commands of God behind in your upward scramble to get there, God will let you get close enough to know and envy others who have made it but keep you an unknown. Do you think that God will not do this? That He is too "kind"? I tell you that God will do it. He is faithful to His nature and will not allow the one He loves to be destroyed through an adulterous infatuation with this world's idols.

Lack of Necessities

When we refuse to respond to God's gracious provision of life's necessities, God begins to remove those necessities. But up to now this has not happened. God has merely withheld the attainment of Gomer's sinful desires, setting a hedge around her. Now God begins to remove the grain and the wine, the wool and the linen. This change is introduced by the second "therefore."

"'Therefore I will take away my grain when it ripens, and my new wine when it is ready. I will take back my wool and my linen, intended to cover her nakedness. So now I will expose her lewdness before the eyes of her lovers; no one will take her out of my hands. I will stop all her celebrations: her yearly festivals, her New Moons, her Sabbath days—all her appointed feasts. I will ruin her vines and her fig trees, which she said were

her pay from her lovers; I will make them a thicket, and wild animals will devour them. I will punish her for the days she burned incense to the Baals; she decked herself with rings and jewelry, and went after her lovers, but me she forgot,' declares the LORD" (vv. 9–13).

When God had first blocked Gomer's path she said, "I will go back to my husband as at first," but she had not done it. Now she must go through hard days.

What a contrast between this and the earlier days of Hosea and Gomer's courtship. Then Hosea had showered his goods on her and had rejoiced with her at the time of Israel's festivals. By removing these things Gomer is now to be brought to the place where she will remember the former days and turn back from her folly.

I think of another case in which this also happened. The prodigal son had asked for his proper share of the father's wealth, and it had been given to him. He then went off to squander his wealth in wild living. He had his fling, but the time came when the money ran out. When this happened he hired himself to a citizen of the country who sent him into the field to feed pigs. The Lord says poignantly, "He longed to fill his stomach with the pods that the pigs were eating, but no one gave him anything" (Luke 15:16). What happened? When he had money and was ensconced in his pleasures, he had no thoughts for his father or his father's home. But later, with the pangs of famine gnawing at his insides, he came to his senses, remembered the days of his youth in his father's house and determined to return to him. He said to himself, "How many of my father's hired men have food to spare, and here I am starving to death! I will set out and go back to my father and say to him: 'Father, I have sinned against heaven and against you. I am no longer worthy to be called your son; make me like one of your hired men'" (vv. 17–19). So he got up and returned to his father.

We cannot say that every case of deprivation fits these categories. The principle we are studying has nothing to do with those who are not yet Christians. It does not even have to do with all who are Christians. Some, like Job, suffer merely that God might be glorified. Still it applies to some, and you know if you are among them. Are you like Gomer at the nadir of her misery? Are you the prodigal son in the foreign country? God has sent the misery to bring you to your senses and draw you back to Him. Profit from your knowledge. Do not say merely, "I will go back to my husband as at first," and then not go. Get up and go to Him. Do not say merely, "I will return to my father," and then sit there without moving. Go to God. Find that He will be waiting with open arms to receive you and shower you with love. The Lord Himself said, "Come to me, all you who are weary and burdened, and I will give you rest" (Matt. 11:28). He said, "Whoever comes to me I will never drive away" (John 6:37).

A DOOR OF HOPE

We come then to the last of the three "therefores" that provide the outline to this chapter. As we do, we come to another of this book's joyous surprises. We have had a series of "therefores" in which the hand of God's judgment has been pressed down ever more firmly on Hosea's rebellious and errant wife. She has been hedged in by a wall. She has been deprived of necessities. We sit in fear as we wonder what further judgment will follow on these inevitable chastisements. Will it be sickness, pain, or death? It could well be; the way of wickedness is hard. But just as we are expecting such things, God opens the hand of His grace and sends forth hope. He says, "Therefore I am now going to allure her; I will lead her into the desert and speak tenderly to her. There I will give her back her vineyards, and will make the Valley of Achor a door of hope" (vv. 14, 15).

"Achor" means "troubling," and the phrase that contains it ("the Valley of Achor") means "the valley of troubling." It occurs three times in the Bible. The first is in Joshua in connection with the story of Achan and his sin. When the people of Israel had conquered Jericho in the first wave of their invasion of the Promised Land, Achan had taken spoil of Jericho that the people had been told by God they were not to do. For this they lost the next battle at Ai. What was wrong? they asked. At last an investigation was made and the sin of Achan was discovered and judged. Achan and his family were stoned in the Valley of Achor, which took its name from this incident (Josh. 7:26).

The second time this valley is mentioned is in Isaiah, when he speaks of a day when it will become a resting place for herds (Isa. 65:10). The third time is in Hosea, and here the place of "troubling" is to become a place of hope for God's people.

How can a place of such swift judgment be hopeful? How can the destructive troubling be changed? We cannot change it certainly. But there is One who can and who does. God sets hope before us when all seems most lost. He does it by taking our trouble on Himself. Do you remember those words of our Lord in the final hours prior to His death as He thought ahead to all that would take place on Calvary? He said, "Now my heart is troubled, and what shall I say? 'Father, save me from this hour'? No, it was for this very reason I came to this hour" (John 12:27). Again we are told that "Jesus was troubled in spirit" (John 13:21). Why was Jesus troubled? He was troubled in our place. God troubled Him with our sin that we might be saved from it and be brought back to God. It is on the basis of His death for that sin that He can now say to us, "Do not let your hearts be troubled and do not be afraid" (John 14:27; cf. v. 1).

The redemptive work accomplished by

Christ is what we will come to in the next chapter, as we study Hosea 3:1–5. But before we turn to that chapter we need to see even here how God pours forth His blessings once again. "'In that day,' declares the LORD, 'you will call me "my husband"; you will no longer call me "my master." I will remove the names of the Baals from her lips; no longer will their names be invoked. In that day I will make a covenant for them with the beasts of the field and the birds of the air and the creatures that move along the ground. Bow and sword and battle I will abolish from the land, so that all may lie down in safety. I will betroth you to me forever; I will betroth you in righteousness and justice, in love and compassion. I will betroth you in faithfulness, and you will acknowledge the LORD'" (vv. 16–20).

"Moreover," says God, "I will restore all that I have taken away. I have taken away the grain and the wine and the oil. I have called the children Jezreel, Lo-Ruhamah, Lo-Ammi. But I will eventually restore it all. I will speak to the skies that have been shut up that they might not give rain, and they will give rain. I will speak to the fields that have been parched and lifeless, and they will bring forth abundantly." The prophecy says, "The earth will respond to the grain, the new wine and oil, and they will respond to Jezreel. I will plant her for myself in the land; I will show my love to the one I called 'Not my loved one.' I will say to those called 'Not my people.' 'You are my people'; and they will say, 'You are my God'" (vv. 22, 23).

There is no greater promise than that. No wider door of hope could possibly be set before us. If you think all is hopeless, hear God as He speaks these words to your heart: "I will betroth you to me forever. . . . I will respond. . . . I will plant. . . . I will show my love to the one I called 'Not my loved one.'" Come to Him and allow Him to restore the years of your life that have been lost.

3

The Greatest Chapter in the Bible

(Hosea 3:1–5)

The LORD said to me, "Go, show your love to your wife again, though she is loved by another and is an adulteress. Love her as the LORD loves the Israelites, though they turn to other gods and love the sacred raisin-cakes."
So I bought her for fifteen shekels of silver and about a homer and a lethek of barley. Then I told her, "You are to live with me many days; you must not be a prostitute or be intimate with any man, and I will live with you."
For the Israelites will live many days without king or prince, without sacrifice or sacred stones, without ephod or idol. Afterward the Israelites will return and seek the LORD their God and David their king.

The third chapter of Hosea is, in my judgment, the greatest chapter in the Bible, because it portrays the greatest story in the Bible—the death of the Lord Jesus Christ for His people—in the most concise and poignant form to be found anywhere. Our study of Hosea's story has already shown that it is a pageant of the love of God for Israel, indeed for His people in every place and age. But when we ask, "Where in the whole of human history is that love most clearly seen?" the answer is obviously, "At the cross of Christ." It is that cross and the work accomplished on that cross that is portrayed in this chapter. Hosea 3 shows us God's work of redemption—the work by which the Lord Jesus Christ delivered us from sin's bondage at the cost of His own life—portrayed in Hosea's purchase of his fallen wife from slavery.

THE CRITICS' OBJECTION

Before we plunge into the dramatization of this story in Hosea, however, we need to answer an objection to this conception of the work of Christ that has been raised by modern scholars. If anything is central to the picture of redemp-

tion provided by Hosea's story, it is the matter of cost—redemption by the payment of a price. But this is precisely what many in our day object to. They say, "If God saves us on the basis of a cost or price, whatever that may be, our salvation is not free, and therefore it is not of grace; but since we know that we are saved by grace, this understanding of redemption must be wrong. To be biblical we have to talk of redemption, not so much as redemption by payment of a price, but simply and exclusively as deliverance."

In honest reaction to this current critical opinion we must acknowledge that it is possible to find passages in Scripture that seem to support it. For example, we recall that when the Emmaus disciples were making their way home after the Resurrection and Jesus appeared to them, they used this word to express their disappointment. Jesus had begun to interrogate them saying, "You look sad. Why is that?"

They answered, "Because of the things that happened in Jerusalem over this weekend."

"What things?" He asked.

They replied, "Don't You know what happened? There was a great prophet. His name was Jesus. He came from Nazareth. He did mighty acts among the people; He was a great teacher. In these last days He was taken by the rulers of the people, tried, condemned, and crucified. He's dead. And you know [this is the sentence in which the word occurs], we had hoped that He was the One who was going to *redeem* Israel" (cf. Luke 24:17–21). Of course, that is what Jesus *was* doing. He was redeeming Israel, and all His people. But they were not thinking in these terms. They were thinking of a political deliverance only. What they meant was, "We had hoped that this was the Messiah who would drive out the Romans."

If I were playing the part of the devil's advocate, I could take that occurrence of the word and say, "You see, in New Testament times redemption no longer had the meaning that is sometimes given to it by some biblical theologians. It meant 'deliverance' only." But if I said that, I would be wrong. One thing wrong with that idea is that the Emmaus disciples obviously misunderstood what Christ had come to do. We know this because Jesus then began to unfold for them out of the pages of the Word of God the things that concerned Himself. He showed that it was necessary that He should "suffer and rise from the dead on the third day, and repentance and forgiveness of sins will be preached in his name to all nations" (Luke 24:46, 47). That is the true interpretation of redemption from the mouth of our Lord.

But there are more reasons for insisting on the matter of the price in redemption than this one story. Let me give four of them.

1. The matter of cost is an Old Testament idea. First, there are the words *gaal* ("redeem") and *goel* (usually translated as "kinsman-redeemer"). It was a principle of Jewish law that property should remain within a family if possible. To be deprived of property was to be deprived of your share of the land, your inheritance. It was disastrous. So provision was made in the law whereby a man, if he had lost his property, could receive it back again through the obligation placed on a kinsman. This would mean that if the man fell into debt and his land was sold to pay off the debt, the duty would fall on his closest kinsman to buy the land back at some point and thus restore it to the family. The man who performed this service was the kinsman-redeemer, and the process was redemption. Boaz did this in the case of the property that had belonged to the husband of Ruth.

A second Hebrew word is *kofer*, which means "a ransom price." Suppose you are a farmer and have an ox that gets free one day, wanders down to your neighbor's farm and kills one of his servants. Under Hebrew law that is a crime for which the animal can be killed. If there was negligence, it is conceivable that you would have to forfeit your life for the one taken. There would not be much advantage to anyone in that, however. So an arrangement was made whereby if the man who owned the animal could settle on a price with the relatives of the man who had been killed, he could redeem either himself or the animal. The price of redemption was the *kofer*.

These words show that the idea of redemption by price was firmly fixed in the Old Testament cultural world and would therefore be natural to the New Testament writers, most of whom were Jews.

2. We find the idea of redemption by the payment of a price in the New Testament world too. The most important Greek word for redemption is *luo*, which means "to loose." It can mean redemption or deliverance, but as time went on and the word group developed (as many basic word groups did), some of the derivatives came to mean deliverance by the payment of a price exclusively. First came the noun *lutron*, which means the

"ransom price." From *lutron* another verb developed, *lutroo*, which always means "to deliver by the payment of a price." From this came the words for "redemption," *lutrosis* or *apolutrosis*.

We also find this idea in the secular culture of this period. For example—I refer to Adolf Deissman's *Light from the Ancient East* and Leon Morris' *The Apostolic Preaching of the Cross*—there was in the Greek world what we would call a standard formula for the manumission of slaves. It had to do with paying a price to one of the gods or goddesses so that a slave might be set free: "_____ pays to the Pithian Apollo the sum of _____ minae for the slave _____ on the condition that he (she) shall be set free." This occurs so frequently that it is evident that the idea of delivering a person by the payment of money was common in the ancient world.

3. We must retain the idea of a price in discussing redemption because the key New Testament texts all refer to it. There is Matthew 20:28, for example. Here our Lord is speaking. He says, "The Son of Man did not come to be served, but to serve, and to give his life as a *ransom* for many." What is He talking about here? Obviously, He is saying that He is going to buy us out of our slavery to sin at the cost of His life. Titus 2:14 speaks of Jesus who "gave himself for us to *redeem* us from all wickedness and to purify for himself a people that are his very own, eager to do what is good." What does this verse mean when it says He gave Himself for us? It does not mean that He gave Himself for us in the sense that He lives for us, though that is also true. It means He died for us. Finally, there is a text that is perhaps the clearest of all: 1 Peter 1:18, 19. It says: "You know that it was not with perishable things such as silver or gold that you were *redeemed* from the empty way of life handed down to you from your forefathers, but with the precious blood of Christ, a lamb without blemish or defect." In this verse

the idea of Christ's life being the cost of our redemption is inescapable.

4. We note that the *luo* word group (*luo, lutron, lutroo, lutrosis*) is not the only word group used for the idea of redemption in the New Testament. We also have the words *agorazo*, which means "to buy in the market place"—and *exagorazo*, which means "to buy out of the market place." Together these words describe how Jesus entered into the market place of sin and at the cost of His own life purchased us to Himself so that we might be brought into that glorious liberty that is ours as children of God.

SOLD TO HOSEA

It is precisely this that is dramatized by the climactic moment in the story of Hosea. Gomer had left Hosea, as we have already seen, and she had sunk lower and lower in the social scale of the day. Now, at the last, she became a slave and was sold in the capital city of Samaria. There were different ways in which a person could become a slave in antiquity. One could become a slave by conquest. To give one illustration, when the Athenians tried to attack Sicily at the time of the Peloponesian war and were defeated, all in the army taken at the Battle of Syracuse became slaves. Second, you could become a slave by birth. That is, if your parents were slaves, you became a slave automatically. Thus, all who descended from the Athenians who were captured at Syracuse became slaves. Finally, you could become a slave through debt. Gomer presumably became a slave in this fashion. Thus, the time came when, at the nadir of her misery, she was sold on an auction block in the capital city, and Hosea was told by God to buy her.

We know quite a bit about the selling of slaves in antiquity because much has been written about it. For example, the slaves were always sold naked. There is a Greek play in which a fat man is put up for sale. The bids are starting, and the men who are buying bid: "Ten cents!" "Fifteen cents!" "Twenty cents!" They begin to joke with one another. One man says, "Why do you bid twenty cents for that fat slave? As soon as he gets in your house he's going to eat up all your food." The man who bid twenty cents justifies his bid, saying, "You don't understand. I've got a squeaky mill; I'm going to cut him up and use him for grease."

At last a beautiful woman is put up for sale. Her clothes are taken off, and now the bidding is not "Ten cents . . . twenty cents." It is: "A hundred dollars . . . a hundred and twenty dollars!" The men are bidding for the body of the female slave.

Thus was Gomer put up for sale. Her clothes were removed, and the men of the city were there to see her nakedness and bid for her. God told Hosea to buy his wife back.

One man started the bidding: "Twelve pieces of silver!"

"Thirteen!" said Hosea.

"Fourteen pieces of silver!"

Hosea's bid was "Fifteen!"

The low bidders were beginning to drop out, but one man continued bidding: "Fifteen pieces of silver and a bushel of barley!"

Hosea said, "Fifteen pieces of silver and a bushel and a half of barley!" The auctioneer looked around and, seeing no more bids said, "Sold to Hosea for fifteen pieces of silver and a bushel and a half of barley."

Now notice, at this point Hosea *owned* his wife. She was his property. He could do anything he wished with her. If he had wanted to kill her out of spite, he could have done it. People might have called him a fool to waste his money on a worthless woman. She might have suffered far more as a slave to some beautiful woman where she would have been obliged to fetch and serve and carry and watch and never enter into the kind of pleasures that brought her to her state in the first place. Still Hosea could have

killed Gomer if he had wanted to. Yet he did not, because at this point Hosea's love, which is an illustration of God's love for us, burned brightest. Instead of seeking vengeance, he put Gomer's clothes on her, led her away into the anonimity of the crowd and claimed that love from her that was now his right. Moreover, as he did so he promised no less from himself.

Here is the way he puts it: "The LORD said to me, 'Go, show your love to your wife again, though she is loved by another and is an adulteress. Love her as the LORD loves the Israelites, though they turn to other gods and love the sacred raisin-cakes.' So I bought her for fifteen shekels of silver and about a homer and a lethek of barley. Then I told her, 'You are to live with me many days; you must not be a prostitute or be intimate with any man, and I will live with you'" (3:1–3).

Does God love like that? Yes, God loves like that! God steps into the marketplace of sin and buys us out of sin's bondage by the death of Christ. We read in our Bibles, "For God so loved the world that he gave his one and only Son . . ." (John 3:16). We ask, "What does *so* mean?" The answer is in Hosea's story. When we see Hosea standing in the market place under orders from God to purchase his wife, who had become an adulteress and a slave, we recognize that this is the measure of God's love.

We are Gomer. We are the slave sold on the auction block of sin. The world bids for us. The world bids fame, wealth, prestige, influence, power—all those things that are the world's currency. But when all seemed lost God sent the Lord Jesus Christ, His Son, into the market place to buy us at the cost of His life. If you can understand it as an illustration, God was the auctioneer. He said, "What am I bid for these poor, hopeless, enslaved sinners?"

Jesus said, "I bid the price of My blood."

The Father said, "Sold to the Lord Jesus

Christ for the price of His blood." There was no greater bid than that.

So we became His, and He took us and clothed us, not with the dirty robes of our old unrighteousnesses, which are as filthy rags, but with the robes of His righteousness. And He said—He says it to you today if you are a believer—"You are to live with me many days; you must not be a prostitute or be intimate with any man, and I will live with you" (v. 3). The Authorized Version says, "So will I also be for thee." That is how God loves us. That is what Jesus did on your behalf.

APPLICATION TO ISRAEL

We must not close our study of this story without applications. The first is to the history of God's dealings with Israel. We admit, as we read this story, that our thoughts slip naturally from the story of Hosea and Gomer to Israel to God's dealings with ourselves and that it is possible in such a flow of thought for the application to Israel to be lost. But we should not do this, particularly since this is the way Hosea himself applies the story in this chapter. He writes, "For the Israelites will live many days without king or prince, without sacrifice or sacred stones, without ephod or idol. Afterward the Israelites will return and seek the LORD their God and David their king. They will come trembling to the LORD and to his blessings in the last days" (vv. 4, 5).

In view of this verse, I do not see how so many scholars can deny that there will be a regathering of Israel and a national repentance of Israel in those last days that are yet to come. Some scholars, particularly Reformed scholars, deny any future national blessing of Israel on the grounds that the promises made to her are fulfilled in the church and that a restoration of Israel would be a retrogression in God's saving work in history. But why is this retrogression? And who are we to say what God must do? Who are we to interpret these passages in any way other than their most obvious meaning?

Some will say that this was indeed a promise to Israel but that it has already been fulfilled. Israel *was* scattered in the period following the falls of Samaria and Jerusalem, but she was regathered at the time the Jews returned to their land under Ezra and Nehemiah. Unfortunately, this regathering does not fit the prophecies. During that period there was no king, as Hosea clearly foretells, and there was no true national repentance. In fact, this period climaxed in the rejection of God's Messiah.

Then perhaps the prophecies will not be fulfilled? Perhaps Israel failed to meet God's conditions when she rejected Christ? That argument does not stand either, for the prophecies of Israel's regathering made by the Old Testament writers (cf. Deut. 28:64–67; Isa. 11:11, 12; 60:21; Jer. 16:14–16; Ezek. 36:24–28; Amos 9:14, 15) are repeated in the New Testament following the rejection of Christ.

The fact that Jesus Christ had come to earth and was largely rejected by the Jews presented a major problem to the early preachers of the gospel. Most of them were Jews, and they had understood that the Messiah was to bring blessing to Israel and to the gentile nations. Jesus was the Messiah. But as they looked at the way things were falling out, it seemed perfectly evident that most of the Jewish people were not believing in Jesus and hence were not entering into the promised blessing. How could that be? We can easily see how it grew into a major theological problem. God has never left His major ways with men unexplained, however. He said to Amos, "Surely the Sovereign LORD does nothing without revealing his plan to his servants the prophets" (Amos 3:7). In this case, God explained the solution of the difficulty to Paul, who recorded it for our benefit. The answer had three parts.

First, as Paul says in the opening verses of Romans 11, it is simply not true that

God has cast off His people utterly. This idea is refuted in his case alone, if no other, for Paul was a Jew and yet believed in Jesus as Lord and Messiah. Paul wrote, "I ask then, Did God reject his people? By no means! I am an Israelite myself, a descendant of Abraham, from the tribe of Benjamin" (Rom. 11:1).

Second, says Paul, he was not the only one who believed. There were many believing Jews. He could have named the eleven disciples, the three thousand and five thousand who believed at Pentecost and the days following, those Jews to whom he had witnessed during his missionary journeys, and others. Moreover, he argued, this is no different from what has always been; for even in the days of Elijah not all Jews believed but only the seven thousand whose existence God revealed to the despondent prophet. "So too, at the present time there is a remnant chosen by grace" (Rom. 11:5).

At this point Paul inserts a parenthesis dealing with the matter of election. He points out that Israel has been removed from a place of special blessing in order that God might deal with the Gentiles. He warns the Gentiles that just as Israel was removed because of her unbelief, so the Gentiles may be removed because of their unbelief. Then he returns to the major argument of the chapter, adding that not only *may* Gentiles be removed from a place of special blessing, they actually *will be* removed as the days of the Gentiles draw to an end. When that happens it will again be a day of Jewish blessing. Paul's actual words are: "I do not want you to be ignorant of this mystery, brothers, so that you may not be conceited: Israel has experienced a hardening in part *until* the full number of the Gentiles has come in [i.e., until all whom God is determining to save from among the Gentiles be saved; cf. 2 Peter 3:9]. And so [at that time] all

Israel will be saved, as it is written: 'The deliverer will come from Zion; he will turn godlessness away from Jacob. And this is my covenant with them when I take away their sins'" (Rom. 11:25–27).

In these words, Paul restates and further defines the Old Testament prophecies of a time of future blessing and future usefulness for Israel.[1]

APPLICATION TO MARRIAGE

The second application of this chapter is to Christian marriage, for the standard of Hosea's love in his union with Gomer is to be the standard of the Christian to his or her spouse within the marriage relationship. At first thought this seems backward . . . and impossible. But then we remember Ephesians 5 and note that this is precisely the standard Paul holds up before Christians. He says in that chapter, "Wives, submit to your husbands as to the Lord. . . . Husbands, love your wives, just as Christ loved the church and gave himself up for her to make her holy, cleansing her by the washing with water through the word." And then, lest we have missed the point, he concludes, "This is a profound mystery—but I am talking about Christ and the church" (vv. 22, 25, 26, 32).

You and I are always ready to abandon the standards of the Word of God and come down to the standards of the world. We are ready to say that such love, demonstrated in the love of Hosea for Gomer, is impossible for us. But it is not impossible if we are truly united to Christ through the Holy Spirit and are allowing Him to love through us.

You say, "Do you mean to tell me that if my wife or my husband runs away from me and commits adultery that I am still to be faithful? Do you mean to tell me that I must continue to love someone like that when I have been wronged and the sanctity of our marriage has been

---

[1] I have discussed the evidence for this future role of Israel at greater length in *The Last and Future World* (Grand Rapids: Zondervan, 1974), pp. 81–97.

violated?" Yes, that is precisely our standard. "But that is not fair!" True, it is not fair—who said anything about being fair?—it is just the expression of true love.

Notice, I do not say that the exercise of a Christian standard in the love of a wife for her husband or a husband for his wife will always hold the home together. It did not do so in Hosea's case. Sometimes—it is happening more and more frequently today—one partner in the marriage will walk out. Sometimes even a Christian will do this. In such a case it is impossible to stop the separation, and the one who loves as God loves and who desperately wants to save the marriage must nevertheless let the faithless one go. There is no sin to the one who wishes to save the marriage in that case. But the faithlessness of the one should not end the true love of the other. That is the point. And the believer (or the one acting by the standards of the believer) should remain free of any second marriage while praying that the love of the erring partner might be restored. You may say, "But I cannot do that. I cannot love like that." The answer is that you can love like that if you will allow God to help you do it. You may say, "But I cannot be happy single." Perhaps not. But God does not promise any of us happiness as we define happiness. We are called to faithfulness, and it is in obedience to God in such difficult situations that the great spiritual victories are won.

I AM THE LORD'S

The final application of this story is to spiritual faithfulness on the part of Christian people. We are unfaithful. But we should be moved to faithfulness by Christ's love for us.

Remember that it was not we who sought Him. It was He who sought us and who joined us to Himself through spiritual marriage. He courted us. He won our love. Then He brought us to that moment when we stood with Him before the Father and recited those spiritual vows that made us His for eternity. He took the vows first of all: "I, Jesus, take thee, sinner, to be My wedded wife; and I do promise and covenant, before God and these witnesses, to be thy loving and faithful Savior and Bridegroom; in plenty and in want, in joy and in sorrow, in sickness and in health, for this life and for eternity." And we looked up into His face and said after Him, "I, sinner, take Thee, Jesus, to be my Savior and Lord; and I do promise and covenant, before God and these witnesses, to be Thy loving and faithful bride; in plenty and in want, in joy and in sorrow, in sickness and in health, for this life and for eternity."

Thus, we took His name and became His. Before, we were Miss Sinner. Now we have become Mrs. Christian, for Christian means "Christ-one." Now we must be careful to keep His name unspotted before the world.

Have you done that? Or have you dishonored His name by the way you have spent your time, by your questionable associations, by your loose talk or blasphemous language? If that is the case, remember that the price He paid for your love was His own death on Calvary. Remember His faithfulness and determine that hereafter you will always be faithful to Him. Ask Him to seal that love, keeping you and perfecting you until the day when you will stand before both Him and His Father at the great marriage supper of the Lamb. There is a hymn that prays along these lines. It was written by Lucy Bennett.

I am the Lord's. O joy beyond expression,
O sweet response to voice of love divine;
Faith's joyous "Yes" to the assuring whisper,
"Fear not! I have redeemed thee; thou art mine."

I am the Lord's. It is the glad confession,
Wherewith the bride recalls the happy day,

When love's "I will" accepted him
forever,
"The Lord's," to love, to honor and obey.
I am the Lord's. Yet teach me all it
meaneth,
All it involves of love and loyalty,
Of holy service, absolute surrender,
And unreserved obedience unto thee.

I am the Lord's. Yes; body, soul and
spirit.
O seal them irrecoverably thine;
As thou, Beloved, in thy grace and fulness
Forever and forevermore art mine.

4

Case for the Prosecution

(Hosea 4:1–19)

Hear the word of the LORD, you Israelites, because the LORD has a charge to bring against you who live in the land: "There is no faithfulness, no love, no acknowledgment of God in the land. There is only cursing, lying and murder, stealing and adultery; they break all bounds, and bloodshed follows bloodshed."

Several times in our study we have applied the story of Hosea's tragic marriage to ourselves saying, "We are Gomer, and Hosea is God." It may be that you found yourself objecting to that identification, and if that was the case, you should now pay particular attention. At this point Hosea's prophecy launches into a formal accusation against Israel in which the sins of the people are brought forward as evidence for the justice of God's judgments. In legal terms we might say that this is the case for the prosecution. We try to excuse ourselves; that is our nature. We say that these things are true of others but not of ourselves. Now we are to be shown that they are indeed true of us, and that we, as well as others, are condemned.

The chapter begins as a formal court proceeding might begin today—"Oyez! Oyez! [Hear! hear!] The court is in session." Hosea expresses the idea by saying, "Hear the word of the LORD, you Israelites, because the LORD has a charge to bring against you who live in the land: 'There is no faithfulness, no love, no acknowledgment of God in the land'" (4:1).

THE BASIC PROBLEM

The opening indictment in this case has three parts, each a "sin of omission." God is charging Israel with having: 1) no faithfulness, 2) no devotion, and 3) no

knowledge of Himself. "No faithfulness" refers to a lack of that very characteristic that God so abundantly shows toward us. It is the firmness and reliability of a person whose word is as good as his bond and who is consistent in his or her responsibility. Faithfulness must be seen in all areas of life but especially in marriage and in the relationship to God that marriage illustrates. Devotion (or "love," NIV) means religiosity or piety in the best sense. It is what man owes to God. Knowledge is that experiential awakening to God in love that affects our conduct.

Each of these three lacks is brought against Israel as a just cause for God's judgment. But when we look at the book as a whole it is apparent that, of the three, the key concern and most important ground of accusation is Israel's failure to acknowledge God.

Hosea tells us many things about this acknowledgment. He tells us that God *desires* it: "For I desire mercy, not sacrifice, and acknowledgment of God rather than burnt offerings" (6:6). We are told that God *commands* it: "But I am the LORD your God, who brought you out of Egypt. You shall acknowledge no God but me, no Savior except me" (13:4). This latter text is a clear reference to the opening phrases of the Ten Commandments. Yet in spite of God's desire and express command, Israel has refused to acknowledge

Him and has instead turned from such knowledge. She has protested, "O our God, we acknowledge you!" (8:2). She has cried out, "Let us acknowledge the Lord; let us press on to acknowledge him" (6:3). But sin has kept her from a true acknowledgment of God and has, in fact, even blinded her eyes to God's goodness: "Their deeds do not permit them to return to their God. A spirit of prostitution is in their heart; they do not acknowledge the Lord" (5:4); "She has not acknowledged that I was the one who gave her the grain, the new wine and oil, who lavished on her the silver and gold—which they used for Baal" (2:8); "They did not realize it was I who healed them" (11:3); "My people are destroyed from lack of knowledge" (4:6). The only hope for Israel is God's promise that as a result of His judgments a day of reconciliation and renewal will come. In that day, says God, "I will betroth you in faithfulness, and you will acknowledge the Lord" (2:20).

To know God in this experiential way was the greatest blessing the ancient Jew could have. To turn from such knowledge to "know" idols was the greatest sin imaginable. It was the spiritual adultery against which the early chapters were protesting.

Although They Knew God

How pointedly this all comes down to us! And how guilty we are in face of this indictment! Here we think of the first chapter of Romans—indeed, we can hardly fail to think of it—for the argument brought against Israel in Hosea 4 is precisely the argument that Paul brings against the race as a whole in his great doctrinal epistle. We may even go further. The similarity of ideas and even verbal echoes between these two chapters indicate that Paul probably had Hosea's chapter in mind as he penned his own indictment of the gentile nations (cf. Hosea 4:6 with Rom. 1:24, 26, 28; Hosea 4:7 with Rom. 1:23; Hosea 4:11 with Rom. 1:21, 22).

"The wrath of God is being revealed from heaven against all the godlessness and wickedness of men who suppress the truth by their wickedness, since what may be known about God is plain to them, because God has made it plain to them. For since the creation of the world God's invisible qualities—his eternal power and divine nature—have been clearly seen, being understood from what has been made, so that men are without excuse. For although they knew God, they neither glorified him as God nor gave thanks to him, but their thinking became futile and their foolish hearts were darkened. Although they claimed to be wise, they became fools and exchanged the glory of the immortal God for images made to look like mortal man and birds and animals and reptiles" (Rom. 1:18–23).

Paul is saying three important things in these verses. First, God has given a *revelation of Himself* to all men from which, however, all men and women have departed.

There is a difference here between Paul's words to the Gentiles and Hosea's words to the Jews, for the Gentiles had less knowledge of God than Israel had. Nevertheless, there is an important similarity, for each has departed from that knowledge, however little or however great it was. In the case of the Gentiles, Paul claims only that there was a knowledge of God's "eternal power and divine nature." That is, the Gentiles knew even without the law of Israel (which they did not possess) that God existed and that He was all-powerful. Israel possessed the bulk of the Old Testament and therefore had greater knowledge. She knew God as the holy One of the Law and the faithful One of the covenant. To turn from such knowledge was greater sin than the sin of the Gentiles. Nevertheless, the sin was the same in nature and the judgment equally justified.

The second of Paul's points has already

been suggested in our discussion of point one, but it needs to be taken separately. It is the heart of the accusation. Having been aware of God and therefore having had at least a rudimentary knowledge of Him (more in Israel's case), people have nevertheless *turned from that knowledge* and suppressed it lest the truth about God rise up to challenge them and lead them in ways they do not wish to go.

This is the true nature of the problem. It is not that men and women have no knowledge of God at all and are condemned for what they "innocently enough" do not know. It is rather that they do have knowledge of God but have rejected it because they do not like the direction in which such knowledge takes them. In the case of the Gentiles, it is the sense that the all-powerful God has a rightful claim over them; and since they do not wish to acknowledge this claim, they reject Him and suppress their knowledge. In the case of Israel, it is the knowledge of God's righteous decrees and standards that the people rejected. They wanted sin: prostitution, adulteries, feasts, and ritual religions (4:10–14). Since these were incompatible with the worship of the true God, they rejected their knowledge of God and served idols.

Paul's last point is that because of their rejection of God through a suppression of the truth about Him, the *wrath of God* is being poured out from heaven. In Romans this is portrayed as the idolatry and moral debasement of the apostle's age. In Hosea the idolatry and immorality are also clearly seen, but in addition there is the specific promise of a future national catastrophe, compared to "a whirlwind" that "will sweep them away" (v. 19). This occurred in the overthrow of Israel and the subsequent deportation of its people.

THE SLIPPERY SLOPE

What happens when a people reject God? What happens when we turn our back on such knowledge? The answer is that we begin a downhill course. God is the source of all good. So if an individual or people will not have God, they will have the opposite in increasing measure. Paul indicates this decline by a threefold reiteration of the phrase "God [He] gave them over"—to the sinful desires of their hearts, to shameful lusts, and to a depraved mind. Hosea describes the same process as: 1) moral depravity, 2) destruction of the environment, 3) the debasement of leadership, particularly religious leadership, 4) personal emptiness, and 5) ruin on a nationwide scale.

The first consequence of a rejection of the knowledge of God is *moral depravity*, as seen in verse 2: "There is only cursing, lying and murder, stealing and adultery; they break all bounds, and bloodshed follows bloodshed." Of all Hosea's statements in this chapter, these words most closely follow Paul's similar description of the Gentiles' depravity. Paul writes, "They have become filled with every kind of wickedness, evil, greed and depravity. They are full of envy, murder, strife, deceit and malice. They are gossips, slanderers, God-haters, insolent, arrogant and boastful; they invent ways of doing evil; they disobey their parents; they are senseless, faithless, heartless, ruthless" (Rom. 1:29–31). It is a horrible picture, but one justly painted of our depraved race.

We do not like to face such descriptions, of course. But there is no accusation in these lists that cannot justly be leveled against our culture or that of any age in history. Let us admit that, although these descriptions are harsh, they are accurate.

Do we need statistics? During the 1960s crime in the United States rose 148 percent, while arrests of persons under 18 nearly doubled. In 1969, the number of reported crimes was 4,989,700, which made the crime rate 2,471 per 100,000 persons. An average of nine major crimes per minute was committed in America during the same period. In 1971, New

York City, with a population of only 8,000,000 persons, recorded more crimes than England, Scotland, Wales, Ireland, Switzerland, Spain, Sweden, the Netherlands, Norway, and Denmark combined. In the following years the crime rate increased. New York now has more than 300,000 alcoholics, affecting the lives of 1,500,000 people and costing more than $1 billion annually. The loss approaches $2 billion for the upward of 100,000 hardcore heroin addicts, who must continually steal to feed their habit. Sexual perversion and sex crimes have also risen rapidly. In one recent year, forcible rape rose 17 percent. One out of four marriages ends in divorce, and in some areas of the country the rate is one in two. Venereal disease is epidemic. Homosexuals clamor for recognition. In 1978, more than one million unmarried girls below the age of sixteen became pregnant. The estimated number of abortions is now over one and a half million annually, and in some areas there are more abortions than live births.[1]

What is the cause of this depravity? Is it not that our nation, like ancient Israel, has rejected the knowledge of God? Is our judgment to be less certain or less swift?

Second, Hosea cites the *destruction of the environment:* "Because of this the land mourns, and all who live in it waste away; the beasts of the field and the birds of the air and the fish of the sea are dying" (v. 3). I am not sure exactly how this is to be taken in regard to Israel. I can understand how the sin of the people in neglecting or denuding the land might cause the ground to become wasteland with due effect on the animals and birds. But I cannot see how Israel's sin could effect even the fish of the sea. Perhaps this was the result of a specific judgment by God. What I do understand is that these sins are pre-eminently true of us.

We may wonder how *Israel* could harm *her* environment; she seems to have lacked the technology. But we *have* the technology, and we are using it to do precisely this. We kill birds. We kill beasts. We kill fish. We have exterminated whole species. Can we be excused for such things? Can we be innocent when Israel, who was capable of so much less, was found guilty?

The third landmark on the slippery slope of Israel's decline was the *debasement of leadership,* particularly religious leadership, in this case the debasement of her priests: "The more the priests increased, the more they sinned against me; they exchanged their Glory for something disgraceful. They feed on the sins of my people and relish their wickedness. And it will be: Like people, like priests. I will punish both of them for their ways and repay them for their deeds" (vv. 7–9).

The period of moral and spiritual decline about which the book is written was not a period of the withering up of "religion." Godlessness is not incompatible with religion. In fact, it goes along with it nicely. Here was a period characterized by cursing, lying, murder, stealing, adultery; but during this period the priesthood grew in numbers as those who were professional religionists moved in to capitalize on the debauchery. Why is this? Again we turn to Romans to discover that when knowledge of the true God is refused, false gods inevitably come in to take the true God's place. True religion is replaced by false religion, godliness by superstition. Paul says, "Although they claimed to be wise, they became fools and exchanged the glory of the immortal God for images made to look like mortal man and birds and animals and reptiles" (Rom. 1:22, 23).

I see another point in these verses: people get the leaders they deserve. Ho-

---

[1]For a fuller list of these and other statistics see, Boice, *The Last and Future World,* pp. 53, 54. For statistics on abortion see C. Everett Koop, *The Right to Live; The Right to Die* (Wheaton, Ill.: Tyndale, 1976), p. 67.

sea puts it in the form of a popular saying: "Like people, like priests" (v. 9). He means that if the people are godly, they will be sent godly leaders. If they are corrupt, God will let them have corrupt leaders. If they are superstitious, God will abandon them to astrologers, palmists, cult figures, and other charlatans. This is happening on a wide scale today.

The fourth step in Israel's decline was *personal emptiness* or dissatisfaction: "They will eat but not have enough [that is, nothing will satisfy them; even their feasts will taste insipid]; they will engage in prostitution but not increase, because they have deserted the LORD to give themselves to prostitution, to old wine and new, which take away the understanding of my people" (vv. 10–12).

It is hard to read this decree of God against the people and their priests without thinking of the shallow reasons why Gomer left Hosea. Hosea indicates that Gomer left him for things and pleasure, both of which were present in the lavish feasts that marked the yearly festivals, new moons, and sabbaths (Hos. 2:11). In this debauchery four things came together: food, sex, wealth, and religion. The world might look to such things and wonder what more one could want. But God tells us that He has arranged life in such a way that if these things are pursued apart from holiness, the result will be frustration rather than satisfaction. There will be food to eat, but it will seem tiring after awhile and the glutton will be searching restlessly for some new titillation. Sex will abound; but it will not satisfy, and the profligate will turn to ever more kinky forms of sex to satisfy his libido. Money will be everywhere; but it will never be enough. Everyone will seem to be religious; but the great questions of life will continue to go unanswered and beneath the formalism of the religious rites will be the gnawing suspicion that God has turned a deaf ear and that all such rites are worthless.

Moreover, God will not even bother to judge such excesses. They will be their own worst punishment: "I will not punish your daughters when they turn to prostitution, nor your daughters-in-law when they commit adultery, because the men themselves consort with harlots and sacrifice with temple prostitutes—a people without understanding will come to ruin!" (v. 14).

That is the final and lowest point of the decline: *ruin on a national scale.* It comes first in individual lives as those who will not have God make shipwreck of themselves. It comes next in families, husbands leaving wives and wives leaving husbands—the children abandoned. Next it is observed in institutions as corruption enters corporate life. At last the entire nation is overcome, as Israel was and our nation most certainly will be— except for national repentance.

A WORD TO JUDAH

This brings us to the concluding section of the chapter. Hosea has presented the indictment of God against Israel, exposing its root cause and tracing it through a declining series of effects of sin and judgments to the point where God will not even intervene to avert the destruction. So far as Israel is concerned, the Rubicon is past. Judgment is certain.

But Israel was not the whole of the Jewish homeland at this stage in history. She was the larger nation, the northern one. But further south there was still the half of the nation known as Judah, and Judah (thanks to the greater faithfulness of her kings) had not slipped so far on the moral scale as Israel. For her there was still hope. Abruptly, therefore, Hosea turns from Israel to speak to this, the southern state, and warn her to shun the nothern kingdom that Judah herself might be spared. "Let not Judah become guilty," cries Hosea. "Do not go to Gilgal; do not go up to Beth Aven. And do not swear, 'As surely as the LORD lives!' The Israelites are stubborn, like a stubborn heifer. How then can the LORD pasture them like lambs in a meadow? Ephraim is joined to idols; leave him alone! Even when their drinks are gone, they continue their prostitution; their rulers dearly love shameful ways. A whirlwind will sweep them away, and their sacrifices will bring them shame" (vv. 15–19).

The references to Gilgal and Beth Aven are significant. When Israel and Judah had divided after the death of Solomon, Rehoboam had taken control in the south while Jeroboam had assumed rule in the north. Each was an adherent to the religion of Jehovah. But the temple and its cult were in the south, and Jeroboam reasoned that if the pious Jews of his northern kingdom went south to the temple worship as the law required, his hold over the north would be weakened. Consequently, he set up rival shrines at Beth Aven (Bethel) and Gilgal—contrary to the law—and encouraged the people of the north to worship at these places. This led quickly to idolatry, as Hosea and (even more forcefully) Amos disclose.

God's warning is to flee from these places: "Do not go to Gilgal; do not go up to Beth Aven."

Is that not the warning He would give us? We live in a declining culture. Sin is apparent on every hand. But it may not be as late for us as it was for Israel. We may not be consigned to judgment irrevocably. If that is the case, then we must hear God's words to Judah and respond as she was encouraged to respond. The word to her is a word of separation, not separation from the world (for she has a witness in the world), but rather separation from the worldliness of the world and particularly from the false and shallow religion that passes so easily as true.

5

The Moth and the Lion

(Hosea 5:1–15)

"I am like a moth to Ephraim, like rot to the people of Judah. . . . For I will be like a lion to Ephraim, like a great lion to Judah. I will tear them to pieces and go away; I will carry them off, with no one to rescue them."

One of the things we tell ourselves when we attempt to run away from God is that if we forget Him He will forget us. But God does not forget us. On the contrary, He knows all things, including all we are and do, and this is frightening.

Actually, it is a cause for resentment and even hatred for God. The greatest theologian America has ever produced, Jonathan Edwards, once wrote a sermon entitled "Man Naturally God's Enemy" in which he listed the attributes of God that sinful men and women dislike and showed why we dislike them. Edwards wrote, "Though they are ignorant of God, yet from what they hear of him, and from what is manifest by the light of the nature of God, they do not like him. By his being endowed with such attributes as he is, they have an aversion to him. They hear God is an infinitely holy, pure, and righteous Being, and they do not like him upon this account. . . . They have greater aversion to him because he is omniscient and knows all things; because his omniscience is a holy omniscience. They are not pleased that he is omnipotent, and can do whatever he pleases; because it is a holy omnipotence. They are enemies even to his mercy, because it is a holy mercy. They do not like his immutability, because by this he never will be otherwise than he is, an infinitely holy God."[1] According to Edwards, all are naturally God's enemies because of five things: God's *holiness*, because we are not holy; God's *omniscience*, because He knows we are not holy; God's *omnipotence*, because this offends our desire for autonomy; God's *mercy*, because it is a holy mercy; and God's *immutability* (unchangeableness), because God will never be other than He is in these "offensive" attributes.

Each of these attributes of God deserves careful consideration and, indeed, has been studied elsewhere.[2] But we mention Edwards here, not for the wider picture, but rather for the light his words throw on God's omniscience.

Unknowing But Known

What a marvelous contrast we have between this theme, in chapter 5, and the complementary theme of knowing God, which we found in chapter 4. In chapter 4 the chief complaint against Israel was that she had abandoned her

---

[1]Jonathan Edwards, *The Works of President Edwards*, Vol. 4 (New York: Robert Carter and Brothers, 1879), p. 38.

[2]Cf. R. C. Sproul, *The Psychology of Atheism* (Minneapolis: Bethany Fellowship, 1974), pp. 81–158, and James Montgomery Boice, *The Sovereign God* (Downers Grove, Ill.: InterVarsity Press, 1978), pp. 149–90.

knowledge of God. God desired her to have such knowledge; it is the greatest of all spiritual blessings. But Israel had chosen sin instead, and the knowledge of God that she once possessed had vanished. Like Hosea's wife, she had been running from God, attempting to put this former knowledge behind her. But although she had forgotten Him, He had not forgotten her. Now he comes to remind her of this holy knowledge. His words are: "Hear this, you priests! Pay attention, you Israelites! Listen, O royal house! . . . I *know* all about Ephraim; Israel is *not hidden* from me. Ephraim, you have now turned to prostitution; Israel is corrupt" (5:1, 3).

In one of his writings A. W. Tozer has spoken of the omniscience of God being a cause of "shaking fear" for the man who has something to hide. But since we all have something to hide, this attribute is a terror to us all.

We have a strange ambivalence at this point. On the one hand, we want to be known. But on the other hand, we do not want to be known too well. The fact that we want to be known comes from our being made in the image of God (Gen. 1:26, 27). That phrase means many things, but one thing it means is that God has made us persons as He is a person. One of the characteristics of persons is that they want to be known by other persons. They want to have relationships. If you come into a room one day and no one bothers to look up and say hello, you feel slighted. If someone regularly slights you, you come to dislike that person. Some who have been slighted or neglected in their childhood develop personality traits that seek to attract attention; they become loud or aggressive, or they are always showing off. Others, who are unable to develop such personality compensations, often become warped and introverted. These behavior patterns show that we want to be known. We have a need to be known by others.

At the same time, we do not want to be known too thoroughly. We have our guard up psychologically and allow ourselves to be known only to the extent that we sense acceptance, and even then never totally.

We may illustrate this by a young couple who are just getting to know each other. On their first date they try to make the best possible impression. She gets all fixed up and then tries to act as intelligent and well-mannered as she can. He tries to be sophisticated. If that first date goes well, each begins to wonder if the relationship is not being based on a false impression and perhaps even worry about what will happen if his or her true self becomes known. So on the next date each one lets down a little and waits to see what will happen. He says, "You know, you probably think I'm a very sophisticated person, and [smugly] it's true, I am. But I wasn't always this way. In fact, about ten years ago—when I was just a kid—I was really quite awkward, and I was afraid of girls." Then he doesn't say any more. He waits. Because what he wants the girl to say is something like, "Oh, I'm glad you told me that because years ago I wasn't very sophisticated either. In fact, I wore braces on my teeth and felt very ugly." That kind of statement means that he is accepted for what he has confessed himself to be and that the relationship can then go a step further. On the next date they might confess a weakness of only five years before or two years before. Eventually they will talk about how things are at the present. I am convinced, however, that at the end of that whole process, even in a good marriage and after years of sharing, no one really tells all that is inside and is always a bit anxious about what might happen if his or her true self were known.

Why is this? Why do we fear exposure? The answer is not an irrational fear at this point, for our fear is not irrational. It is rather that we do have something to hide. We are not what we ought to be. We are sinners, and whether we admit it openly or not we know it and develop psychological defense mechanisms. We hide on three levels: 1) we hide from ourselves; the proof is our failure to face the facts about ourselves squarely, to make excuses; 2) we hide from others; our posturing is the evidence; 3) we hide from God.

But here is the problem. We can hide from others. We can even do a good job of hiding from ourselves. But how do you hide from One before whom "all hearts are open, all desires known" (Anglican collect)? How do you deal with One of whom it is written, "Nothing in all creation is hidden from God's sight. Everything is uncovered and laid bare before the eyes of him to whom we must give account" (Heb. 4:13)? We cannot. We cannot hide from God. The only thing we can do is accept the reality of God's nature as it is and come to Him on the basis of Christ's atonement.

WHAT GOD KNOWS

Israel was unwilling to face the fact that God really did know her—sin blinds us even to such obvious facts as this. Therefore, God follows the statement that He knows Israel with specifics. These occupy the next four verses.

Taken in logical sequence (though not the sequence in the verses), the first thing that God knows about Israel is her *"seeking" God*. The reference is in verse 6: "When they go with their flocks and herds to *seek the* LORD. . . ." This is not a true seeking after God. It corresponds to the universal religiosity of the Gentiles who, having turned from the knowledge of the true God, substitute idols in His place (Rom. 1:22). Still, it is seeking of a sort— seeking for something while they are actually running away from God—and God is pointing out that He sees it. He knows what is happening, and He is not fooled by it.

If the question were put to Israel—

"What are you doing?"—they would say, "We are seeking Jehovah." They probably would point to their flocks and herds dedicated for sacrifice as proof of the sincerity of their intentions. If the question were put to many people today, they would claim the same thing: "We are seeking God. Look how religious we are." But God says that they are not seeking; and the reason He knows they are not seeking is that they are refusing to abandon the sin that always keeps a person from actually coming to Him. The text says, "Their deeds do not permit them to return to their God. A spirit of prostitution is in their heart; they do not acknowledge the LORD" (v. 4).

This is the same thing Paul says in Romans: "There is no one righteous, not even one; there is no one who understands, no one who seeks God. All have turned away, they have together become worthless; there is no one who does good, not even one" (Rom. 3:10–12). "But," says someone, "I *have* sought God. I have sought Him everywhere, but I have not been able to find Him. I was born in a Baptist home and attended a Baptist church. But I couldn't find God in the Baptist church, so I left that church and became a Methodist. When I couldn't find God in the Methodist church, I became a Presbyterian. After that I became an Episcopalian, and finally I joined the Roman Catholic communion. I've sought God everywhere, but I can't find Him." God says that this is not true. The truth is rather that you have been running away from God. When God got close to you in the Baptist church you left it and became a Methodist. When He got close to you in the Methodist church, you became a Presbyterian. When He met you there, you became an Episcopalian, and then a Roman Catholic. You have been running away. And if He gets close to you in the Roman Catholic church, you are likely to look around to make sure no one is watching and slip back into the Baptist church once again.

The second thing God says about the religiosity of Israel (indeed, of the race as a whole) is that He knows it is *not satisfying*. In fact, He tells them about it in advance saying that it will not be satisfying: "When they go with their flocks and herds to seek the LORD, *they will not find him;* he has withdrawn himself from them" (v. 6). No doubt the people professed otherwise. As true religion declined they seem to have made more of their sacrifices, worship, high holy days, and festivals. They would have said "how meaningful," "how moving," "how spiritual an experience" it all was. But God says that it is actually worthless because it had nothing to do with Him. He was not in it; and if He is not in it, it is not true worship no matter how "meaningful," "moving," or "spiritual" it may be.

I am persuaded that this is what much of the new liturgicalism is producing— emptiness and dissatisfaction—because it does not actually have to do with God. Professor Donald G. Bloesch speaks of such liturgical innovation in a chapter entitled "Burying the Gospel." "The new liturgy, like the new theology which informs it, also tends to bury instead of exalt the gospel. New liturgical experiments that feature agape meals, guitar masses, audio-visual aids, and religious drama often leave out the one thing that is most important as far as evangelical theology is concerned—the preaching and hearing of the Word of God. The heart of the gospel, say the avant-garde liturgists, is not a rational message but an experience of community or a style of life. The Catholic lay theologian Leslie Dewart contends in his *The Future of Belief* that Christianity has a '*mission, not a message.* . . . What it communicates is its reality and existence, not an idea.'

"In contradistinction to the liturgical tradition, the new style liturgy is centered not in God's revelation but in man's faith. It is geared to the celebration of the festivity of life instead of the Word made flesh. Its concern is with the search for identity rather than the worship of a living, personal God."[3]

I cannot say whether your worship, prayer, Bible reading, or other religious activity is like that. But *you* know whether it is the real thing or not. You know whether or not your soul is being satisfied by true fellowship with the living God. If it is not, then you must turn from the sin that is barring you from God's presence and come to Him in Christ where that sin has been forgiven and a door of access into the presence of the Father has been opened.

There is one more thing God says He knows about these people: their *hypocrisy*. The chapter does not use the word, but this is what is meant when God speaks against them for turning to the king of Assyria for help. "When Ephraim saw his sickness, and Judah his sores, then Ephraim turned to Assyria, and sent to the great king for help. But he is not able to cure you, not able to heal your sores" (v. 13). This is hypocrisy because in their worship they had been voicing confidence in God, while practically, in their politics, they had been depending on their alliances with the godless statesmen around them.

Many do today. They come to church to sing, "Our God, our Help in ages past, our Hope for years to come." But they go out and act exactly like pagans as they scramble, cheat, scheme, and use every device at their disposal to get what they want out of life.

WHAT WE SHOULD KNOW

Thus far in our study we have seen two types of knowledge: 1) knowledge of God, which we have rejected—because we do not like the God who is to be known—and 2) the knowledge that

---

[3]Donald G. Bloesch, *The Invaded Church* (Waco, Tex.: Work Books, 1975), p. 44. Bloesch also points to certain kinds of social activism, psychological analysis, cultural preaching, and concern for church mergers as things that tend to bury the gospel and exclude true worship.

God has of us. This second area of knowledge is unsettling, for we are not right with God and we fear to have that wrong relationship and its cause, our sin, exposed. But there is also a third kind of knowledge. It is the knowledge of God's ways with sinners, which He now reveals (in spite of our rejection of Him) so that we might see His hand in the things that come into our lives and be led back to Him by that discovery.

God uses an illustration to make this truth stick in our minds. It concerns a moth and a lion. After having spoken clearly of Israel's sin, which had turned the heart of the nation from Him, God says that He will first be like a moth to the people: "I am like a moth to Ephraim, like rot to the people of Judah" (v. 12). There are two things a moth does. First, a moth *distracts* us or bothers us in a harmless way. If you have had the experience of reading outdoors on a porch on a summer evening, you know how a moth can be attracted by the light and suddenly flutter in front of you. It is only a light touch, but it diverts your attention and perhaps even makes you stop reading. By comparing Himself to a moth God may be saying that at the beginning of our path of disobedience He is like that. He distracts us from sin, bothers us, tries to get us away from it and back to thinking of Him once again.

Second, many moths are *destructive*. It is in the larva or caterpillar stage that the damage is done. The young feed off plants, crops, woolen clothing, upholstery, fur, or carpets on which the eggs have been laid by the female moth. These things can rot away, as Hosea suggests: "like rot to the people of Judah." Here is a case where we, having resisted the fluttering of the moth, now find it to have gotten into the things we value and to have destroyed them. God says that He will also do that to turn us to Him.

But suppose we do not turn to God when He sends insect troubles? Suppose we resist these warnings? Two verses farther on we find a word that is much more terrible: "For I will be like a lion to Ephraim, like a great lion to Judah. I will tear them to pieces and go away; I will carry them off, with no one to rescue them" (v. 14). One commentator writes, "This is the progress of God's love. He will not let us lose ourselves without exhausting all of the resources of his love. The moth may have eaten valuable possessions, but we can turn the rug around, we can put the couch against a wall where the ravages cannot be seen, we can move a lamp so that the light will not shine upon the destruction. Then he is forced to send the lion. With no warning at all, great trouble springs upon us like a beast of prey. Fear grips us. Our blood runs cold. Happy are we, if we realize that this is the Lord of love, who calls us to turn from the path where lions lurk and to run to the path of his will where no enemy can assail us."[4]

Let me ask this one last question: What happens if even then we do not turn to Him? What happens if, our garments and food destroyed by insects and our bodies mangled to the point of death, we still will not hear Him? In that case, says God, He reluctantly pours out on us the greatest judgment of all: *He leaves us.* He turns away from us. He abandons us to precisely what we want: "Then I will go back to my place until they admit their guilt. And they will seek my face; in their misery they will earnestly seek me" (v. 15). I can think of no more horrible judgment than to be abandoned by God in the very depths of our wretchedness and misery.

ROBES OF RIGHTEOUSNESS

Yet that is our hope, for even at this point God is being good to those who are His. He will hide His face. We will grope in our darkness. But even this, dreadful as it is, exists only "until" we

[4]Donald Grey Barnhouse, *Let Me Illustrate: Stories, Anecdotes, Illustrations* (Westwood, N. J.: Fleming H. Revell, 1967), p. 20.

admit our guilt and turn to Him (v. 15). Thus it is that even in the darkest hour there is a glimmer of hope and love in God's judgments.

What happens when we do turn to Him? We feared His omniscience because it meant exposure of ourselves as we truly are. We have done everything possible to avoid admitting our guilt. But when we finally come to God and allow Him to remove the robes of our self-righteousness, to which we have clung so desperately, we find that He is waiting with the blood of Christ to cleanse our sin, the oil of His spirit to anoint our wounded bodies and the robes of His own righteousness to clothe us. When Adam and Eve sinned, they ran from God when they heard His voice in the garden. But God sought them out, confronted them in their sin and then clothed them with skins of animals that He Himself killed. When Hosea found Gomer, she was exposed on the auction block of Samaria, naked in the sight of all the people. But Hosea purchased her for himself and clothed her again. So it is with us. We have hidden from God. But in Christ we can now stand before Him. We can be known and yet clothed at the same time. Indeed, we can cry with Isaiah, "I delight greatly in the LORD; my soul rejoices in my God. For he has clothed me with garments of salvation and arrayed me in a robe of righteousness, as a bridegroom adorns his head like a priest, and as a bride adorns herself with her jewels. . . . The Sovereign LORD will make righteousness and praise spring up before all nations" (Isa. 61:10, 11).

6

Repentance That Does Not Count

(Hosea 6:1–7:16)

"Come, let us return to the LORD. He has torn us to pieces but he will heal us; he has injured us but he will bind up our wounds. After two days he will revive us; on the third day he will restore us, that we may live in his presence. Let us acknowledge the LORD; let us press on to acknowledge him. As surely as the sun rises, he will appear; he will come to us like the winter rains, like the spring rains that water the earth."

A convict was released from a Kansas prison after serving seven years for fraud. Upon his release he immediately acquired someone else's credit cards and went on a spending spree that took him across the state in first-class hotels, gourmet restaurants, and private planes. He was caught and brought to trial. In court the man confessed what he had done. But he asked the judge to pardon him on the ground that he had now learned his lesson. "It was wrong," he said. "I know that now, and I will never do anything like that again."

The judge was unimpressed. He said, "I have learned that courtroom confessions last only until the criminal gets to the door." Then he committed the man to prison again.

This story introduces the sixth and seventh chapters of Hosea's prophecy, for the repentance with which these chapters open is as ungenuine as the "about face" of this thief. Israel had rebelled against God and had suffered for it. A cry for repentance went out: "Come, let us return to the LORD. He has torn us to pieces but he will heal us; he has injured us but he will bind up our wounds" (6:1). This call was probably voiced with great intensity and even conviction, but it was not genuine.

SIN AND PRESUMPTION

Look over these verses and see if you can detect what is wrong with this confession. Does Israel seem to be honest, forthright, orthodox? They have the right vocabulary. The two main verbs, "return" and "acknowledge," are certainly what God had been calling on the people to do. There is recognition that the hand of God was in their calamities, for He is the One who has "torn . . . to pieces" and "injured" the people. These words even have a proper sense of God's sovereignty and appeal to Him, not on the basis of Israel's deeds, but of His mercy.

If you are a careful reader and understand biblical theology, you will recognize that the essential elements of a true confession are missing. The first element that is missing—indeed, the obvious and almost inescapable element—is a *reference to sin*. There is acknowledgment of the consequences of Israel's sin: injury and the absence of God Himself. But there is total non-acknowledgment of the sin that caused them. There is nothing of the acceptable prayer of the publican, referred to by Jesus, who cried out, "God, have mercy on me, a sinner" (Luke 18:13).

This has great current application. In

recent years in America media attention has focused on evangelicals and their "born again" experience. Key government officials and others have been identified in this way. Gallup poll people even identified one recent year as "the year of the evangelical." But in many interviews between reporters and known evangelical leaders the reporters have asked, "If evangelicals really are as numerous as the polls indicate, why is it that there seems to be so little impact upon the country? Crime continues to increase. Divorce statistics climb. It is the same in all other areas so far as we are able to judge. Is it that there are really not as many evangelicals as you claim, or is it the case that being 'born again' actually makes no difference in how a person lives?"

What *is* the problem? The problem is that the evangelical movement in America in the twentieth century is shallow. It speaks of salvation, but it does not grapple with sin. And since it does not grapple with sin, there can be no true repentance. I am often asked whether we are witnessing a revival today, and I always answer that we are not. We are seeing many persons converted; to that extent I take the Gallup poll seriously. But there is no revival and will be no revival until there is an acute awareness of sin and a genuine turning from it. Until that happens any national profession of faith will be hollow, and the country will continue to decline, just as Israel did.

A second missing element in the alleged "repentance" recorded in Hosea 6:1–3 is a *personal relationship with God.* This is not as easy to detect as the first omission, the confession of sin, but it is there nonetheless. It is seen in the mechanical way the people conceive of God's restoring them.

Voltaire, the brilliant French atheist, once said sarcastically of God's forgiveness, "Pardonner? C'est son métier!" ("Forgiveness? That's his job!") That glib rejoinder is on Israel's tongue in these verses. True, God has judged them. But He will restore them again. That's the way He always does it. They have been down for two days, but they will rise on the third. The sun sets; the sun also rises. God will be like that with His people. The presumption of this form of thought is captured by James Luther Mays in his excellent commentary on Hosea: "That Yahweh alone kills and makes alive, wounds and heals, was an old dictum of faith in Yahwism (Deut. 32:39), originally a way of saying that in effect Yahweh alone is God. But the ancient affirmation is twisted to link the acts of wounding and healing together as though they were an automatic sequence, an expected cycle of divine work on which the devotees of Yahweh could rely willy-nilly. There is no mention of the iniquity of the nation as in 14:1ff., no word of the change that must be wrought through judgment. 'When he is "worshipped" he will tend our wounds, for that is his business and nature.' The call is issued in presumptuous confidence that Yahweh will be quick to respond."[1]

It is always an error to presume thus on God. We try to force Him into our little boxes, thinking that in that way we can somehow control Him and get Him to do what we want. But God cannot be thus controlled, and it is the case rather that He conforms us to His wishes. We are never in greater danger than when we assume that He will always forgive us as long as we go through the outward forms of repentance.

There are two terrible consequences of our doing this. First, we depersonalize God. Rather than allowing Him to be for us the great personal God who discloses Himself in history and in His written Word, He becomes for us something like a great scientific equation, which can

---

[1]James Luther Mays, *Hosea: A Commentary* (Philadelphia: Westminster, 1976), p. 95.

always be expected to work so long as we get the ingredients of the chemical reaction right. We do not worship a God like that; we use Him. Second, we empty the biblical vocabulary—in this case, the words "return" and "acknowledge"—of meaning. Mays writes, "Once Yahweh is thought of in this unhistorical impersonal fashion, the notions of 'return' and 'know God' lose their validity and power for reformation, because they have no focus on the saving history and covenant relation, and so can only stir the current religiosity of Israel."[2]

This is true for vast segments of so-called Christianity today. There is no real awareness of sin and turning from it; consequently the biblical terms lose meaning. "Sin" no longer means rebellion against God and His righteous law, for which we are held accountable, but rather ignorance or the kind of oppression that is imagined to reside in social structures. "Jesus" becomes our pattern or example, the highest evolutionary peak of humanity, rather than the incarnate God who came to die for our salvation. "Salvation" ceases to be "getting right with God," as the old theology would say, or even "God moving to redeem us in Christ." Rather it is liberation from the oppression of this world's structures. "Faith" is awareness. "Evangelism" is helping people to become aware. So it goes! It will always go thus until men and women see themselves as sinners before a holy God, and turn from that sin to God through faith in Jesus Christ. Until that happens our little "repentances" do not count. We can "repent." We can go through all the rituals of religion—going to church, singing hymns, giving money, serving on church boards, even doing "good" deeds—but it will all be worthless so far as finding God is concerned.

A CHARGE REPEATED

This is precisely what God says in chapters 6 and 7. God acknowledges that

the people are crying out. But "they do not cry out to me from their hearts," He expostulates (7:14). They wail, but they do not turn from their evil way.

In 6:4–7 there is a reiteration of the charge God brought against the people in 4:1. In the earlier verse God said, "There is no faithfulness, no love (devotion), no acknowledgment of God in the land." Now, in spite of the protests of repentance with which chapter 6 began, God says that the charge still stands: "What can I do with you, Ephraim? What can I do with you, Judah? Your love is like the morning mist, like the early dew that disappears. Therefore I cut you in pieces with my prophets, I killed you with the words of my mouth; my judgments flashed like lightning upon you. For I desire mercy, not sacrifice, and acknowledgment of God rather than burnt offerings. Like Adam, they have broken the covenant—they were unfaithful to me there."

Let us take these accusations in the order in which they occur in chapter 6. The first is a *lack of love for God*, the second item mentioned in 4:1. God says that it is like "the morning mist" or "the early dew that disappears." This does not mean that the people have a genuine love for God but only that what they do have does not stand the test of time. It means that this "love" is inadequate. In fact, it is so inadequate it cannot really be called love.

What the people of Israel probably had in this period was an emotional attachment to the ancient God of their fathers, much the way some people today consider themselves "Christians" because of the genuine faith of their parents or grandparents. The people of Israel were worshipers of Jehovah, much like those in America, Britain, Canada, and other western nations are "worshipers" of Christ. It is all meaningless, says God. It is as passing as morning mist or dew.

I remember a trip through Bavaria by auto many years ago in which, on one

[2]Ibid., p. 96.

particular morning, the dew clung so closely to everything that the world seemed transformed. Everything was dull gray—houses, fences, fields, roads. Even the cattle seemed coated and their cow bells muffled by the enveloping shroud. I thought at the time that it was as if a giant painter had used an immense spray can to cover everything with a flat gray paint. Even time seemed frozen. But that was at 7:00 or 8:00 A.M., and before long the sun began to come up. When it did everything sprang to life before my eyes. Colors reappeared. Dampness vanished. By 10:00 A.M. no one would have known that the entire countryside had been covered with dew just hours before. God says that this is what our "love" for Him is like . . . without repentance.

The second item in God's charge is the absence of any true *knowledge of Himself.* At first glance this seems a strange and even unfair accusation, for the earlier repentance of the people had contained this very word: "Let us acknowledge the LORD; let us press on to acknowledge him" (v. 3). The people seem to want to do that. But God explains the apparent unfairness by showing that they want wrongly to define this knowledge in their own way, that is, ritualistically but without any true transformation in their lives. What they want is "sacrifice" and "burnt offerings" (v. 6), ceremony. God wants confession of sin and practice of righteousness and justice by those who claim to know Him.

In these ancient days sacrifice was the essential religious act. So it must have sounded strange indeed for Hosea's hearers to be told that God loves "mércy" and "knowledge" of Himself rather than burnt offerings. Still, it was true then and is also true today. In fact, we find the same emphasis at many other points in the biblical revelation.

Amos says it forcefully. Speaking on behalf of God, he declares, "I hate, I despise your religious feasts; I cannot stand your assemblies. Even though you bring me burnt offerings and grain offerings, I will not accept them. Though you bring choice fellowship offerings, I will have no regard for them. Away with the noise of your songs! I will not listen to the music of your harps. But let justice roll on like a river, righteousness like a never-failing stream!" (Amos 5:21–24).

Isaiah writes, "I have more than enough of burnt offerings, of rams and the fat of fattened animals; I have no pleasure in the blood of bulls and lambs and goats. When you come to meet with me, who has asked this of you, this trampling of my courts? Stop bringing meaningless offerings! Your incense is detestable to me. New Moons, Sabbaths and convocations—I cannot bear your evil assemblies. Your New Moon festivals and your appointed feasts my soul hates. They have become a burden to me; I am weary of bearing them. When you spread out your hands in prayer, I will hide my eyes from you; even if you offer many prayers, I will not listen. Your hands are full of blood; wash and make yourselves clean. Take your evil deeds out of my sight! Stop doing wrong, learn to do right! Seek justice, encourage the oppressed. Defend the cause of the fatherless, plead the case of the widow" (Isa. 1:11–17).

David captured it when he said, "You do not delight in sacrifice, or I would bring it; you do not take pleasure in burnt offerings. The sacrifices of God are a broken spirit; a broken and contrite heart, O God, you will not despise" (Ps. 51:16, 17).

The third and final item in God's charge against the people is *unfaithfulness,* the first charge leveled in chapter 4. Here it is carried back to the fall of the race in Adam: "Like Adam, they have broken the covenant—they were unfaithful to me there" (v. 7).[3] The point is that the

---

[3] The KJV translates the words "like Adam" as "like men," since the word "Adam" does mean man. But there is a fuller meaning (and the passage as a whole makes better sense) as the NIV renders it. The RSV and NASB have preceded the NIV in this wording. The NEB regards the noun as a place name, saying, "At Admah they have broken my covenant, there they have played me false."

rebellion of Israel is something that lies deep in human nature, having been inherited from Adam, and therefore does not surprise God. This does not excuse Israel; for it is "they" who have broken the covenant . . . like Adam. It is merely that they have inherited their unfaithful nature from Adam and may therefore also be said to have broken the covenant "there."

What is the consequence? It is the same twofold consequence seen in the early history of our race. On the one hand, there was an attempt to cover up sin (Adam tried to blame Eve; Eve tried to blame the serpent). On the other hand and at the same time, sin began to abound. God says, "Gilead is a city of wicked men, stained with footprints of blood. As marauders lie in ambush for a man, so do bands of priests; they murder on the road to Shechem, committing shameful crimes. I have seen a horrible thing in the house of Israel. There Ephraim is given to prostitution and Israel is defiled. . . . They practice deceit, thieves break into houses, bandits rob in the streets." God concludes, "They do not realize that I remember all their evil deeds. Their sins . . . are always before me" (Hos. 6:8–10; 7:1, 2).

One of sin's tragedies is that it causes us to think it can be hidden. It cannot. God reminds us that it is ever before Him. The only escape from judgment for sin is a true repentance and a turning to God for salvation through the death of Christ.

Four Images

The remaining parts of chapter 7 give four images to show how God regards those who confess His name while nevertheless continuing their rebellious way of life: an oven, a half-baked cake, a dove, and a faulty weapon.

The first image, "an oven" (vv. 4, 6, 7), is common both in the Bible and in secular sources. It refers to inordinate sexual desires primarily, portraying them

as intense fires that drive the adulterer and eventually consume him. No doubt there are overtones of that spiritual adultery that the story of Hosea and his wife Gomer were to illustrate. But as God speaks in these verses we also sense that there were very literal adulteries occurring all over the nation and at all levels of society. The verses immediately before this speak of murder, robbery, deceit and prostitution. Again, they refer to intoxicating feasts, where such adulteries were most likely to occur. What God is saying is that these were not the innocent or harmless acts between "consenting adults" that our society makes them out to be but were actually passions inflamed by sin that eventually destroyed the one affected by them.

There is also a direct political reference in these verses (vv. 1–7), a description of what we would call a coup. It begins with flattery of the king and his princes (v. 1). It contains a plot in which the rulers are encouraged to become drunk at a festival (v. 5). Then there is the stealthy approach (v. 6) as the result of which the king and rulers fall (v. 7). Something similar to this occurred several times in the waning days of Israel's political life. King succeeded king, and the nation suffered in the accompanying uncertainty. In her quest for autonomy she was literally burning herself up. Yet neither she nor her kings called to God for help.

The second image that God uses of the rebellious nation is "a flat cake not turned over" (v. 8). We would say "half-baked," that is, cooked more than enough on one side but completely undone on the other. This suggests two things: first, that Israel in her present state was useless; second, that she might be said to make God sick. We think of the description of the church at Laodicea in Revelation. She is described as being "lukewarm—neither hot nor cold," as a result of which God was about to spit her out of His mouth (Rev. 3:16). If that is true of this church, which was merely lukewarm, how much more must it be true of Israel at this stage—a cake, half of which was raw dough.

Israel did not even seem to be aware of what it was. Hosea says, "His hair is sprinkled with gray, but he does not notice" (v. 9). In other words, Israel was in national old age but did not know this or fear for it, so blinding is sin's power. G. Campbell Morgan wrote of this blindness, "Signs of decadence, which are patent to others, are undiscovered by ourselves; and we go on, and on, and on, the victims of ebbing strength, spiritually and morally becoming degenerate, without knowing it! We are blind to the signs which are self-evident to onlookers. There is no condition more perilous to our highest well-being than this of unconscious decadence."[4] It was of Israel as it had been of Samson so many years before: "He did not know that the LORD had left him" (Judg. 16:20).

The third image is of *"a dove"* (v. 11). A dove brings thoughts of beauty. Symbolically it means "peace." But this is not the meaning here. In these verses the dove suggests a helpless creature "easily deceived and senseless." Having forsaken God, who was her only true source of national security, Israel now does not know where to turn. She looks to Egypt, the great power to the south. She looks to Assyria in the east. God says that He will now pull her down: "When they go, I will throw my net over them; I will pull them down like birds of the air. When I hear them flocking together, I will catch them" (v. 12).

Finally, God compares Israel to *"a faulty bow"* (v. 16). In this case she is not only useless but even downright dangerous. The one who puts his trust in a weapon like this will fall to his enemies.

TRUE REPENTANCE

What is to be done? Israel, we know, did nothing and judgment came. But that does not need to be our story or that of our nation. What should we do? The answer is obvious. We should repent of sin and turn to God as He reveals Himself in Jesus of Nazareth. Fortunately we have an example of what such repentance ought to be at the end of this prophecy. It is as good an example of genuine repentance as the opening verses of chapter 6 are of a repentance that does not count. We read, "Return, O Israel, to the LORD your God. Your sins have been your downfall! Take words with you and return to the LORD. Say to him: 'Forgive all our sins and receive us graciously, that we may offer the fruit of our lips.'" This is a true confession, and where it occurs God promises, "I will heal their waywardness and love them freely" (14:1, 2, 4).

That is the secret—"Take *words* with you and return to the LORD. Say to him: 'Forgive all our *sins* and receive us *graciously.*'" First, confession of sin. Second, an appeal to God on the basis of His abundant grace.

It is the same in the New Testament. "If we claim to be without sin, we deceive ourselves and the truth is not in us. If we confess our sins, he is faithful and just and will forgive us our sins and purify us from all unrighteousness" (1 John 1:8, 9). "If you confess with your mouth, 'Jesus is Lord,' and believe in your heart that God raised him from the dead, you will be saved. For it is with your heart that you believe and are justified, and it is with your mouth that you confess and are saved" (Rom. 10:9, 10).

---

[4]G. Campbell Morgan, *Hosea: The Heart and Holiness of God,* original ed. 1948 (Grand Rapids: Baker, 1974), p. 57.

7

Reaping the Whirlwind

(Hosea 8:1–14)

"They sow the wind and reap the whirlwind. . . . But I will send fire upon their cities that will consume their fortresses."

Only once in my life have I been close to the eye of a hurricane. I was a young boy at the time and had gone with my family to Atlantic City for a late August vacation. While we were there a hurricane moved up the coast passing within ten or twenty miles of where we were staying. As news of the approaching storm reached the vacation community, many of those staying in the various hotels and motels went home. My family stayed, and I will never forget the storm.

The wind was intense, the rains torrential. The streets surrounding our motel were flooded. My father and I waded through these streets to the boardwalk where we stood watching the fury of the elements. The tides were many feet higher than normal so that most of the beach was covered with water. The waves were gigantic, and they pounded on the beach and parts of the boardwalk with devastating force. At any moment the winds threatened to blow us off the boardwalk and back into the flooded streets.

As I stood watching the storm I asked myself what could ever produce winds of such intensity and waves of such violence. Today I still do not know everything that goes into the making of a hurricane. But because of the Book of Hosea I do know what produces similar scenes of spiritual force and destruction.

It is not big things. It is "little" things, like forgetting God and then trusting in our own resources rather than in Him. This neglect seems small at the beginning, but it grows big and ends in destruction.

This is the meaning of the two proverbs that lie at the heart of Hosea 8. "They sow the wind and reap the whirlwind. The stalk has no head; it will produce no flour" (v. 7). The first of these sayings expresses the principle that there is a correspondence between what a person does and what happens to him or her later. One commentator expresses it by saying, "Deed is seed, which is multiplied in harvest."[1] Since "wind" in Scripture often refers to what is empty or illusive, the proverb means that Israel has sown the seed of meaningless religion and shall therefore reap a harvest of judgment at the hand of God. The second saying reinforces the first. A headless stalk of wheat is worthless. Since it will produce no flour it is fit only to be carted away and burned. According to Hosea, the enemy that will be set on Israel will prove the truth of this principle.

FORGETTING GOD

The specifics of what Israel has done are spelled out in the chapter. But these specific sins flow from that more basic sin mentioned at the end: "Israel has for-

---

[1]Mays, *Hosea: A Commentary*, p. 119.

gotten his Maker" (v. 14). Does this mean that Israel has forgotten that there is a God? Has she forgotten who the true God is? No. That is not the meaning of the word. Not only had Israel not forgotten God—she still knew that He existed and even thought that she was worshiping Him—it is actually the case that no one ever forgets God in the absolute, intellectual sense. It is our inescapable knowledge of God coupled to our unreasonable and sinful rejection of that knowledge that makes us guilty before Him (Rom. 1:18–20). What the word "forget" actually means is "neglect." Israel knew God intellectually, but she had neglected Him by pushing Him aside. She had allowed other, lesser things to become central in the national life.

G. Campbell Morgan relates this problem to the warning given to Israel by Moses shortly before his death. It is found in the early chapters of Deuteronomy. In these chapters Moses reviewed the mighty acts of God on Israel's behalf—bringing them out of Egypt and giving them a land that they were then to go in and possess. But he repeatedly warned them not to forget these things after they were established in the land: "Be careful not to forget the covenant of the LORD your God that he made with you; do not make for yourselves an idol in the form of anything the LORD your God has forbidden" (Deut. 4:23); "When the LORD your God brings you into the land he swore to your fathers, to Abraham, Isaac and Jacob, to give you—a land with large, flourishing cities you did not build, houses filled with all kinds of good things you did not provide, wells you did not dig, and vineyards and olive groves you did not plant—then when you eat and are satisfied, be careful that you *do not forget* the LORD, who brought you out of Egypt, out of the land of slavery" (6:10–12); "When you have eaten and are satisfied, praise the LORD your God for the good land he has given you. Be careful that you *do not forget* the LORD your God, failing to observe his commands, his laws and his decrees that I am giving you this day. Otherwise, when you eat and are satisfied, when you build fine houses and settle down, and when your herds and flocks grow large and your silver and gold increase and all you have is multiplied, then your heart will become proud and *you will forget* the LORD your God, who brought you out of Egypt, out of the land of slavery" (8:10–14); "*If you ever forget* the LORD your God and follow other gods and worship and bow down to them, I testify against you today that you will surely be destroyed. Like the nations the LORD destroyed before you, so you will be destroyed for not obeying the LORD your God" (8:19, 20).

These verses and others show that the problem involved was not an intellectual forgetting of God but a moral "forgetting" in which a genuine worship of God and a rigorous obedience to His commands are neglected. This was in danger of coming about when the people became settled in the land and were prosperous. Morgan writes of Moses' sense of the danger of that time saying, "He saw this nation, and he saw it down the coming years, and he knew its supreme peril would be that God should be forgotten. If they could not intellectually forget God, they could put him out of calculation, they could mislay him."[2]

A similar situation prevails today in many "Christian" circles. It is not that God is denied. On the contrary, He is acknowledged, sometimes with great ceremony and by the most beautiful of services. The problem is that worshipers forget that God must be obeyed and that they must therefore live their lives differently.

Do you think this does not happen? I tell you it does happen even in the most evangelical churches. There are people

[2]Morgan, *Hosea: The Heart and Holiness of God*, p. 71.

who could be very useful in the Lord's work but who are useless simply because they are taken up with their jobs, families, cars, or houses. They have no time for service. Others are made useless by sin. They have forgotten God by the way they are living, wrongly thinking that they can profess Christ as Savior while ignoring Him as Lord. I know church members who are committing adultery or are engaging in premarital sex, who do not want to change but who nevertheless come to church and make a profession of godliness. They are unhappy, yet they will not stop. Is it not true that in such churches (even evangelical churches) we are sowing the seed of the neglect of God and will reap the whirlwind?

GROUNDS FOR JUDGMENT

Five sins resulted from Israel's forgetting of God: 1) the breaking of His covenant, 2) the choice of kings and other national leaders without His direction or consent, 3) idolatry, 4) the formation of alliances with ungodly nations, and 5) the construction of false altars. These are brought forward in this chapter as grounds for God's judgment.

1. *The breaking of God's covenant* (vv. 1–3). "Put the trumpet to your lips! An eagle is over the house of the LORD because the people have broken my covenant and rebelled against my law" (v. 1). The word "covenant" means "agreement." It is essentially personal. "Law" is an objective standard. In some circles it has been customary to set these two ideas over against one another as two conflicting definitions of sin. It is said that the old orthodoxy defined sin as a transgression of law, as in the Westminster Shorter Catechism: "Sin is any want of conformity unto, or transgression of, the law of God" (Q. 14). It is said that the new orthodoxy defines sin more correctly as a broken relationship. But

these two ideas cannot be set over against one another. To break God's covenant *is* to break God's law. Similarly, to break the law of God is to offend against God personally.

The problem with making a separation between these two definitions is that we can easily delude ourselves into thinking that our relationship with God is intact while we are nevertheless sinning, and this only adds hypocrisy and hardness of heart to our other sins. Some time ago *The Wittenburg Door* published an interview with a self-confessed homosexual clergyman, which is a case in point. He justified his life style. Then, when asked whether the law of God did not condemn his sexual practice as sin, he replied, "Sin . . . is separation from God."[3] He meant that sin should not be defined by the law of God but only by relationships.

This is false, though widespread. So when our text combines the breaking of God's covenant with rebellion against God's law it is saying something very timely and significant. It is saying that we cannot call God, God, without obedience. Jesus indicated the same thing when He asked, "Why do you call me, 'Lord, Lord,' and do not do what I say?" (Luke 6:46). This question is immediately followed by the parable of a man who built his house on sand and suffered the loss of everything when the storm struck.

There is one more thing we need to notice about this breaking of God's covenant. It is the reaction of God to the hypocrisy. We see His reaction in the tone of the passage, primarily in the emphasis on the words "my" and "me" (also "you") in these verses. Read them with that emphasis and you will see what is being said: "The people have broken *my* covenant and rebelled against *my* law. Israel cries out to me, 'O our God, we acknowledge *you*!' But Israel has rejected what is good; an enemy will pursue him.

---

[3]*The Wittenburg Door* (October-November, 1977), p. 31.

They set up kings without *my* consent; they choose princes without *my* approval" (vv. 1–4). God is saying that He hates the hypocrisy of it all. They dare to claim that they are acknowledging Him when actually they are disregarding *His* law.

2. *The choice of kings and other national leaders without God's direction or consent* (v. 4). One of the great gifts of God to a nation is upright and godly leadership. But how are we to have that leadership, particularly in a democracy, unless we ask God for it? We cannot see into human hearts. Character is known to God alone. So to choose leaders without the direction of God is not only sinful, it is foolish. Those who follow their own wisdom in the choice of leaders inevitably get what they deserve.

3. *Idolatry* (vv. 4–6). The choice of bad rulers leads to bad religion, and vice versa. So it is no surprise that the next step in Israel's rebellion against God is idolatry. The chapter says, "With their silver and gold they make idols for themselves to their own destruction. Throw out your calf-idol, O Samaria! My anger burns against them. How long will they be incapable of purity? They are from Israel! This calf—a craftsman has made it; it is not God. It will be broken in pieces, that calf of Samaria" (vv. 4–6).

God condemns the worship of the "calf-idol" at the cult centers of the northern kingdom as idolatry, but we miss the point if we think of this calf-worship as an outright rejection of Jehovah for idols. The sin was far more subtle. What had happened was quite similar to what had happened in the days of Moses and Aaron when the people were gathered around Mount Sinai. In those days the people clamored for a god like the gods of Egypt, and Aaron made them a little calf out of the gold they had brought from Egypt. Aaron did not think of this as an idol— that is the point. He thought of the calf

as a representation of the strength of Jehovah and even proclaimed the dedication feast (which turned into an orgy) as "a festival to the LORD" (Exod. 32:5). But the people missed the distinction, identified the calf with the fertility bull-gods of Egypt, and behaved accordingly.

Now it was all happening again. In theory the calves of the cult centers were not gods. They were actually calf-pedestals on which the true and invisible god was supposed to stand. But because the people could not see the invisible god, while they could see the calf, it inevitably happened that the true God was debased and the "idol" worshiped.

This interesting use of the calves has been traced by the well-known dean of archeologists William Foxwell Albright in *From the Stone Age to Christianity*. He writes, "It is true that the 'golden calves' have been assumed by most scholars to have been direct representations of Yahweh as bull-god, but this gross conception is not only otherwise unparalleled in biblical tradition, but is contrary to all that we know of Syro-Palestinian iconography in the second and early first millennia B.C. Among Canaanites, Aramaeans, and Hittites we find the gods nearly always represented as standing on the back of an animal or as seated on a throne borne by animals—but never as themselves in animal form. . . . The storm-god of Mesopotamia is actually represented on seal-cylinders of the second millennium B.C. as a schematic bolt of lightning set upright on the back of a bull, and this iconographic device may go back to Sumerian seals showing the bull who was the central figure in the ritual of consecration on a sacred drum with the winged shrine of music (so labelled!) on his back. The bull on which the storm-god stood is sometimes represented as a bullock of two or three years."[4]

You do not have to say "I am wor-

---

[4]William Foxwell Albright, *From the Stone Age to Christianity: Monotheism and the Historical Process*, second edition (Baltimore: John Hopkins Press, 1957), pp. 299, 300.

shiping an idol" to be actually worshiping an idol. We can say that we are worshiping God but be worshiping an idol—our money, homes, cars, position, wife, husband, children—even when we associate those things with God or think of them as the gift of God. It is a question, not of what we say, but of that to which we actually give our time and allegiance.

4. *The formation of alliances with the ungodly nation of Assyria* (vv. 8–10). Hosea quotes God as saying, "They have gone up to Assyria like a wild donkey wandering alone. Ephraim has sold herself to lovers. Although they have sold themselves among the nations, I will now gather them together. They will begin to waste away under the oppression of the mighty king" (vv. 9, 10).

This drift of policy was all quite literal in the northern kingdom's last days. Hoshea, Israel's last king, ascended the throne through the murder of his predecessor Pekah, and his first act after his assumption of the throne was to submit to Assyria. He submitted by paying tribute, his only chance of remaining king. The same thing had been done by Menahem some years before. No doubt these kings would have pleaded "political expediency" or "emergency measures." They would have said, "It is all we can do." But God is not impressed with this reasoning. Instead of congratulating them on their astute political wisdom, He compares such leadership to a wild ass and a prostitute. Political expediency will not work. Instead of surviving, Israel will become scattered among the nations to whom she looked for support (v. 8).

5. *The construction of false altars* (vv. 11–13). The final ground of God's pending judgment on Israel cited in this chapter is the construction of false altars, false not because they were dedicated to a god other than Jehovah but because they contributed to the mere formality of Israel's religious practices and thus became a cause of further sinning. "Though Ephraim built many altars for sin offerings, these have become altars for sinning. I wrote for them the many things of my law, but they regarded them as something alien. They offer sacrifices given to me and they eat the meat, but the LORD is not pleased with them. Now he will remember their wickedness and punish their sins" (vv. 11–13).

Our equivalent to these altars 'could be churches and other Christian "monuments": endowed chairs of theology, gifts to Christian institutions, pulpit Bibles, choir robes, stained-glass windows or any of the other paraphernalia of mere organized religion.

"BIGNESS EQUALS BLESSING"

Each of these five items, which flow from a forgetfulness of God, bring judgment. This is the way verses 13 and 14 end. But there is one more thing to be noted before we close our discussion of this chapter. At the beginning we looked at the root cause of these five deviations and found them explained in summary form by the first phrase of verse 14 ("Israel has forgotten his Maker"). That is true. But in the space between that summary and the concluding words of judgment ("I will send fire upon their cities that will consume their fortresses"), God notes one other item of the people's behavior that flows from their forgetfulness.

What God says in these interim phrases is that "Israel . . . built palaces" and "Judah has fortified many towns." On the surface this does not seem to be too meaningful, perhaps even a bit out of place. But we see why this is included when we realize that the basic idea of the word translated "palaces" is "spaciousness" or "bigness." (The Authorized Version of the Bible translates this word as "temples." The Revised Standard Version and the New International Version say "palaces." Because the central idea is "bigness" the word may actually mean either.) What God is talking about in these phrases is the passion of the nation at that time to build big things.

Having forsaken God, who alone was big enough for her need, Israel tried to compensate by the construction of big things without Him.

This is so contemporary! And so true of humanity in general! If we have God, we can be content with however little (or much) He gives us. But if we have lost Him, we find ourselves striving to build big things to take God's place.

Let me give three examples. First, a well-known poem by Oliver Wendell Holmes. It is called "The Chambered Nautilus," and is about a sea creature who builds his house ever larger as he himself grows. Holmes applied this to human beings and regarded his discovery as one of the secrets of life.

Build thee more stately mansions, O my soul.
As the swift seasons roll!
Leave thy low-vaulted past!
Let each new temple, nobler than the last,
Shut thee from heaven with a dome more vast,
Till thou at length are free,
Leaving thine outgrown shell by life's unresting sea.

What Holmes desired and expressed so eloquently cannot be done. Yet the desire is there, and people earnestly try to do it. They are compensating for a misplaced relationship to God.

A second example is from contemporary popular culture. In recent years there has been a discovery of science fiction movies on a scale not previously experienced, initially *Star Wars* and *Encounters of the Third Kind*. These movies have set new records for attendance and gross receipts, and the question has been asked: "Why are these films so popular?" It has been suggested by some that it is because they are a rediscovery of the old adventure film. Some speak of their new visual effects. I do not believe that these are the real reasons. I think their appeal is religious. For decades we have experienced an increasing secularization of our culture in which God has been progressively banned from the thinking of contemporary people. As God has retreated from view, it has seemed in increasing measure that we must then be a small, insignificant speck in the infinite sea of space. The result is that we feel overcome, terrified, worthless, without hope of ever successfully dealing with our problems. In such a state, it is a relief (almost a religious experience) to believe that somewhere "out there" are beings who have "made it" and who, just possibly, might arrive here one day to save us or at least point the way forward. This is the explicit moral of *Encounters of the Third Kind*.

The third example comes closest home: the preoccupation of evangelicals with bigness. Actually, we are a shallow movement—shallow in our commitment, knowledge, morality, and service. But lest this become apparent to others or even to ourselves, we launch bigger and bigger projects, build larger and larger churches, raise more and more money. If we could put it in a formula, we would probably say: "Bigness Equals Blessing," meaning that size is a proof of God's presence.

But it is not so. Sometimes God does bless in this way. He prospers His people. Again, we rightly desire to see much rather than little happen. We desire to see many converted and much good done. But it is the equation that is wrong; for it is often in the smallest things that the greatest blessing is given, and it is in the insignificant things that God is often most present. If God gives bigness, fine. But whenever we find ourselves longing for this and struggling for it, we had best be on guard. Just as in the secular world, it is often the case that we strive for bigness when God is least present—in order that, by that means, we may cover up the moral poverty and spiritual futility of our lives.

What should we do if that has happened? Remember God! Come back to

Him! It is as simple as that. Turn from what is empty, meaningless, and vain. Turn to God as He is revealed in Jesus Christ, and allow Him to be to you all that you could ever want to have.

8

The God Who Is *Not* There

(Hosea 9:1–17)

"Even if they rear children, I will bereave them of everyone. Woe to them when I turn away from them!"

Francis Schaeffer of L'Abri Fellowship has written a book on the inescapable reality of God entitled *The God Who Is There*. It is true that God is always there and is ultimately inescapable, but there is a certain sense in which He sometimes judges His people by turning from them so that He is *not there for them* when they cry to Him. In Hosea 9 this is what God says He is about to do to Israel. For years they had benefited from His presence, even though they did not honor Him. Now He is to withdraw, and the result will be the end of their blessings. He says of this moment, "Ephraim's glory will fly away like a bird—no birth, no pregnancy, no conception. . . . Woe to them when I turn away from them!" (9:11, 12).

Woe to us as well should this happen! In the midst of sin even Christians sometimes think how nice it would be if God would simply go away and leave them alone. They think of Him as being oppressive and His commands as being burdensome. But what if He should go? Ah, then the blessing we think we could and ought to have would go too. The Bible says, "You will fill me with joy in your *presence*" (Ps. 16:11). If we are not in His presence, joy and all other blessings will vanish.

There are four important parts to this chapter: 1) a prophecy of what is coming

as a result of God's departure, 2) a proof from the contemporary behavior of the people that these things are coming, 3) a truncated prayer by Hosea, and 4) God's final word on the subject, followed by Hosea's response.

PUNISHMENT FOR ISRAEL

The immediate effect of God's withdrawal from Israel's affairs is to be the fall of the people to their enemies. God is their strength; if He is withdrawn their fortresses must inevitably be taken. This is not said in language as prosaic as this, however. Instead, Hosea couches it in terms of the current feasts of Israel, in which they were relishing.

It is probably the case, though we do not know this for sure, that Hosea delivered the opening part of this oracle as a sermon on the occasion of a harvest festival.[1] The autumn festival of Sukkoth was a time of joy at the conclusion of the harvest. It was characterized by feasting, mirth, and dancing. A coming disaster would have been the last thought to enter anyone's mind. Yet at this point Hosea probably stepped forth to demand that the revelry cease and to call the people to accountability. He cried, "Do not rejoice, O Israel; do not be jubilant like the other nations. For you have been un-

---

[1]For an elaboration of this point see E. B. Pusey, *The Minor Prophets*, Vol. 1 (New York: Funk and Wagnalls, 1885), p. 87, and Mays, *Hosea: A Commentary*, p. 125.

62

faithful to your God; you love the wages of a prostitute at every threshing floor. Threshing floors and winepresses will not feed the people; the new wine will fail them. They will not remain in the LORD's land; Ephraim will return to Egypt and eat unclean food in Assyria. They will not pour out wine offerings to the LORD, nor will their sacrifices please him. Such sacrifices will be to them like the bread of mourners; all who eat them will be unclean. This food will be for themselves; it will not come into the temple of the LORD. What will you do on the day of your appointed feasts, on the festival days of the LORD?" (9:1–5).

This message may be difficult to accept, but it is easy enough to understand. It is simply that because the people have forsaken God, God has forsaken them. And because God has forsaken them, the blessings that the harvest symbolized would soon come to an end.

The reason this message is difficult to accept is that we do not normally think of the blessings of life as being a direct result of God's favor. We think mechanistically and materially—without God entering into much of that thinking—with the result that it is for us as it was for the skeptics who are reported as saying: "Everything goes on as it has since the beginning of creation" (2 Peter 3:4). But it is not true that all things continue on unchanged. Judgments do come in history, and beyond that there is the final judgment. The reason things seem mechanical and free from judgment to us is that God is extremely patient "not wanting anyone to perish, but everyone to come to repentance" (2 Peter 3:9).

We may think here of that well-known sermon of Jonathan Edwards entitled "Sinners in the Hands of an Angry God." It is based on the text: "In due time their foot will slip" (Deut. 32:35), which Edwards correctly expounded as a threat of the vengeance of God on unbelievers.

But though he expostulated earnestly and eloquently on the coming judgment of God in that sermon, Edwards' purpose was not to terrify but rather to turn sinners back to God by assuring them that it was only because of the present mercy and grace of God that they were not then in hell's judgment. He wrote: "The God that holds you over the pit of hell, much as one holds a spider, or some loathsome insect, over the fire, abhores you, and is dreadfully provoked: his wrath towards you burns like fire; he looks upon you as worthy of nothing else, but to be cast into the fire; he is of purer eyes than to bear to have you in his sight; you are ten thousand times more abominable in his eyes, than the most hateful venomous serpent is in ours. You have offended him infinitely more than ever a stubborn rebel did his prince: and yet, it is nothing but his hand that holds you from falling into the fire every moment. It is to be ascribed to nothing else, that you did not go to hell the last night; that you were suffered to awake again in this world, after you closed your eyes to sleep. And there is no other reason to be given, why you have not dropped into hell since you arose in the morning, but that God's hand has held you up." At the end Edwards concluded, "Now you have an extraordinary opportunity, a day wherein Christ has thrown the door of mercy wide open, and stands calling. . . . How awful it is to be left behind at such a day!"[2]

Today these words seem so harsh that it is next to impossible to preach along these lines. Yet the principles they enunciate are true. (And who is to say that the power and success of Edwards' preaching was not due in large measure to proclaiming these things fearlessly.) Hosea preached the same, maintaining that the blessings that Israel enjoyed, even in their apostasy, were from God, and warning that the day of reckoning was at hand.

[2]Jonathan Edwards, *Select Works of Jonathan Edwards*, Vol. 2, *Sermons* (London: The Banner of Truth Trust, 1959), pp. 191, 192, 197.

PROOF OF GOD'S JUDGMENT

The second section of this chapter contains a proof from the behavior of the people that the judgments about which Hosea was speaking were indeed coming. Significantly enough the proof is in their reception of Hosea. Hosea had spoken of the coming invasion in clear and passionate terms. He was concerned for the people and sincerely wanted them to repent of sin and return to God. But at first the people neither agreed nor became angry. Instead they laughed at Hosea. They said he was a fool and crazy. Only after that, when he persisted in his preaching, did they become hostile and do him harm. The prophecy says, "Because your sins are so many and your hostility so great, the prophet is considered a fool, the inspired man a maniac. The prophet, along with my God, is the watchman over Ephraim, yet snares await him on all his paths, and hostility in the house of his God" (vv. 7, 8).

We have something similar to this in the Book of Amos. Amos says that when he came preaching against Israel, as Hosea did, he was met at Bethel by Amaziah, the official head of the northern kingdom's religious establishment. Amaziah regarded his words as treachery. So he reported them to the king, saying, "Amos is raising a conspiracy against you in the very heart of Israel. The land cannot bear all his words. For this is what Amos is saying: 'Jeroboam will die by the sword, and Israel will surely go into exile, away from their native land.'"

Then Amaziah reported back to Amos, presumably with the king's message: "Get out, you seer! Go back to the land of Judah. Earn your bread there and do your prophesying there. Don't prophesy anymore at Bethel, because this is the king's sanctuary and the temple of the kingdom" (Amos 7:10–13).

I say this is similar, but it is not identical, for in Hosea's case there was no official dismissal from the northern kingdom. Instead, they called him a madman,

a lunatic. They said in effect, "Who in his right mind would prophesy a judgment like this when we are in the midst of such a bountiful harvest, in itself a proof of God's blessing?"

This reaction to the prophets was not at all uncommon. We think of Isaiah, probably the greatest of the prophets. Early in his career he seems to have carried on a more or less private ministry. But the time came when he began to speak openly about the decaying political situation, and at this point his listeners began to mock him. We find it in chapter 28. Isaiah had spoken of judgment saying, "Woe to that wreath, the pride of Ephraim's drunkards, to the fading flower, his glorious beauty. . . . That wreath, the pride of Ephraim's drunkards, will be trampled underfoot" (vv. 1, 3). But the people break in to mock him:

> Who is it he is trying to teach?
>   To whom is he explaining his message?
> To children weaned from their milk,
>   to those just taken from the breast?
> For it is:
>   Do and do, do and do,
>   rule on rule, rule on rule;
>   a little here, a little there (vv. 9, 10).

Isaiah's answer is that, if they will not listen to such plain Hebrew (we would say "plain English"), then God will speak to them in foreign languages, meaning that He would send foreigners to overrun the country. Still they did not listen. They considered Isaiah crazy.

Jeremiah got the same treatment. Shemaiah, the false prophet of his day, called him a "madman who acts like a prophet" and counseled that he should be put in "stocks and neck-irons" (Jer. 29:26).

Even our Lord did not escape. He had been teaching the people, and they had disagreed with His teaching. "You are demon-possessed," they argued (John 7:20). It was a way of saying that He was not in His right mind.

Why is it that people can make such foolish and irresponsible judgments where the prophets, and even the Son of God, are concerned? It is certainly not the inherent "foolishness" of the prophetic message or the mode in which it was delivered. Considered objectively, it is hard to think of any words in history that bear more the marks of being sane, passionate, and constructive discourses. Besides, the things they prophesied came true. How is it that such words can be so totally disregarded? Hosea gives the answer: "Because your sins are so many and your hostility [to God] so great" (v. 7). Sin separates from God. Isaiah, Hosea's contemporary, wrote, "Your iniquities have separated you from your God" (Isa. 59:2). When we are separated from God by sin, the spiritual perception that comes from God is taken away and spiritual and moral blindness ensues.

Yet we must say this. It is true that the people had sinned and that they had grown spiritually deaf as a result of their transgressions. The word of God had been spoken to them by the prophets. The word seemed foolish, and they had laughed at the messengers. It is a grim picture. But it is not as grim as it was soon to become, for the very reason that the word of God was at least still being spoken at that point in Israel's history. The prophets might be laughed at. Their word might be disregarded. But as long as the prophets were there (whether they were respected or not), as long as the word of God was spoken (whether it was listened to or not), as long as those things were present there was hope. The word of God is powerful. "Sharper than any double-edged sword, it penetrates even to dividing soul and spirit, joints and marrow; it judges the thoughts and attitudes of the heart" (Heb. 4:12). So long as God speaks all things are possible.

But when God removes Himself—as Hosea says He is about to do—then the word of God is removed too, and there is no hope. There is only a famine for the word of God (Amos 8:11), and despair.

Today we do not have primary revelation as Israel did when the biblical writers spoke God's word to them. But we do have many preachers and other witnesses who speak the word faithfully on the basis of Scripture. Thus, although ours is not a very responsive age and although the word of God is not always heard, there is still hope so long as we have those who are called by God and sent forth by Him to proclaim it.

An Interesting Prayer

The third part of chapter 9 is the prayer of Hosea in verse 14. It is interesting because it is broken off after the first phrase due to the fact that although Hosea earnestly wants to pray for the people, he finds that he does not know what to ask. He begins his prayer well: "Give them, O Lord—" But he breaks off because he does not know what God should give them. He even asks, "What will you give them?" At last the only thing he can think of is childlessness in order that the miseries of the day of judgment be as limited as possible. So he concludes: "Give them wombs that miscarry and breasts that are dry."

There is a prayer in the Book of Exodus that likewise breaks off in the middle. It is a prayer of Moses. Under his direction the people who had left Egypt had come to Mount Sinai where God was to give them the law, and Moses had been called up into the mountain to receive it. Moses spent forty days on the mountain receiving the Ten Commandments and much of the Old Testament legislation. As the hours turned to days and the days to weeks, the people who were left in the valley gradually overcame their awe of the mountain, as people will do, and they grew increasingly cynical and impatient. They said, "Where is this man Moses, the man who brought us up out of the land of Egypt? We do not know what has become of him." Before long they began to remember the worship of Apis the bull and Hathor the cow that they had known in Egypt, and they approached Moses' brother Aaron to ask him to make an image of Apis or Hathor for them. This he did, as we pointed out in the previous chapter. He did not have enough of the precious metals to make a bull, but he made a calf and the people were satisfied.

On the mountain God was still speaking to Moses, but He knew what was going on in the valley and angrily interrupted the giving of the law to send Moses back down to the nation. How ironic the situation was! How horrible! God had just given Moses the Ten Commandments. But while God was giving the Ten Commandments the people of Israel were breaking them. The Commandments say: "I am the LORD your God, who brought you out of Egypt, out of the land of slavery. You shall have no other gods before me. You shall not make for yourself an idol in the form of anything in heaven above or on the earth beneath or in the waters below. You shall not bow down to them or worship them; for I, the LORD your God, am a jealous God, punishing the children for the sin of the fathers to the third and fourth generation of those who hate me" (Exod. 20:2–5). But while God was saying that, the nation He had delivered from Egypt was making the image and worshiping it in direct violation of this the first and greatest of all God's commandments.

Moses went down to deal with the sin as best he knew how. In anger he had first smashed the stone tablets of the law that God had given him. Now he entered the camp, rebuked Aaron publicly, and called for all who still remained on the Lord's side to come and stand beside him. The tribe of Levi responded, and Moses commanded them to go into the camp with drawn swords to kill those who had led the rebellion. He called on the rest to reconsecrate themselves to God.

From a human point of view Moses had dealt with the sin. The leaders were punished, and the loyalty of the people was at least temporarily reclaimed. All seemed to be well. But Moses did not only stand in a special relationship to the people. He also stood in a special relationship to God, and God still waited in wrath on the mountain. What was Moses to do? By this time not all the law had been given, but Moses had received enough of it to know something of the horror of sin and something of the uncompromising righteousness of God. Had God not said, "You shall have no other gods before me"? Had He not promised to punish the children for the sin of the fathers to the "third and fourth" generations? Who was Moses to think that the limited judgment he had begun would satisfy the holiness of this God?

On the mountain Moses had said that the people were God's people, but he knew that they were his people too, and that he loved them. The night passed, and the morning came on which he was to reascend the mountain. He had been thinking during the night, and he had thought of a way that might possibly divert the just wrath of God. He had remembered the sacrifices of the Hebrew patriarchs and the newly instituted sacrifice of the Passover. Certainly God had shown by these sacrifices that He was prepared to accept an innocent substitute in place of the just death of the sinner. Perhaps God would accept. . . . At this point Moses would hardly have voiced his idea. But when morning came he reascended the mountain with great determination.

Moses began to speak to God. It must have been in great anguish, for this is the prayer in which (like the prayer of Hosea) the sentence breaks off without ending. This is indicated by a dash in the NIV and other translations. The prayer is a strangled cry, a gasping sob welling up from the heart of a man who is asking to be sent to hell if only it can mean the salvation of the people he had come to love. Moses prayed, "Oh, what a great sin these people have committed! They have made themselves gods of gold. But now, please forgive their sin—but if not, then blot me out of the book you have written" (Exod. 32:31, 32).

Something like this happened in the experience of Hosea. Hosea too knew that God was a God of righteousness and that he had been given a message of judgment by Him. But Hosea also loved the people, and it is this that causes him hardly to know what to pray. "Give them, O LORD—" But what can God give them? If they will not repent, there is nothing for them but God's judgment.

GOD'S FINAL WORD

This is the way the chapter ends. God reiterates the judgment, and Hosea bows to God's pronouncement. God says, "Because of all their wickedness in Gilgal, I hated them there. Because of their sinful deeds, I will drive them out of my house. I will no longer love them; all their leaders are rebellious. Ephraim is blighted, their root is withered, they yield no fruit. Even if they bear children, I will slay their cherished offspring." Hosea concurs sadly, "My God will reject them because they have not obeyed him; they will be wanderers among the nations" (vv. 15–17).

Is this the end? Is this the final word for the people of Israel for this point in their history? In their case it was. The judgment prophesied by Hosea and the other prophets came. The people were carried away into slavery, and the word of God through the prophets ceased until that fresh outpouring of revelation of the new covenant established by the Lord Jesus Christ.

But what was true for that generation is not yet true for us. We have the word of God in the gospel, and where that word exists there is hope. Go back to Moses. Moses, at the finest moment of his life (recorded in Exod. 32) offered himself for the people, who were sinners. But the offer was no good, for Moses himself was a sinner. He was actually a murderer and so could not die for another, let alone for an entire people. Still there was One who could die . . . and did. That One is Jesus, of whom it is written, "But when the time had fully come, God sent his Son, born of a woman, born under law, to redeem those under law, that we might receive the full rights of sons" (Gal. 4:4, 5).

Thus it is for those who live in this present day of God's grace. God was in His holy mountain, and while He was in His holy mountain we were in the dark valley of this world breaking His commandments and turning our backs on the very One who has given us life and who sustains us on this earth. We were children of God's wrath, and the wrath was soon to fall. We were oblivious to the danger and unaware of the heinous character of our sin. Christ came. He spoke out of love for you and me. He said to God, "I am willing to be sent to hell, to be separated from You, My Father, if only it can bring about the salvation of these sinful, rebellious, unbelieving people that I love." God said, "This sacrifice I will accept. You will be cursed for others. My wrath will fall on You rather than on them. You shall be cut off from My presence. On the basis of Your sacrifice, I will deal mercifully with them. I will cleanse their sin. I will make them a kingdom of priests to Me forever."

If you believe that, God will spare you the just consequences of your sin. Indeed, He has already cleansed you of all unrighteousness and He has given you a new spirit formed by His love, capable even of sacrificing your own salvation for that of others—if that were possible.

9

The Divided Heart of Israel

(Hosea 10:1–15)

Israel was a spreading vine; he brought forth fruit for himself. As his fruit increased, he built more altars; as his land prospered, he adorned his sacred stones. Their heart is deceitful, and now they must bear their guilt. The LORD will demolish their altars and destroy their sacred stones.

Over and over again in the Old Testament, Israel is portrayed as God's choice vine or vineyard. Isaiah wrote, "My loved one had a vineyard on a fertile hillside. He dug it up and cleared it of stones and planted it with the choicest vines. He built a watchtower in it and cut out a winepress as well. Then he looked for a crop of good grapes, but it yielded only bad fruit. . . . The vineyard of the LORD Almighty is the house of Israel, and the men of Judah are the garden of his delight" (5:1, 2, 7). Jeremiah recorded, "I had planted you like a choice vine of sound and reliable stock. How then did you turn against me into a corrupt, wild vine?" (2:21). Ezekiel 15 compares Israel to a vine also, as does Ezekiel 19: "Your mother was like a vine . . . fruitful and full of branches" (v. 10). One of the best-known passages is from the psalms: "You brought a vine out of Egypt; you drove out the nations and planted it. You cleared the ground for it, and it took root and filled the land. The mountains were covered with its shade, the mighty cedars with its branches" (Ps. 80:8–10). The extraordinary thing about the use of this image in the Old Testament, however, is that it is always brought forward as a symbol of Israel's degeneration, rather than of her fruitfulness. The point of Isaiah's reference is that the vine has run

wild, producing sour grapes. "What more could have been done for my vineyard than I have done for it?" God asks. Yet it brought forth "bad" grapes (5:4). Jeremiah calls Israel "a corrupt, wild vine." The eightieth psalm is set in the context of a plea for God's renewed favor after the vine has been burned in judgment and the hedges broken down.

It is the same in Hosea. In chapter 10 Israel is termed a "spreading" or "luxuriant" vine. But her fruit is not what God desires. It is the fruit of idolatrous religion, fruit unto herself. Hosea writes, "Israel was a spreading vine; he brought forth fruit for himself. As his fruit increased, he built more altars; as his land prospered, he adorned his sacred stones. Their heart is deceitful, and now they must bear their guilt. The LORD will demolish their altars and destroy their sacred stones" (vv. 1, 2).

NEITHER COLD NOR HOT

In each chapter of his book Hosea has been analyzing the people's sin in a slightly different way. He does so here on the basis of Israel's divided or deceitful heart. The NIV begins verse 2 with the words "Their heart is deceitful." But the word translated "deceitful" is *chalaq*, which literally means "smooth." Applied to a person's speech, we would translate *chalaq* as "oily," "slick" or "double-tongued." The idea is that the people went through the motions of doing one thing when actually they were intent on doing something else. Do we have that today? Of course we do. Consequently, we must see the examples that Hosea gives in terms of our own hypocrisy.

The first area in which Israel may be said to have had a divided or deceitful heart is her purported *love for God contrasted with her true unfaithfulness.* This is the burden of the first two verses where the issue is Israel's idolatrous worship. The whole background of the book, Hosea's marriage, comes into view here, for in Hosea love or faithfulness (hate or unfaithfulness) is illustrated by faithfulness or unfaithfulness in marriage. No doubt, when Hosea's wife Gomer went off with her lovers, she would have said that she was not being entirely unfaithful to Hosea. She may have said that she did "still love him." But "love" like that has no place in marriage. By its very nature and by the law of God marriage is an exclusive affair. It is one man and one woman, faithful to each other—"in plenty or in want, in joy or in sorrow, in sickness or in health, until death us do part." When another comes into the marriage what happens is that love is betrayed and the vacillating partner is seen to be unfaithful.

This is what Israel was doing. She was coming to the shrines of Jehovah and was pretending to worship Him. She would have said that Jehovah was her God. But even while she was saying this, Israel was multiplying false altars and dedicating "sacred stones." She would have said that these were for God. But God had not commanded them. He did not desire them. Israel was really committing spiritual adultery with the idols of the land.

Today millions of so-called Christians do the same thing. They would not think of denying the existence of the Christian God. They would even claim to be His people, to worship Him. "We go to church," they would claim. "We are not Jews or Buddhists or Muslims. We are Christians." But instead of worshiping and serving Him, such people are actually often in church only because of what people will think of them if they do not go or in order to make a good impression so that they might be able to do better in their business. Let us make sure that we do not have a divided heart at this point. Let us make sure that we do not merely say that we love God but actually love Him and show it by the way we order our lives.

The second area of Israel's deceit concerns her profession of *truth versus actual falsehood.* This is discussed in verse 4, where Hosea says, "They make many promises, take false oaths and make agreements; therefore lawsuits spring up like poisonous weeds in a plowed field." His point is that the people pretended to speak truthfully, making agreements that supposedly could be trusted as befitting those who are followers of the God of truth. But actually they were attempting to cheat others for the sake of their own private gain.

How strange this was for a people who identified themselves as followers of the true God. Jehovah is a God of truth. His Spirit is the Spirit of truth. His word is truth. To operate by any other standard while saying that one is a follower of this God is hypocrisy. Yet professing Christians do this too. No doubt Israel would have claimed that this is just the way business was conducted in their time. Many would say the same today. But what is this but another case of the church (or Israel) taking its standards from the world rather than from the clear principles and standards of the Word of God?

The only way we will be people of truth is when we are people of "the Book." In theory we are. We say we are. We acknowledge that this is what our standard is or should be. But in practice many so-called Christians operate exactly the way other people do. We have to recover the biblical standard. This means that we cannot say, as I have heard evangelical men say on important issues, "Well, that particular thing just does not bother me." That response is not good enough. Instead, we have to get to what the Word of God says. We have to study it, do our homework. Then we must ask: On the basis of this Word, what does God want for the church in this age?

We are going to have to do that sooner or later anyway, or else we are going to have to go the world's way entirely. This is so because history does not allow us to stand long in an ambiguous position. Someone has pointed out that in Germany, in the Nazi period, the church went in one of two ways: either it capitulated to the Nazi point of view (and most of the established church did), or it became increasingly a church of the Book. Those who lived by the Book eventually established a communion of their own. They signed documents identifying themselves as the "confessing church." Why did they go this way? They did so because, when the whole drift of society and the culture is contrary to biblical standards, it is impossible to appeal to any external norms. You cannot say, "This is backed up in the area of psychology or science or social relations," because it is not. The things that are being written in those areas are contrary to biblical truth. So the church must increasingly fall back on the divine revelation. Has God spoken to His people in this Book? Does He speak? If God does speak, then we must be clear and say, "Let God be true and every man a liar." We must try to be like Him in this important characteristic.

The third area of Israel's duplicity was her profession of *righteousness while actually practicing evil.* In going to her high altars she undoubtedly pretended to be the very epitome of goodness. Who else but "the good" would be so religious? God was not fooled by this profession.

He saw the evil that was done in secret— and sometimes not even in secret. He calls the altars "high places of wickedness" that will soon be destroyed (v. 8). Notice that God is not talking here about what we would call mere shortcomings or failures. He is talking about real wickedness, the category in which He places the people's transgressions.

We must give attention to a reference that we have overlooked up to this point. It is the reference to Gibeah, referred to twice previously (in 5:8 and 9:9) and now here at greater length. It is a serious reference, for, as God says, "Since the days of Gibeah, you have sinned, O Israel, and there you have remained" (v. 9). What is Gibeah? Well, if you take a concordance of the Old Testament and look up this word, you will discover that Gibeah was a town occupied by the tribe of Benjamin and that it comes into history through a terrible deed that was performed there. During the days of the Judges a priest or Levite, who was on a trip, was on his way home with his concubine and found as nighttime neared that he was not going to be able to reach home that evening. He did reach Gibeah, so he went in and looked for a place to stay for the night. None would open their home to him. At length an old man came in from the fields and invited the Levite and his concubine to stay with him.

Soon a band of the depraved youth of the town gathered outside the old man's door and demanded that he send the Levite out. They wanted to have homosexual relations with him, precisely the sin and circumstances that had occurred much earlier when the angelic visitors had entered Sodom to get Lot and his family to leave the city. The old man resisted. In the end the concubine was sent out to face the young men. They used her all that night, and in the morning she staggered back to the house where she fell on the doorstep. When the Levite emerged the next morning she was dead. This man took his concubine home, cut up her body into twelve pieces, and then sent the parts to each of the tribes of Israel. He intended to shock the tribes, and he succeeded. They rallied and eventually attacked the people of Benjamin and almost wiped them out. It was a black day in Israel's history. The people were dismayed at what had happened and equally dismayed at the near loss of one of the tribes of Israel. As we read the chapters of Judges that contain this story (19–21) we discover that God was also dismayed. Not just because of the atrocity performed by the Benjamites! He was dismayed because the moral tone of all the people was at such a low ebb. Not all had participated in the Benjamites' sin, but all were so insensitive to sin that it took an act such as the Levite's to rouse them. Besides, as Judges tells us, "in those days . . . *everyone* did as he saw fit" (21:25). The Authorized Version says, "Every man did that which was *right in his own eyes.*"

God goes back to this horrible period to portray vividly how He regards Israel's sin, saying, "Since the days of Gibeah, you have sinned, O Israel, and *there you have remained.*" That is, "Don't think of what happened at Gibeah as an exception to your normal moral conduct. That is the level on which you have been operating constantly."

THOSE WHO ARE HIS

God says something else too: His people must and will live differently. One good statement of the principle is in Paul's second letter to Timothy: "Nevertheless, God's solid foundation stands firm, sealed with this inscription: 'The Lord knows those who are his,' and 'Everyone who confesses the name of the Lord must turn away from wickedness'" (2:19). In Hosea the theme comes through as an appeal to God's people. To those whose hearts were divided—who spoke of love when they were actually unfaithful, who pretended to be truthful while practicing falsehood, who posed as righteous while

indulging in sin—God appeals for love, righteousness, and truth. "Sow for yourselves righteousness, reap the fruit of unfailing love, and break up your unplowed ground; for it is time to seek the LORD, until he comes and showers righteousness on you" (v. 12).

These three themes—truth, righteousness, and love—are precisely the items that the apostle John introduces in his first letter as evidence that a person has been born again. Some time before John's writing, some of the more intellectual members of the Christian community had withdrawn from the believers' fellowship to found a "church" of their own (cf. 1 John 2:19). They claimed that their understanding of the faith represented an improvement on what had been taught before. Many of the regular members were confused. Were the new teachers right? Was the old teaching to be abandoned? Where did the truth lie? John wrote his first epistle to assure the believers that they really were Christians and at the same time give them three tests by which spiritual claims might be evaluated.

The first test is the presence of practical *righteousness* in the believer's life. This does not mean that a Christian must be without sin. In fact, John says that a person who claims to be without sin deceives himself and makes God out to be a liar, for God says that all sin (1:8, 10). It means that the one professing to know God must be progressing in righteousness so that his profession is increasingly matched by his conduct (2:3–6; 3:4–10). Any claim to a higher experience of Christianity that is not matched by superior moral conduct is to be rejected (1:6). The second test is *love*, which John considers in terms of a Christian's relationship to other Christians. Does he love them in noticeable ways? Since God is love and since love comes from Him, anyone claiming to know God but failing to show love for others is either self-deceived or is attempting to deceive (2:7–

11; 3:11–18; 4:7–21). The third test is a theological test, the test of *truth*. It is John's claim that no one who fails to believe that the pre-existent Son of God, the second person of the Trinity, became flesh at a fixed point in time and history and died for our sin can be a Christian (2:18–27; 4:1–6).

These tests challenge presumption. They are tests by which everyone who claims to be in a right relationship to God may examine himself to determine whether this profession is actually matched by reality. On the other hand, they are also tests that can and should lead a Christian into that holy boldness in approaching God which is his or her privilege and right and can endow his speech with that note of authority needed as he attempts to bear witness to other persons.

I cite these verses in 1 John to counter a tendency we have when we read the Old Testament. We read a prophecy like Hosea's and say, "It is all so strange and far away. Think of the digging you have to do even to understand the reference to Gibeah. How can any of this be relevant to me?" Well, you do not have to dig all that much. But whether you do or not, the message is very simple and is the same from the beginning of the Bible to the end. God saves us by grace. He draws us into a spiritual union with Himself by grace. But those who are so drawn must, by the very fact of their union with Him, be changed. We must be marked by truth, as He is truth; by righteousness, as He is righteous; and by love, as He is love. If we have a divided heart at those points, we are either saved but terribly far from God, or else we have never tasted the life of the Lord Jesus Christ in the first place, regardless of our profession.

ABIDE IN ME

We may ask at this point, "But how can I live as I should? I talk about love, but I know that I am unfaithful. I talk about truth, but I speak falsehood. I strive for righteousness, but I carry sin within me. How can we who are marred by sin actually live to God?"

The answer comes from the mouth of the Lord Jesus Christ, who put Himself forward in the fifteenth chapter of John, as we well know, not as the degenerate vine that Israel had become because of her divided heart, but as that "true vine" to which those who are His have been joined. To such He speaks this encouraging word: "Remain in me, and I will remain in you. No branch can bear fruit by itself; it must remain in the vine. Neither can you bear fruit unless you remain in me. I am the vine; you are the branches. If a man remains in me and I in him, he will bear much fruit; apart from me you can do nothing" (John 15:4, 5).

The key sentence in these two verses can mean any one of three things. It can be a simple declarative with the sense, "You *must* remain in Me, and I *must* remain in you." It can be a promise: "Remain in Me, and I *will* remain in you." It can be a command, meaning "Remain in Me and, thus, see to it that I for My part also remain in you." Probably, as Leon Morris points out, the third of these should be preferred. "Jesus means that the disciples should live such lives that he will continue to abide [remain] in them. The two 'abidings' cannot be separated, and 'abiding' is the necessary prerequisite of fruitfulness. No branch bears fruit in isolation. It must have vital connection with the vine. So to abide in Christ is the necessary prerequisite of fruitfulness for the Christian."[1] Union with Christ is the secret of all fruitfulness, and this means that the essential element is new life. Religion stands over the cripple and says to him, "You are not walking properly. In fact, you are not

---

[1]Leon Morris, *The Gospel According to John* (Grand Rapids: Eerdmans, 1971), pp. 670, 671.

walking at all. Here is how you should do it." But he cannot; he simply lies there. Christianity takes hold of his hand and says, "In the name of Jesus Christ rise up and walk." As a result, new life surges through his twisted body. It is union with Christ (and only union with Christ) that gives us power to live a godly and fruitful life in this world.

A great promise is given to us, if we do abide in Jesus. It is that we shall be fruitful. I do not know if you ever get discouraged in your Christian work or witness, but I assure you that I do. When we get discouraged it is good to turn to a verse like this and find Christ saying that if we abide in Him, as He tells us to do, then we will be fruitful, whether we see the fruit of our efforts or not.

I am not a horticulturist, but I am told by those who know such things that a vine needs to be cultivated at least three years before being allowed to produce fruit at all. That is, it must be trimmed and allowed to grow, then be trimmed and allowed to grow again, and so on for a considerable length of time. Only after this does it become useful for bearing fruit. In the same way, there are times in our lives when we seem to go for considerable periods, undergoing rather radical treatment at the hands of the Father, and seeing very little fruit come from it. In such times we doubt if there will ever be the fruit of righteousness, truth, and love. But that is only because we cannot see as God sees. We do not have His perspective. Do not get discouraged if that has happened to you. Instead, remember that Jesus promises fruit in due time if we truly abide in Him. Ultimately, God is the One responsible for the vineyard; and He has determined that His vineyard will be fruitful.

10

The Troubled Heart of God

(Hosea 11:1–12:1)

"When Israel was a child, I loved him, and out of Egypt I called my son. . . . How can I give you up, Ephraim? How can I hand you over, Israel? How can I treat you like Admah? How can I make you like Zeboiim? My heart is changed within me; all my compassion is aroused. I will not carry out my fierce anger, nor devastate Ephraim again."

After the first three chapters of Hosea, which tell the story of Hosea's marriage, it is difficult to distinguish any large segments of the prophecy and thus show movement in the book. Hosea seems rather to be a collection of short oracles grouped loosely around the themes highlighted by my chapter titles. If there is any place where a new movement can be detected, however, it is at the beginning of chapter 11. Beginning with this chapter and continuing to the end a new emphasis on the sovereign and ultimately triumphant love of God can be found.

In this, the prophecy of Hosea comes full circle and parallels in its structure the story of the marriage on which it is built. The story of the marriage had three phases. There was an initial period of love and happiness. There was the period of Gomer's unfaithfulness in which the course of her life was continually downward. During this phase Hosea continued to love his wife and provide for her, but her dissolute and promiscuous life led her into increasing poverty and eventually into slavery. The third phase is seen in Hosea's act of redemption in which he purchased his wife in the slave market and thereby made her his forever. He said in that day, "You are

to live with me many days; you must not be a prostitute or be intimate with any man, and I will live with you" (3:3). On the basis of that analysis we may say that the last four chapters of Hosea correspond to stage three. The love of God has been present all along, but from chapters 4 to 10 the notes of discipline and judgment predominate. Now, although judgment is still present, the emphasis falls on God's prevailing and unquenchable love.

What an amazing love this is! In chapter 11 Hosea writes of the love of God in reference to Israel's past, present, and future. But in each case there are surprises. The love of God does not operate as we might think it should. It is because God is "God, and not man" that He acts differently (v. 9).

A BLISSFUL PAST

Verses 1–4 tell of Israel's past. It is not the first time in the book in which God has looked to this early and blissful period of His relationship to the people. The story of the marriage suggests it. There is a brief reference in 9:6. But in spite of these earlier suggestions of a happy past we are not quite prepared for the intensity and pathos of these verses. It is impossible to read them without being moved. God compares Himself to a father who has called and trained a son; but the son has turned out to be unresponsive and ungrateful, and He is about to lose him through judgments soon to come.

If this passage is moving to us, it must have been even more stirring to Hosea, who wrote it, and to the people who heard and read it, for the idea of God being a father was not at all common in that day. It has been pointed out by a number of Old and New Testament specialists that before the coming of Jesus Christ no individual Jew ever seemed to have thought of God as his or her personal father. This was a new idea brought into the world by Jesus. Apparently Jesus habitually called God "my Father"— which made a great impression on the minds of His disciples—then toward the end of His life authorized His followers to do the same: "Go . . . to my brothers and tell them, 'I am returning to my Father and your Father, to my God and your God'" (John 20:17), and "This is how you should pray: 'Our Father . . .'" (Matt. 6:9). In the Old Testament God is only called the father of Israel as a whole, never of individuals, and even that is seldom.[1]

In view of this, the passage before us is remarkable. True, it is of Israel as a whole. But the portrayal of God as a father calling and caring for His son is so tender in its detail that it is hard to imagine anyone (particularly a Jew) reading this and not feeling personally the object of such divine compassion.

There are two main parts to these verses, each of which contributes to the intensity of the portrayal. First, there is the call or election of God: "When Israel was a child, I loved him, and out of Egypt I called my son" (v. 1). Here are two references, one historical (to the national deliverance from Egypt at the time of Moses) and one literary (to the Book of Deuteronomy). The text in Deuteronomy to which these words probably look back is particularly instructive, for they are an explanation (such as it is) of why the Lord chose Israel. They say, "The LORD did not set his affection on you and choose you because you were more numerous than other peoples, for you were the fewest of all peoples. But it was because the LORD loved you and kept the oath he swore to your forefathers that he brought you out with a mighty hand and redeemed you from the land of slavery, from the power of Pharaoh king of Egypt" (Deut. 7:7, 8). What claim did Israel have on God? None at all! That is what these verses teach. She was not more numerous and therefore useful. She was not more moral or devoted. There was nothing in Israel that in any way made her superior or more desirable to God than the other nations round about. So the explanation of God's electing love is to be found in the love itself and in no other place. He loved them because He loved them. That is all.

That is the point of the opening sentence in Hosea 11. For here, as God begins to speak of His father-love for Israel, He reminds the people that they became His, not by birth, but by an adoption based on election. He loved them and called them, and therefore they should love Him.

Moreover, God did not just adopt His people. He also cared for them in the days of their spiritual infancy, as a father cares for his son. He taught them to walk when they could only crawl. He healed them when they became sick. He bent down to feed them when they were unable to feed themselves. Here is the way God says it: "It was I who taught Ephraim to walk, taking them by the arms; but they did not realize it was I who healed them. I led them with cords of human kindness, with ties of love; I lifted the yoke from their neck and bent down to

---

[1]Only fourteen times in all. See, for example, Exodus 4:22; Psalm 103:13; Isaiah 64:8, and Jeremiah 3:19, 20.

feed them" (vv. 3, 4). Anyone who has ever lived in a house with a baby can easily visualize these pictures: a father or mother bending over a child to hold its upraised arms as, laughing, it takes its first steps; the anxious face of the parent administering medicine to the helpless infant who is sick and crying; a parent leaning over the highchair to shovel pablum into the mouth of a baby who has not yet learned to feed itself. God says that this is what He has been doing. He has been caring for Israel like a doting parent. Without this care Israel would surely have died. Yet in spite of His devoted care, Israel turned away from God as she grew older. Like the prodigal son, she went her own way into a far country. Like Hosea's wife, she turned prostitute. God says, "The more I called Israel, the further they went from me. They sacrificed to the Baals and they burned incense to images" (v. 2).

So have we all. We said earlier that this is not merely Israel's story. It is the story of the race and of ourselves in particular. There is not one who has not run from God in spite of His common and abundant grace, and there are others (believers in Christ) who have turned from Him even though they have been adopted into His family. Only sin's horror explains how we can scorn such love.

IMMINENT DISASTER

The next section of the chapter (vv. 5–7) deals with Israel's present, but it is a theme we have heard again and again throughout the prophecy. Israel has turned from God. Hence, in place of the bliss of her infant years there is now to be the harsh and dreadful reality of God's judgments. We note, moreover, that it is not merely Israel's sin that is the problem, but rather the grim fact that she will not repent of it: "Will they not return to Egypt and will not Assyria rule over them because they refuse to repent? Swords will flash in their cities, will destroy the bars of their gates and put an end to their

plans. My people are determined to turn from me. Even if they call to the Most High, he will by no means exalt them."

Here is the place at which we may also take up the last verse of chapter 11 and the first verse of chapter 12, which stand by themselves and are not closely attached either to chapter 11 or the one following. They are a further description of the people's guilt. "Ephraim has surrounded me with lies, the house of Israel with deceit. And Judah is unruly against God, even against the faithful Holy One. Ephraim feeds on the wind; he pursues the east wind all day and multiplies lies and violence. He makes a treaty with Assyria and sends olive oil to Egypt" (11:12; 12:1). Wind symbolizes vanity, as we saw earlier. The east wind probably refers to Assyria and to the people's attempt to gain an imagined security through alliances with her. At the same time apparently Israel was hedging her bets by sending produce south to Egypt.

God's words are firm: judgment will come in the form of a destructive invasion, and the people will be carried off to Assyria while others flee to Egypt from which God had delivered them so many centuries before. Full circle! The end!

SOVEREIGN LOVE

Yet it is not the end, for at this point God steps forward to disclose the conflict in His own heart and shows that the day will yet come when He will reclaim His people and have them worship Him.

I confess that I hardly know how to treat this section, for in a chapter full of tenderness, pathos, and surprises, this is undoubtedly the most amazing part. God has been comparing Himself to a man, a human father. He has spoken of His love and of the ingratitude and irony of having Israel go her own way rather than remain with Him. It is a striking image, but in the back of our minds we are always thinking that it is, after all, an image and not to be pressed too far. God loves us, yes! But surely not with the full emotions that a human father would have at the rebellion of his son! No? Yet that is what God says in verses 8 and 9. And not only this, He also portrays Himself as being inwardly divided—uncertain what to do, vacillating. Can this be God saying, "How can I give you up, Ephraim? How can I hand you over, Israel? How can I treat you like Admah? How can I make you like Zeboiim? My heart is changed within me; all my compassion is aroused"?

Israel's sin has brought her to the brink of irrevocable judgment, the very theme that has occupied the center section of the book (chs. 4–10). "Giving them up" and "handing them over" refer to total destruction. Admah and Zeboiim were two of the cities of the plain destroyed when Sodom and Gomorrah were likewise blotted out (cf. Gen. 10:19; 14:2, 8; Deut. 29:23). Their names stand for swift annihilation. But on the brink of such judgment it is God rather than Israel who hesitates. "How can I do it?" He says, as wrath against sin and love for the people do battle within Him.

At last the answer comes: "I will not carry out my fierce anger, nor devastate Ephraim again. For I am God, and not man—the Holy One among you. I will not come in wrath" (v. 9).

What do you think of this verse? It is a welcome note. The second half is given as an explanation of the first half. God says that He will not destroy Israel utterly. Although the judgment will come, this will not be the end. Rather, it will be followed by a second regathering of the people: "'They will follow the LORD; he will roar like a lion. When he roars, his children will come trembling from the west. They will come trembling like birds from Egypt, like doves from Assyria. I will settle them in their homes,' declares the LORD" (vv. 10, 11). The reason God gives for this final resolution of His internal conflict is that He is "God, and not man." But I ask: What do you think of this? Does it seem natural? Correct? On the surface it seems anything but correct. When God says, "I am God, and not man," what we should naturally expect is swift repression of all vacillating sentiment for Israel and immediate execution of the judgment that must come. Does He not call Himself the Holy One? Shall not the judge of all the earth do right?

The answer is clear. Sin must and will be punished. But that is not all there is to God, and for this we must thank Him eternally. True, God is a God of justice. But He is also a God who acts in love to spare His people. We think back to the opening verse where He speaks of His sovereignty in choosing Isarel in the first place. He appeals to this same characteristic now. They have not chosen Him. But He has chosen them, and so set is His choice that He will not allow them to be utterly destroyed but will speak to call them forth from the lands into which they have been driven.

JUST AND JUSTIFIER

This comes at great cost, and the cost is the death of Jesus. Hosea probably did not know much about how God would eventually solve the difficulty of refusing to condemn sinners and yet remain the Holy One. He knew the problem. He must have wondered how God could say on the one hand, "I am God, and not man—the Holy One among you," and on the other hand, "I will not come in wrath." He knew that there is no lowering of God's just standard and also that there is a love that saves. These are possible because with God all things are possible. Still Hosea must have wondered how such love could triumph.

Today we know the answer. Jesus paid the price of our transgression, with the result that God can be both "just and the one who justifies the man who has faith in Jesus" (Rom. 3:26).

G. Campbell Morgan has some excellent words on this theme. He writes, "When God, in spite of sin, says, How can I give you up? My heart is stirred, My compassions are stirred, but I am holy; how can I give you up? and yet says, I will not give you up, I will not, I will not, we are in the presence of some possibility wholly of God. It must have been a great word for trembling and troubled hearts even then.

"But our Bible does not end in Hosea. The name Hosea meant salvation. I do not know who named him. The father or mother, or both, in all probability; but they called that boy Hosea, a sob and sigh and song merging in a name. There came one in the fulness of time, whose name was Jehovah and Hosea: Jesus. So in the fulness of time the gleams and glints of glory broke out into full manifestation; and we find out at last in Jesus, how God can be just and the justifier of the sinning soul.

"The way of accomplishment Hosea did not see. In communion with God he had learned facts about the divine nature which seemed to be conflicting, and he delivered his message and uttered the words; but at last he came, who is the brightness of the Father's glory and the express image of his person, and in him I see how righteousness and peace meet together, and God can be just and the justifier. Through him the claims of justice which are against my soul are all met. Through him the glory of holiness is maintained; for his redemption of the human soul is not a pity that agrees to ignore sin; but a power that cancels it and sets it free from its dominion. Through him the loved one is regained, restored, renewed, and all the lights that flash and gleam upon the prophetic page, astonishing my soul, come into focused unity in Jesus. God says of you, of me, 'How can I give thee up? I will not . . . I will not . . . I will not.'

"But how? 'I am God and not man, I am the Holy One.' Through Christ he has made the way by which sinning souls can be conformed to his image, his likeness, his will. The gospel is gleaming in Hosea. It is shining in full radiance in Christ."[2]

That gospel is present in its fullness today. God is no less a God of justice. His wrath burns no less fiercely against our sin than it did against the sin of Israel. But God has shown where that wrath is quenched—in Christ—and He has commanded those who are yet in their sins to turn to faith in the Savior. Will you not turn to Him? There is nothing in you that can possibly commend you to God—not your works, not your character, not even your repentance or faith. God's choice is apart from human merit. Therefore, salvation is to be received as a free gift through Christ; and it is in Christ alone—crucified, dead, buried, and risen again—that you will find it. If you have never come to Him, come now. Say, "Lord Jesus Christ, I want You to be my Savior, and I now turn from sin to follow You." If you have already believed but have been drifting away, hear as He calls after you and come trembling back to Him. He will receive you again. He will settle you in your true spiritual home.

---

[2]Morgan, *Hosea: The Heart and Holiness of God,* pp. 105, 106.

11

Judah at the Jabbok

(Hosea 12:2–14)

The LORD has a charge to bring against Judah; he will punish Jacob according to his ways and repay him according to his deeds. . . . He found him at Bethel and talked with him there—the LORD God Almighty, the LORD is his name of renown!

During the fifty or so years of Hosea's ministry as prophet to Israel, the northern kingdom of Israel and the southern kingdom of Judah had gone their separate ways. They had been one nation once—under David and his successor Solomon. But after Solomon's death the unwise policies of young King Rehoboam quickly pushed the northern tribes to rebellion. Solomon had taxed the people heavily. The northerners asked Rehoboam to grant relief from the burdensome taxation. He replied that, rather than lightening their load, he would increase it. He said that his father had lashed them with whips but that he would lash them with scorpions. This spark ignited the rebellion, and from that time on the ten northern tribes were known as Israel and the two southern tribes as Judah, from the name of the larger. At their own pace and according to their own individual sins, each went its own course to destruction.

By the time of the writing of Hosea's prophecy, shortly before the fall of the northern kingdom to Assyria in 721 B.C., the two nations had been separate for nearly 200 years. Yet in spite of their separate history over this long period of time, Israel and Judah were still one people whose destinies were inseparably connected. True, they declined at different rates and fell to their enemies at different times (Jerusalem fell to the Babylonians in 587 B.C.), but the pattern was similar and the cause identical. Each forgot God.

Because of this intertwined history and common destiny the prophecy of Hosea, which up to this point has been directed almost exclusively against Israel, now includes a brief word regarding Judah also. The word begins with 12:2, and is present in one form or another throughout the chapter.

A PARALLEL CHARGE

The verses dealing with Judah begin: "The LORD has a charge to bring against Judah" (v. 2). These words make the reader think of the beginning of chapter 4, which reads: "Hear the word of the LORD, you Israelites, because the LORD has a charge to bring against you who live in the land." In the earlier passage there is the statement of God's formal case against Israel, a case presented from 4:1 to the end of the prophecy (exclusive of 12:2–6). This passage is a deliberate reference to that. It is briefer—only five verses plus some indirect references later on—but the idea is the same. Though Judah is not as far along the slippery path of decline as Israel, she is nevertheless on that path and is therefore likewise endangered. She must repent. Apart from repentance her doom will be as certain as the doom of Israel.

One senses that the fate of Judah is not yet fixed. Israel's fate is fixed. Although it will not mean the final annihilation of the people and will be followed by a future calling of them out of their places of captivity, judgment is coming. Not so with Judah. In her case, there is still time to repent of sin and avoid the destruction.

What would it take for her to do this? Hosea answers by a review of the life and spiritual experiences of Israel and Judah's common ancestor, Jacob, the grandson of Abraham. Apparently, Hosea identifies Jacob with Judah primarily—"The LORD has a charge to bring against *Judah*; he will punish *Jacob* according to his ways" (v. 2)—but Jacob was a common ancestor, and his association with the northern site of Bethel makes him a basis on which to appeal to Israel also. Hosea alludes to three episodes in his life.

The first episode concerns Jacob's birth, with which his original name is associated. Jacob was a twin, born to Isaac and Rebekah. His brother was Esau. Genesis tells us that the two babies were struggling with each other in Rebekah's womb before the birth and that when they were born, although Jacob was born second and was therefore technically the younger brother, he emerged grasping Esau's heel. Genesis 25:26 indicates that his name came from this incident. In Hebrew the word "heel" is *'āqēb*, and "Jacob" is *ya'aqōb*. It means "heel grasper."

"To grasp the heel" also meant to go behind one's back in order to deceive or trick him, and this became the dominant characteristic of the man. Jacob was always second—second in his birth, in strength, in the favor of his father. But he was always trying to use his wits to trick and thus get ahead of the one before him. Although Hosea does not mention it specifically, every Jewish reader would be aware of Jacob's cheating his brother Esau of his birthright and of the all-important deathbed blessing of their father.

What Hosea does say is that Jacob "struggled with God" (v. 3). He thought he could handle God the same way he was always trying to handle other people. He thought he could trick God or at least manipulate Him to do what he wanted.

This is the point at which the story comes home. For what better describes the religion of Israel and Judah (and at times unfortunately even of ourselves) than the attempt to use God. Israel and Judah thought that if they went through the prescribed religious rituals—prayer, sacrifice, feast days—this would inevitably bind God to them and oblige Him to prosper and protect them, regardless of what their true spiritual or moral state should be. People think like this today. They think that if they go through the forms of religion, God will be obliged to prosper them. Thus, although they do not really love or faithfully obey Him, they are always shocked when disciplines of any sort come on them.

JACOB AT THE JABBOK

The second episode in Jacob's life is the crucial one, for it was the turning point in his otherwise undistinguished career: his struggle with the angel of God at Jabbok. This story involves a bit of background. Having cheated his brother of his birthright and blessing, Jacob had been forced to run for his life. At this point, with nowhere else to go, he went back toward Haran, the country from which his ancestors came. Here he met his uncle Laban, married two of Laban's daughters and worked for him as a shepherd for more than twenty years.

In time the Lord spoke to Jacob. He said, "Go back to the land of your fathers and to your relatives, and I will be with you" (Gen. 31:3). This was good news to Jacob, for it coincided with a period of particularly bad relations between himself and Laban. Immediately he started off. He probably did so with a spring in his step, for he had more or less forgotten what he had done in cheating his brother. Back then Esau had said he would kill him. But that was twenty years before, and twenty years is a long time. Surely Esau had forgotten! Perhaps he was even dead!

But suppose he was not. Suppose he remembered. Jacob began to have doubts, and the closer he got to the land from which he had come and in which Esau was still living the more doubtful he became. He became anxious and then frightened. Each step became more difficult. Finally Jacob came to the brook Jabbok, which marked the border of Esau's territory, and he was petrified. If he could have gone back, he would have. But things had become so difficult with Laban that retreat was cut off. He had nowhere to go but forward.

As he stood on the east bank of the Jabbok, Jacob asked himself what he was going to do. He reasoned that the wise thing would be to find out what the situation was. So he sent some of his servants over the Jabbok ahead of him to find out about Esau. If they found him they were to identify Jacob as his "servant," tell briefly about the past twenty years and ask Esau for a favorable reception. The servants went, met Esau and came back with this news: "We went to your brother Esau, and now he is coming to meet you, and four hundred men are with him" (Gen. 32:6). Four hundred men! This was an army to the mind of shepherd Jacob. He was even more frightened than before. Resourcefully but "in great fear and distress Jacob divided the people who were with him into two groups, and the flocks and herds and camels as well. He thought, 'If Esau comes and attacks one group, the group that is left may escape'" (vv. 7, 8).

He began to pray, asking God to protect him. But even while he was praying his mind began to work on plans that might overcome his brother's antagonism, so little was he really trusting God even in this extremity. He decided to begin to give up his possessions.

First, he took a flock of 200 female goats and sent them ahead of him toward Esau. He put a servant in charge and instructed the servant in this way: "When my brother Esau meets you and asks, 'To whom do you belong, and where are you going, and who owns all these animals in front of you?' then you are to say, 'They belong to your servant Jacob. They are a gift sent to my lord Esau, and he is coming behind us'" (vv. 17, 18). He thought that he might soften Esau's heart in this fashion and thus escape with his life.

But suppose the flock of 200 female goats was not enough? Suppose Esau was not satisfied? He decided to send 20 male goats after them, again in the keeping of a servant who was instructed to convey the same message.

After the 20 male goats Jacob sent 200 ewes.

After the ewes there were 20 rams.

After the rams he sent 30 female camels with their young.

Then came forty cows.

Ten bulls.

Twenty female donkeys.

Ten male donkeys.

Jacob thought, "I will pacify him with these gifts I am sending on ahead; later, when I see him, perhaps he will receive me" (v. 20). We are told that Jacob's gifts went on ahead of him and that he spent that night in the camp.

When morning came he carried out more of the same strategy, this time with his family since the flocks were gone. He sent his two wives, their children and the closest family servants ahead of him over the Jabbok. Apparently, as the next chapter indicates, he sent the servants first—since he valued them least. Then he sent Leah, who was the least favored wife, with her children. Finally, he sent Rachel. Everything was stretched out in bands across the desert toward Esau. Last of all, at the very back of the procession, was Jacob—all alone and trembling. He had given up his possessions, even his family. But he was still the same old Jacob. He had not given up himself.

That night God sent a messenger, probably an angel, who wrestled with Jacob until daybreak. At first Jacob prevailed. But the angel touched his hip so that it was wrenched, shriveled, or damaged in some way. Jacob, now at the point of true personal surrender, cried out for a blessing and was blessed. He was now changed. As a symbol of that surrender and resulting blessing the messenger changed his name. Before, it had been Jacob—"heel grasper," "cheat," "supplanter." Now it became Israel, which meant "one who has struggled with God" and been overcome.[1]

Many do what Jacob did. God gets close to them, and they are afraid of what He might require. So they say, "I'll pacify Him; I'll give Him some money." When God doesn't seem to be satisfied with that, they say, "I'll serve on a church board; I'll teach a Sunday school class." At last they give Him their family. They do not give themselves. Finally the time comes when they are standing alone, naked in the sight of Him with whom we have to do, and God sends His angel to wrestle them to the point of personal submission.

GOD OF BETHEL

The third and final episode from Jacob's life referred to by Hosea is the patriarch's meeting with God at Bethel, recorded in Genesis 35. Jacob had been at Bethel once before. In fact, he had named it. Bethel means "house of God," and Jacob had named it this because he had received a vision there of a staircase reaching to heaven. On that earlier occasion Jacob had been his old self. He had bargained with God, promising Him a tenth of his possessions if God would prosper him: "If God will be with me and will watch over me on this journey I am taking and will give me food to eat

and clothes to wear so that I return safely to my father's house, then the LORD will be my God. This stone that I have set up as a pillar will be God's house, and of all that you give me I will give you a tenth" (Gen. 28:20–22). How noble of Jacob!

On his return he was a different man. He did not bargain with God. On the way he had instructed his household and servants to get rid of whatever idols they may still have had, to purify themselves and change their clothes. That is all he is reported as saying. Now he stands before God humbly to hear what God will say and to receive whatever instructions He has for him.

This is the point to which Judah must come, according to Hosea. She is not there yet. On the contrary, she is far from it. But she can go in that direction if she chooses. She must "return to . . . God; maintain love and justice, and wait for . . . God always" (12:6). In her current state she is like Jacob at the Jabbok, still bargaining with God but able to surrender to Him if she will only learn from her present needs and setbacks.

THE LATER HISTORY

So much for Judah. What about Israel—Ephraim, as Hosea likes to call her? The word for Ephraim is not good. She is dishonest, rich, and arrogantly confident that no one will ever be able to prove her guilty of any sin (vv. 7, 8). She will be driven from God's land.

There is a word in the Hebrew of verse 7 that is obscured in most of the English translations. It is the word "Canaan" or "Canaanite," translated "merchant" in most instances, though footnotes sometimes indicate the other possibility (see KJV, ASV). This word stands first and isolated in verse 7, so that we could read: "Canaanite! He uses dishonest scales; he loves to defraud. Ephraim boasts, 'I am very rich; I have become wealthy. With

---

[1]Israel (*yisrĕ'ēl*) is much like the word for "struggle" (*sārā*), plus "God" (*'ēl*).

all my wealth they will not find in me any iniquity or sin.'" (Canaanite also means merchant, with an emphasis on being dishonest in trade, but by translating it "merchant" Hosea's deliberate reference to the people of the land is obscured.)

The point is this. Before Israel settled in the land promised to them by God the land was called Canaan. It was an abominable place. Not only was it a center for all types of commercial dishonesty; it was also notorious for its sexual and religious depravity. Cultic prostitution was common. People worshiped symbols of the sexual organs. At times children were sacrificed to Canaan's gods. "Canaan" meant depravity. When Israel was sent into Canaan under Joshua, she was given the task of rooting out this corruption and establishing a culture marked by holiness instead. Israel's task was to make Canaan Israel. What happened? Canaan made Israel Canaan! Mays says of this deplorable transformation, "Israel has taken on the character of the dwellers in the land and has lost his identity as Israel. . . . The old Jacob of greed and trickery lives on in the people and makes them a better Canaanite than Israelite. The ethic of the covenant has given way to the ethos of the unscrupulous trader."[2]

This happened in spite of God's gracious dealings with His people, as the chapter goes on to show. God had revealed Himself to them; there are two references to prophets (vv. 10, 13). He had delivered them from Egypt (vv. 9, 13). He cared for them (v. 13), but they rebelled. Hosea puts it together at the end: "The LORD used a prophet to bring Israel up from Egypt, by a prophet he cared for him. But Ephraim has bitterly provoked him to anger; his LORD will leave upon him the guilt of his bloodshed and will repay him for his contempt" (vv. 13, 14).

REASONABLE SERVICE

Thus far in our study of Hosea 12 we

have had two pictures: a picture of the southern nation standing on the brink of decision, at her own personal Jabbok, and a picture of the northern kingdom as having passed beyond the point of recovery. Two pictures! But there is also a third to be considered, though it is not presented in this chapter. It is the proper picture, the one to which these pictures point by comparison. What is it? It is of faithful, reasonable service to the God of salvation. I find it in Romans: "Therefore, I urge you, brothers, in view of God's mercy, to offer your bodies as living sacrifices, holy and pleasing to God— which is your spiritual worship" (12:1).

Why do I call such service reasonable? There are four explanations. First, *because of what God has done for us.* This is the significance of the word "therefore" that begins this chapter. "Therefore" refers back to everything that Paul has already said in the epistle. He had begun in the early chapters to talk of our sin and need, our spiritual depravity before God. He has rehearsed our inability to please Him, the fact that none of us is righteous, that none understands spiritual things, that none seeks after God. Yet when we were in that state, God sent His Son, Jesus Christ, to die in our place to provide a magnificent salvation that answers our need on all levels. We were not righteous, but we are made righteous in Christ. We did not understand spiritual things, but He gives us understanding. We did not seek after Him, but He sought us. Paul unfolds this great plan of salvation, and when he gets to chapter 12 he says, "It is reasonable for us to serve God."

Second, it is reasonable *because of what God is presently doing in us.* Salvation is not just a past thing. Salvation is also a present experience. It is not only under the penalty of sin that we suffer. There is also the power of sin. We know how difficult it is to make changes in life, break habits, live a life pleasing to God. The Holy Spirit provides us with that

[2]Mays, *Hosea: A Commentary,* p.167.

present salvation so that as we come to Him, pray, study His Word and share with other Christians, we do grow. Paul says that for that reason too it is reasonable to serve God.

Third, he says that it is reasonable *because such service is God's will for us.* This is what the second verse of Romans 12 goes on to articulate: "Do not conform any longer to the pattern of this world [Phillips says, 'Don't let the world force you into its mold'], but be transformed [that is, from within] by the renewing of your mind. Then you will be able to test and approve what God's will is—his good, pleasing and perfect will."

What is God's will for you? God's will expresses itself in many particulars; they differ in every case. But fundamentally God's will is that you might be like Jesus Christ and serve Him. That is what this verse says. Furthermore, lest we think that this will is something hard, difficult, abstract, or irrational, Paul gives three adjectives to tell us what the will of God is. It is "good," he says. God is the master of the understatement. So if God says His will is good, it is good with a capital G. Furthermore, it is "pleasing," that is, pleasing even to us. Do not say that God's will is hard. You do not understand what God is doing if you think in those terms. God's will is the most acceptable thing there is. Finally, it is "perfect." When Paul says perfect, what he is really saying is that it cannot be improved upon. Our ways are not God's ways. There are always going to be circumstances in which we do not understand what God is doing. But God says, "Know this, believe it, accept it as a fact: My will is good, My will is pleasing, My will is perfect. You find that will in My service."

Finally, service makes sense *because God is worthy of our efforts.* We read in the fourth chapter of Revelation: "You are worthy, our Lord and God, to receive glory and honor and power, for you cre-ated all things, and by your will they were created and have their being" (v. 11). Or in the fifth chapter of Revelation: "Worthy is the Lamb, who was slain, to receive power and wealth and wisdom and strength and honor and glory and praise!" (v. 12). Again in the next verse: "To him who sits on the throne and to the Lamb be praise and honor and glory and power, for ever and ever!" We read those words; we sing those words; we even talk about those words. But do we believe them? Do we believe that God the Father, God the Son, and God the Holy Spirit are really worthy of all praise, honor and *service?* If we do, then it makes sense to serve God.

We indicate whether we really think God is worthy of our service by what we do. Take a girl who is just engaged. She has a ring. She wants to show that ring to everyone. If she begins by being not the most attractive person, perhaps a bit homely, as her friends look at her and notice her joy in the engagement they also notice that she seems to glow with this love. If she is a little overweight, they notice that she is making an effort to slim down in order that she might be a little more attractive to the man whom she is going to marry. They will say, "The engagement is certainly doing worlds for her, improving her." They have a measure of the worth in which she holds her husband-to-be in the ways she acts and the things she does.

It is the same spiritually. You can come to church and say "God is worthy of honor." But if you go out and do not live any differently, your actions deny your profession. On the other hand, if your life has changed—if it has changed in such a way that you have given yourself to God first of all, have given your body and all aspects of your activity to Him to use as He desires, and then have given sacrificially—you are testifying that our God is worthy to be praised by everyone.

12

Death of a Nation

(Hosea 13:1–16)

When Ephraim spoke, men trembled; he was exalted in Israel. But he became guilty of Baal worship and died. Now they sin more and more; they make idols for themselves from their silver, cleverly fashioned images, all of them the work of craftsmen. It is said of these people, "They offer human sacrifice and kiss the calf-idols. . . ." "Like a lion I will devour them; a wild animal will tear them apart. I will destroy you, O Israel, because you are against me, against your helper."

In the sixth chapter of Romans there is a verse that should be memorized early and repeated often by every Christian: "For the wages of sin is death, but the gift of God is eternal life in Christ Jesus our Lord" (v. 23). These words deal with individual salvation, but they also express a principle that goes beyond the individual. True, sin brings death individually. But sin also causes the death of family life, culture, movements of the Spirit of God in history . . . even the death of nations. An example is in the thirteenth chapter of Hosea's prophecy.

Oswald Spengler in his massive two-volume work, *The Decline of the West*, views civilizations by use of an image that recognizes that these die. Spengler was attempting to write a universal history of the human race. But as he turned his massive learning and ability to this task, attempting to distill the principles of historical development and decay into a pattern that would enable him to understand the vast movements of past history, what impressed him most was their similarity to biological life. He found four stages based on this analogy. Civilizations are born. They grow strong. They deteriorate. They die. Spengler made no attempt to link this inevitable

death to what we would call sin, and he knows nothing of redemption in history. But so far as his analysis goes it is both interesting and accurate. Sin brings death, and it is not only the sinning soul but also the sinning nation or culture that "will die" (cf. Ezek. 18:4, 20).

This is what God says to Israel as He contrasts the people's youthful days with their present old age: "When Ephraim spoke [past tense], men trembled; he was exalted in Israel. But he became guilty of Baal worship *and died*" (Hos. 13:1).

SPIRITUAL AUTOPSY

To say that God is contrasting Israel's former days of youth and health with her present old age is technically inaccurate since Israel is already dead. But it is a strange death. We need to follow the hand of the divine surgeon as He conducts a spiritual autopsy. In medicine an autopsy is conducted to determine the cause of death and establish the condition of the corpse for the record. God does this in the first three verses of chapter 13.

As Hosea writes about the death of Israel he is probably thinking along the lines in which the fall of the race is described in the early chapters of Genesis. God told Adam and Eve, "I am placing

84

a tree in the middle of the garden of which you are not to eat. You may eat of all the other trees of the garden. But you are not to eat of this tree as a symbol of the fact that I am the Creator and you are the creatures, that I alone am autonomous and that you are subject to Me. Moreover, that you may know how serious this matter is, I warn you that in the day you eat of it you shall surely die."

Adam and Eve may not have understood completely what dying meant, but they knew it was serious and still disobeyed. Eve ate first. Then she got her husband to eat of the tree too. *And they died.*

Some have objected that Adam and Eve did not die the same day in which they ate of the tree. They lived many hundreds of years after that, according to Genesis. But the objection betrays a misunderstanding of what death is. The objection would be valid if death were only a physical thing, but death is more than physical. Death is also spiritual, and the spiritual death (though not the physical death) took place instantly.

Actually, death affects each part of the human constitution. When God created the man and woman He created them in His image, and one of the things this means is that He created them a trinity, as He is a Trinity. God is three: Father, Son, and Holy Spirit. Adam and Eve possessed a body, soul, and spirit. When they sinned, each of these either died or began to die. The first part to die was the spirit. The spirit is that part of the human being that has awareness of and is capable of communion with God. It is what sets the human being apart from animals, who have something like a personality but who do not have communication with God. Animals do not worship. People worship, and this is due to their spiritual nature. However, when Adam and Eve sinned this part of their constitution died.

They proved it by hiding from God when He came to them in the garden.

It had been God's custom to visit Adam and Eve in the garden in the cool of the day and this had apparently been a joyous time for them. Having sinned, it was now anything but joyous; so rather than come to Him, they hid from Him in the shrubbery. God is the holy One. When we sin a barrier is erected, and the communion that we originally had in Adam and which we are still meant to have is broken. We may describe this by saying that the spirit died. It died instantly.

Something else also happened: the soul began to die. The word "soul" is often used in the Old and New Testaments as if it were synonomous with "spirit," that is, as descriptive of the nonmaterial part of the human constitution. But it is also distinguished from spirit in that it is used for animals, which is not the case with the word "spirit." Spirit always relates to God, as we have indicated. Soul refers more broadly to what we might call individuality or personality. It has to do with our likes and dislikes, our dispositions, our ambitions or lack of them, the way we see ourselves. Above all, it concerns the moral or ethical side of our nature. This part of Adam and Eve began to die, which they demonstrated by their sinful answers to God and by their treatment of one another.

When God came to Adam He asked Adam what he had done: "Have you eaten from the tree that I commanded you not to eat from?" Adam could not deny the fact, but he pleaded extenuating circumstances, blaming the woman who had given him the fruit and, indirectly, God who had given him the woman: "The woman you put here with me—she gave me some fruit from the tree, and I ate it." Likewise, the woman blamed the serpent. Here was the first evidence of their dying in soul. They were trying to excuse themselves, rather than admit their wrongdoing. From this point things went downhill. In the next generation one of the sons of Adam and Eve, Cain, killed his brother. Within several generations the world of that day had become as wicked as our own.

Finally, the body died too. God said, "Dust you are and to dust you will return" (Gen. 3:19).

How Nations Die

This pattern of biblical teaching was in mind as Hosea began to write this section of his prophecy. For the death of the nation described in these verses closely parallels the death of our first parents. How do nations die? The answer is that they die in spirit first. Next they die in soul. Eventually the body of the nation also dies and vanishes.

This needs to be looked at in greater detail, however. So we ask first: How does a nation die *in spirit*? A nation dies in spirit when it forgets God and begins to worship that which is not God. Hosea describes this in the case of Israel by saying, "He became guilty of Baal worship and died" (v. 1). In more recent times the worship of Baal has been replaced by worship of the race (as in the case of Nazi Germany) or material prosperity (as is happening in most of the western nations).

When we talk about the death of a nation's spirit we do not mean that there has ever been a nation on the face of the earth, including Israel, in which every individual was regenerate. No nation has ever had a total awareness of God, involving every one of its citizens. Nevertheless, there is such a thing as God-consciousness in a nation, and it has sometimes been the case, particularly at the birth of a nation or at some period of special religious awakening, that many people have been aware of God and have been so anxious to serve Him that they have impressed truly spiritual principles and standards on their corporate life. This was true of the United States of America. Not all our founding fathers were Christians. On the contrary, many were mere deists. Some probably believed almost nothing biblical. But these views were not formative for the nation and did not dominate its first organization. In those days, people who did not believe the principles of the Christian revelation did not express their disbelief or fight for their secular outlook as people do today. Consequently, a certain God-consciousness was present and expressed. Prayer was part of national life. "In God we trust" was a genuine slogan. In the schools the Bible was read and taught by thousands.

Unfortunately that ended. The first step in a nation's death takes place when its God-consciousness dissipates or, worse yet, is deliberately removed. We cannot speak of other nations at this point—we can speak only for ourselves—but we can say that this is precisely what has happened in America. In our country, particularly in recent years, there has been a deliberate attempt to remove any kind of overt dependence on God from national life. Prayer and Bible reading have been removed from the schools. Public figures have become afraid of identifying policies with Christian principles. Trust in weapons or diplomacy has replaced dependence on God.

Second, *the soul* of the nation dies. This means that the national character deteriorates. We see this in the lowering moral climate of our citizenry, the accelerated corruption of business, the breakup of families, materialism, the increase in crime. We also see it at the national level in the failure of government to keep faith with its people and those of other nations.

One example of how governments break faith with their people is by permitting inflation, particularly on an epic scale (which happens in periods of decline). In the days of their greatest vitality and earning power people save money to see them through their old age. The money they lay aside is worth something when they save it. But as the years go by the value of their dollars is deflated so that the money is actually worth much less when they come to use it. In ten years (figuring from a base year of 1967), inflation in the United States has topped one-hundred percent, meaning that a dollar saved in 1967 was worth less than fifty cents in 1977. Therefore, the working, saving people of America were half as well off as they thought they would be and have a right to be.

Governments break faith with the people of other nations when they fail to honor treaties or trade agreements. The United States did this when it broke treaties with Taiwan. Why? Because mainland China demanded it as a condition for establishing diplomatic relations with us, and it seemed to our financial and political advantage to have such new relations.

Hosea talks about this stage of Israel's decline in verse 2, saying, "Now they sin more and more; they make idols for themselves from their silver, cleverly fashioned images, all of them the work of craftsmen. It is said of these people, 'They offer human sacrifice and kiss the calf-idols.'" Hosea's point is that, although Israel is spiritually dead (v. 1), she nevertheless goes on sinning. She is a walking, sinning corpse. It is what Paul says of the former life of the Christians at Ephesus. They were "dead in . . . transgressions and sins." Nevertheless they sinned, following "the ways of this world and of the ruler of the kingdom of the air" (Eph. 2:1, 2).

At last, *the body* of the nation dies. By degrees! To use the analogy of a body, it is as if one organ after another fails to function properly and the body as a whole gradually sinks down until it collapses utterly. Nations seldom die cataclysmically by sudden and total overthrow at the hands of an enemy. They break down bit by bit. The police cease to be effective. The courts become technical battlegrounds and so cease to perform their proper function of punishing the guilty and exonerating the innocent. Politicians become no longer worthy of the trust

committed to them. Schools cease to educate. Workers cease to work. Managers cease managing. Eventually the whole thing caves in, the country becomes a third- or fourth-rate power, and at last the nation is taken over or is dominated by another country whose star is rising.

This is what Hosea refers to in verse 3. He has spoken of the death of the spirit of the nation, which is past. He has spoken of the present moral decline, the death of the soul. Now he looks to the future and sees the eventual disappearance of the body: "Therefore they will be like the morning mist, like the early dew that disappears, like chaff swirling from a threshing floor, like smoke escaping through a window." Mist! Dew! Chaff! Smoke! It is hard to think of four images better calculated to express how light, weak, and empty the nation had become. It is difficult to picture more graphically how she was to vanish at the first ray of heat or breath of air.

GOD THE DESTROYER

There is an important question to be raised at this point, and Hosea does not fail to raise it. From what source does the death about which he has been writing come? Who sends it? What is the source of the prophesied destruction? Some, wishing to preserve the name of God from any imagined tint of dishonor, speak as if death is merely in the nature of things. This is not what Hosea says or what the Bible as a whole teaches. Hosea says that God sends death. He is the destroyer. The One who previously has preserved the nation now brings judgment on it.

This idea is graphically portrayed in verses 4–16. They begin with a reminder of the deliverance of the people from Egypt by God's hand. In fact, they begin with a direct verbal echo of the opening phrases of the Ten Commandments in which the deliverance is brought forward as the moral basis of the people's obligation to serve God: "But I am the LORD your God, who brought you out of Egypt. You shall acknowledge no God but me" (v. 4). The passage continues with a reminder of the care God gave during the days of the people's desert wanderings: "I cared for you in the desert, in the land of burning heat. When I fed them, they were satisfied" (vv. 5, 6). Nevertheless, the people forgot God. Now, says God, He who has been their deliverer will become their destroyer: "I will destroy you, O Israel, because you are against me, against your helper" (v. 9).

Hosea makes the point by three images. The first is of *a shepherd* who turns himself into the very enemies of the sheep he would normally be concerned to drive away. This image is slightly hidden in most English versions, but it is noticeable as soon as one realizes that the words "I cared for you" at the beginning of verse 5 are actually "I pastured you," which is what a shepherd does. God says that He was like a shepherd to Israel. He led them into the wilderness as a shepherd might lead sheep. He cared for them like sheep. But they forgot Him. Therefore, He will attack them like those animals that are the sheep's natural enemies: "So I will come upon them like a lion, like a leopard I will lurk by the path. Like a bear robbed of her cubs, I will attack and rip them open. Like a lion I will devour them; a wild animal will tear them apart" (vv. 7, 8).

It is interesting—though I am not certain of the exact literary connection—that these four animals (the lion, leopard, bear, and wild beast) are found in the seventh chapter of the Book of Daniel, which forecasts gentile world history from the period of the fall of Jerusalem up to the coming of Jesus Christ. The order is slightly different. Daniel has the bear and leopard reversed. But with this slight exception the passages seem to be parallel. In Daniel's vision the lion represents the kingdom of Babylon, the state that overthrew the last remnants of the Jewish nation in 587 B.C. The bear rep-

resents the kingdom of Media-Persia, which under King Darius overthrew Babylon. The leopard stands for the empire of Alexander the Great. The fourth animal, the unnamed wild beast, stands for Rome. Repetition of these four animals in the prophecies of Hosea and Daniel can hardly be an accident, and what it suggests from the perspective of Hosea's prophecy is that God works through the heathen to cause Israel's defeat.

God can do the same today. And He will! We look at Russia, Red China, or the various Muslim nations, and in our imagined self-righteousness we sometimes feel we have no use for them. They are not godly. We feel that they are only fit for God's judgment. They are. But that does not mean that God cannot or will not use them to destroy those who have once professed His name but have died spiritually.

The second image in these verses is of *an unborn child*, a fetus, who refuses to be born. Hosea writes, "The guilt of Ephraim is stored up, his sins are kept on record. Pains as of a woman in childbirth come to him, but he is a child without wisdom; when the time arrives, he does not come to the opening of the womb" (vv. 12, 13). What is Hosea saying? Is he comparing Israel to a woman in labor or to the child who refuses to be born? The answer is, both . . . and neither. Actually, it is the situation itself that is his focus. When a woman's time comes a child is expected to be born. This is the natural course of events. If the baby cannot be born, it is unnatural, dangerous, and eventually fatal. This is Israel's state. Her rejection of God is unnatural, for the one who has been delivered and kept by God should be thankful. It is dangerous because it invites judgment. It is ultimately fatal because God will judge the nation that rejects Him.

The final image is one that would be well understood by the inhabitants of Palestine: *a destructive wind from the des-*

ert. It represents the invasion that was to come from Syria. Hosea writes, "An east wind from the LORD will come, blowing in from the desert; his spring will fail and his well dry up. His storehouse will be plundered of all its treasures. The people of Samaria must bear their guilt, because they have rebelled against their God. They will fall by the sword; their little ones will be dashed to the ground, their pregnant women ripped open" (vv. 15, 16). It is from the Lord that this destruction comes.

A NEW CREATION

If the death of a nation unfolded along these lines for Israel, if it became true for Judah later, if this unfolding of spiritual death has characterized nations throughout history and seems to be descriptive of our own nation in the present day—is it nevertheless possible to say at any point that there is hope? Is there a gospel of salvation?

It is hard to answer this where nations are concerned, though there is always the possibility of grace. A people can always turn to God and find that He is ready and willing to receive them and will gladly postpone or forego judgment. There have been examples of this in history both in biblical times and since. With God all things are possible. Still, this is not the same as saying that repentance of this scope will occur or that judgment will be stayed where our particular nation is concerned. Will we be spared? Perhaps. But we must note that for every nation that has experienced repentance on a national scale and been spared, there are hundreds of others that have continued on their sinful way oblivious to the whirlwind coming upon them. I doubt if we will see a major turning to God again in America, though we may.

At the same time we can say this: although repentance may not occur nationally so that the nation is saved, it can always happen to and for the individual so that the individual is saved. It can happen to you personally. The death I have described—the death of the spirit, soul, and body—is something each of us has experienced, for all have sinned and died. But each can also experience salvation in those areas. You can be a new creation. This is what God does; He makes us new creations. He does not take the old dead spirit and patch it up. What would He do with a patched-up corpse? He does not take that old soul, decaying under the weight of its sin, and plug up the holes. What would He do with a plugged-up soul? He does not keep alive that old body. God gives us a new spirit, a new soul, and a new body, and each is far better than what we had before.

God works with the spirit first of all. Our old spirit died. God gives us a new spirit when we are born again. That is what the new birth means; it means to be made alive in spirit, reanimated by the Holy Spirit of God. Our old soul has been dying. God gives us a new soul known as the new man. He brings about an inward transformation so that we begin to think and act differently. It is what Paul is speaking about when he writes, "Do not conform any longer to the pattern of this world, but be transformed by the renewing of your mind" (Rom. 12:2). At last we are given a new body—at the moment of the resurrection. We become new creations.

Christians have an opportunity to live, serve, and pray for the nation of which they are a part. If we do that, by the grace of God we may be instrumental in bringing about the repentance and revival of our nation. It may be that, at least in this generation, we will not die . . . but live to the glory of God.

13

The Death of Death

(Hosea 14:1–9)

Who is wise? He will realize these things. Who is discerning? He will understand them. The ways of the Lord are right; the righteous walk in them, but the rebellious stumble in them.

In the thirteenth chapter of Hosea there is a verse that is ambiguous: verse 14. The ambiguity is significant. Because of the form of the Hebrew words, the first part of the verse can be translated either as a statement that God will deliver the people from death's powers, or as a question that in the context might be answered in the negative. We see the contrast by comparing the translation of the New International Version with the Revised Standard Version, to give just two examples. The NIV views the statements positively: "I will ransom them from the power of the grave; I will redeem them from death. Where, O death, are your plagues? Where, O grave, is your destruction?" The RSV reads: "Shall I ransom them from the power of Sheol? Shall I redeem them from Death?" If this refers to the impending destruction of Samaria, which did come, the answer to the question apparently is No, in which case the next questions are to be read as an appeal to Death and Sheol to do their worst. "O Death, where are your plagues? O Sheol, where is your destruction?"

How should the verse be taken? As I say, the matter is ambiguous. To be sure, in 1 Corinthians 15:54, 55 the apostle Paul refers to these verses in speaking of the destruction of death through the work of Christ—"When the perishable has been clothed with the imperishable, and

the mortal with immortality, then the saying that is written will come true: 'Death has been swallowed up in victory.' 'Where, O death, is your victory? Where, O death, is your sting?'"—but that is not the same thing as saying that this is the meaning of the similar verses in Hosea.

Does verse 14 refer to the defeat of death? The immediate context would suggest No, for the verses on either side speak of the destruction that did come. On the other hand, the greater message of the book is of an eventual restoration in which the death of the nation will be overcome. This is the meaning of the story of Hosea and Gomer with which the prophecy began. Though fallen, Gomer was eventually restored. It is also the message of the Word of God generally. Though ruined by sin, we (who believe on Christ) are to be completely restored in spirit, soul, and body that we might be new creations in which God alone is glorified.

One thing is certain. Restoration will not be apart from a genuine repentance, involving both a frank confession of sin and a radical return to God. Sin brings death. It is only the grace of God received through faith that brings blessing.

Call to Repentance

In view of this truth, we are not surprised to find an appeal in the last chap-

90

ter of Hosea to Israel to return to God. In a sense it is God's last word—a word that is to sustain the people during the coming days of captivity. In that day they will undoubtedly wonder if God has cast them off utterly. They will feel forsaken. But God wants them to know that their captivity is due, not to His wishes for them or abandonment of them, but to their sin, and that in spite of their sin the way of return stands open. "Return, O Israel, to the LORD your God. Your sins have been your downfall! Take words with you and return to the LORD. Say to him: 'Forgive all our sins and receive us graciously, that we may offer the fruit of our lips. Assyria cannot save us; we will not mount war-horses. We will never again say "Our gods" to what our own hands have made, for in you the fatherless find compassion'" (vv. 1–3). If they will make such a confession, God will restore them, as the next verses show.

What strikes us first about this appeal is how different it is from the false confession of 6:1–3. That confession has many of the same words as this latter, true confession. But the tone is entirely different. It lacked a true awareness of sin and a true turning to God. It thought of God mechanically: "Come, let us return to the LORD. He has torn us to pieces but he will heal us; he has injured us but he will bind up our wounds. After two days he will revive us; on the third day he will restore us, that we may live in his presence. Let us acknowledge the LORD; let us press on to acknowledge him. As surely as the sun rises, he will appear; he will come to us like the winter rains, like the spring rains that water the earth." These words are offensive, because they are shallow and presume on God. They assume that if the people only acknowledge God verbally He will inevitably restore them because—so the argument runs—that is the way it works. God will appear as surely as the sun rises. He is

like the seasons. Spring will follow winter. You can depend on it!

But God is not nature. He is not a machine. He is the holy God, who will bless—but only as His people turn from their sin to righteousness. He will bless only when their repentance is along the lines of that with which the book closes.

There are three things that make this confession a true one, things lacking in the false repentance of chapter 6. First, there is an *awareness of sin* and that in two ways: 1) that sin is sin, and 2) that it is serious. We see this in the word that is used for sin, literally "iniquity" (v. 1). It is an ugly word, but it rightly describes sin's nature, which is ugly. True repentance begins with an acknowledgment that sin is sin and that it is ugly and terribly offensive in God's sight.

In his study of the Book of Hosea for the English Keswick Week meetings of 1963, J. Graham Miller contrasted this true confession with what he had observed during a tour of missionary duty in the New Hebrides some years before. He wrote: "It was the custom in the New Hebrides, if you did something trifling, to call it in pidgin English: 'Mistake, mistake.' If it was something serious, you still called it, 'One small mistake'; and if it was some dastardly act, and you were later found out, you shrugged it off by saying, 'Oh, me fella me make one small mistake no more.'" This is the tendency of the human heart, but it is not true repentance, as Miller goes on to show. "When we are truly contrite, the smallest sin becomes an offence which is mountainous in the sight of God, and dreadful in the view of our own hearts. We remember what is said in Isaiah 53, that 'He was bruised'—not for our mistakes, but 'for our iniquities,' 'Mistake' is one of Satan's vocabulary to fit the impenitent who thinks that he can bluff God; but God says, 'I remember all their works.'"[1]

---

[1]*Keswick Week 1963* (London and Edinburgh: Marshall, Morgan & Scott, 1963), p. 117.

The second thing that makes the confession of chapter 14 a true repentance is its *turning from specific sins*. In this case it is a repudiation of those foreign alliances, which the people have trusted, and the idols, which they made in the days of their apostasy: "Assyria cannot save us; we will not mount warhorses. We will never again say 'Our gods' to what our own hands have made" (v. 3).

Two things regarding repentance are easy to do: 1) repent of someone else's sins, and 2) repent of sin generally. To repent of one's own, specific sin is so difficult that it is actually impossible apart from the grace of God. We think here of the repentance that took place in Nineveh under the preaching of Jonah. Nineveh was the capital of Assyria, then the dominant power in the near east. She was known for her violence in dealing with those she conquered. Nahum wrote of this city: "Woe to the city of blood, full of lies, full of plunder, never without victims! The crack of whips, the clatter of wheels, galloping horses and jolting chariots! Charging cavalry, flashing swords and glittering spears! Many casualties, piles of dead, bodies without number, people stumbling over the corpses" (Nah. 3:1–3). But revival came to the city through Jonah's preaching, and we know it was true revival because it was exactly of these sins that the populace repented. The decree of the king tells it all: "Do not let any man or beast, herd or flock, taste anything; do not let them eat or drink. But let man and beast be covered with sackcloth. Let everyone call urgently on God. Let them give up *their evil ways and their violence*. Who knows? God may yet relent and with compassion turn from his fierce anger so that we will not perish" (Jonah 3:7–9). The specific sin of the Ninevites was violence, and it was from this that they repented.

We must do the same. If our specific sin is covetousness or greed—one of the dominant sins of the western world—we must repudiate that sin. This means we must not buy that extra car, house, or stereo. If our greed is great, we must even give away what we have and adopt a simpler life style. We must remember that it was to the *rich* young ruler that our Lord said, "Sell everything you have and give to the poor, and you will have treasure in heaven. Then come, follow me" (Luke 18:22). Perhaps ours is a sexual sin. In that case we must turn from it rigorously, because until we do all forms of religious practice will be mere hypocrisy. The one thing we must not do is pretend that our specific sin—whether greed, immorality, anger, pride, gluttony, dishonoring of our parents, or whatever it may be—is not sin, or think that we can retain it while nevertheless serving God.

The third element in the true repentance of these verses is an *appeal to the grace of God*. This is involved in verse 2: "Forgive all our sins and receive us graciously." It means that we must come to God solely on the basis of His grace, not imagining that in spite of our sins there is nevertheless some merit in us to commend us to God—not even the fact that we have repented of our sins and appeal to His mercy.

There is probably nothing that is harder for us to do. It is hard to admit that we are sinners and that sin is serious. It is harder to admit to specific sins and turn from them. Hardest of all is to admit that apart from these sins there is still nothing in us to commend us to God or compel Him to be favorably disposed toward us. What we usually do, even when we are confessing our sin, is immediately rush on to remind God that although we have sinned there are nevertheless other areas in which we have been true to Him. This is not true repentance. It may be true that there have been areas of faithfulness, but the areas of unfaithfulness spoil even those ("A little yeast works through the whole batch of dough," 1 Cor. 5:6). We only truly repent when we admit, as the old Anglican collect has it, that "there is no health in us."

How do we repent? Hosea hits on something important when he answers, "With words." "Take words with you and return to the LORD" (v. 2). We must not merely assume that God knows of our repentance, though He does if we are repentant. Rather we must express our repentance verbally. Without this open confession we can never be fully sure that we have done what God requires. But "if we confess our sins," we can know that "he is faithful and just and will forgive us our sins and purify us from all unrighteousness" (1 John 1:9).

GOD'S PROMISE TO RESTORE

This is the point to which the last chapter of Hosea's prophecy now comes. Having called on the people genuinely to repent of their sins, God now promises a full measure of restoration for when they do. God says He will do three things. First, He will heal their waywardness. That is, He will not only forgive them for their sins; He will actually cure the waywardness so that they will not wander from Him again. Second, God says He will love them. The pattern here is the love of Hosea for Gomer even after her fall into slavery. The life of slavery had taken its toll, but Hosea loved Gomer anyhow and acted to redeem her—which is how God acts with us and with Israel. Third, God says that He will cause His people to prosper again.

This last promise is couched in a series of images that may well be the most beautiful and poetic section of the book. They are all pastoral in nature. The judgment of which the earlier chapters speak is harsh and sudden. Ruin results. But from the ruins, like plants or trees gradually forcing down their roots and rising above the destruction, the people would again begin to grow under God's divine presence and blessing. He would be like the early dew of morning—quiet but effective. They will be like flowers, trees, vines, and fields of grain. God says, "I will be like the dew to Israel; he will blossom like a lily. Like a cedar of Lebanon he will send down his roots; his young shoots will grow. His splendor will be like an olive tree, his fragrance like a cedar of Lebanon. Men will dwell again in his shade. He will flourish like the grain. He will blossom like a vine, and his fame will be like the wine from Lebanon" (vv. 5–7).

When God says that His blessing will result in the growing of blossoms like a lily, He is saying that He will restore *beauty* to the nation. Israel was beautiful once. But sin is ugly, and sin had ruined Israel. Sin likewise makes us ugly, and none can change that ugliness but God. Has sin made you ugly—ugly in face and temperament? Repent of your sin and turn to God. He is able to restore "the years the locusts have eaten" (Joel 2:25). He can bring a beauty to your life that you thought could not be restored.

When God speaks of sending down roots like one of the great cedars of Lebanon, He is saying that He will restore *strength* to the nation. This too is important. Sin not only makes us ugly; it also weakens us, and this weakness becomes increasingly apparent as we grow older. Has sin made you weak? Has it taken away the strength you once had? Repent of that sin and turn to God. He can make you strong again. Isaiah knew this and wrote: "Even youths grow tired and weary, and young men stumble and fall; but those who hope in the LORD will renew their strength. They will soar on wings like eagles; they will run and not grow weary, they will walk and not be faint" (Isa. 40:30, 31).

When God speaks of the splendor of the olive tree, He is saying that He will restore the nation's *value*. The splendor of the olive is oil. It was highly valuable in ancient times. It would be the equivalent of petroleum today. In their sin the nation had ceased to have value, even in its own eyes, but the love and blessing of God would make it valuable again. Has sin robbed you of your value? Has it made you feel worthless in your own eyes and in the eyes of others? Repent of that sin and turn to God. He can teach you to bring forth fruit that will last forever. When you appear before Him in the day of your death you can hear Him exclaim, "Well done, good and faithful servant! You have been faithful with a few things; I will put you in charge of many things. Come and share your master's happiness!" (Matt. 25:21).

When God speaks of the fragrance of the cedars of Lebanon, He is saying that He will again make the nation a *delight*. Fragrance has no utilitarian value, but it is a pleasure to all who breathe it. If you have ceased to be a pleasure to God or others through sin, repent of that sin and turn to God. It can be said of you as Paul said it was of the Christians of his day: "God . . . always leads us in triumphal procession in Christ and through us spreads everywhere the fragrance of the knowledge of him. For we are to God the aroma of Christ among those who are being saved and those who are perishing" (2 Cor. 2:14, 15).

In verse 7 a number of images are combined: the shade of a tree, the flourishing of a field of grain, the luxuriant blossoming of a vine. It is a way of talking about *abundance*, which God says He will cause to be true of Israel in the day of their return to Him. If sin has robbed you of the abundant life that God intended you to have, repent of that sin and return to God. He will make you fruitful in His service, as Jesus said to His disciples: "I am the vine; you are the branches. If a man remains in me and I in him, he will bear much fruit. . . . You did not choose me, but I chose you to go and bear fruit—fruit that will last" (John 15:5, 16).

Does the scope of this promise of God surprise us? It should not, because God is the source of every good gift and all fruitfulness. Beauty! Strength! Value! Delight! Abundance! These are in Him. He is beauty, strength, value, delight, and abundance. He is the answer to our need.

An End to Idols

We must come the whole way. We want to come part way which is, in our thinking, far enough to get what we want while nevertheless preserving the greatest measure of freedom to do our own thing. This will not do in dealing with God. It might work with our employer, parents, husband, or wife. But it does not work with God for the simple reason that He is God. He says to us, "I am the Lord; that is my name! I will not give my glory to another or my praise to idols" (Isa. 42:8). If we would have God, we must renounce our idols entirely (Hos. 14:8).

What will cure us of the idols of our lives? Not another idol certainly. Not will power, for we are dead in trespasses and sins and therefore have no will at all in spiritual matters. The only thing that will do it is a vision of Him whose glory eclipses all else and whose love draws us to Himself alone. Have you seen that one? Have you seen Jesus—not with the eyes of physical sight but with the eyes of faith and the vision of the heart? One of our hymn writers asks that poignant question:

> Hast thou heard Him, seen Him, known Him?
> Is not thine a captured heart?
> Chief among ten thousand own Him,
> Joyful choose the better part.
>
> Idols once they won thee, charmed thee,
> Lovely things of time and sense;
> Gilded thus does sin disarm thee,
> Honeyed lest thou turn thee thence.
>
> What has stript the seeming beauty
> From the idols of the earth?
> Not a sense of right or duty,
> But the sight of peerless worth.
>
> Not the crushing of those idols,
> With its bitter void and smart;
> But the beaming of His beauty,
> The unveiling of His heart.

Who extinguishes their taper
   Till they hail the rising sun?
Who discards the garb of winter
   Till the summer has begun?

'Tis that look that melted Peter,
   'Tis that face that Stephen saw,
'Tis that heart that wept with Mary,
   Can alone from idols draw.

Draw and win and fill completely,
   Till the cup o'erflows the brim;
What have we to do with idols
   Who have companied with Him?

Hosea ends with an appeal to those who have wisdom to discern the truthfulness of such teaching. "Who is wise? He will realize these things. Who is discerning? He will understand them. The ways of the LORD are right; the righteous walk in them, but the rebellious stumble in them" (v. 9).

It is the same today. Sin brings death, but obedience is the path to life. If you have never come to the Lord Jesus Christ as your Savior, come to Him. Confess your sin and throw yourself on His abundant mercy displayed in His dying for you. If you are already His, be sure to live for Him. The apostle John wrote to those of his day: "Dear children, keep yourselves from idols" (1 John 5:21).

JOEL

14

Sign of the Times

(Joel 1:1–20)

The word of the LORD that came to Joel son of Pethuel. Hear this, you elders; listen, all who live in the land. Has anything like this ever happened in your days or in the days of your forefathers? Tell it to your children, and let your children tell it to their children, and their children to the next generation. What the locust swarm has left the great locusts have eaten; what the great locusts have left the young locusts have eaten; what the young locusts have left other locusts have eaten.

On the first day of November, 1755, one of the great earthquakes of modern times struck the city of Lisbon, Portugal. The epicenter was located several miles off the Portuguese coast, in the Atlantic, so tremendous tidal waves struck the city and contributed to the damage. The earthquake came at 9:40 A.M. and lasted for six minutes. In those six minutes all public buildings and 12,000 dwellings were demolished. Sixty thousand people died, including those who were killed as a result of the tidal waves and a fire, which raged for six days. Heavy damage occurred in Fez, Morocco, to the south, and in Algiers, 700 miles to the east. On the coast the tidal waves were sixty feet high. At the island of Martinique, 3,740 miles away, which the waves passed ten hours later, the crest was twelve feet above normal.

There had been earthquakes before, of course, and there have been many since—in Europe, the Pacific, San Francisco, Nicaragua. But there were facets to this earthquake that have not been present to the same degree either before or since. For one thing, the first half of the eighteenth century had been a time of relative peace and prosperity in Europe, a condition particularly welcome following the religious wars of the seventeenth century. Moreover, the era had been marked by a philosophy of optimism associated with the name of Gottfried Wilhelm Leibnitz (1646–1716), who had died less than forty years before. Leibnitz argued that this is "the best of all possible worlds." He viewed evil as mere imperfection and argued that the best of all worlds proves the existence of a wise and benevolent Creator. His view had been popular among so-called "Christian" thinkers. But suddenly optimism was shaken. How could a good God allow such an evil as the Lisbon earthquake? If God is good, He must have lacked power to prevent it; if He had power, He must not be good.

As if to dramatize the uniquely spiritual dimensions of this tragedy the earthquake had occurred on All Saints' Day, which meant that many pious people had been in the churches at the very hour the earthquake struck. The churches collapsed along with the other public buildings.

Christians responded by trying to find a reason for the tragedy. In England many argued that Lisbon was destroyed because its inhabitants were Catholics. In Lisbon clerics said that God was angry because the people had tolerated a few Protestant heretics to live among them. Some of these were subsequently executed. In general, non-Christians ridiculed the entire affair, among them François Voltaire (1694–1778), who attacked the views of the orthodox, first in verse, in 1756, and then in the brilliantly urbane novelette *Candide*, published in 1759. It was Voltaire who had argued that within fifty years of his death Christianity would have been forgotten and the Bible have become an unknown book. *Candide* made fun of the "best of all possible worlds" idea (and Christianity) through the foolishness of the philosopher Pangloss. "All this is for the best," said he. "For if there is a volcano at Lisbon, it cannot be anywhere else; for it is impossible that things should not be where they are; for all is well."[1] Unfortunately for Pangloss, the philosopher became one of the victims of the Catholic reaction in Lisbon—Voltaire's way of saying that this should be the fate of all who utter such nonsense.

Is it nonsense? Indeed it is! For although this is God's world, it is certainly not the best of all possible worlds. Or to paraphrase another writer, although God's in His heaven, all is not right with the world. Having said this, however, we still have not dealt with the problem of evil. Can we deal with it? The answer is that we probably cannot understand all the problems involved with the existence of monstrous evil in a world created and governed by a good God, but we can understand parts of the problem, as the Book of Joel indicates.

DATE AND AUTHOR

We do not know much about Joel or the circumstances of the writing of his book, except that an invasion of locusts had swept through Judah, and that in its own way this was as terrifying and unsettling as the Lisbon earthquake was for the Portuguese.

The name Joel means "Jehovah is God" and therefore constitutes a short confession of faith, somewhat like the primary New Testament confession "Jesus is Lord." The name probably points to genuine faith on the part of Joel's father Pethuel, but aside from this nothing further is known about either Joel or Pethuel. (There are at least twelve other men in the Bible called Joel.) All we can assume is that Joel lived in Jerusalem and appeared there as a prophet of God on the occasion of the locust invasion.

We do not even know when this invasion occurred or when Joel prophesied. There are three main possibilities. The first and probably the oldest of the modern views is that Joel wrote in the early part of the reign of Joash in the ninth century B.C. This was argued first by K. A. Credner in 1831 and was then adopted by such well-known nineteenth-century conservative commentators as Carl Friedrich Keil (1861), E. B. Pusey (1885) and Hans Conrad Von Orelli (1897). The view has been taken up by such modern writers as E. J. Young (1949) and Theo. Laetsch (1956). These men argue that the nonmention of such prominent national enemies of Judah as Syria, Assyria, or Babylon requires an early date. It is assumed that Amos quotes Joel 3:16 at the beginning of his prophecy (Amos 1:2) and that Isaiah borrows a sentence from Joel 1:15 in Isaiah 13:6. If so, Joel must have been written before the age of either of these later prophets. The references to Egypt and Edom in 3:19 are explained by reference to Shishak's attack on Jerusalem in Rehoboam's reign (1 Kings 14:25–28). Joel's placement as the second of the Minor Prophets in the Hebrew canon is also said to suggest an early period.

The second possibility is to date Joel in the postexilic period, around 400 B.C. This possibility was elaborated by the

---

[1]François Voltaire, *Candide or Optimism*, trans. by Richard Aldington (Norwalk, Conn.: The Heritage Press, n.d.), p. 19.

nineteenth-century critical German scholars, beginning with W. Vatke in 1835. In general this school tended to date most biblical books as late as possible, in this case arguing that the nonmention of Syria, Assyria, and Babylon shows that the nations of Israel and Judah had already fallen to these powers and that the references to Egypt and Edom involve atrocities committed by these nations at the time of the fall of Jerusalem to Babylon in 587 B.C. Joel's concern for the temple cult (Joel 1:13, 14; 2:13–17) is said to reflect the postexilic period. It is argued that the parallel wording of certain texts in Isaiah, Joel, and Amos shows Joel's dependence on the other two prophets rather than the reverse.

The third position is a mediating one— late pre-exilic—but it contains much variety within itself. A. S. Kapelrud dates the book about 600 B.C., probably in the reign of Zedekiah. Carl A. Keller argues for the period between 630 and 600 B.C. Wilhelm Rudolph's dates are between 597 and 587 B.C. Bo Reicke and Jacob M. Myers put the book about 520 B.C. Gösta W. Ahlström has it as late as 515 to 500 B.C. An excellent recent work, *The Books of Joel, Obadiah, Jonah and Micah* by Leslie C. Allen (1976), sides with the last of these scholars.[2]

It is obvious from the variety of these positions that a consensus of scholarship is hardly possible and that the matter therefore remains uncertain. Conservatives will probably reject a postexilic dating, but they will not necessarily come down either on a ninth-century B.C. or a sixth-century B.C. setting. Fortunately the teaching of the book is unaffected by either. Calvin noted, "As there is no certainty it is better to leave the time in which he taught undecided; and as we shall see, this is of no great importance. Not to know the time of Hosea would

be to readers a great loss, for there are many parts which could not be explained without a knowledge of history; but as to Joel there is less need of this, for the import of his doctrine is evident, though his time be obscure and uncertain."[3] The important point is that Joel had witnessed a devastating invasion of Judah by locusts and that he had recognized that it was God Himself, and not mere chance, who was responsible.

THE LOCUST INVASION

Today in America, where a locust invasion is quite remote, we can hardly imagine the desolation and desperation that would accompany a locust plague. But there have been similar invasions in relatively modern times from which we can make an assessment.

In 1915 a plague of locusts covered Palestine and Syria from the border of Egypt to the Taurus mountains. The first swarms appeared in March. These were adult locusts that came from the northeast and moved toward the southwest in clouds so thick they obscured the sun. The females were about two and one-half to three inches long, and they immediately began to lay eggs by digging holes in the soil about four inches deep and depositing about 100 eggs in each. The eggs were neatly arranged in a cylindrical mass about one inch long and about as thick as a pencil. These holes were everywhere. Witnesses estimated that as many as 65,000–75,000 eggs were concentrated in a single square meter of soil, and patches like this covered the entire land from north to south. Having laid their eggs the locusts flew away.

Within a few weeks the young locusts hatched. These resembled large ants. They had no wings, and within a few days they began moving forward by hopping along the ground like fleas. They

[2]Leslie C. Allen, *The Books of Joel, Obadiah, Jonah and Micah* (Grand Rapids: Eerdmans, 1976). Allen has a valuable and balanced discussion on the dating problem on pages 19–25.

[3]John Calvin, *Commentaries on the Twelve Minor Prophets*, Vol. 2, *Joel, Amos and Obadiah* (Edinburgh: Calvin Translation Society, 1846), p. xv.

would cover four to six hundred feet a day, devouring any vegetation before them. By the end of May they had molted. In this stage they had wings, but they still did not fly. Instead they moved forward by walking, jumping only when they were frightened. They were bright yellow. Finally the locusts molted again, this time becoming the fully developed adults that had invaded the land initially.

According to a description of this plague by John D. Whiting in the December, 1915, issue of *National Geographic Magazine*, the earlier stages of these insects attacked the vineyards. "Once entering a vineyard the sprawling vines would in the shortest time be nothing but bare bark. When the daintier morsels were gone, the bark was eaten off the young topmost branches, which, after exposure to the sun, were bleached snow-white. Then, seemingly out of malice, they would gnaw off small limbs, perhaps to get at the pith within." Whiting describes how the locusts of the last stage completed the destruction begun by the earlier forms. They attacked the olive trees, whose tough, bitter leaves had been passed over by the creeping locusts. "They stripped every leaf, berry, and even the tender bark." They ate away "layer after layer" of the cactus plants, "giving the leaves the effect of having been jackplaned. Even on the scarce and prized palms they had no pity, gnawing off the tenderer ends of the swordlike branches and, diving deep into the heart, they tunneled after the juicy pith."[4]

This is precisely what Joel and his contemporaries experienced in their day, and the various stages of the molting insects probably explain the four different Hebrew terms Joel uses. In the Authorized Version the Hebrew words are: "palmer worm," "locust," "cankerworm" and "caterpillar." The New International Version says: "locust swarm," "great locusts," "young locusts" and "other locusts" for lack of adequate English words. Probably these are all stages of the same insect, and if so, Joel certainly captures the nature of the utter destruction by reporting, no doubt with perfect accuracy:

> What the locust swarm has left
>   the great locusts have eaten;
> what the great locusts have left
>   the young locusts have eaten;
> what the young locusts have left
>   other locusts have eaten (v. 4).

Whiting, who quotes this and other opening verses of Joel's prophecy in his article, writes, "We marvel how this ancient writer could have given so graphic and true a description of a devastation caused by locusts in so condensed a form."[5]

A CALL TO MOURN

The most remarkable thing about Joel's prophecy is not that he describes the locust invasion so accurately, however. The remarkable thing is how he deals with it.

To begin with, he does not treat the disaster lightly, as certain kinds of Christian people tend to do. That is, he does not imbibe the "best of all possible worlds" philosophy. In *Candide*, the philosopher Pangloss is unshaken by the evil of the Lisbon earthquake. He argues that since the earthquake occurred in Lisbon, it did not occur anywhere else. And since this is the best of all possible worlds, the fact that it did not occur anywhere else and occurred only in Lisbon is good. This thinking is entirely alien to Joel and indeed to any other of the Hebrew prophets. These men described evil as evil, and far from playing down the disaster, they actually magnified it. So far as the locust invasion is concerned, Joel calls it the worst thing that has ever

[4]John D. Whiting, "Jerusalem's Locust Plague," *National Geographic Magazine*, Vol. 28, No. 6 (December, 1915), pp. 511–50.
[5]Ibid., p. 511.

happened to Israel: "Has anything like this ever happened in your days or in the days of your forefathers?" (v. 2). The answer clearly is No. In Joel's mind the invasion is an unprecedented and unmitigated disaster.

Moreover, Joel is concerned that everyone see the disaster as he does, which means that he would not even have sympathy with an optimistic philosophy. Instead of slighting the problem, he accepts it in its full horror and calls on various groupings of people within the land to mourn with him. First, he calls on the *elders*. They are the leaders of the people. They are to take the lead in facing up to the enormity and meaning of this disaster. They are to measure it fully and then remember it so they can tell it to their children that they in turn might tell it to theirs (v. 3).

The second group Joel appeals to are *drunkards*. At first sight this seems strange, but it is soon clear that the appeal is made ironically. Others might shrug the disaster off, but the drunkards at least will not do this since the invasion means the destruction of the tender vines from which come the grapes to make wine: "Wake up, you drunkards, and weep! Wail, all you drinkers of wine; wail because of the wine, for it has been snatched from your lips" (v. 5). Joel's concern is broader than this, however. For, as he points out, it is not only the vines that are affected; the fig trees are also destroyed (v. 7); the grain is devoured (vv. 9, 10); the oil of the olive is lost (v. 10); the pomegranate, palm, and apple tree are ruined (v. 12). Even the ground is dried up (vv. 10, 12). Nor is it only the fields that are affected: "Surely the joy of people is withered away" (v. 12).

Pity the *farmers*, the third group! "Despair, you farmers, wail, you vine growers; grieve for the wheat and the barley, because the harvest of the field is destroyed" (v. 11).

The last of the groups addressed by Joel are *priests*. He calls on them to lead the nation in mourning:

Put on sackcloth, O priests, and mourn;
    wail, you who minister before the altar.
Come, spend the night in sackcloth,
    you who minister before my God;
for the grain offerings and drink offerings
    are withheld from the house of your God.
Declare a holy fast;
    call a sacred assembly.
Summon the elders
    and all who live in the land
to the house of the LORD your God,
    and cry out to the LORD.

What a dreadful day!
    For the day of the LORD is near;
it will come like destruction from
    the Almighty (vv. 13–15).

At the end of the chapter Joel, who was perhaps himself a priest, leads the way with a sample prayer of mourning:

To you, O LORD, I call,
    for fire has devoured the open pastures
and flames have burned up all the
    trees of the field.
Even the wild animals pant for you;
    the streams of water have dried up
and fire has devoured the open
    pastures (vv. 19, 20).

Christians need to learn from Joel's approach to suffering. We may not have a "best of all possible worlds" philosophy in our day, but we do often tend to treat disaster lightly—especially when it does not happen to us. We tend to use euphemisms. When we go to the dentist to have a tooth filled and he tells us to "open wide," we know what is coming. The dentist says, "This may cause a bit of discomfort." "Discomfort" is a euphemism. The dentist actually means, "This is going to hurt. I'm going to make you suffer." We all tend to use euphemisms. But this is not the approach of the biblical writers. They call evil, evil, and suffering, suffering. They even cry out in their pain. So did Jesus. He is called "a man of sorrows" and one "familiar" with suffering (Isa. 53:3). Jesus wept over Jerusalem (Luke 19:41). In His agony in the garden He sweat, as it were, great drops of blood (Luke 22:44). On the cross He cried out in a loud voice, "My God, my God, why have you forsaken me?" (Mark 15:34). In none of these cases is there any attempt to glorify pain, but neither is there any attempt to deny it.

THE PROPER QUESTION

The most important thing about Joel's handling of disaster is that he sees God as responsible for it. This does not mean that God is the author of sin, as if He were directly responsible for the rebellion of Satan or the original transgression of Adam and Eve. But it does mean that, given the sin-sick, evil world in which we live, God Himself does not hesitate to take responsibility for the occurrence of natural disasters and the resultant suffering.

This is the reason why Joel is dealing with the disaster caused by the invasion of the locusts. To be sure, the first chapter merely bemoans the disaster. But as we get farther into the book we discover that the locust invasion is a foretaste of the coming day of God's judgment and is sent in advance of that day as a warning of it. In chapter 2, where the locust invasion is treated as a symbol of the coming Day of the Lord, Joel makes very clear that God causes both: "The LORD thunders at the head of his army; his forces are beyond number, and mighty are those who obey his command" (v. 11). Will Judah repent? This is the goal of Joel's writing: "'Even now,' declares the LORD, 'return to me with all your heart, with fasting and weeping and mourning.' Rend your heart and not your garments. Return to the LORD your God, for he is gracious and compassionate, slow to anger and abounding in love, and he relents from sending calamity" (vv. 12, 13).

There will always be people who object to such teaching, arguing, as many did in Europe in the eighteenth century, that such judgments are selective and therefore unjust. "Why should Lisbon be destroyed and not other cities?" they ask. "Why should Judah be judged and not other nations?" Many would conclude that this objection presents insurmountable problems for Christianity. But it does not trouble the biblical writers, and this is because they have a far higher vision of the majesty and holiness of God and a far more accurate estimation of the sin and depravity of men and women than do those who raise this objection.

On one occasion a question along these lines was asked of Jesus. Some time before, Herod's soldiers had fallen upon a group of Galileans at the moment when they were offering their sacrifices at the temple in Jerusalem, and the problem suggested by this was raised with Jesus. How could this happen in a world run by a good God? These worshipers were killed at the very moment they were apparently being most devout. Again, there was the case of the collapse of the tower in Siloam. It killed eighteen people. How could that happen? Are we to suppose that these were more sinful or more deserving of God's judgment than the many others about them who were spared? We know how Jesus answered. He did not argue, as Job's comforters did, that those who were killed were more evil than those about them—whatever the outward appearances might be. He did not say, as we might, "Well, accidents will happen. I suppose that God merely nodded for a moment, and the tower fell. I'll speak to Him and see if He can't be a bit more careful in the future." We know Jesus did not respond that way.

Jesus actually said, "Do you think that these Galileans were worse sinners than all the other Galileans because they suffered this way? I tell you, no! But unless you repent, you too will all perish. Or those eighteen who died when the tower in Siloam fell on them—do you think they were more guilty than all the others living in Jerusalem? I tell you, no! But unless you repent, you too will all perish" (Luke 13:2–5).

What is Jesus saying? When we listen carefully we hear Him saying that those who object to tragedies like Lisbon or the locust plague err because they ask the wrong question. They are asking, "Why should disaster fall upon these? Why should God strike such innocent people?" But what they should be asking is: "Why haven't these disasters come on us? Why haven't they destroyed us?" Our problem is that we have forgotten how sinful we are. We have forgotten that it generally takes a disaster of unparalleled proportions to wake us from sin's lethargy.

This brings us to the bottom line, which is the point of Joel's prophecy. Both the delays in God's judgment (the periods of grace) and the previews of judgment in such catastrophic events as locust plagues and earthquakes are for our good, that we might repent.

In America we have not seen many disasters of this magnitude. But few would deny that times are not good and that even worse times may lie ahead. We have not had earthquakes of the size of the one at Lisbon, but our cities have been ravaged by blight and riot, by corruption and other forms of decay. We have not been destroyed by locusts, but we have seen our economy weakened by the declining value of the dollar, an intolerable balance of payments deficit and shortages of oil and other necessities. We have had droughts. Are we to make light of such things? Are we to dismiss them and then merely go our normal way until even greater judgments overtake us? Are we to say, "Such things just happen"? Are we to blame Russia or communism or Iran or Islam? No doubt God does use causes, and the opposition of these or other countries may be among them. But the wise will see these things as having come from God and lead us in personal and national repentance.

15

Torn Hearts, Torn Garments

(Joel 2:1–17)

"Even now," declares the LORD, *"return to me with all your heart, with fasting and weeping and mourning." Rend your heart and not your garments. Return to the* LORD *your God, for he is gracious and compassionate, slow to anger and abounding in love, and he relents from sending calamity. Who knows? He may turn and have pity and leave behind a blessing—grain offerings and drink offerings for the* LORD *your God.*

When the locust invasion of 1915 struck Palestine and Syria the desolation was as great as anyone could possibly have imagined. The first swarms appeared in March. The final stages did not depart until early summer. During that four-or five-month period the land was stripped of every green thing: vines, fig trees, grain. Still, bad as the destruction was, the locusts did move on and in time the land recovered. Since the invasion of Judah in Joel's day was undoubtedly similar, we might suppose that Joel would have had at least a few encouraging words. "Hang in there!" he might have said. "Things are bad, but they will get better. The important thing is to have hope. Look up! After all, every cloud has its silver lining." Joel did precisely the opposite. Instead of suggesting that things would get better, he argued that the worst was to come. The destruction of the locusts was total, but it was as nothing compared to the final judgment of God, which was almost around the corner.

This is the explanation of the apparent shift in imagery in chapter 2. The description in chapter 1 is literal. The various stages of the locusts are specified (v. 4). The destruction of vines, grain, and trees is described quite clearly (vv.

7–12). Judah is to mourn for the land. In chapter 2 this literal description is suddenly heightened by the use of stirring imagery, and the locusts begin to take on overtones of even greater invaders. They are described as "a large and mighty army" (v. 2).

They have the appearance of horses;
  they gallop along like cavalry.
With a noise like that of chariots
  they leap over the mountaintops,
like a crackling fire consuming stubble,
  like a mighty army drawn up for battle.
At the sight of them, nations are in anguish;
  every face turns pale.
They charge like warriors;
  they scale walls like soldiers.
They all march in line,
  not swerving from their course.
They do not jostle each other;
  each marches straight ahead.
They plunge through defenses
  without breaking ranks.
They rush upon the city;
  they run along the wall.
They climb into the houses;
  like thieves they enter through the windows.
Before them the earth shakes,
  the sky trembles,
the sun and moon are darkened,
  and the stars no longer shine.

Joel concludes by saying,

> The LORD thunders
>   at the head of his army;
> his forces are beyond number,
>   and mighty are those who obey his
>   command (vv. 4–11).

Some scholars think that Joel is talking about a military invasion, perhaps by the Syrian or Babylonian armies. Others have taken both chapters as referring only to locusts. Probably neither is right. Joel is saying that the original literal invasion of locusts is a warning of even worse things to come.

THE DAY OF THE LORD

There is an important clue to Joel's purpose in the way he begins this chapter: not with a view to the past, as he did in chapter 1 ("Has anything like this ever happened in your days or in the days of your forefathers?" v. 2), but in anticipation of the future ("Let all who live in the land tremble, for the day of the LORD *is coming.* It is close at hand," v. 1). The invasion described in chapter 1 has happened. The invasion described in chapter 2 is not present, though it is threatening. Joel wants to sound the alarm so that those who are threatened by the second, greater invasion might get ready for it.

Again, there is mention of "the day of the LORD." We find this at the beginning of chapter 2 ("the day of the LORD is coming," v. 1) and again at the end of the opening section ("The day of the LORD is great; it is dreadful. Who can endure it?" v. 11). This is the first mention of the Day of the Lord in the Minor Prophets, since it is absent from Hosea, at least by name. But it is a major idea both in these prophets and in other biblical literature.

"The day of the LORD" (literally, "the day of Jehovah") is a technical phrase used initially by the Old Testament prophets to designate a future period of catastrophic judgment. Sometimes the references are to destructive events then present, as to the locust plague in Joel. But always there is overriding reference to an even more intense, final judgment by God. It is a day in which Jehovah will break silence and intervene in history to judge both Israel and the gentile nations. This twofold use of the phrase is illustrated by the way we use the word "Armageddon," which is also a biblical term. Armageddon refers to the great, final conflict to be fought between the powers of good and evil on the plain of Megiddo in northern Palestine. It is the final holocaust. General Douglas MacArthur used the word in this way in his observations on World War II. "We have had our last chance. If we will not devise some greater and more equitable system, Armageddon will be at our door."[1] But the word is also used of any particularly destructive conflict, as we know.

The characteristics of the Day of the Lord are seen in the following quotations. Isaiah writes, "Wail, for the day of the LORD is near; it will come like destruction from the Almighty. . . . See, the day of the LORD is coming—a cruel day, with wrath and fierce anger—to make the land desolate and destroy the sinners within it. The stars of heaven and their constellations will not show their light. The rising sun will be darkened and the moon will not give its light" (Isa. 13:6, 9, 10). Ezekiel says, "The day of the LORD is near—a day of clouds, a time of doom for the nations" (Ezek. 30:3). Amos is most explicit:

> Woe to you who long
>   for the day of the LORD!
> Why do you long for the day of the LORD?
> That day will be darkness, not light.
> It will be as though a man fled from a
>   lion
>   only to meet a bear,
> as though he entered his house
>   and rested his hand on the wall
>   only to have a snake bite him.

---

[1]Douglas MacArthur, *Reminiscences* (New York: McGraw-Hill, 1964, p.276.

WOMAN - WHAT SINS

> Will not the day of the LORD be darkness,
> not light—
> pitch-dark, without a ray of bright-
> ness? (Amos 5:18–20).

Zephaniah says,

> The great day of the LORD is near—
> near and coming quickly.
> Listen! The cry on the day of the LORD
> will be bitter,
> the shouting of the warrior there.
> That day will be a day of wrath,
> a day of distress and anguish,
> a day of trouble and ruin,
> a day of darkness and gloom,
> a day of clouds and blackness,
> a day of trumpet and battle cry
> against the fortified cities
> and against the corner towers.
> I will bring distress on the people
> and they will walk like blind men,
> because they have sinned against the
> LORD (Zeph. 1:14–17).

It is obvious from the references to the darkening of the sun, moon, and stars in several of these passages that this is the event referred to by Jesus in Matthew 24:29–31. In that passage Jesus quotes the verses in Isaiah dealing with the Day of the Lord and applies them to the time when He will Himself judge the world. Peter also refers to this day, saying, "But the day of the Lord will come like a thief. The heavens will disappear with a roar; the elements will be destroyed by fire, and the earth and everything in it will be laid bare" (2 Peter 3:10). In the liturgy of the church this theme is expressed by the *Dies Irae*, which means the "day of [the] wrath" of God.

From an examination of these and other texts (cf. Jer. 46:10; Lam. 2:22; Zech. 14:1–7; Mal. 4:5) several things are clear. First, the Day of the Lord is a day of God's judgment. Second, the day is still future. Third, it is accompanied by a time of great trouble on earth. Fourth, it is to be followed by the reign of God through His Messiah, the Lord Jesus Christ. That day is coming, as Joel indicates. The disasters of this life—locust invasions, plagues,

famines, wars, and natural catastro-phies—are little judgments compared to it, but they are warnings of the wrath to be revealed.

REPENTANCE

This is the goal of Joel's writing, of course—to lead people to repentance. So we are not surprised that the next section of chapter 2 contains a direct and moving appeal for repentance. It contains: 1) an analysis of true repentance (vv. 12, 13) and 2) incentives for it (vv. 13, 14).

As Joel speaks of repentance his em-phasis is on the heart. That is, he wants a true repentance and not merely a formal one. True, Joel does speak of outward expressions: "fasting and weeping and mourning" (v. 12). Outward expressions of an inward state are both right and valuable. But what Joel is against is out-ward expression that does not corre-spond with reality, for God looks on the heart (1 Sam. 16:7). Therefore the people of God are to rend their hearts, not their garments (v. 13). It is easier to do the opposite, to rend our garments rather than our hearts. But God wants us to be "heartbroken" over sin. Only that will actually turn us from sin and enable us to find God's favor again.

Joel's discussion of repentance re-minds us of the similar discussion of re-pentance in Hosea, which occurs just pages earlier in the Bible. In chapter 6 of Hosea there is a description of repen-tance that is not genuine. It has the out-ward form. The people say, "Come, let us return to the LORD. He has torn us to pieces but he will heal us; he has injured us but he will bind up our wounds. After two days he will revive us; on the third day he will restore us, that we may live in his presence" (vv. 1, 2). There is no true acknowledgment of sin here, and as a result there is a rather glib treatment of God. Of course, He will pardon! He always does! The passage is disturbing because the confession of sin rings false. On the other hand, at the end of Hosea, in chapter 14, there is a description of true repentance: "Return, O Israel, to the LORD your God. Your sins have been your downfall! Take words with you and return to the LORD. Say to him: 'Forgive all our sins and receive us graciously, that we may offer the fruit of our lips'" (vv. 1, 2). These words acknowledge sin, confess it, and appeal to God, not on the basis of good works (not even repentance), but on the basis of God's great grace.

This is the kind of repentance Joel wanted to see among his people and which we should seek today. What should we expect if repentance of this kind were actually taking place in our churches and in other centers of our national life?

One thing we should expect to see is open *confession of the specific sins* we have committed, for until we confess sins specifically we are not really repenting. Charles Haddon Spurgeon tells of a woman who went to see her minister, affecting to be a great sinner in whom he should take an interest. He suspected that her confession was not genuine. So he said to her, "Well, if you are a sinner, of course you have broken God's laws; let us read the Ten Commandments and see which you have broken." He began to read, "'Thou shalt have no other gods before me.' Did you ever break that?" he asked.

"Oh, no," she said, "not that I know of."

"'Thou shalt not make unto thee any graven image.' Did you ever break that?"

"Never, sir" she said.

"Then 'Thou shalt not take the name of the Lord thy God in vain'" The woman was very particular on that point. She could not think that she had ever offended by taking God's name in vain.

"'Remember the sabbath day, to keep it holy.'" She never worked on Sunday. "'Honor thy father and thy mother.'"

She did that. So it was with the sixth, seventh, eighth, ninth, and tenth commandments. In the end it turned out that what her minister suspected was true. She did not really consider herself to be a sinner, and she was only "repenting" as a pious and praiseworthy thing to do.[2]

The second element in true repentance is *contrition,* that is, genuine sorrow for sin. The Bible says, "The sacrifices of God are a broken spirit; a broken and contrite heart, O God, you will not despise" (Ps. 51:17). Contrition is deeper than regret. We may all regret something we have done but still not sorrow over it. Judas regretted his sin of betraying Jesus to such a degree that he returned the blood money given to him by the priests and then committed suicide. But he did not repent of his sin and so suffered for it.

Mariano Di Gangi writes in his study of Joel, "Do we know what it means to be contrite? God desires that sinners sense their guilt and weep within for what their sins have done to defile self, destroy neighbor, and dishonor Christ. When we experience poverty of spirit, we are on the right road to everlasting enrichment from the treasury of divine grace. When we mourn over our sins, we pass through spiritual winter. Then comes the springtime of God's comfort."[3]

The final element in repentance is *conversion,* the point Joel most emphasizes. Joel uses the word "return" ("Return to me with all your heart," v. 12; "Return to the LORD your God," v. 13), but the meaning is the same as "convert." Convert is from the Latin words *con,* meaning "around," and *verto, vertere,* meaning "to turn." It means "to turn around." Return means "to turn again." In both cases there was a right relationship to God (in Adam before the Fall), but the person has turned away from God and now needs to turn back.

---

[2]*Spurgeon's Illustrative Anecdotes,* edited and condensed by David Otis Fuller (Grand Rapids: Zondervan, 1945), pp. 87, 88.

[3]Mariano Di Gangi, *The Book of Joel* (Grand Rapids: Baker, 1970), p. 36.

This is the essential meaning of repentance too. Repentance comes from a Latin word (*paeniteo, paenitere*) that refers to a change of mind, a change so basic that the direction of one's life is altered. In a Sunday school class one day a little boy said that repentance was being sorry for your sins. But a little girl added that it was being sorry enough to quit. She was right. Repentance is essentially an about-face. It is a military command. One commentator writes, "A group of men are facing south and the officer gives the command. There is an immediate pivoting and the group comes to its new position facing north." He concludes, "You, today, are facing yourself, and your hope and confidence lie in your character and your good works. Behind you is the Lord Jesus Christ, despised and rejected by you. If you hear God's command to repent—if you are drawn by the sweet wooing of the riches of His grace—there will be an 'about face' that will change the direction of your walk forever. Now you will know values in their true light. You shall put all your hope and confidence in the Lord Jesus Christ, and in him alone."[4]

SPIRITUAL RECOVERY

Joel does not only show the nature of true repentance. He also gives incentives, arguing that God is "gracious and compassionate, slow to anger and abounding in love, and he relents from sending calamity" (v. 13). Because of this, "Who knows? He may turn and have pity and leave behind a blessing" (v. 14).

That God often changes His intention to judge sin and instead "repents" and shows mercy is a problem for some persons. They ask, "How can the unchanging God change His mind? How can God repent?" That may be a problem for our thinking, but it is important to note that it is no problem for God. God does not explain His repentance. He simply states

that He does repent, and He holds this possibility out to get us to turn from sin. God *is* gracious. God *does* relent from sending calamity. He *has* delayed His judgments and turned back His wrath.

At the end of our last study the judgments of the locust plague in Judah and the earthquake in Lisbon were applied to the current judgments on the western world, particularly on the United States of America. It would be wrong to compare shortages of oil and other necessities and our declining position in the world to these catastrophies, as if mere shortages are equal to a national disaster. But these are warnings, and the trend will inevitably be downhill unless we repent. Sin always leads the sinner downhill. Sometimes it is rapid, like a mountain stream twisting and splashing downward over rocks and crags. Sometimes it is slow, like the nearly imperceptible course of a glacier. But it is still downhill. America is going downhill and will continue to go downhill to ever greater judgments unless there is a national confession of sin and a turning around.

Can the glacier be halted? Can the stream be damned up? Certainly. It has happened before and can happen again, if the God of the Bible is again held up before us to convict us of sin and turn us back.

We can think of such former periods. Revival occurred in the eighteenth century under the influence of Jonathan Edwards (1703–1758), George Whitefield (1714–1770) and other later Puritans. It was called the Great Awakening. It happened in the revivalism of the nineteenth century under the preaching of such men as D. L. Moody (1837–1899) and others. According to Edward L. R. Elson, a former minister of the National Presbyterian Church in Washington, D.C., America experienced at least a partial spiritual recovery in the late 1940s and early 1950s. In his book, *America's Spiritual Recovery*,

[4]Donald Grey Barnhouse, *God's Wrath*, Vol. 2 in the exposition of the Epistle to the Romans (Grand Rapids: Eerdmans, 1953), pp. 29, 30.

published in 1954, Elson analyzed the breakdown of American society following the second world war but concluded that he had witnessed a remarkable renaissance of faith in recent years. He wrote, "There have been intermittent periods of religious renaissance in our past, but we are living today in what probably is destined to be the greatest religious awakening in the history of our nation. There is convincing evidence that in the present epoch we are experiencing a moral resurgence and spiritual awakening of national proportions. The evidence is both overt and covert, but its total impact is not to be denied."[5]

From the perspective of twenty-five more years of history we may say that Elson's estimate was perhaps a bit too optimistic, or we may argue that America has slipped backward again. But the point remains that a true spiritual repentance and recovery is possible and should be urged on all who will attend the preaching of the gospel.

Early in 1980, I attended an "Authority of Scripture" seminar sponsored by the International Council on Biblical Inerrancy and heard Bruce H. Wilkinson, founder of Walk Through the Bible Ministries, speak on the stages of a genuine national revival . He had been conversing with specialists in revivals and had noted five stages through which revivals come: 1) mass evangelism, 2) widespread dissemination of Christian literature, 3) effective Christian education, 4) personal repentance and renewal, and 5) transformation of society. In his view, we have already witnessed the first three of these in America. We see the fourth, personal repentance and renewal, in pockets. The fifth, transformation of society, is not yet happening and will not happen until renewal at the personal level is widespread. What is his point? He argues that revival is possible—judgment can be averted—but only at the price of broken hearts and changed lives.

WHERE ARE THE LEADERS?

There is one last point: the need for leaders. Joel points to this in the closing verses of this chapter. Having spoken of the judgment to come and of the nature and incentive for repentance, he turns to the priests, the leaders of Israel, and calls on them to set the pattern. These verses are marked by imperatives: *"Blow* the trumpet . . . , *declare* a holy fast, *call* a sacred assembly, *gather* the people, *consecrate* the assembly; *bring together* the elders, *gather* the children . . ." (vv. 15, 16). Who is to blow, declare, call, gather, consecrate and bring together? The priests! They are to "weep between the temple porch and the altar." They are to say,

Spare your people, O LORD.
Do not make your inheritance an object
   of scorn,
   a byword among the nations.
Why should they say among the peoples,
   "Where is their God?" (v. 17).

This is a special word for those in spiritual authority. But it is also a word for all God's people, for in this day all are priests in God's service (Rev. 1:6). We are all to lead the way in repentance. If we do not do this, who will do it? We are the watchers on the wall. If we do not see the approaching danger and sound the alarm, who will sound it? No one! People will perish, and the blame will be ours (Ezek. 33:2–6).

When Albert Einstein, the great physicist and mathematician, saw the rising tide of Nazism in Germany between the world wars, he said that he expected the chief opposition to come from the press and men of letters. That did not happen. The press was strangely silent, and sometimes, which was even worse, it was on the side of Hitler's socialism. The men of letters were also silent. Next, Einstein placed hope in the universities, in the liberal minds of discriminating scholars; but these were submissive too.

[5]Edward L. R. Elson, *America's Spiritual Recovery* (Westwood, N.J.: Fleming H. Revell, 1954), p. 33.

Where then could he look for opposition? In the end it was only in the churches that Einstein found those of sufficient courage to make vigorous resistance to the Nazi movement, and he came to respect the church as he had not respected it before[6]

That is the way repentance will come today—if it is to come. May God grant it for the good of all.

[6]Ibid., p. 122.

16

No Other God

(Joel 2:18–27)

"I will repay you for the years the locusts have eaten—the great locust and the young locust, the other locusts and the locust swarm—my great army that I sent among you. You will have plenty to eat, until you are full, and you will praise the name of the LORD your God, who has worked wonders for you; never again will my people be shamed. Then you will know that I am in Israel, that I am the LORD your God, and that there is no other; never again will my people be shamed."

In my early teen years I had an experience that comes to mind at this point. I had grown up in a church where it was customary to have altar calls, especially at the evening service. Sometimes they were for those who wished to accept Christ as Savior. At other times they were for the dedication of people's lives to Christ's service. On this occasion I had been in church, but my mind had been drifting. I knew the service was directed toward young people, but I had not followed what was being said. The end came. Heads were bowed. The pastor was praying. Suddenly I realized that the other young people, my peers, were going forward to the front of the church. I was confronted with this dilemma: if I did not join them, I would be thought to be resisting the leading of the Holy Spirit, which I really did not want to do; but on the other hand, if I went forward, I would not really know what I was doing. In the end I went up and stood with the others, most uneasily—willing, but not sure what I was willing to do.

Joel has brought us to a similar point. He began with a description of a locust plague that did heavy damage to Judah in his day. He amplified on the horrors of this plague and spoke of it as a pre-

cursor of the even more terrible Day of the Lord, which is pending. This led him to call for repentance, which he did by quoting the Lord directly for the first time:

"Even now," declares the LORD,
"return to me with all your heart,
with fasting and weeping and mourning" (2:12).

The following verses analyze repentance, encourage it and call on the leaders of the people, the priests, to lead the people in a rejection of sin and a return to God.

But here is the problem. We may assume that some at least have heard Joel's call and are moved by his warning. They are willing to repent, to turn back to God. But what is the sin or sins for which they are to repent? We have already seen that repentance involves confession of specific sins. What are they? Unless this question is answered, the situation of Judah would be similar to the personal dilemma with which I began. The people would be standing humbly before God but with no clear knowledge of why they were there or what they were to do.

In the middle section of chapter 2 (vv. 18–27), the center and heart of the book, we see the sin and its remedy. It is Israel's old sin of spiritual adultery or idolatry. This is made clear toward the end of the section where God is promising restoration after repentance. He concludes, "Then you will know that *I* am in Israel, that *I* am the LORD your God, and that *there is no other*" (v. 27).

THE FIRST COMMANDMENT

One does not have to know the Old Testament very well to realize that this is a reference to the first of the Ten Commandments, which says, "I am the LORD your God, who brought you out of Egypt, out of the land of slavery. You shall have no other gods before me" (Exod. 20:2, 3). This commandment stood at the head of Israel's laws and in a sense summed them all up. If one worships the true God and Him only, the moral standards of this God will inevitably guide the worshiper in other areas.

This law was well known in Israel, as we have said. It guided the people's understanding of religion and morality. But it is not just a guide for Israel. It is a guide for us as well, and since we are studying Joel for what it says to us today as well as for what it said to Judah in Old Testament times, we must see this law in a contemporary light. Clearly, to worship any God but Jehovah is to break this commandment. But it is not necessary to worship a clearly defined god to break it—Baal, Zeus, Minerva, a Roman emperor, or one of the idols of the many pagan tribes of our own day. We break it whenever we give some person or something that first place in our affections that belongs to God alone. Quite often this substitute god is ourselves or our opinion of ourselves. Sometimes it is such things as success, material possessions, fame, or personal dominance over others.

What would the keeping of this commandment be? John Stott writes, "For us to keep this first commandment would be, as Jesus said, to love the Lord our God will all our heart and with all our soul and with all our mind (Matt. 22:37); to see all things from his point of view and do nothing without reference to him; to make his will our guide and his glory our goal; to put him first in thought, word and deed; in business and leisure; in friendships and career; in the use of our money, time and talents; at work and at home." He adds correctly, "No man has ever kept this commandment except Jesus of Nazareth."[1]

But why should we do this? Why should we have no other gods but Jehovah? The answer is in the preface to this commandment, a preface that is at the same time a preface to the whole of the Decalogue. It is in two parts: one, because of who God is, and two, because of what He has done.

The first of these, dealing with who the true God is, is expressed in the words "I am the LORD your God." In Hebrew they are the words *Yahweh Eloheka*. The reason we should obey these commands is that the God who is speaking in the commandments is Jehovah, the true God. He is the God who is without beginning and end—"I am who I am" (Exod. 3:14). He is self-existent. No one created Him; He is responsible to no one. He is self-sufficient. He needs no one; He does not depend on anyone for anything. Quite obviously, any god less than this is not God. It is because of who He is that He can demand such worship.

Second, we should obey these commandments because of what God has done. He indicates this in the words "who brought you out of the land of Egypt, out of the house of bondage." This applies primarily to Israel, who alone of all nations was literally delivered out of slavery in Egypt. Even if God were only a limited tribal god, Israel would owe Him reverence for this deliverance. But this reference does not exhaust the commandment. For one thing, it must

---

[1]John R. W. Stott, *Basic Christianity* (Grand Rapids: Eerdmans, 1959), p. 65.

apply to *any* who have experienced deliverance, whether from death or slavery or poverty or disease. There is no one who has not been blessed by God in at least one of these areas, even though he or she may be unaware of it and not acknowledge God as the source. In addition, the deliverance must apply to *spiritual* as well as material matters. Even in the case of Israel, the deliverance was not physical merely but rather deliverance from Egyptian idolatry. It was a deliverance from false gods. In the same way, the calling of Abraham is noteworthy as a call to serve Jehovah rather than the strange and unworthy gods of Mesopotamia (Josh. 24:2, 3, 14).

The reasoning behind the first commandment applies to every human being. All have been blessed by God. All have benefited from the progressive advance of truth over superstition through the revelation conveyed to the world through Judaism and Christianity. Do we worship God wholly and exclusively as a result? No, we do not! Consequently, the first commandment virtually shouts to us that we are ungrateful, disobedient, rebellious, and ruled by sin.

Repentance and Blessing

As we said in our first study of Joel, we do not know precisely when Joel was written. So we cannot say at what point of Israel's apostasy these warnings and the accompanying promises were given—whether before the Exile or after it. But the message is nevertheless clear. If the people of God will return to Him with all their heart, then He will hear from heaven, turn back His wrath, restore them, and heal their land.

Earlier in this chapter Joel had expressed this desirable outcome tentatively. He was writing in his own name (though at the direction of the Holy Spirit) and said, "Who knows? He [that is, the Lord] may turn and have pity and leave behind a blessing" (v. 14). Now he quotes God directly, saying that blessing will

indeed be in the fullest measure. It will be in three areas: first, *material prosperity* ("The LORD will reply to them: 'I am sending you grain, new wine and oil, enough to satisfy you fully,'" v. 19); second, *national security* ("I will drive the northern army far from you, pushing it into a parched and barren land, with its front columns going into the eastern sea," v. 20); third, a *restoration of the lost years* ("I will repay you for the years the locusts have eaten—the great locust and the young locust, the other locusts and the locust swarm," v. 25).

When we speak of *material prosperity* (v. 19), we have to be careful of two things. First, we must not attribute everything we have, particularly our excess or what we have gained at the expense of other people, to God in the sense of justifying our avarice or injustices by God's name. Second, we must not attribute all we have to ourselves and our ability, rather than acknowledging God and thanking Him for it. The first is probably the characteristic sin of God's people. The second is the sin of the godless.

We have a strange idea in American Christianity, though it has been present in other cultures and other ages too, that the closer we are to God the more He will bless us physically and the richer we will become. The obvious conclusion of this train of reasoning is that the wealthy Christian is closer to God than the poor one and that the poor one is farther away. But nothing is farther from the truth. It is true, as Joel clearly says, that if we seek God's face He will provide the "grain, new wine and oil, enough to satisfy [us] fully." But the promise is only that we will be satisfied, not stuffed. We will have enough but not necessarily an excess, particularly when that is achieved at the expense of other people.

This does not mean that one cannot be wealthy. Job, Abraham, David—all were wealthy men who were nevertheless upright and fully obedient to God.

But they are the exceptions, and it would be true to say that most of God's people, in biblical times as well as in other periods of history, were not wealthy and yet were fully provided for both physically and spiritually. The believer's duty is to be careful that what he has really comes from God, that his priorities regarding material and spiritual things are right and that whatever he has does not control him.

The other problem concerning material prosperity is the sin of the godless: attributing what is possessed to human strength and ability and not to God. Nebuchadnezzar is an example. He stood on the roof of his palace and, looking out over the magnificent city of Babylon, said, "Is not this the great Babylon I have built as the royal residence, by my mighty power and for the glory of my majesty?" (Dan. 4:30). Nebuchadnezzar took credit for his accomplishments while refusing to recognize that God was the ultimate source of these and that he held his possessions in trust for God. His was an intolerable sin, and God responded to it by taking his "things" away. In that hour Nebuchadnezzar became insane and was driven from the palace to live with the wild animals, which he did for seven years. At the end of that time his sanity was restored, both physically and spiritually, and he praised God: "Now, I, Nebuchadnezzar, praise and exalt and glorify the King of heaven, because everything he does is right and all his ways are just. And those who walk in pride he is able to humble" (Dan. 4:37).

The second blessing that God says will follow on repentance is: *national security* (v. 20). Unfortunately, the language of the verse in which this is mentioned is obscure, for when Joel mentions "the northern army" he can be speaking of: 1) the locusts, 2) actual physical armies from the hostile nations round about, or 3) the metaphorical army of God to be unleashed at the final judgment. The precise meaning is probably unimportant and, indeed, all three may be in view. Nevertheless, what Joel is saying is that God will keep all enemies away and that He will throw up a hedge of protection around His people.

That is the only security any people or any nation has, for there is no wall, no army, no weapons system that can be counted on ultimately for salvation. Decades ago the United States spent billions of dollars constructing an extensive military radar network called the DEW line—Distant Early Warning—that stretches across the North American continent. It was designed to limit to a minimum the breakthroughs of Russian long-range bombers coming to attack the United States. It was good in its time, but it was quickly outmoded by the proliferation of long-range ballistic missiles. Today it is useless against sophisticated low-flying missiles, multiple warheads, nuclear armed submarines, and other probably little-known devices of destruction. The psalmist said, "No king is saved by the size of his army; no warrior escapes by his great strength" (Ps. 33:16).

The final blessing of the three that God says will follow genuine heart repentance is *restoration of the lost years* (v. 25). This is a special blessing. Many of us have run from God and have wasted many years. It is only by returning to God that the loss of those years can be made up.

When we disregard God and run away from Him we enter upon a downhill course, like Hosea's wife Gomer. We do not think this will happen when we start out. But it does happen, because God has established this as one of the laws governing spiritual disobedience, and He is faithful to His laws. When we disregard God, life inevitably goes downhill. We miss our opportunities. We fail in small and then in greater things. We become hardened by sin. We increasingly live for ourselves and disregard others. We lose friends. Eventually we are all alone and are totally miserable in our loneliness. God can change all that. *We* cannot undo what is done. Sin is sin, and the effects of sin often continue for long periods. But God can restore what the locusts have eaten. Opportunities may have been lost, but God can give new and even better opportunities. Friends may have been alienated and driven away, but God can give new friends and even restore many of the former ones. God can break the power of sin and restore a personal holiness and joy that would not have been dreamed possible in the rebellion.

Are you one whose life has been destroyed by the locusts of sin? Has sin stripped your life of every green thing, so that it seems a spiritual desert? If so, you need to return to the One who alone can make life grow fruitful again. Only God can restore the years that have been eaten away.

THE BIBLE'S GOD

Do you ask where you can find Him? There is only one place. That is in the Bible, where He has made Himself known. If you do not know the Bible— if you do not study it—then you are not worshiping the one true God who is found there, but rather a God of your own making or imagination, whatever you may call Him. If you are doing that, you are committing that first and original sin against which the second chapter of Joel was written. You must ask: Do I really know the Bible? Am I worshiping God on the basis of the truths I find there? Those truths are centered in Jesus Christ, who is the theme of the Bible. In Him the invisible God is made visible. In Him the immaterial God is revealed in space and time. It is said of some that "although they knew God, they neither glorified him as God nor gave thanks to him" (Rom. 1:21). Let us determine that this shall not be said of us. We see God in Jesus. Let us know Him as God, love him as God, serve Him as God, worship Him as God. We cannot do these things fully as we ought, but by God's grace we can keep from doing them to some other.

17

Peter's Text at Pentecost

(Joel 2:28–32)

"And afterward, I will pour out my Spirit on all people. Your sons and daughters will prophesy, your old men will dream dreams, your young men will see visions. Even on my servants, both men and women, I will pour out my Spirit in those days. I will show wonders in the heavens and on the earth, blood and fire and billows of smoke. The sun will be turned to darkness and the moon to blood before the coming of the great and dreadful day of the LORD. And everyone who calls on the name of the LORD will be saved; for on Mount Zion and in Jerusalem there will be deliverance, as the LORD has said, among the survivors whom the LORD calls.

It is hard to handle prophecy. This is because the prophecies often seem obscure to us; and even if their meaning is clear, we cannot always be sure to what period of history the words apply. To confuse matters further, the Bible itself sometimes takes the prophecies in more than one way. They can be applied to a current event in Israel, for example; but they can also be referred to a future Day of the Lord.

While recognizing this, we know nevertheless that many Old Testament prophecies are interpreted to us by the New Testament, so that, whatever our problems may be with other passages, these at least are certain. Of these clear passages, none is more certain than Joel 2:28–32, a passage interpreted by the apostle Peter as applying to the events at Pentecost. After the ascension of Jesus the apostles waited in Jerusalem for the coming of the Holy Spirit, as Jesus had told them to do (Acts 1:4, 5). On Pentecost, the second of the three chief Jewish festivals, these were gathered together in one place, when suddenly, as Acts says, "a sound like the blowing of a violent wind came from heaven and filled the whole house where they were sitting" and "they saw what seemed to be tongues of fire that separated and came to rest on each of them." Then "all of them were filled with the Holy Spirit and began to speak in other tongues as the Spirit enabled them" (Acts 2:2–4).

When the people of Jerusalem heard the sound they came together, and Peter preached the first sermon of the Christian era. Briefly, he denied that the disciples were intoxicated, which is what some were saying, and instead interpreted the event as the fulfillment of Joel's prophecy. "This is what was spoken by the prophet Joel: 'In the last days, God says, I will pour out my Spirit on all people. Your sons and daughters will prophesy, your young men will see visions, your old men will dream dreams. . . . And everyone who calls on the name of the Lord will be saved'" (Acts 2:17, 21).

Quite clearly, we cannot interpret Joel 2:28–32 apart from Peter's interpretation. We need to see: 1) the need for this particular outpouring of God's Spirit, 2) Joel's promise of it, 3) the fulfillment of the promise in Acts, and 4) the result of that fulfillment.

A WISTFUL LONGING

The roots of the promise are in Numbers 11:29, in the midst of a story about Moses. It was a bad time for Moses. The people had been complaining of their wilderness diet of manna, and Moses, perhaps in sheer physical weariness, was overcome with the burden of leading the people and dealing with their complaints. God sympathized with him and told him to select seventy of the elders of Israel and bring them with him to the Tent of Meeting. God promised, "I will come down and speak with you there, and I will take of the Spirit that is on you and put the Spirit on them. They will help you carry the burden of the people so that you will not have to carry it alone" (Num. 11:17). That is what happened. These men received the Holy Spirit and began to prophesy. It was a sign to the people that they had received this gift and were therefore chosen by God to minister alongside Moses.

Two of these elders were not with the others at the Tent of Meeting, but the Spirit of God came on them as well, and they also prophesied. This bothered some who were closest to Moses. One young man ran up to him saying, "Eldad and Medad are prophesying in the camp."

Joshua, who had been Moses' close aid since youth, said, "Moses, my lord, stop them!"

Moses' reply was the roots of the promise found in Joel. He answered wistfully, "Are you jealous for my sake? I wish that all the LORD'S people were prophets and that the LORD would put his Spirit on them!" (vv. 27–29).

The incident shows that in this early period God's Spirit was not given to all His people in the way He is now. God was with His people, but His Spirit did not come on them or dwell in them. Instead, He came on certain individuals for specific purposes. Sometimes He left them, as happened in the case of Saul (1 Sam. 16:14). The first reference in the Bible to any individual's possession of the Holy Spirit is in Genesis 41:38, where Pharaoh asks concerning Joseph, "Can we find anyone like this man, one in whom is the spirit of God?" This was because of Joseph's ability to interpret Pharaoh's dream. The craftsmen who helped build the tabernacle are said to have been "filled . . . with the Spirit of God" (Exod. 31:3). Joshua is described as a man "in whom is the spirit" (Num. 27:18). The judges Othniel (Judg. 3:10), Gideon (Judg. 6:34), Jephthah (Judg. 11:29) and Samson (Judg. 13:5; 14:6, 19; 15:14) were also in this category. So probably was Deborah, who served as a judge and functioned in the name of the Lord, though it is not specifically said of her that she was filled with the Spirit (cf. Judg. 4:4–7). The Holy Spirit indwelt both Saul and David (1 Sam. 10:9, 10; 16:13) and presumably all the prophets, though (like Deborah) this is not said specifically in every case.

In the Old Testament period the Holy Spirit was not the common gift of God to all His people. So when Moses intoned, "I wish that all the LORD'S people were prophets and that the LORD would put his spirit on them," he was expressing a very real need and longing. It was not until God had spoken to the people through Joel that there was even a promise of such universal blessing.

A GLORIOUS PROMISE

God's promise through Joel is striking because it is the book's first mention of spiritual rather than mere physical blessing. It is understandable that material things are emphasized—material prosperity (v. 19), national security (v. 20), the restoration of lost years (v. 25)—because the locust plague was a material disaster and it formed the focal point and occasion of the prophecy. Still, we are glad to find spiritual blessings too, for we know, as our Lord taught, that it is folly for a man "to gain the whole world, yet forfeit his soul" (Mark 8:36).

Joel's emphasis is on the universal nature of this gift, for he shows that it is for "all people" as opposed to being for some only as it had been previously. Lest we miss this, the point is spelled out in detail. It will be for the young ("your sons and daughters") and the old ("your old men"), the strength of the nation ("your young men") and servants ("even on my servants, both men and women").

This is truly a momentous thing, for it is a way of saying that in the church age, which the coming of the Holy Spirit would inaugurate, *all* would be ministers of God, not merely a special corps of workers. Of course, there will be different tasks to do and different gifts given to enable God's people to do them. Some will prophesy. Some will dream dreams. Still others will see visions. Men and women, young and old, slaves and free men will not necessarily do the same work. But all will have work to do and will be indwelt by God's Spirit so that the work can be done effectively.

In the Reformation era this was termed the "priesthood of all believers," and it was seen to establish a proper relationship between clergy and laity. John R. W. Stott points out in *One People* that there had developed within the church (as today) a division between "clergy" and "laity" in which the clergy were supposed to lead and do the work of Christian ministry while the people (which is what the word "laity" means) were to follow docily—and, of course, give money to support the clergy's work. This is not what the church is to be, and where this view prevails the church and its ministry suffer. They suffer by the loss of the exercise of those gifts given to the laity. The Spirit is to help each serve others. The laity serve the church and the world. The clergy serve the laity, particularly in helping them to develop and use their gifts (Eph. 4:11–13).

Stott points out that three false answers have been given to the question of the relationship of clergy to other Christians. The first is *clericalism*. It is the view already referred to, namely, that the work of the church is to be done by those paid to do it and that the role of the layman is at best to support these works financially. How did this false picture arise? Historically it resulted from the development of the priesthood in the early Roman church. In those days the professional ministry was patterned after the Old Testament priestly system with the mass taking the place of the blood sacrifices. Only "priests" were authorized to perform the mass, and this meant that a false and debilitating distinction between clergy and laity was drawn. Those who favor this view say that it goes back to the days of the apostles. But this is demonstrably false. As reflected in the New Testament, the early church often used the word "minister" or "ministry" to refer to what *all* Christians are and must do and never used the word *hiereus* ("priest") of the clergy. Elton Trueblood points out that "the conventional modern distinction between the clergy and laity simply does not occur in the New Testament at all."[1]

There are historical reasons for the development of clericalism then. But these in themselves are not the whole or even the most significant things. The real causes of clericalism lie in human failures. Sometimes the clergy want to run the show, to dominate those who attend church. This often leads to outright abuse or tyranny. If we need an example, we can find one in the New Testament in the person of Diotrephes "who loves to be first," according to the apostle John who wrote about him (3 John 9). A warning against this pattern is found in 1 Peter in a passage conveying instruction to church elders: "Be shepherds of God's flock that is under your care, serving as overseers—not because you must, but

---

[1]Elton Trueblood, *The Incendiary Fellowship* (New York, Evanston, and London: Harper & Row, 1967), p. 39.

because you are willing, as God wants you to be; not greedy for money, but eager to serve; not lording it over those entrusted to you, but being examples to the flock" (5:2, 3). The chief biblical example is the Lord Jesus Christ who, though Lord of creation, nevertheless put on a servant's garment and performed a servant's job in washing His disciples' feet.

Again, there is the willingness of laymen to "sit back" and "let the pastor do it." Stott quotes a remark of Sir John Lawrence to this effect: "What does the layman really want? He wants a building which looks like a church; a clergy dressed in the way he approves; services of the kind he's been used to, *and to be left alone.*"[2] This is not what Joel 2:28–32 envisions.

The second false answer to the relationship of clergy to laypersons is *anticlericalism*. Since the clergy sometimes despise the laity or think them dispensable, it is no surprise that the laity sometimes return the compliment by rejecting the clergy.

This is not always bad. We can imagine situations in which the church has become so dominated by a corrupt or priestly clergy that a general housecleaning is called for. Again we can think of areas of the church's work that are best done by laymen, for which the clergy is not at all necessary. But these are not grounds for anticlericalism as the normal stance of Christian people. On the contrary, where the church wishes to be biblical it must recognize not only that gifts of teaching and leadership are given to some for the church's well-being but also that there is ample biblical teaching about the need for such leadership. Judging from Acts and the various Pauline epistles, it was the apostle Paul's regular practice to appoint elders in every church and entrust to them the training of the flock for

ministry (Acts 14:23; 20:17). In the pastoral epistles the appointment of such leaders is specifically commanded (Titus 1:5), and the qualifications are given (1 Tim. 3:1–13; Titus 1:5–9).

Some who have captured the idea of ministry as belonging to the whole church have begun to wonder on *this* basis whether there is room for clergy. But their insight, good as it is, does not lead to this conclusion. As Trueblood says, "The earliest Christians were far too realistic to fall into this trap, because they saw that, if the ideal of universal ministry is to be approximated at all, there must be some people who are working at the job of bringing this highly desirable result to pass."[3]

The final false model of the relationship between the professional clergy and laymen is what Stott calls *dualism*. Dualism says that clergy and laymen are each to be given their sphere, and neither is to trespass on the territory of the other. This describes the traditional Roman Catholic system in which a "lay status" and a "clerical status" are very carefully delineated. It is also true of certain forms of Protestantism. In such a system the sense of all being part of one body and serving together in one work evaporates and rivalry enters in instead.

What is the true pattern? Ephesians 4:11–13 describes it well, for in pointing out that apostles, prophets, evangelists, pastors, and teachers are to equip the saints for the work of ministry, it is saying that the proper relationship of clergy to laypersons is *service*. The clergy are to equip the saints, that is, assist them and train them to be what they should be and do the work they should do, which is the proclamation of the gospel to the world. In this pattern of service we have no lesser example than that of Jesus who, as noted above, "did not come to be served, but to serve, and to give his life

---

[2]John R. W. Stott, *One People* (London: Falcon Books, 1969), p. 30. Stott discusses the proper pattern on pp. 42–47.

[3]Trueblood, *The Incendiary Fellowship*, p. 40.

as a ransom for many" (Mark 10:45).[4]

FULFILLMENT

Joel's prophecy was fulfilled at Pentecost when the Holy Spirit came on all believers. All began to speak and witness to others. A new era was inaugurated. It is said of the church at this period that "all the believers were together and had everything in common. Selling their possessions and goods, they gave to anyone as he had need. Every day they continued to meet together in the temple courts. They broke bread in their homes and ate together with glad and sincere hearts, praising God and enjoying the favor of all the people" (Acts 2:44–47).

In each of nine cases in which it is said that the disciples were filled with the Holy Spirit, the consequence of that filling was a witness to Jesus Christ. The first of these cases is Pentecost. We are told that "all of them were filled with the Holy Spirit" and that they at once began to witness (Acts 2:4–13). Peter did so officially and most effectively. The second case is Peter's being "filled with the Holy Spirit" just before he addressed the Sanhedrin on the occasion of his first arrest (Acts 4:8). He preached Jesus. The third case is the description of a prayer meeting in which the believers "were all filled with the Holy Spirit and spoke the word of God boldly" (Acts 4:31). Acts 6:3, the fourth reference, says that deacons were chosen on the basis of their being "full of the Spirit." At first glance this seems to be an exception, for nothing tells us that they then witnessed to Christ. But it is important to note that the verse does not describe them as being filled with the Spirit but only says that they gave evidence of *having been filled* with the Spirit (past tense). How was this known? The passage does not say how specifically, but it may well have been because they were already active as witnesses. Besides, the account of the choice

of these deacons is immediately followed by the story of the death of the deacon Stephen, which certainly contains an effective witness to the grace of God in Christ's ministry.

The fifth example of a person being filled with the Spirit is Stephen who, "full of the Holy Spirit, looked up to heaven and saw the glory of God, and Jesus standing at the right hand of God" and testified of this fact: "Look, . . . I see heaven open and the Son of Man standing at the right hand of God" (Acts 7:55, 56). Paul is twice said specifically to have been "filled with the Holy Spirit" (Acts 9:17; 13:9). The first time was at his conversion when Ananias came and placed his hands on him. Paul recovered his sight, was baptized and "at once . . . began to preach in the synagogues that Jesus is the Son of God" (Acts 9:20). The second time was when Paul confronted Elymas, the sorcerer, and pronounced a judgment on him in the name of Jesus. Barnabas is said to have been "full of the Holy Spirit." He was a preacher. The ninth example is the company of disciples at Antioch who were "filled with joy and with the Holy Spirit" and who doubtless revealed this by continuing to spread the gospel even after Paul and Barnabas had been expelled from their region (Acts 13:52).

This is the clear and distinguishing mark of a person being filled with the Holy Spirit, and it is the sense in which the words in Joel—"Your sons and daughters will prophesy"—must be taken. There may be prophecy in the sense of foretelling things to come. Paul, Peter, John, and some others did that. But in the sense that *all* will prophesy, what is involved is proclamation of God's truth concerning the Lord Jesus Christ as Savior.

Jesus said that this was to be the Spirit's work. "I have much more to say to you, more than you can now bear. But when

---

[4]This discussion is borrowed in part from James Montgomery Boice, *God and History* (Downers Grove, Ill.: InterVarsity Press, 1980), pp. 137–41.

he, the Spirit of truth, comes, he will guide you into all truth. He will not speak on his own; he will speak only what he hears, and he will tell you what is yet to come. He will bring glory to me by taking from what is mine and making it known to you. All that belongs to the Father is mine. That is why I said the Spirit will take from what is mine and make it known to you" (John 16:12–15).

A BLESSED RESULT

The result of the coming of the Holy Spirit and the consequent testimony to Jesus by those who were so filled was repentance. We are told that after Peter preached, "about three thousand" repented of their sin, were baptized, and were added to the number of the early Christians (Acts 2:37–41). Later we read, "And the Lord added to their number daily those who were being saved" (Acts 2:47).

Repentance brings us back to Joel and the purpose of Joel's prophecy. Joel had been calling on the people to repent of specific sin, the sin of worshiping other gods and of failing to give the true God the worship and obedience He deserves. God had promised blessing if the people would repent. Would they? Could they? The answer to that question is perhaps unknown in the context of the prophecy itself. But it is important to note that at the same time that God calls for repentance He promises a day in which He will pour out His Spirit on all people, and when that happens, as it does at Pentecost, repentance is the first evidence in the lives of people generally. Thousands are convicted of sin, repent of it, and turn to Jesus.

It is the same today. Repentance is always the first visible evidence of the Holy Spirit's presence and activity. Where He is at work, repentance and a resulting belief in Jesus as Savior follow. We should pray for repentance first in our own hearts and then in those of our contemporaries.

18

Valley of Decision

(Joel 3:1–21)

Multitudes, multitudes in the valley of decision! For the day of the LORD is near in the valley of decision. The sun and moon will be darkened, and the stars no longer shine. The LORD will roar from Zion and thunder from Jerusalem; the earth and the sky will tremble. But the LORD will be a refuge for his people, a stronghold for the people of Israel.

Peter lived many centuries after the prophet Joel. But if Joel had been able to know Peter and had become familiar with his writings, he would have echoed Peter's words about judgment: "It is time for judgment to begin with the family of God; and if it begins with us, what will the outcome be for those who do not obey the gospel of God?" (1 Peter 4:17). Joel's book has been a warning to God's people of such judgment.

But the fact that there will be a judgment of God on His disobedient people does not mean that God is forgetting about the sins of the ungodly or that He will neglect to mete out judgment to them. On the contrary, like waters collecting behind a great dam, God's wrath has been gathering and increasing as it awaits the day when it will be released in fury against individuals and nations. Paul spoke of this day when he told the Athenians: in the past God overlooked the ignorance of pagan worship but "now he commands all people everywhere to repent. For he has set a day when he will judge the world with justice by the man he has appointed [that is, by Jesus]. He has given proof of this to all men by raising him from the dead" (Acts 17:30, 31). This is what Joel speaks of as he closes his prophecy. He has warned Israel of God's judgment. Now he reminds even pagans that they will be called to account for their offenses.

The idea of God's wrath is unpopular for obvious reasons. Yet this is the only point in God's final dealings with sinful people that has real logic to it. In most theological systems the doctrine of the last things centers around three great truths: the return of Jesus Christ, the resurrection of men and women, and the final judgment. But it is only the last of these that is logical. There is nothing logical about the return of Jesus Christ. Jesus came once and was rejected. If He went away and never came again, it would be only what we should expect. There is nothing logical about the resurrection either. "Dust you are and to dust you will return" is God's word to sinners (Gen. 3:19). Yet God promises "unlogically" to raise us to life. The only really sensible thing is God's judgment.

Why? Because we have broken God's laws and have sinned against Him in thought, word, and deed. And the Judge of all the earth must do right! If we will not repent of sin and return to God in the way He has provided—through Christ—that judgment is even now waiting at the door.

THE CHARGE

The first six verses of chapter 3 give God's charge against the heathen nations, and the point of concern is that they have attacked God's people and divided His land. The most prominent feature is God's repeated emphasis upon "my people" and "my land." We read, "I will enter into judgment against them concerning *my inheritance, my people Israel,* for they scattered *my people* among the nations and divided up *my land.* They cast lots for *my people*" (vv. 2, 3). Again, "You took *my silver* and *my gold* and carried off *my finest treasures* to your temples" (v. 5).

The people of God are His by two acts: creation and redemption. They are His because He made them. This applies to all, but there is a special application to Israel (in the Old Testament period) and to the church (in the New Testament period). God brought each into being. He created Israel by calling Abraham and giving him descendants as numerous as the stars of heaven (Gen. 15:5). Of the New Testament community Jesus said, "I will build my church" (Matt. 16:18).

Again, the people of God are His by redemption. That is, they are purchased with the blood of Christ. The word "redemption" is an interesting one. It is a Latin derivative based on the words *re,* which means "again," and *emo, emere,* which means "to acquire." Redemption means "to acquire again" or "to buy again." In its full biblical usage redemption means deliverance from the bondage of sin by Christ at the cost of His life—because He loved us.

The idea of *deliverance* is easy to understand, especially deliverance from slavery, which is the kind of deliverance that is meant. I think of the book *Ben Hur.* After a privileged upbringing in Jerusalem the hero of the book, Judah Ben Hur, falls afoul of the Roman authorities. He is arrested, condemned, and finally sentenced to serve out his life on one of the Roman slave ships. There is a great scene in which Judah, having fallen from his position of privilege, is now in the bowels of the Roman ship rowing his life away with other con-

demned and equally hopeless men. They are hanging on by sheer determination. Some are beginning to despair. At this point the Roman admiral explains the reason for their existence, saying, "We keep you alive to serve this ship." It is hard to think of any better words to epitomize the hopelessness of such slavery.

Then the story unfolds, and there comes a moment when there is a battle and the slaves on this particular ship are set free. Ben Hur rescues the admiral and is later adopted as his son. He thus rises to a position of privilege and authority again. This story symbolizes what redemption means. It is to be delivered from slavery. In spiritual terms we are slaves to sin, but Jesus breaks the power of sin and sets us free.

Charles Wesley sang about it in his great hymn "And can it be that I should gain."

Long my imprisoned spirit lay
Fast bound in sin and nature's night.
Thine eye diffused a quick'ning ray:
I woke—the dungeon flamed with light!
My chains fell off, my heart was free,
I rose, went forth, and followed Thee.

The second element in redemption is the most important part, for it tells us that redemption is not merely deliverance from sin but deliverance from sin *by Christ at the cost of His life.* It was by dying for us that Christ set us free.

Some biblical scholars would pull back at this point, arguing that any idea of a cost or price of salvation is unworthy of God, whatever that price may be. They would argue that "if God saves us on the basis of a price, then our salvation is not free, and therefore it is not of grace; but since we know that we are saved by grace through faith, this understanding of redemption must be wrong. It must mean deliverance only." Some might even cite the use of the word by the Emmaus disciples, who explained that "Jesus of Nazareth . . . was a prophet, powerful in word and deed before God and all the people. The chief priests and our rulers handed him over to be sentenced to death, and they crucified him; but we had hoped that he was the one who was going to *redeem* Israel" (Luke 24:20, 21). The Emmaus disciples were obviously thinking of redemption as deliverance from the power of Roman domination in that reply.

But they were mistaken. Christ had indeed come to redeem Israel, though not in the way they were thinking. They were thinking only of a physical, national deliverance. He was thinking in spiritual terms, for it was in order to accomplish that spiritual deliverance that He died. Jesus asked, "Did not the Christ have to suffer these things and then enter his glory?" And beginning with Moses and all the Old Testament writings "he explained to them what was said in all the Scriptures concerning himself" (vv. 26, 27).

This is the way redemption is referred to throughout the New Testament. In Matthew 20:28 Jesus says, "The Son of Man did not come to be served, but to serve, and to give his life as a ransom for many." What is He talking about? Obviously, this is redemption from sin at the cost of His life. Titus 2:14 speaks of Jesus as One who "gave himself for us to redeem us from all wickedness and to purify for himself a people that are his very own, eager to do what is good." This verse does not mean that He gave Himself for us in the sense that He lives for us, though that is also true. It means that He gave His life that we might be delivered. Finally, there is that classic text in 1 Peter 1:18, 19. "For you know that it was not with perishable things such as silver or gold that you were redeemed from the empty way of life handed down to you from your forefathers, but with the precious blood of Christ, a lamb without blemish or defect." In this passage the idea of Christ's life being the cost of our redemption is inescapable.

Besides all this, it was because of His great love that Christ redeemed us. The Bible says, "For God so loved the world that he gave his one and only Son, that whoever believes in him shall not perish but have eternal life" (John 3:16).

It is true that from the point of history in which Joel stood this redemptive work of Christ was still future. The Old Testament saints looked forward to it, just as we look back. But it is nevertheless on this basis, future or past, that the people of God are God's. God has delivered them from the bondage of sin by Christ at the cost of His life—because He loves them.

THE CHALLENGE

The next section of Joel's chapter is a challenge, and an ironic one at that. In these verses God challenges the nations that have made war on His people to turn their plows into swords and their pruning hooks into spears and marshal their forces to do battle against Him in the Valley of Jehoshaphat.

There are two great ironies in this challenge. First, the challenge to beat plows into swords and pruning hooks into spears is a reversal of the promises God makes elsewhere concerning the future Golden Age. In Isaiah 2:4 God speaks of a day when many will go to the mountain of the Lord to learn His ways and walk in His paths. In that day, says God, "They will beat their swords into plowshares and their spears into pruning hooks. Nation will not take up sword against nation, nor will they train for war anymore." Similarly, in Micah 4:3 the words of Isaiah's prophecy reappear in a passage concluding, "Every man will sit under his own vine and under his own fig tree, and no one will make them afraid" (v. 4). Here truly is a Golden Age in which the God of peace has abolished war and the instruments of war have been made into agricultural instruments. But men do the opposite. They turn tools into swords.

The second irony is the obvious one:

mere men marshaling forces to do battle with God. There is a recent drama by a black playwright entitled "Your Arms Too Short to Box with God," which expresses a profound biblical principle. No man can hope to fight God successfully. Yet many try. God here challenges them to come out against Him for this last, decisive confrontation.

We can hear the derisive laughter of God as this is spoken, for the second psalm tells us explicitly that God laughs at such presumption. "Why do the nations rage and the peoples plot in vain?" God asks. Why do "the kings of the earth take their stand and the rulers gather together against the LORD and against his Anointed One"? They say, "Let us break their chains and throw off their fetters" (Ps. 2:1–3). In these verses God is describing the cosmic rebellion of the human race which, in this particular expression, involves the kings of the earth and the nations. They regard God as their enemy and His rightful rule over them as oppressive. They want to cast off His rule. They want to be answerable to no one. So they make their tools into weapons, gather their arms and warriors, and march defiantly out to do battle against God. What is God's reaction to this act of treason? Does He cower in fear? Does He retreat to His heavenly barricades? Does He capitulate? We know He does not. God laughs! "The One enthroned in heaven laughs; the Lord scoffs at them. Then he rebukes them in his anger and terrifies them in his wrath, saying, 'I have installed my King on Zion, my holy hill'" (vv. 4–6). The Lord's reaction is utter scorn, for nothing is so preposterous as puny mortals marching out to do battle with the Omnipotent.

This is God's picture of the final judgment: men and women marching out to battle and God laughing as justice is administered and judgment falls on the ungodly.

I have spoken of two ironies in God's challenge to the rebellious nations: the irony of making plows into swords and pruning hooks into spears and the irony of mere men fighting God. But there is also a third irony conveyed in the image God uses to describe His judgment. It is the image of God trampling out the grapes of His wrath:

> Swing the sickle,
>   for the harvest is ripe.
> Come, trample the grapes,
>   for the winepress is full
>   and the vats overflow—
> so great is their wickedness! (v. 13).

Why is this image ironic? It is ironic because in the normal life of an agricultural people the time of harvest was the most joyous occasion of the year. At harvest time the grain was gathered in and the grapes were thrown into the wine vats to be trampled into wine. At that time the hard work of the long hot summer was done. The fruits of labor were now to grace the people's tables throughout the winter. At harvest time laughter would be heard; harvest festivals would be common. Macaulay, in his famous poem, "Horatius at the Bridge," describes the joy of harvest even though in his story the men of the country have left the fields to go to war and the work at home is being done by women.

> This year the must shall foam
> Round the white feet of laughing girls
> Whose sires have marched to Rome.

But there will be no joy when the Lord Jesus Christ comes to tread out God's wrath. In God's day the scene of rejoicing is changed to one of sorrow.

This scene is also described in Revelation. "I looked, and there before me was a white cloud, and seated on the cloud was one 'like a son of man' with a crown of gold on his head and a sharp sickle in his hand. Then another angel came out of the temple and called in a loud voice to him who was sitting on the cloud, 'Take your sickle and reap, because the time to reap has come, for the harvest of the earth is ripe.' So he that was seated on the cloud swung his sickle over the earth, and the earth was harvested.

"Another angel came out of the temple in heaven, and he too had a sharp sickle. Still another angel, who had charge of the fire, came from the altar and called in a loud voice to him who had the sharp sickle, 'Take your sharp sickle and gather the clusters of grapes from the earth's vine, because its grapes are ripe.' The angel swung his sickle on the earth, gathered its grapes and threw them into the great winepress of God's wrath. They were trampled in the winepress outside the city, and blood flowed out of the press, rising as high as the horses' bridles for a distance of 1,600 stadia" (14:14–20).

Having this picture before us, we may apply it personally. Our nation is among those that are challenged to appear in the Valley of Jehoshaphat (Jehoshaphat means "the Lord judges"). What nation has ever been as richly blessed in material and even spiritual things as our own? We have been blessed beyond measure, and blessing such as this is the gift of God. Has such goodness led our nation to God? It has not. On the contrary, it has made us indifferent to Him. One commentator writes, "We have wealth surpassing all the nations of the earth, but the masses throw their surplus to the gambler's syndicates or waste it on liquor or amusement. How we have been blessed! Yet we despise the blessings as a nation, taking them all as belonging to us instead of realizing that we would be as the nations that are overrun by war, but for the grace of God."[1]

Are we to think that such ingratitude and irresponsibility will go unnoticed or be unpunished by God? Dare we think that the challenge of God to the nations is for others only and not also for ourselves?

The Crisis

Beginning in verse 13 there is a de-

scription of "multitudes in the valley of decision." This text has been used thousands of times in evangelistic meetings to portray people needing to make decisions for Christ. The evangelist will say, "You stand tonight in the valley of decision, and you need to decide for Christ." But this is not the kind of decision Joel is thinking of. This is not the decision of the evangelistic meeting. It is the decision of the court, and the one making the decision is not the one who has rejected Christ but the Christ he or she has rejected. This is God's decision, a decision that will determine people's destinies forever.

In what direction will yours be determined? When we think of a division between persons we cannot forget Christ's great sermon on the Mount of Olives before His arrest and crucifixion. In that sermon Jesus borrowed language from this very chapter of Joel ("the sun will be darkened, and the moon will not give its light," Joel 3:15; cf. Isa. 13:10; 34:4) and elaborated on the judgment, warning His hearers to get ready for it. He told three parables: of the ten virgins, of the talents, and of the sheep and the goats. These vary in details, but the points of each are similar. In each there is a sudden appearance of the Master that catches the people involved by surprise. In each there is a separation: the five wise from the five foolish virgins, the ones who used their master's talents wisely from the one who did not, the sheep from the goats. Finally, in each there is utter surprise on the part of those who receive punishment. The foolish virgins are astounded that the Master will not admit them to the wedding banquet. The wicked steward is amazed that the Master is not satisfied with his lack of performance. The goats ask Jesus, "Lord, when did we see you hungry or thirsty or a stranger or needing clothes or sick or in prison, and did not help you?" (Matt. 25:44).

[1]Barnhouse, *God's Wrath*, pp. 27, 28.

As we read those parables we think of many people today. They have despised the grace of God while "storing up wrath against [themselves] for the day of God's wrath, when his righteous judgment will be revealed" (Rom. 2:5). But they are unaware of what they are doing and will be surprised when God's decision is made. They will have despised the very thing that was given to lead them to repentance (Rom. 2:4).

The Consolation

Yet the outcome need not be that of the foolish virgins, the wicked steward, or the uncharitable goats. There are also those others whose destiny is as sure and blessed as the end of the others is miserable. Joel speaks of these in this great chapter, for he goes on to say, "But the LORD will be a refuge for *his people,* a stronghold for the people of Israel" (v. 16). For them the earth will be replenished, and sin will be pardoned (vv. 18–21).

How is that possible? It is not that the sins of God's people are necessarily any less than those of the surrounding nations. Joel's prophecy was occasioned by a locust plague in Israel that was a warning by God of an even greater judgment to come—precisely on Israel. Israel was not innocent. Nor is the church. We are all guilty sinners. If we are saved, it will be, not because of our guiltlessness (which does not exist), but because the Lord Jesus Christ, our Savior, bore the guilt and suffered the consequences of sin for us.

Years ago in California there was a farmer who had been growing fields of grain. The locomotives of those days burned coal and wood, and it often happened that as the trains passed through the countryside sparks from their stacks would ignite the fields and set them on fire. The farmer was aware of this. So he kept his eyes on the trains and fields. One day when the grain was ripe and ready for harvest, a train passed by. A short time later the farmer saw that the worst had happened. Off in the distance, upwind, there appeared a wisp of smoke. The farmer knew that his field was burning and that, unless he moved quickly, the fire would soon sweep down over the fields and destroy his entire crop. He rushed to the blaze. Part way there he stopped and started another fire that eventually produced a fire wall across his acreage. The fire roared down, reached this break and burned itself out.

Half the farmer's crop had been destroyed. The man walked dejectedly through the burned fields, wondering why this had happened to him. What purpose could God have in it? As he walked through the ashes thinking about these things he noticed the charred body of a hen that had been caught in the inferno. The farmer kicked it over, and when he did, five little chicks ran out from underneath it.

The Bible tells us that the wrath of God is as a consuming fire. Nevertheless, it need not touch those who are covered by the Lord Jesus Christ. There is refuge in Him. The full wrath of God is revealed at two points in history: at the final judgment, described by Joel and other biblical writers, and at the cross of Christ, where it has already been poured out for those who trust Jesus. If you wait until the final judgment, you will face it alone and be condemned by Jesus. If you take refuge in Christ, He has faced your judgment for you. The Bible says, "There is now no condemnation for those who are in Christ Jesus" (Rom. 8:1).[2]

---

[2]The story of the farmer is borrowed from a telling by Donald Grey Barnhouse and is reprinted from an earlier use in Boice, *The Last and Future World,* pp. 122, 123.

AMOS

19

The Prophet From Tekoa

(Amos 1:1, 2; 7:10–17)

The words of Amos, one of the shepherds of Tekoa—what he saw concerning Israel two years before the earthquake, when Uzziah was king of Judah and Jeroboam son of Jehoash was king of Israel.

He said: "The LORD roars from Zion and thunders from Jerusalem; the pastures of the shepherds dry up, and the top of Carmel withers."

The Book of Amos is one of the most readable, relevant, and moving portions of the Word of God. But in much of church history (until very recent times) little or no attention has been paid to it. Why? It is because the book speaks powerfully against social injustices and religious formalism, and many who would otherwise read the book have been implicated in such sins and are condemned by it.

Frank E. Gaebelein, a wise and experienced observer of the American church scene, wrote, "Since the 1920s I have attended evangelical churches and participated in many Bible conferences. Yet never have I heard at a Bible conference a responsible treatment of Amos' strong words about the injustices done through the misuse of wealth or an exposition of the great passages in Isaiah and the other prophets that stress God's concern for the poor and oppressed. Not, in fact, till this year [1979] have I heard in a conservative evangelical church any really forthright preaching about these things, which are so important in God's sight. Prophecy, yes—but only in its predictive, eschatological aspect with little or nothing about the major witness of the prophets against the idolatry of

things and the oppression that may be entailed in accumulating them."[1]

The church's neglect of Amos might be understandable if we lived in a world of little injustice, little poverty, and little misuse of wealth—or even if we lived in a world in which the conditions Amos speaks of were recognized but were gradually being righted. But this is not the case. In 1977 the National Academy of Science published a report saying that 750 million people in the poorest nations live in extreme poverty with incomes of less than seventy-five dollars per year. The United Nations' *Development Forum* reported in 1974 that "at least 460 million are actually starving." Roughly a billion persons, chiefly in third- and fourth-world countries, are malnourished. Yet in spite of efforts to deal with such great problems in some quarters, the gap between the rich and poor countries is widening as the years go by. In 1965 the per capita Gross National Product of developed countries was twelve times as large as that of developing countries taken as a group. But that figure has already increased, and it is predicted by Professor Bhagwati of the Massachusetts Institute of Technology that the rich will have

[1]Frank E. Gaebelein, "Challenging Christians to the Simple Life," *Christianity Today*, Sept. 21, 1979, p. 23.

fifteen times as large a Gross National Product by the year 2000.

This is not merely a feature of the relationship between rich and poor *nations* either. It holds true for relations between individuals within nations, even in the United States. Recent U.S. government studies show that in spite of improvement in living conditions of some members of minority groups, the gap between rich and poor is widening.[2]

THE "BEST" OF TIMES

Amos is the first of the writing prophets. That is, he is the earliest prophet who has left literary remains and whose dates are not in serious dispute. Amos says that he wrote during the reigns of Uzziah of Judah and Jeroboam of Israel "two years before the earthquake" (Amos 1:1). We have no independent record of this earthquake (cf. Zech. 14:5), so *that* phrase is no help to us in dating. But the Jeroboam who reigned in Israel at the time Uzziah reigned in Judah was Jeroboam ben Joash, generally known as Jeroboam II. He reigned from 786 to 746 B.C.[3] Since the conditions Amos describes developed during the reign of Jeroboam, it is likely that the prophet appeared in Israel toward the end of that period, around 750 B.C.

The importance of this dating is that this was a period of unusual prosperity in the northern kingdom of Israel. Israel had come into existence after the death of Solomon (during his son Rehoboam's reign over Judah), at which time the kingdom had split into two parts. Judah continued to exist in the south, ruled by the heirs of Solomon. The northern kingdom went its own way and was ruled by various kings. In the beginning Israel was hemmed in by the neighboring kingdom of Syria. There were frequent border skirmishes. Times were hard. But a decade or so before the accession of Jeroboam, the Assyrian king Adad-Nirari III defeated Syria, thus disposing the power that more than any other had hindered Israel's expansion, and then, having unwittingly served Israel's interests, Assyria entered a decline from which it did not awaken until the accession of Tiglath-Pileser III in 745 B.C.

Jeroboam used this period profitably, effecting conquests that restored the older, Solomonic boundaries for the one and only time since the great king's death (cf. 2 Kings 14:23–29). By this he ushered in a period of materialistic prosperity such as Israel had never before known. Wealth accumulated. Leisure became possible. Most people said that God was evidently blessing the nation. Indeed, they had a state religion to say this formally. The state religion was popular—at least with the wealthy classes.

The only difficulty was that the blessings for which the rich were thanking God had come at the expense of the poor and, as a consequence, the religion was no true religion but a sham. It looked good on the surface, but it was corrupt beneath, just as the land appeared prosperous on the surface but was groaning under the injustices inflicted on it. God sent Amos with his prediction of judgment and coming doom into this climate.

Have you ever heard a lion roar? The sound frightens you and makes the chills run up and down your spine, even when

---

[2]See Ronald J. Sider, *Rich Christians in an Age of Hunger* (Downers Grove, Ill.: InterVarsity Press, 1977).

[3]There is some difference of opinion regarding these exact dates. The years given are those cited by John Bright in *A History of Israel* (Philadelphia: Westminster, 1959, Chronological Charts), Bernhard W. Anderson in *Understanding the Old Testament* (Englewood Cliffs, N. J.: Prentice-Hall, 1957, p. 240), Martin Noth in *The History of Israel* (New York: Harper & Row, 1958, p. 237) and James Luther Mays in *Amos: A Commentary* (Philadelphia: Westminster, 1969, p. 1), Richard S. Cripps in *A Critical and Exegetical Commentary on the Book of Amos* (London: S.P.C.K., 1969, p. 34) places Jeroboam's reign in the years 783 to 745 B.C. J. A. Motyer uses the dates 793 to 753 B.C. in *The Day of the Lion: The Message of Amos* (Leicester, England: Inter-Varsity, 1974, p. 16).

you know the lion is behind strong bars in a zoo. That is what Amos says God was now doing. The Lord was roaring from Zion, thundering from Jerusalem. The roar was to frighten those who were about to become the lion's prey. Amos said that God would roar from *Zion* (v. 2).

One problem with the religion of the northern kingdom was that it was conducted at the cult shrines of Bethel, Beersheba, and Gilgal. These were not authorized by God and were actually an abomination to Him, as becomes clear in the prophecy. So Amos states the place from which God speaks: from Jerusalem. Then too, Amos indicates the scope of God's judgment. It will extend from Zion to the pastures of the shepherds, that is, from the best to the poorest and most remote areas of the land. Mount Carmel was high, caught the moisture-laden winds, and so produced the best farm and grazing lands. Nevertheless, it was to wither in the days to come.

THE "LEAST" OF MEN

From a human point of view Amos was an extraordinary man. He had a great moral consciousness, surpassing that of all but a few people who have ever lived. He was perceptive. He was courageous. Yet, so far as we can tell, he was a man without any formal religious training, and perhaps without any formal training at all.

In the first sentence of the prophecy and in chapter 7, where Amos includes an incident involving the chief priest of Bethel, Amaziah, Amos uses three words to describe what he was. In Amos 1:1 and 7:14 he says he was a shepherd, "one of the shepherds of Tekoa." Some who have wondered how a man of such origins could produce the knowledgeable and very moving verse of which the prophecy consists imagine that the word "shepherd" refers to an owner of great flocks, a man who would have many shepherds under him. Although that is possible, it is not likely. It is not a normal use of the

word, and the other words Amos uses of his profession suggest something quite different. The second word is "caretaker," a caretaker of sycamore trees (7:14). Again, it is possible that Amos owned the trees and was therefore a rather prosperous farmer. But he does not say that. He says simply "caretaker." Besides, the sycamore produced a very poor kind of fruit, which only the poorest people ate. This does not suggest prosperity. The third word is "tender," a tender of sheep (7:15). The words all suggest a poor man who worked hard for his living.

This gives us the first and perhaps one of the greatest lessons of this book: God's use of the insignificant. It is true that God sometimes uses the great of this world. We are pleased that He does. But it is more often the case—almost the rule—that He uses the insignificant so that the glory might go to Himself and not to mere men and women. The principle is stated in 1 Corinthians 1:26–29: "Brothers, think of what you were when you were called. Not many of you were wise by human standards; not many were influential; not many were of noble birth. But God chose the foolish things of the world to shame the wise; God chose the weak things of the world to shame the strong. He chose the lowly things of this world and the despised things—and the things that are not—to nullify the things that are, so that no one may boast before him."

Take the three most significant men of the Old Testament as examples. Abraham is the father of the Jewish people and the chief Old Testament example of one who lived by faith. Who was Abraham? He was a man who lived in Mesopotamia, in Ur of the Chaldees, and who had many possessions. But he was not a particularly spiritual man. In fact, there is every reason to think that he was like every other pagan of his day in that he worshiped the demon gods of the Mesopotamian culture. It was from this background that God called him to be the father of that nation from which Jesus Christ came. When Joshua wanted to humble the people and remind them to continue to love and serve God, he pointed back to Abraham, saying, "Long ago your forefathers, including Terah the father of Abraham and Nahor, lived beyond the River and worshiped other gods" (Josh. 24:2). God took Abraham from that, and the people were to remember that background in order that they might be humble before God.

The second figure is Moses, the great lawgiver. Moses became a great leader and was possibly the best-educated man of his day. It is conceivable that he had been trained to be the next Pharaoh of Egypt. But he was not born in a palace or even in the home of one of Egypt's noble families. He was born of slaves and belonged to a nation that had been in bondage for nearly four hundred years. Even more, he was under sentence of death. The government had declared that all Jewish males should be killed at birth. Yet God took this baby, a nobody, and used him as the chief figure of the Exodus. He was the one through whom the Old Testament law was given.

The third example is David, the greatest of Israel's kings. David was an attractive youth. He had a forthright and winsome personality. But he was the youngest in his family, and as a result, no one expected him to be important. Even the prophet Samuel did not expect it. God sent Samuel to the house of Jesse of Bethlehem to anoint the next king, and Samuel naturally looked to the oldest, a tall, good-looking man named Eliab. Samuel thought, "Surely the LORD's anointed stands here."

But God said to Samuel, "Do not consider his appearance or his height, for I have rejected him. The LORD does not look at the things man looks at. Man looks at the outward appearance, but the LORD looks at the heart."

After this Jesse called his second son, Abinadab. But Abinadab was not the Lord's choice either. After this there was Shammah, and so on with seven of Jesse's sons. At last Samuel asked Jesse, "Are these all the sons you have?"

Jesse answered that there was still another, an insignificant one. He explained that he was the youngest and that "he [was] tending the sheep." Samuel insisted that David be called for, and when he arrived the Lord indicated to Samuel that he was the chosen one. From that humble beginning God raised up the greatest of Israel's kings (cf. 1 Sam. 16:1–13).

Here are three: Abraham, the pagan who became the greatest of the Hebrew patriarchs; Moses, the slave who became the great liberator and lawgiver; and David, the eighth son who became the greatest king. All were insignificant. But all were totally given over to God, as Amos was, and God therefore accomplished much through them in their time. The awareness of that gives me hope. If we are looking for those who have great stature in this world's eyes and are looking to them for what needs to be done, I am afraid we are in great trouble. There are "not many wise . . . not many influential . . . not many of noble birth." If that is what God needs, the church is in trouble. But if, on the other hand, God is able and actually does use the nobodies of this world, this means that He is able to use us and will use us if our lives are really given over to Him. It is from people like us that God does great things in order that honor and glory might be given to His own great name.

AMOS AND AMAZIAH

The fact that God used Amos does not mean that His message was well received, however. In fact, the opposite was the case. God called Amos when he was a shepherd and caretaker of sycamore trees in Tekoa, about ten miles from Jerusalem. He said, "Go, prophesy to my people Israel" (7:15). So Amos left his flocks and trees and started northward from Judah to Israel. Apparently he began to preach as soon as he crossed the border at Bethel, the first Israelite city of any size.

It was significant that Amos began to preach at Bethel. But in order to understand why, it is necessary to understand something of what happened after the division of the nation into two parts following the death of Solomon. In the south, Rehoboam continued to reign. But in the north, Jeroboam I became the new king. He had the task of consolidating the kingdom under his rule, but this was difficult due to the previous focus of Israel's political and spiritual life at Jerusalem. It was to Jerusalem that the people went annually (and sometimes more often) to offer their sacrifices. Jeroboam recognized that if this continued, there would be a gradual lessening of loyalty to his kingship. The Bible quotes him as saying, "The kingdom will now likely revert to the house of David. If these people go up to offer sacrifices at the temple of the LORD in Jerusalem, they will again give their allegiance to their lord, Rehoboam king of Judah. They will kill me and return to King Rehoboam" (1 Kings 12:26, 27). At last, after seeking advice, he established several religious sites for his kingdom. One was on the southern border at Bethel and another on the northern border at Dan. He placed a golden calf in each and instructed the people to do their worshiping there. In addition, Jeroboam appointed other shrines and instituted festivals to match those of the southern kingdom. Each site became a focus for the official state religion and a home for the official priests of Israel.

This was exactly what God had told the people not to do. Sacrifices were to be made only at Jerusalem, and there were most certainly not to be any high places, shrines, or golden calves. Jeroboam's move, though shrewd politically, was outright disobedience to God's laws

and therefore had predictably evil results. The state religion naturally propped up the state and became a tool of repression rather than a voice for righteousness in the land.

It was to the southern center of this state cult, Bethel, that Amos went, and that is why his preaching there was so significant. We do not know precisely what Amos said on this occasion, but presumably it was the gist of the message found in the prophecy. He spoke about immorality and social injustice. He spoke of false religion and the oppressive use of wealth. He said that judgment was coming. None of this would have been received well anywhere at the time, but it was particularly offensive at Bethel, the state shrine, and to Amaziah, the priest entrusted with the smooth running of this branch of the government. Like a true state functionary, Amaziah sent a report to Jeroboam: "Amos is raising a conspiracy against you in the very heart of Israel. The land cannot bear all his words. For this is what Amos is saying: 'Jeroboam will die by the sword, and Israel will surely go into exile, away from their native land'" (7:10, 11).

In J. A. Motyer's excellent commentary on Amos, the author views this response as the first of three temptations pressed on Amos. He calls it the test of *misrepresentation*.[4] Amos did say that Israel would be taken away into exile, but nowhere in the prophecy does Amos say that Jeroboam would be killed. In fact, that did not happen. Jeroboam died a natural death at home, and his son Zechariah succeeded him.

That often happens when the word of God is spoken. People will allow us to speak the truth of God so long as we speak it to ourselves or to those who agree with us, or if we do it vaguely enough so that they do not understand what we are saying. But let the message be heard and understood, and immediately the opposition and misrepresen-

[4]Motyer, *The Day of the Lion*, pp. 170, 171.

tation begin. Speak about sin, and they say, "Oh, those hypocrites think they're better than everyone else." Speak of Jesus as the way of salvation, and they call us "narrow-minded" or "bigoted." Speak of judgment, and they claim that you have had a bad upbringing and could not get along with your mother or father. It is misrepresentation all the way.

The second temptation is *self-interest.* Amaziah says, "Get out, you seer! Go back to the land of Judah. Earn your bread there and do your prophesying there" (7:12). Motyer suggests that the Hebrew verbs translated "Get out," and "Go back" contain the added emphasis "for your own sake." That is, "If you want success and security, preach in Judah, where you are from; let them pay your salary." Since Amaziah was in the religious business for money, he assumes that Amos is in it for money too and tells him (as one professional to another) that he will do far better in his own land if he wants to preach against Israel.

That temptation is also with us today. I have had religious functionaries warn me—as if they were on my side—that if I wanted to get ahead in the church I should be careful not to identify myself with this or that evangelical organization. I suppose they meant this in my best interest, as they conceived it. But words like these were not in my best interest, nor are they in the best interest of anyone. They are actually the words of the devil, who told the Lord Jesus Christ in similar language that if He wanted to get ahead in His work He should do things the devil's way rather than God's: "All this I will give you if you will bow down and worship me" (Matt. 4:9). He did not understand that those who have heard the word of God must do as God demands and that they can be content and secure only in so doing. A person who exchanges that contentment for the favor of Satan is a fool. The one who forfeits the bread of God's

Word for physical bread is the greatest of all imbeciles.

The third test was a confrontation with *authority:* "Don't prophesy anymore at Bethel, because this is the king's sanctuary and the temple of the kingdom" (7:13). Motyer states that "Amaziah clothes himself with all his ecclesiastical pride of position" and declares that since "Bethel is a Royal Chapel and a National Cathedral . . . people like Amos are decidedly out of place!"[5] In man's sight, perhaps! Not to God! In God's sight Amos was precisely where He had placed him, and Amos, who knew that he had been placed there by God, stood firm.

WHEN JUDGMENT COMES

Indeed, he did more than stand firm. He talked back, and the words of his rebuttal were a judgment on the devil's priest: "Now then, hear the word of the LORD. You say, 'Do not prophesy against Israel, and stop preaching against the house of Isaac.' Therefore this is what the LORD says: 'Your wife will become a prostitute in the city, and your sons and daughters will fall by the sword. Your land will be measured and divided up, and you yourself will die in a pagan country. And Israel will certainly go into exile, away from their native land'" (7:16, 17). Amaziah's rejection of Amos' message did not affect the message or its outcome in the slightest. What Amos said would happen did happen. And the results were disastrous for Amaziah.

In 735 B.C., shortly after Amos prophesied, the weakened kingdom of Syria and the strengthened kingdom of Israel joined in an attack on Ahaz, king of Judah in the south, to try to force him into an alliance against Assyria which was then rising again under the rigorous leadership of Tiglath-Pileser III. Instead of joining them, Ahaz appealed to Assyria against his two neighbors. By 733 B.C. Tiglath-Pileser had responded and overrun the northern and eastern parts

[5]Ibid., p. 171.

of Israel. In this attack Damascus was totally destroyed and its population deported. A little more than ten years later, Tiglath-Pileser's successor, Shalmaneser V, overran the central area of the country and beseiged Samaria. In 721 B.C. the city fell to his successor, Sargon, and 27,000 of its inhabitants were deported. The king and his nobles were taken, and although we have no independent record of the fate of Amaziah, presumably he was also taken into exile and died in Assyria, as Amos said.

The lessons of this book are at least three. First, God is a righteous God who requires righteousness in His people. We are all good at imposing God's standards on others, but we need to remember that God's standards apply first of all to us. Are we righteous? Do we live as God wants us to live, particularly toward others?

Second, God is not satisfied by formalism in religion and actually hates religion when it is used to justify the status quo and oppress the unfortunate. In Amos, God says, "I hate, I despise your religious feasts; I cannot stand your assemblies. Even though you bring me burnt offerings and grain offerings, I will not accept them" (Amos 5:21, 22). There was much of this in Amos' day, and the people no doubt thought themselves to be quite spiritual because of their formal adherence to such practices. After all, God had commanded these practices, and they were obeying cheerfully. But God says it was all a sham! If religion is to be acceptable to God, it must be a religion of the heart that begins with genuine repentance for sin and issues in a life that is transformed in ways that please Him.

Finally, we need to accept Amos' challenge to do good. It is not enough just to speak our religion. We must act it out, as I have indicated. Here is how Amos says it: "Seek good, not evil, that you may live. Then the LORD God Almighty will be with you, just as you say he is. Hate evil, love good; maintain justice in the courts. Perhaps the LORD God Almighty will have mercy on the remnant of Joseph" (5:14, 15). May God give each of us grace to do just that and may He have mercy on us for Jesus' sake.

20

Everyone Equal Before God

(Amos 1:3–2:16)

This is what the Lord says: "For three sins of Israel, even for four, I will not turn back my wrath. They sell the righteous for silver, and the needy for a pair of sandals. They trample on the heads of the poor as upon the dust of the ground and deny justice to the oppressed. Father and son use the same girl and so profane my holy name. They lie down beside every altar on garments taken in pledge. In the house of their god they drink wine taken as fines."

A woman attended an evangelistic meeting and was delighted when she learned that the preacher would talk about sin. When he preached against strong drink she cried, "Preach it, brother!" When he declaimed against tobacco she shouted, "Amen!" The minister's third point was a condemnation of gossip, and she leaned over to her neighbor and said, "Now he's not preachin'; he's meddlin'."

This is the way those who first listened to Amos must have reacted as they heard the sermon recorded in the first two chapters of his prophecy. We do not know what portion of the book Amos first preached when he arrived at the cult city of Bethel from Tekoa, or even whether we have that material. But it is not hard to imagine that Amos might have begun with the material in these opening chapters because, more than anything else, this is perfectly structured to gather an audience and lead it to the chief points the later chapters develop. These chapters contain eight oracles: one against each of the six nations that surrounded Judah and Israel (Syria, Philistia, Tyre, Edom, Ammon, Moab) and one each against Judah and Israel themselves. These are not a random collection. The list is carefully constructed so that the

judgment net slowly and inexorably closes around the very people to whom Amos was speaking. At the beginning of his talk the people would presumably have been pleased to hear his condemnation of the neighboring hostile nations. They may even have been willing to hear judgments against Judah, the southern Jewish kingdom. But at last the net tightens, judgment is pronounced against Israel, and the people probably said, "This man is no longer preaching; he's meddling in our affairs."

It is as though Amos were preaching to us and began his sermon by a condemnation of ungodliness in Russia. Afterward he would talk about violence in Iran, and then racial discrimination in South Africa. We could bear that easily. But what would be our reaction if he should then begin to talk about ungodliness, violence, and discrimination in the country and even in the city in which we live?

No Respect of Persons

The background is that in Amos' view "God does not show favoritism," as the apostle Paul later claimed in Romans 2:11. The reason He does not show favoritism is that He is the God of the whole world, each individual of which is equally responsible before Him. This cuts two ways. On the one hand, it means that Israel does not have any privileged position just because she has benefited from God's past acts on her behalf. She is not God's pet. If any irregularity exists, it is in the opposite direction, for the benefits of her history imply a greater obligation. On the other hand, the principle of equality applies to the pagan nations too, for although they are not Israel and have not received Israel's blessing, they are nevertheless responsible for their violations of the law of God implanted in every mind and conscience.

J. A. Motyer writes: "It is the crowning evidence that Amos is speaking of the God of the whole Bible, the God of the Bible-loving Christian, that in the name of his God he faces a whole world, in all the reality of its cruelties, its unresolved injustices, its privileged and under-privileged peoples, and submits it totally and without reserve to the sway and judgment of the one and only God. . . . Feel the weight of the monotheism of Amos! When he reviews the world of the have-nots, the nations who have never received any revelation of Yahweh (1:3–2:3), he takes absolutely no cognizance of the fact that each worshipped a god of its own. Such information was quite irrelevant. It was not to that god that they were answerable, nor could that god save them in the day of Yahweh's wrath. There was only one God over the whole earth, and to him they must and would render account.

"But much more is it the message of Amos that this truth has its foremost and more abundant application to the people of God themselves (2:4–3:2). To whom much is given, of him much shall be required. Judgment will not only come but will begin at the house of God, and will be manifest there in a seemingly pitiless and all-destroying intensity."[1]

MULTIPLE TRANSGRESSIONS

As soon as we begin to speak of God's judgment on the pagan nations we have to give an explanation. For the question immediately arises, "If they are pagan nations and if, as you have just acknowledged, they have not received Israel's blessing, including the Old Testament law, then how can they be held responsible for failing to do those things they did not know they were to do?" The answer to this question is that they are *not* judged for failing to do what they did not know to do but for failing to do what they knew very well was required of them.

The one common denominator of the oracles against Syria, Philistia, Tyre, Edom, Ammon, and Moab is that each involves a sin against basic human relations. Damascus is condemned for cruelty to Gilead. Gaza is judged for enslaving and selling whole communities to Edom. Tyre broke a treaty of brotherhood. Edom "pursued his brother with a sword" (1:11). Ammon exhibited fury in the murder of the pregnant women of Gilead. Moab desecrated the bones of Edom's king. These are not violations of any specific provision of the law of God, though the Old Testament law covers these as well as other items. They are violations of that basic code of human behavior written in the hearts of all people and expected of all, whether friend or foe, kinsman or stranger, neighbor or member of a distant nation. God holds even the pagan nations responsible for merciful behavior, but these, as others, had acted without mercy to their foes.

Moreover, they had done it on more than one occasion and in multiple ways. For the sake of his oracle Amos lists just one violation. But we are not to think that these nations had been exemplary in their conduct up to this point, had slipped just once and were now to ex-

---

[1]Motyer, *The Day of the Lion*, pp. 31, 32.

perience God's harsh judgments. On the contrary, they were responsible for multiple atrocities and were to be judged at last by the God who had already been more than merciful. This is the point of the idiom that begins each oracle: "For three sins of _____, even for four, I will not turn back my wrath" (1:3, 6, 9, 11, 13; 2:1, 4,6). The idiom refers to repeated violations, atrocity upon atrocity. The item cited is merely one illustration.

There are interesting patterns to Amos' use of these six nations. The first is geographic. Syria, the first nation mentioned, was situated to the northeast of Israel. Philistia, the second, was to the southwest, directly opposite Syria. Tyre was to the northwest, Edom to the southeast. In other words, the first four nations form an "X" marking four points of the compass relative to the people Amos is addressing. Ammon and Moab round out the pattern by filling in the nations to the east between Syria to the north and Edom to the south.

A more important pattern in Amos' use of these six nations is what he chooses to say against them. Each of the condemnations concerns violations of human rights, but these denunciations are no random collection. On the contrary, they fall into three groups of two each, in which each new group intensifies the horror of what has gone before.

The first group contains the nations of Syria and Philistia, embodied in their two main cities: Damascus and Gaza. The sin of these nations is cruelty. Against *Damascus* Amos says, "For three sins of Damascus, even for four, I will not turn back my wrath. Because she threshed Gilead with sledges having iron teeth" (1:3). We do not know what precise historical incident this refers to, though the people of Israel undoubtedly knew. But we can get an idea of what is involved from the metaphor. In ancient times threshing was done with a sled-like object that was dragged over the freshly harvested grain by animals. It would be of wood, but the bottom could be cov-

ered with iron bands to protect the wood and do the work more thoroughly. The sledge would crush the grain, separating the kernels of wheat from the chaff; then the mixture would be winnowed by allowing the wind to blow the chaff away. Since Amos uses this image of Syria's military campaigns in Gilead, we can conclude that Syria did something like this to the conquered communities. Perhaps the armies destroyed whole villages. Perhaps they massacred the people. Whatever the details were, they were beyond what was necessary even in warfare, and Damascus was to be judged for those atrocities.

This is quite up to date. It is said that in war there is only one rule: Hit the enemy with all you've got, and do anything you can to win an absolute and unconditional victory! This is good logic from a human perspective. Syria has not been the only nation in the long history of human warfare to make use of it. But it is wrong from God's point of view. God condemns it. He says that even in warfare there are certain obligations that mercy imposes, and the victors must not be ruthless either after the victory or on their way to achieving it.

In the case of *Gaza*, the chief city of Philistia, the area of offense is commerce, but its nature is the same: unnecessary cruelty. "For three sins of Gaza, even for four, I will not turn back my wrath. Because she took captive whole communities and sold them to Edom" (v. 6). The condemnation here is not against slavery in and of itself, just as the previous oracle was not against war in and of itself. The crime is not that soldiers were enslaved after being taken in battle, which was the standard practice, but that the Philistines used their temporary supremacy to enslave whole populations—soldiers and civilians, men and women, adults and children, young and old—for commercial profit. Gaza did not even need the slaves. She merely sold them to Edom for more money.

Today literal slavery is outlawed in

virtually the entire world. But there are various forms of slavery, and the judgment of God would apply to any oppression of other people merely to increase one's wealth. We are not to profit at the expense of other people.

The next pair of nations consists of Tyre, the great seaport community to Israel's northwest, and Edom, the desert fortress to the southeast. The condemnation against these nations is in the same category as that against Damascus and Gaza: a violation of basic codes of human behavior. But here it is intensified. The word that is common to these two oracles is "brotherhood" (v. 9) or "brother" (v. 11). This means that, although the judgment against the first two nations was for a general cruelty against others, in this case it is for a more specific cruelty against those to whom the nation should have been particularly merciful.

Tyre is condemned because "she sold whole communities of captives to Edom"—the same offense for which Philistia was judged—and because she disregarded "a treaty of brotherhood." We do not know what nation was involved in this latter offense. But there was some nation to which Tyre was related, with whom a treaty of mutual defense had been made, and it was against this nation that the offense was committed.

The sin of *Edom* was similar. Amos says that Edom "pursued his brother with a sword, stifling all compassion" (v. 11). This offense must have been particularly heinous, because the next book in the collection of the minor prophets, Obadiah, is concerned entirely with this sin. Obadiah writes,

> Because of the violence against your
> brother Jacob,
> you will be covered with shame;
> you will be destroyed forever.
> On the day you stood aloof
> while strangers carried off his wealth
> and foreigners entered his gates
> and cast lots for Jerusalem,
> you were like one of them.
> You should not look down on your
> brother

> in the day of his misfortune,
> nor rejoice over the people of Judah
> in the day of their destruction (vv. 10–
> 12).

Apparently, during some attack on Jerusalem by a foreign power (we do not know which one), Edom joined with the attackers to profit from Judah's temporary misfortune. This was doubly offensive because of Edom's blood relationship to the Jewish people. Both were descended from Isaac, the son of Abraham. Edom came from Esau, Israel (Judah) from Jacob. Edom should have stood with Judah. At the very least the Edomites should have refused to profit from Judah's misfortunes. But they did not and are judged for it.

These two oracles are a warning against what we would call "pragmatism" in international affairs. It is a political doctrine in some places that nations should act in their own self-interest and that nothing should ever take precedence over that. The French are well known for this philosophy. No doubt Tyre and Edom argued on the basis of self-interest also. But God replies that this is not valid and that historical ties are important. Treaties should be honored. Nations should not take advantage of others' misfortunes.

The last part of chapter 1 and the first part of chapter 2 introduce two more nations, the third group. They are also cited for cruelty, but in these cases the sins are most offensive since they are against the helpless. *Ammon* is judged "because he ripped open the pregnant women of Gilead in order to extend his borders" (1:13); *Moab* is condemned "because he burned, as if to lime, the bones of Edom's king" (2:1). The first offense is against the future. Ammon particularly sought out the pregnant women and killed them so that the rising generation of the inhabitants of Gilead might be destroyed and the future task of assimilation of Gilead by Ammon might be made easier. The second offense is against the past. So spiteful were the Moabites that they heaped insult and sacrilege on defeat by desecrating the remains of one of the national heroes of Edom.

We are to honor the past. We are to protect the future. This is an obligation binding on all nations whether they are the beneficiaries of the laws of God or not. Ammon and Moab had not done this. As judgment was pronounced, the people must have responded warmly to Amos's theme.

GOD'S PEOPLE

Agreement must have faded away as Amos continued and the thrust of his message became clear. Beginning with 2:4 he has words against Judah. In verse 6, he begins a long series of judgments against the northern kingdom.

It is worth taking these two nations together. Not only do they form a fourth pair; they actually belong together as the one people of God, and the oracles against them form one continuing exposition of their sin and decline. The first step of the decline is found in verse 4 as part of the oracle against Judah: "For three sins of Judah, even for four, I will not turn back my wrath. Because *they have rejected the law of the LORD* and have not kept his decrees." Amos did not say this about Damascus; they did not have God's law. He did not say this about Gaza. He did not say it about Tyre or Edom or Ammon or Moab. These were pagan nations. So they were condemned, not on the basis of their violation of the law of God given to Israel, but on the basis of their violation of the law of God written on each human mind and conscience. God says this to those to whom the law had been given. They were much more culpable, for "from everyone who has been given much, much will be demanded; and from the one who has been entrusted with much, much more will be asked" (Luke 12:48).

Do we reject the laws of our God? We say, "No, we wouldn't do that. We love the laws of our God. Don't we sing 'O how love I Thy law; it is my meditation all the day'?" Well, we may sing it, but it probably is not true that God's law is our meditation all the day. Our minds are too filled with other things. What is more, we probably also often reject it, just as Judah had done. We reject it by equivocation. Whenever we come across something that requires a change in our behavior or life style, we say, "I wonder what it says in the Hebrew." Or we argue, "That must have been written for another age." Failing that, we just refuse to read it. One preacher said of God's Word, "This book will keep you from sin, or sin will keep you from this book." Many have rejected the law of God because they do not want to relinquish sin.

The second step in the people's decline is linked to the first. Having said that people rejected the law of the Lord, Amos adds that they have also been "led astray by false gods, the gods their ancestors followed" (v. 4). This follows what has gone before, in that: 1) if you reject the Bible, you will reject the Bible's God, and 2) if you reject the Bible's God, other gods, idols, will come in to take the true God's place. We have a saying, "Nature abhors a vacuum." That is also true of spiritual matters. We cannot exist without a higher being. So if we put the true God out, a lesser god will come in. If we put true morality out, a lesser morality, which is actually an immorality, will come in. If we reject the Bible, other trashy books will take the Bible's place.

The third step appears in the first words Amos specifically addressed to Israel. They concern Israel's morality, and his point is this: having rejected the Bible and consequently also the God of the Bible, *Israel next rejected this God's morality*. And they became like . . . what? Precisely like the heathen over whom they were voicing their enthusiastic amens! The heathen used people for their own selfish ends, but this is precisely what Israel has done. Amos says,

For three sins of Israel,
even for four, I will not turn back my
    wrath.
They sell the righteous for silver,
and the needy for a pair of sandals.
They trample on the heads of the poor
as upon the dust of the ground
and deny justice to the oppressed.
Father and son use the same girl
and so profane my holy name.
They lie down beside every altar
on garments taken in pledge.
In the house of their god
they drink wine taken as fines (2:6–8).

There are a number of sins here, but they are not to be taken merely as a list of examples. They are a composite picture of multiple and overlapping corruption. The first sin is economic oppression and that even for small gains: "They sell the righteous for silver, and the needy for a pair of sandals." In this verse "selling" the righteous probably does not refer to slavery but to what we mean when we talk of "selling someone out." It means betraying him, using him, cheating him out of his just desserts for gain, whether large (silver) or small (a pair of sandals).

The second sin is denying "justice to the oppressed." This relates to what is said before. Israel's rich oppressors did not stoop to steal from the poor physically. Why risk that when they could easily get what they wanted through the courts? They ran the courts. So when the poor appealed to the courts for justice they found that justice was denied them.

The third sin is immorality: "Father and son use the same girl and so profane my holy name." There is some question as to how this accusation should be taken. Some commentators feel that the word "same" should be omitted, giving the sense: "Both father and son are womanizers."[2] But the passage goes on to talk about "every altar" and "the house of their god," and for this reason most interpreters see it as a reference to cultic

prostitution. Both father and son visit the shrine, sleep with the same girl on different occasions, and thus violate the laws of Leviticus 18:7, 15; 20:11 and Deuteronomy 22:30, as well as commit idolatry.[3]

Fourth, there is the sin of keeping garments of poor people taken in pledge. According to Exodus 22:26, 27, these were to be returned at nightfall, since they were the only thing the poor had to keep warm and they were not to be cruelly deprived of necessities.

Finally, there is the sin of enriching oneself through fines imposed on the innocent. Although the details are not spelled out, we are probably to think of these fines as mere subterfuges by which the poor were stripped of what little they possessed in order to further the opulent life style of the rich.

This is not merely a collection of examples of social injustice and immorality but rather a composite picture of a most corrupt society. Let me explain what I mean. First, it is necessary to know something about the Hebrew word translated "they lie down." As translated, this is a reflexive verb. That is, the action turns back on the subject with the meaning "they lie *themselves* down" or, as we would say, simply "they lie down." However, this verb is never used elsewhere in the Hebrew Bible in a reflexive way. It is always transitive; and if this is the case, the object of the verb should be supplied. Who is it that these so-called worshipers of God lay down beside the altars? It can be none other than the temple girls. So the translation should be, "They lay *them* down beside every altar on garments taken in pledge."

Here is where the description gets interesting as a composite picture of multiple sins. Several years ago I was listening to a message given by John Gerstner of Pittsburgh Theological Seminary in which he painted a picture of a thoroughly corrupt individual. He de-

[2]Ibid., p. 58.
[3]Mays, *Amos: A Commentary*, p. 46.

scribed him as drunk and in bed with a prostitute while underneath the bed he was hiding a pot of stolen gold. That is quite graphic. But in these verses Amos outdoes John Gerstner. He describes the practice of sexual immorality in a temple dedicated to the God of Israel, in comfort, with objects extorted from the poor. Moreover, these sinners are so pleased with themselves that they even toast their success with wine dishonestly acquired through their corrupt legal system. This makes Amos sick and makes God so angry that His wrath will now come.

When we put it like this almost anyone can recognize how bad things were. We are inclined to say, "Preach it to them, brother!" But in doing this it is fatally easy to miss the fact that Amos is also preaching to us. Is it never the case that in America, in the city in which we live, justice is perverted and the poor oppressed? Is it never the case that the rich get off because they can afford better lawyers and impress the judges, while the poor are condemned because they cannot afford good lawyers and do not impress the judges? Is it never the case that people come to church to praise God, knowing that the week before they used questionable but "legal" means to cheat someone out of their business or livelihood? Is it never the case that we ourselves have profited at the expense of the unfortunate?

The Logic of Judgment

The first great sermon of the Book of Amos now rushes to its inevitable conclusion: the people are guilty, and judgment must come. But on the way to this conclusion Amos zings the people one more time. They are guilty; that is bad enough. But, as he reminds them in verses 9–11, they have done these things in spite of the marvelous acts of God on their behalf. God brought them out of Egypt. He drove the inhabitants of Canaan out of the land before their advancing armies. He raised up prophets to rebuke their sin and teach them God's ways. They had no memory for these things, and when the prophets were sent to recall them to the God who had saved them from slavery and made them a nation, they commanded the prophets not to prophesy and even got them drunk when possible (v. 12).

What was to happen now? The outcome was to be the most logical thing in the world:

"Now then, I will crush you
    as a cart crushes when loaded with grain.
The swift will not escape,
    the strong will not muster their strength,
    and the warrior will not save his life.
The archer will not stand his ground,
    the fleet-footed soldier will not get away,
    and the horseman will not save his life.
Even the bravest warriors will flee naked on that day,"
    declares the LORD (2:13–16).

This is not hyperbole. This is simple truth, and an understatement at that. You cannot fool God. God means business. He is righteous and just, and those who are His people must live by the standard that flows from His own character. If we will not do it, He will bring His judgment on us. He will not be accused of being two-faced. He will not judge the heathen and spare His people—if His people are guilty of the same sins, as they so often are.

But how in the world can anyone live up to that standard? In ourselves we cannot. But the God who drove out the Amorites and defeated the Egyptians will help us, if we want to walk in His way.

21

Judgment on God's Elect

(Amos 3:1–15)

Hear this word the LORD *has spoken against you, O people of Israel—against the whole family I brought up out of Egypt: "You only have I chosen of all the families of the earth; therefore I will punish you for all your sins."*

If Amos is a collection of sermons preached in Israel in the days of Jeroboam, it is clear that a new sermon begins with chapter 3. The first contained judgments on Israel's neighbors, gradually narrowing to a judgment on Israel herself. Its theme was: Heathen nations have no special exemption from God's judgments, and Israel has no special position. The sermon that begins in chapter 3 picks up at that point, showing not only that Israel has no special position on the basis of which she can sin with impunity, but she actually has a higher obligation for holiness because of God's dealings with her and will therefore be judged more severely for her rebellion against God's law.

It is the point of privilege implying responsibility. William Shakespeare treated this theme in four of his historical plays: *Richard II* and the plays involving King Henry V (*Henry IV, Parts I and II,* and *Henry V*). In the first play we follow the career of Richard II who began his reign with great privilege and opportunity. Richard is impetuous and arbitrary. He does not administer justice properly. His course is downhill, and he dies as the play ends. Henry's course is in the opposite direction. In his youth the prince is profligate. He spends his time carousing with old John Falstaff. But when the king, his father, dies, Henry changes

his goals and begins to live in a manner expected of leaders. He knows he did nothing to merit being king. At one point he speaks to his dying father about England's crown: "You won it, wore it, kept it, gave it me." But having become king through no achievement of his own, he now nevertheless determines to live in a manner worthy of that status:

. . . The tide of blood in me
Hath proudly flowed in vanity till now.
Now doth it turn and ebb back to the
  sea,
Where it shall mingle with the state of
  floods,
And flow henceforth in formal majesty.

This is what God wanted to see concerning Israel, but Israel had not lived up to its responsibility.

A CHOSEN PEOPLE

In a sense, Amos says everything needful in verses 1 and 2. They contain three truths about Israel and one conclusion about the coming judgment.

The first truth is that *Israel is God's chosen people*. The very name Israel implies this, for it is a covenant name: "God said to him, 'Your name is Jacob, but you will no longer be called Jacob; your name will be Israel. . . . The land I gave to Abraham and Isaac I also give to you, and I will give this land to your descendants after you'" (Gen. 35:10, 12). Amos

3:2 says the same thing: "You only have I chosen of all the families of the earth." Israel traced its ancestry to Abraham, and, as we saw in the first of these studies of Amos, Abraham had nothing by which to commend himself to God. God did not look down from heaven to find a man who had a little bit of faith or a little bit of spiritual understanding and then say, "Oh, good; here is someone with a little bit of faith. I'll blow on that little spark and coax it along, and perhaps if things go right, I can build an elect people from Abraham." It was entirely the other way. Abraham was a pagan, living among pagans. Left to himself he would have continued in his pagan ways and would have died in heathen ignorance without God. But God did not leave Abraham to himself. He revealed Himself to Abraham, calling him out of darkness into His own marvelous light. Abraham was God's chosen person.

We see the same principle in the next generation. Abraham had no children, and as the years rolled by he reached the age when it was impossible for him to generate them. Moreover, Sarah was past the age when she could conceive children. Abraham had to believe that God would give him an heir even though both he and Sarah were past the age of having children. He did believe. Isaac was born when Abraham was one hundred years old. But it took a miracle!

The third generation also makes the point, again in a way entirely different from the previous two cases. In this generation, Isaac's wife Rebecca had twins: Esau and Jacob. Either could have been the heir of promise. But God intervened to choose one and not the other. "Rebecca's children had one and the same father, our father Isaac. Yet, before the twins were born or had done anything good or bad—in order that God's purpose in election might stand: not by works but by him who calls—she was told, 'The older will serve the younger.' Just as it is written: 'Jacob I loved, but

Esau I hated'" (Rom. 9:10–13). In other words, in the cases of Abraham, Isaac, and Jacob (Israel) we have denials that the election of Israel was based on anything in these men and the affirmation, by contrast, that it was due entirely to the free pleasure of God. Abraham shows that election is not by merit. Isaac shows that it is not by physical strength. Jacob shows that it is not even by inheritance. It is by grace alone, and grace demands accountability.

The second truth about Israel is that *it had been delivered from bondage in Egypt.* In this case the matter is not election but redemption. Not only did God choose Israel on the basis of grace alone, He also redeemed the nation on the same basis. Apart from the grace and power of God displayed profusely in the days of Moses, the people would have been in Egypt to this day, probably assimilated into the ancient Egyptian races. But God sent Moses and worked through him to deliver the people.

The third truth is that *this amazing election and redemption were unique to Israel among all the families of the earth.* Every nation is the recipient of what is called common grace. Each exists by God's favor and is blessed with life, food, health, and limited success as a unique people. But the favor spoken of in these verses is not universal. It was not true of Egypt or Syria or Edom or the nations at large. It was only true of Israel: "You *only* have I chosen of all the families of the earth." Nothing could demand a higher level of accountability.

There is a classic statement of this principle in Deuteronomy. The passage discusses election and makes the point that election is really of grace—just as we have been showing from the lives of the three Jewish patriarchs. "The LORD did not set his affection on you and choose you because you were more numerous than other peoples, for you were the fewest of all peoples. But it was because the LORD loved you and kept the oath he swore to your forefathers that he brought you out with a mighty hand and redeemed you from the land of slavery, from the power of Pharaoh king of Egypt." Thus far the points are precisely what we have already seen in Amos: election and redemption. But the passage goes on: "Know therefore that the LORD your God is God; he is the faithful God, keeping his covenant of love to a thousand generations of those who love him and keep his commands. But those who hate him he will repay to their face by destruction; he will not be slow to repay to their face those who hate him. Therefore, take care to follow the commands, decrees and laws I give you today.

"If you pay attention to these laws and are careful to follow them, then the LORD your God will keep his covenant of love with you, as he swore to your forefathers. He will love you and bless you and increase your numbers. He will bless the fruit of your womb, the crops of your land—your grain, new wine and oil— the calves of your herds and the lambs of your flocks in the land that he swore to your forefathers to give you. You will be blessed more than any other people; none of your men or women will be childless, nor any of your livestock without young. The LORD will keep you free from every disease. He will not inflict on you the horrible diseases you knew in Egypt, but he will inflict them on all who hate you."

The writing goes on in this way for several chapters, then concludes, "If you ever forget the LORD your God and follow other gods and worship and bow down to them, I testify against you today that you will surely be destroyed. Like the nations the LORD destroyed before you, so you will be destroyed for not obeying the LORD your God" (Deut. 7:7–15; 8:19, 20).

This is the point Amos makes at last. Because the people have not lived up to their responsibility as God's people, obeying His commands, "therefore I [God] will punish you for all your sins." Because they have sinned, they will be destroyed just as the nations were that God destroyed at the time of Israel's conquest of the Promised Land.

This applies to us also. Just as Israel was chosen by grace, so have we been chosen—if we truly are believers in Jesus Christ. Just as Israel had been redeemed, so have we been redeemed. Therefore, much is required of us. If we do not follow in God's way, worshiping Him only and obeying His holy and just commands, judgment will fall on us, too. It is precisely because we have been chosen that God will punish us most severely for all our sins.

A PLEA FOR SOUND THINKING

How hard it is to listen to this kind of reasoning! We want to plead the privileges of our position and say that God must deal with us differently—because we are His. No doubt many did this in Amos' day as they listened to this preaching. In Judah the people later rejected the warnings of prophets such as Jeremiah on the grounds that they were God's people, that God had promised that a king would never cease to sit on the throne of David and that Jerusalem could therefore never fall to an invading army. But Jerusalem did fall. In the same way, Samaria (and all Israel) was about to fall precisely because the people were not living as God's people.

Amos 3:3–8 calls for clear thinking on the part of the prophet's hearers. In this section Amos uses nine questions, plus one interjected statement in verse 7, to speak of cause and effect.

Do two walk together
  unless they have agreed to do so?
Does a lion roar in the thicket
  when he has no prey?
Does he growl in his den
  when he has caught nothing?
Does a bird fall into a trap on the ground
  where no snare has been set?
Does a trap spring up from the earth
  when there is nothing to catch?

When a trumpet sounds in a city,
    do not the people tremble?
When disaster comes to a city,
    has not the LORD caused it? . . .

The lion has roared—
    who will not fear?
The Sovereign LORD has spoken—
    who can but prophesy? (3:3–6, 8).

Amos' points are quite obvious. If people meet in order to go walking, it is by prior arrangement. If they have not agreed to meet, the walk will not take place. A lion does not roar if he is about to seize his prey. If he growls in his den, it is because he has caught it. A bird falls into a trap only because someone has first set the trap. If a trap springs up, it is because it has been tripped. Trumpets sound when danger threatens. Disaster comes because the Lord has sent it.

We need to notice three things about this sequence. First, there is a noticeable progression from the lesser to the greater, from something that is not threatening to something that is. This is not an identical technique to that which Amos used in chapters 1 and 2, in which the noose of judgment slowly tightened around the throats of the Israelites. But it is similar in that the sequence is carefully worked out and leads step by step to the point Amos wants to make. That point is in verse 6: A warning is never given unless disaster is imminent, but a warning is being given and God is sending disaster. The first part of that is amplified in verses 7 and 8. The second part is amplified in the remainder of chapter.

The second thing to notice is Amos' emphasis on the warning. It is the warning God was giving the people through him. If we had only the questions of verses 3–6, we would have but one side of the story, namely, that where the warning is given the attack soon follows. But the amplification in verses 7 and 8 gives another side as well, namely, that the God of grace does not send the disaster without sending a warning first.

This is the point of preaching. If a pastor speaks on the authority of the Bible to say that judgment is coming, that judgment is coming. But the situation involved in such preaching is not mere denunciation. It is warning, given precisely so the judgment might be averted.

Amos' reference to a lion—"Does a lion roar in the thicket when he has no prey?"—echoes Hosea where the same image occurs (ch. 5). In that chapter God describes Himself as a moth, and then later as a lion. He says He will come to Ephraim first as a moth (v. 12). But if Ephraim will not listen, He will then come as a lion (v. 14). This means that when we get out of God's will He warns us about it gently. He does not like to be harsh with us. So He comes into our lives as a moth. A moth flutters around and distracts us. God says He comes that way first, fluttering about, trying to distract us from what is getting us off the right course. However, if we do not respond when God comes as a moth, He comes as a lion, because He is determined that His people will be holy and will walk in His way.

God is no patsy! He is no weak-livered, pathetic figure wringing His hands on the ramparts of heaven as He witnesses our sin, wondering what He is going to do. He is the Lion-God! He is the God who marches at the head of the alien armies to judge His unholy people.

The third thing to notice is that God sends disasters. Christian people seem very reluctant to admit this, and instead of admitting it seem to be trying to get God off the hot seat by blaming the devil, distinguishing between primary and secondary causes or referring to the simple but impersonal "acts" of nature. The strange thing is: the Bible does not do this. No doubt there are primary and secondary causes. There is a devil. But the Bible teaches that God controls the secondary as well as the primary causes and that He even controls the devil. The story of Job is an example of the latter.

Although the devil wanted to injure Job, he was unable to do so until God called attention to Job and actually gave the devil permission to remove his possessions and inflict him with boils. Even in this, God fixed the points beyond which the devil could not go: "Everything he has is in your hands, but on the man himself do not lay a finger" (Job. 1:12), "He is in your hands; but you must spare his life" (Job 2:6).

In Isaiah 45:7 we find the claim that God controls and sends disasters. "I form the light and create darkness, I bring prosperity and create disaster; I, the LORD, do all these things."

It is here that Amos speaks directly to the setbacks and shame that America has experienced in recent years. Once our currency was "as good as gold." It was prized by the world. Today in many countries it is a quarter of what it once was. Once Americans who traveled abroad were respected. Today both they and their government are scorned, and hostile governments think nothing of taking our citizens hostage. Once our armed forces were the strongest the world has ever seen. Today we are on the way to becoming a second-rate power. Once we could be counted on to keep our treaty obligations. Today even our allies wonder if we will risk anything for their security. And what of natural disasters: fires in the west, drought in the south, winter fuel shortages in the north? What about beef and poultry prices? What about inflation generally? These things are not the results of mere chance. They are from God, and they are warnings of even greater judgments.

One commentator has written: "War, drought, famine, pestilence do not come by accident! They are sent as snares, as instruments of [our] destruction! . . . Local and national calamities are not due merely to natural causes, are not only the consequence of human mistakes, or faulty

legislation, or political folly, or inadequate statesmanship. These and other matters may be contributory causes. [But] the final author of all evil (and of good) is the *Lord*. He has done it!"[1]

WHEN DISASTER COMES

There are two ways of looking at the final section of chapter 3, in which the day of final disaster predicted in verse 6 comes. The emphasis could be on its thorough nature. It will consume the rulers and army (v. 11), the priests (v. 14), the rich (v. 15). It will be so terrrible that others, even the traditional enemies of Israel, will hear of it and be frightened (v. 9). If this is the emphasis, then the thematic verse is verse 12: "As a shepherd saves from the lion's mouth only two leg bones or a piece of an ear, so will the Israelites be saved, those who sit in Samaria on the edge of their beds and on the corner of their couches." The judgment will be as thorough as a lion's consumption of a sheep.

On the other hand, the emphasis could be God's comment on the people's attempt to escape the disaster. If that is the point, the lesson is that there will be nowhere to hide. In times of war the first place one would seek shelter is in a fortress or armed camp. The forces of Israel had been successful during these prosperous years under Jeroboam, and great defensive fortifications had been set up. Samaria was one of them. Situated high on a mountain, protected by steep cliffs and thick encircling walls, the rulers of Samaria must have thought themselves safe from any army that could possibly be brought against them. They were so safe they could even lie down on their beds and take it easy. But God says that their fortresses will be inadequate: "An enemy will overrun the land; he will pull down your strongholds and plunder your fortresses" (v. 11).

Assuming that the country was over-

---

run, the next places one would look for safety were the temples and altars at which one could seek sanctuary. In that day a fugitive could seek safety by clinging to the horns of an altar, since it was considered sacrilege to kill him there. Perhaps the people could find sanctuary on the horns of those altars on which they had offered God sacrifices! Not so! says God. God remembers how corrupt that worship was. He remembers that it was beside those very altars that the people lay down on stolen garments to drink their fill and commit their cultic prostitution. God will see to it that those altars are torn down: "On the day I punish Israel for her sins, I will destroy the altars of Bethel; the horns of the altar will be cut off and fall to the ground" (v. 14). No matter that those altars had been dedicated to Jehovah. "The Lord, the LORD God Almighty" Himself will tear them down (v. 13).

Well, the fortresses are gone and the temples are gone. Where can the people flee to next? There is only one place left, pathetic though it may be. The people go home—home to those beautiful winter and summer houses they constructed with their extorted earnings. They go home, dismiss the servants, lock the doors, slip into their bedrooms and hide under their beds. But it is all of no use! "'I will tear down the winter house along with the summer house; the houses adorned with ivory will be destroyed and the mansions will be demolished,' declares the Lord" (v. 15).

Incidentally, archaeologists have found these very houses. In the age prior to Jeroboam II (and even earlier, in the tenth century B.C.), the houses in Israel's cities were of roughly uniform size. But in the eighth century B.C., by contrast, a city such as Tirzah contained a quarter with large, expensive houses, and one of small huddled structures—even smaller than the uniform houses of earlier years.[2] The larger houses were filled with beautiful inlaid ivories and other marks of prosperity. The people who occupied such houses no doubt thought themselves to be at the pinnacle of earthly success. They must have considered themselves inviolable. But God knew how their gains had been made, and he had no respect for their houses. They would be destroyed along with their owners in that coming terrible day.

Where can you hide from "the Lord, the LORD God Almighty"? There is nowhere to hide! There is nowhere now. Above all, there will be no place in the day of His final judgment when kings, princes, generals, the rich, the mighty, every slave and every free man will flee to the mountains and will cry to the mountains and rocks, "Fall on us and hide us from the face of him who sits on the throne and from the wrath of the Lamb! For the great day of their wrath has come, and who can stand?" (Rev. 6:16, 17).

Who can stand? Only those who stand in Christ. For He first stood where we stand and bore the wrath of God in our place. Only in Him will anyone be sheltered from the inevitable judgment.

---

[2]Mays, *Amos: A Commentary*, p. 2. Mays refers to R. de Vaux's *Ancient Israel* (New York: McGraw-Hill, 1961). See also C.C. McCown, *The Ladder of Progress in Palestine* (New York: Harper, 1943).

22

How God Views Religion

(Amos 4:1–5:15)

"Go to Bethel and sin; go to Gilgal and sin yet more. Bring your sacrifices every morning, your tithes every three years. Burn leavened bread as a thank offering and brag about your freewill offerings—boast about them, you Israelites, for this is what you love to do," declares the Sovereign LORD.

I do not know what part of God's revelation is hardest for the human mind to accept, but I suspect that every point is difficult. I would go so far as to say that nearly every important biblical truth is the direct opposite of what the human mind thinks naturally. The Incarnation is a difficult concept. It was so offensive to the Greeks, who thought that God was totally other than matter, that they laughed when the early preachers proclaimed Christ as God come in human flesh. The Resurrection is difficult. Many laugh at that. For most people the greatest difficulty is the Bible's insistence that we must be saved by grace apart from human works. This is so difficult and yet so important that it needs to be proclaimed again and again in the churches and in the world generally.

In the fourth and fifth chapters of Amos we come upon another of those areas in which the mind of God and the minds of fallen human beings diverge. It is the matter of religion. In most people's minds religion is a very good thing. Depending on their training, they would prefer one or another of the world's religions or even one or another of the many forms of Christianity. But to their way of thinking even the less desirable forms of religion are better than no religion at all. They suppose, on the assumption that God thinks as they do, that God is basically pleased with all religious practices.

This is not how God thinks. On the contrary, not only is God not pleased with our religious practices, He is actually very much displeased. Even more, He hates, He despises religion. In Amos 5 God says,

> I hate, I despise your religious feasts;
> I cannot stand your assemblies.
> Even though you bring me burnt offerings and grain offerings,
> I will not accept them.
> Though you bring choice fellowship offerings,
> I will have no regard for them (vv. 21, 22).

This does not mean that there is no worship whatever that *is* pleasing to God, of course. In other places, God instructs us how we should worship and informs us of what is pleasing to Him. But religion as religion is abhorrent. That is the point. The only thing that is pleasing is a genuine, thankful, and obedient response to God growing out of a life that has been transformed by Him.

BETHEL, GILGAL, BEERSHEBA

God's hatred of religion includes religion that goes by the name of Judaism (or Christianity), for that is the point of Amos' prophetic denunciations in these chapters. Amos is not talking about the religion of Syria at this point. In chapter 1 he condemned Syria for its cruel, inhuman behavior; he will not mention that nation again. He is not talking about Philistia or Philistia's gods. He is not talking about the religious practices of Edom or Moab. Amos is talking about Israel—Israel who professed to worship Jehovah, the God of the Old Testament, and who apparently did so enthusiastically and joyfully at this very time in its history.

In Jeroboam's day the religion of Israel was focused at the land's cult shrines, from Bethel in the south to Dan in the north (cf. 1 Kings 12:28–30). In Amos 4 and 5 Amos concentrates on three of them. The first is Bethel, where he apparently began to speak and perhaps did most of his prophesying (see 7:10–17). Bethel is mentioned in 4:4; 5:5, 6. The second is Gilgal, mentioned in 4:4 and 5:5. The third, mentioned only in 5:5, is Beersheba. Each site had its own history and probably its own distinct forms of worship—all in the name of Jehovah, the God of Israel—but Amos speaks of each with sarcasm. The people can go to these shrines. They can call on Jehovah. But all they will do is increase their sins and pile up wrath against the day of God's judgment (4:4; 5:6).

In his helpful commentary, J. A. Motyer studies the significance of each of these sites and finds the clue to the book's specific statements in their history. *Bethel* was associated with the patriarch Jacob, who rested there on his flight from home after cheating Esau of his birthright. That night, as he slept, Jacob had a vision of angels ascending and descending on a stairway that reached from earth to heaven, and God spoke to him to reestablish the covenant previously made with Abraham and Isaac (his grandfather and father). God said, "I am with you and will watch over you wherever you go, and I will bring you back to this land. I will not leave you until I have done

what I have promised you" (Gen. 28:15). When Jacob woke up he was impressed with the fact that God had been in that place though he had been unaware of it. So he set up an altar and named it Bethel, which means "the house (or dwelling) of God" (Gen. 28:19). Later, when he was returning home from Paddan Aram, he visited the place again and remembered that it was "where God had talked with him" (Gen. 35:15).

Bethel was the place where God was supposed to be, where people could meet Him. But Bethel had been corrupted. Jeroboam I had set up a golden calf in Bethel, appointed priests to serve it and made it the center for a special national festival to be held on the fifteenth day of the eighth month of every year (1 Kings 12:31–33). This was religion, but it was no true worship of Jehovah. It was sin. So Amos says sarcastically, "Go to Bethel and sin" (Amos 4:4). Or again, with reference to the inability of anyone to find God at Bethel while it was in this state, he quotes God as saying, "Seek me and live; do not seek Bethel" (5:4, 5).

The second cult city was *Gilgal*. The history of Israel's contact with this place begins at the time of the Conquest when, having crossed the Jordan River and having entered the Promised Land, they paused at Gilgal to erect a monument to their crossing and reconsecrate themselves as God's elect people. There they circumcised the sons who had been born during the years of their desert wandering. They observed the Passover together at Gilgal. It was while they were encamped at Gilgal that the manna stopped and they began to eat of the fruit and grain of Canaan (Josh. 5:1–12). Gilgal symbolized possession of the Promised Land. But Amos says sarcastically, "Do not go to Gilgal. . . . For Gilgal will surely go into exile" (5:5). The God of Gilgal was the guarantee of the promises. But Gilgal without God, religion without the reality, meant nothing.

Beersheba, the third of these three religious centers, was in Judah. At first glance it seems strange that Amos mentions it, since he is focusing his attention on the apostasy in Israel, not Judah. But Judah is not excluded from his warnings, and besides, the people of Israel apparently journeyed to Beersheba even though it was in Judah and apparently also practiced their empty religion there.

Beersheba was associated with the very roots of the nation, for it figured in the lives of each of the three great patriarchs: Abraham, Isaac, and Jacob. The first biblical mention is in Genesis 21:22–33. In that passage Abraham visits Beersheba and participates with pagans in the naming of it. The theme of the story is in Abimelech's and Phicol's words to Abraham: "God is with you in everything you do" (v. 22). Five chapters later Abraham's son, Isaac, comes to Beersheba and hears God promising the same thing to him: "I am the God of your father Abraham. Do not be afraid, for I am with you; I will bless you and will increase the number of your descendants for the sake of my servant Abraham" (Gen. 26:24). At last Isaac's son, Jacob, visits Beersheba on his way to Egypt at the invitation of Joseph. On that occasion God spoke to Jacob in a vision, saying, "Do not be afraid to go down to Egypt, for I will make you into a great nation there. I will go down to Egypt with you, and I will surely bring you back again" (Gen. 46:3, 4). In each of these incidents, God promises to be with the person involved. But in Amos God tells the people not to "journey to Beersheba" (5:5), for He will not be with them in their depraved, self-satisfied worship.

Motyer calls Amos 5:1–5 a funeral dirge. "The dirge . . . speaks of death where there should have been life: *Fallen, no more to rise* (2a). Here is the failure of Bethel: the house of God, the location of the promise 'God is in this place' as the giver of hope and new life, the one who can make the name 'Israel'

a reality. Secondly, the dirge speaks of abandonment where there should have been companionship: *The virgin Israel; forsaken . . . with none to raise her up* (2b). Here is the failure of the Beersheba promise 'God is with you.' Israel has been carried off in death as a virgin who has never known the joys of married companionship and who, even in her virgin state, could find none to befriend her in the hour of need. Thirdly, the dirge speaks of dispossession where there should have been inheritance: *Fallen, . . . forsaken on her land, with none to raise her up*, the failure of the Gilgal promise, the people of God lying in defeat, dead, where in the heyday of Joshua's Gilgal they had shouted in triumph over dispossessed foes."[1]

Autopsy of a Dead Faith

These important middle chapters of Amos do not merely say that God hates empty religion. They also tell why, and in this respect they are an autopsy of Israel's dead faith. They tell us several things about it.

First, they tell us that Israel's religion co-existed with widespread moral corruption. As is true of Amos' style, he does not detail every offense Israel had committed, though quite a few are mentioned in the course of the prophecy. Rather, he paints another of his gripping pictures, in this case focusing on the women of the "upper crust" of Samaria. He regards them as indolent, bestial, indifferent to the poor and needy, tyrannous in their relationship to their husbands, preoccupied only with their own physical pleasure. He calls them "cows of Bashan"—part of a good breed, but still cows. In verses 2 and 3 he says to them,

The Sovereign LORD has sworn by his holiness:
"The time will surely come
when you will be taken away with hooks,
the last of you with fishhooks.

[1]Motyer, *The Day of the Lion*, pp. 108, 109.

You will each go straight out
through breaks in the wall,
and you will be cast out toward Har-
    mon," declares the LORD.

It is interesting that Amos paints a fresh
portrait of moral corruption at this point,
for it is a way of saying that corruption
like this can coexist with a highly developed sense of religion. Amos has already talked about corruption in Israel.
Chapters 1 and 2 led up to it, showing
that it was the same as and equal to the
corruption found in the pagan countries
round about. The end of chapter 3 suggests it by reference to the extraordinary
wealth of the people. Now the corruption
is shown to exist alongside Israel's fer-
vent religious practice.

We find a list of details in chapter 5.
There are: injustice in the courts, hatred
of truth, disregard of the poor, oppression, and corresponding vices:

You who turn justice into bitterness
    and cast righteousness to the ground
    . . .

you hate the one who reproves in court
    and despise him who tells the truth.

You trample on the poor
    and force him to give you grain. . . .

You oppress the righteous and take bribes
    and you deprive the poor of justice in
    the courts.

Therefore the prudent man keeps quiet
    in such times,
    for the times are evil (vv. 7, 10–13).

Israel's injustices existed quite peacefully
with its popular religion.

This seems surprising, but it is not
really so. Similar corruption has existed
alongside religion in all ages. It was true
at the time of Christ. There has probably
never been a period or place in history
where religion was more carefully developed or more thoroughly adhered to
than by the scribes and Pharisees in Israel at the time of Christ. So far as these
religious leaders were concerned, the law
was to be kept and they kept it. Yet when
they wanted to do away with Christ, they
were capable of carrying out their mur-
derous designs and religious duties all
at the same time.

The difficulty they faced was that the
arrest of Jesus came at the time of the
Passover, the most holy week of their
religious year, and they needed to get rid
of Him without defiling themselves and
thus rendering themselves unfit to par-
ticipate in the week's activities. They
concluded that it could be done this way.
First, there would be a trial by night
(which was illegal, but not so wrong, in
their judgment, as failing to keep the
Passover). Next there would be an official
trial by day, in the early morning hours.
There would be an approach to Pilate,
though they needed to make sure that
none of them actually went into his quarters since that would defile any Jew and
prohibit him from eating the Passover.
Finally there would be the execution. The
whole thing could be over by noontime,
and everyone involved could then go
home and worship Jehovah. They
marched along the narrow path of their
own regulations, thinking themselves
quite proper and religious. When it was
necessary they stepped out of the rules
just enough to kill Jesus. Then they
stepped back in and went on with their
religious performances.

It is possible to illustrate this truth in
other periods of history as well: in the
atrocities practiced by nominal Christian
people at the time of the Crusades, in the
greed and perversions of the organized
church during the decadent Dark Ages,
in modern, organized religion. In each
case there is much visible religion side
by side with much obvious corruption.

The second thing God hates about this
kind of popular religion is that there is
no sense of sin on the part of the worshiper. This is very clear in Amos 4, for
the one glaring omission in the list of
offerings that the people are said to have
brought to God at Bethel and Gilgal is
the sin offering. They bring "thank offerings" and "freewill offerings." They

even boast about them (v. 5), so that everyone will know how generous and pious they are. But there are no sin offerings, presumably because they had no sense that they were sinful.

Charles Wesley once met a woman like this. She wanted some of his attention, so she asked him to pray for her because, she said, "I am a great sinner." She added, "I am a Christian, but sometimes I fail so dreadfully. Please pray for me."

Wesley suspected that much of this was hypocrisy. So he looked at her rather sternly and used her own words against her, saying, "Madam, I will pray for you; for truly you are a great sinner."

She was aghast. She answered, "What do you mean? I have never done anything very wrong."

Much religious practice is like this. The apostle Paul faced it in his day in those who claimed to know the law and keep it, but who actually broke it and were known to have done so. He wrote to them: "If you rely on the law and brag about your relationship to God; if you know his will and approve of what is superior because you are instructed by the law; if you are convinced that you are a guide for the blind, a light for those who are in the dark, an instructor of the foolish, a teacher of infants, because you have in the law the embodiment of knowledge and truth—you, then, who teach others, do you not teach yourself? You who preach against stealing, do you steal? You who say that people should not commit adultery, do you commit adultery? You who abhor idols, do you rob temples? You who brag about the law, do you dishonor God by breaking the law? As it is written: 'God's name is blasphemed among the Gentiles because of you'" (Rom. 2:17–24). As Paul goes on to show, all are sinners—the religious person as well as the pagan or non-religious person. Consequently, any religious practice without a sense of sin and a need for atonement for sin and forgiveness from God is hypocrisy and an offense both to God and man.

The third cause of offense is that the worshipers were not seeking God. At first glance this seems to be preposterous, for what is religion if it is not a seeking after God? Are not all religions attempts to find Him?

Not in God's opinion! In fact, the opposite is the case. Religions are really attempts to get away from God. That is why there are so many of them. When God begins to get close to a person, one of the easiest ways to still the insistent prodding of His Holy Spirit and thus continue to hang on to sin and the control of one's own life is religion.

Is there anything he is seeking? Yes, a person like this may be seeking praise from other people. That is why Amos says that the people of his day bragged about their freewill offerings. They *boasted* about them (4:5). They were into religion for the glory it would bring them. Again, such people may be seeking a feeling of importance by associating with something that seems to be important in other people's eyes. When Amos says that the people were seeking Bethel and Gilgal, rather than the God of Bethel and Gilgal, he may be thinking of this (5:5). Finally, it may be the case that people like this seek religion for the cloak it provides. We know this to have been true in Israel, for the Bethel worshipers were actually at Bethel to meet the temple girls.

WARNINGS AND AN INVITATION

What difference does it make what worshipers are seeking so long as they are finding answers to a felt need? God answers that it makes all the difference—not only for this world but for eternity. We see this in the warnings God gave Israel to turn them from this false religious path: famine, drought, crop blight, disease and war (4:6–11). These were given so the people would return to God, yet they did not.

"I gave you *empty stomachs* in every city
    and lack of bread in every town,
    yet you have not returned to me,"
    declares the LORD.

"I also *withheld rain* from you
    when the harvest was still three months
    away.
I sent rain on one town,
    but withheld it from another.
One field had rain;
    another had none and dried up.
People staggered from town to town for
    water
    but did not get enough to drink,
    yet you have not returned to me,"
    declares the LORD.

"Many times I struck your gardens and
    vineyards,
I struck them with *blight and mildew*.
Locusts devoured your fig and olive trees,
    yet you have not returned to me,"
    declares the LORD.

"I sent *plagues* among you
    as I did to Egypt.
I killed your young men with the sword,
    along with your captured horses.
I filled your nostrils with the stench of
    your camps,
    yet you have not returned to me,"
    declares the LORD.

"I *overthrew* some of you
    as I overthrew Sodom and Gomorrah.
You were like a burning stick snatched
    from the fire,
    yet you have not returned to me,"
    declares the LORD.

These verses contain an elaboration of the theme first introduced in Amos 3:6—"When disaster comes to a city, has not the LORD caused it?" One commentator writes, "The striking feature of the narrative is its presentation as a Yahweh-history. The God of Israel speaks in first-person style and proclaims these disasters as his own deeds in the past. . . . The proclamation of the Exodus, the leading through the Wilderness and the Conquest was heard as a promise of protection and benevolence. But Amos' history spoke of the very opposite of security

and blessing. His oracular narrative takes the separate sporadic hardships of Israel's life in Canaan and makes them coalesce into a continuous cohesive record in which Yahweh's personal dealings with Israel are disclosed. And it is a history with a rationale. Its purpose is insistently stated in the refrain which interprets the disasters as Yahweh's quest for Israel's return to him. The cogency of reciting this narrative as a record of Israel's failure to respond to Yahweh presupposes that Amos had a basis for recognizing the blows as the personal overtures of Yahweh, and that the people should have recognized them as such and responded."[2]

Disasters are given by God so that people may awake from their lethargy, turn from sin and seek Him.

This is where the section we are dealing with ends. Early in chapter 5, Amos tells the people not to seek Bethel, Gilgal, or Beersheba, for these will be reduced to nothing when judgment comes. They should seek God: "Seek me and live" (v. 4), "Seek the LORD and live" (v. 6). He now ends on this note:

Seek good, not evil
    that you may live.
Then the LORD God Almighty will be
    with you,
    just as you say he is.
Hate evil, love good;
    maintain justice in the courts.
Perhaps the LORD God Almighty will
    have mercy
    on the remnant of Joseph (vv. 14, 15).

There is no seeking after God that is not at the same time a seeking after good and a shunning of evil. There is no seeking after God that is not at the same time a seeking after justice. Anything else is hypocrisy. But where God is sought, there is life. He is the source of life. Jesus said, "I am the way and the truth and the life" (John 14:6). Even though we have sinned in the past, there is abundant mercy with the Lord.

---

[2]Mays, *Amos: A Commentary*, p. 79.

23

The Day of the Lord

(Amos 5:16–27)

Woe to you who long for the day of the LORD*! Why do you long for the day of the* LORD*? That day will be darkness, not light. It will be as though a man fled from a lion only to meet a bear, as though he entered his house and rested his hand on the wall only to have a snake bite him. Will not the day of the* LORD *be darkness, not light—pitch-dark, without a ray of brightness?*

It is important to understand two steps in the spiritual decline of nominally religious people. Such people do not live for God, though they think they do. They live for self, and the first stage of their decline is to put off the day of reckoning. At this stage they know what is right and expect to do the right someday. But in the meantime they want the imagined benefits of a life of sin. The second stage comes when sin has so trapped them and distorted their thinking that they lose sight of what is right or wrong and imagine their sin to be right conduct. At this point, far from putting off the day of reckoning, they actually desire it. They imagine that their deeds will be vindicated and that the people they have wronged will be shown to be deserving of their conduct.

SIN IN ISRAEL

This is what had happened in Israel as those who had grown rich by exploiting the poor became religious. They knew from their law and the traditions of Israel that what they were doing was wrong. That is one reason why they became so religious; religion was a cloak for their sin. But after they had practiced their injustices for a long enough period, they eventually lost sight of the fact that what

they were doing was wrong. They considered it right and began to look forward to the day when their "hard but necessary" decisions and "right but misunderstood" conduct would be vindicated.

They centered their hope on what was called "the day of the LORD." In the later prophets this phrase appears quite often (Isa. 2:12; 13:6, 9; 22:5; 34:8; Jer. 46:10; Ezek. 7:19; 13:5; 30:3; Joel 1:15; 2:1, 11, 31; 3:14; Obad. 15; Zeph. 1:7, 14–18; Zech. 14:1; Mal. 4:5), but this is the first mention of the idea in any of the historical writings of Israel. We are not to think that Amos invented it, however. The very way in which Amos mentions the Day of the Lord shows that it was already a common idea that had been seized upon by the people in precisely the sense I have been sharing. Briefly, the Day of the Lord was the day in which Jehovah would return in judgment to punish sin and set things right. The people longed for this day. They thought it would mean judgment on their enemies, blessing for Israel and, above all, vindication for themselves. Amos' point is that it would be anything but that. If they were standing in a right relationship to God, which they would show by their faithful pursuit of justice and righteousness, the Day of the Lord would be a day of light for them. But since they were not doing this, the day they longed for would actually be a day of doom.

> Woe to you who long
>   for the day of the LORD!
> Why do you long for the day of the LORD?
> That day will be darkness, not light.
> It will be as though a man fled from a lion
>   only to meet a bear,
> as though he entered his house
>   and rested his hand on the wall
>   only to have a snake bite him.
> Will not the day of the LORD be darkness,
>   not light—
> pitch-dark, without a ray of brightness? (5:18–20).

These verses are filled with irony, as even the casual reader can tell. But they are preceded by a short section that may contain the greatest irony of all. Twice in the preceding chapters Amos has explicitly mentioned Egypt. In chapter 3 he summoned Egypt to assemble with Philistia to observe the injustices practiced on the mountains of Samaria (3:9). In chapter 4 he says that God will be sending plagues on Israel, just as He did on Egypt at the time of the Exodus (4:10). In view of these references, it is reasonable to think that Amos has Egypt and the Exodus in mind as he writes about Israel in 5:16, 17. At the time of the Exodus God passed through Egypt and killed the first-born. This was the tenth and most devastating of the plagues. Anguish filled Egypt. From the palace of the Pharaoh to the poor in the fields— all lost their first-born sons, and there was wailing and mourning everywhere. This is what is going to happen to Israel, says Amos: "There will be wailing in all the streets and cries of anguish in every public square."

The people of Amos' day thought the coming Day of the Lord would be another Exodus for them. They looked forward to it. Amos shows that while it will indeed be an exodus for God's people, Israel's conduct had placed them, not in the camp of the just, but in the camp of the Egyptians. They would be judged as the heathen when the Lord passed through their land.

TWO GREAT DAYS

The same idea is present in the New Testament. It is presented in a contrast between "the day of Jesus Christ," which is a new idea, and "the day of the Lord," which is carried over from the prophets. The day of Jesus Christ refers to Jesus' return for His people. This is a joyous thing for believers, and they are told to anticipate it eagerly. Paul writes about it in 1 Thessalonians saying, "The Lord himself will come down from heaven, with a loud command, with the voice of the archangel and with the trumpet call of God, and the dead in Christ will rise first. After that, we who are still alive and are left will be caught up with them in the clouds to meet the Lord in the air. And so we will be with the Lord forever. Therefore encourage each other with these words" (4:16, 17).

Jesus described this event, saying, "Two men will be in the field; one will be taken and the other left. Two women will be grinding with a hand mill; one will be taken and the other left. Therefore keep watch, because you do not know on what day your Lord will come" (Matt. 24:40–42). In biblical theology this event is the first in a long list of events prophesied for the end times.

On the other hand, the New Testament also knows of the Day of the Lord, which it picks up from the Old Testament. Isaiah had said,

> Wail, for the day of the LORD is near;
>   it will come like destruction from the Almighty.
> Because of this, all hands will go limp,
>   every man's heart will melt.
> Terror will seize them,
>   pain and anguish will grip them;
>   they will writhe like a woman in labor.
> They will look aghast at each other,
>   their faces aflame.

See, the day of the LORD is coming—
a cruel day, with wrath and fierce anger—
to make the land desolate and destroy the sinners within it (13:6–9).

Ezekiel wrote, "This is what the Sovereign LORD says:

'Wail and say,
"Alas for that day!"
For the day is near,
the day of the LORD is near—
a day of clouds,
a time of doom for the nations'" (30:2,3).

Joel, Amos' contemporary, declared:

What a dreadful day!
For the day of the LORD is near;
it will come like destruction from the Almighty (1:15).

Let all who live in the land tremble,
for the day of the LORD is coming.
It is close at hand—
a day of darkness and gloom,
a day of clouds and blackness.

The LORD thunders
at the head of his army;
his forces are beyond number,
and mighty are those who obey his command.
The day of the LORD is great;
it is dreadful.
Who can endure it?

The sun will be turned to darkness
and the moon to blood
before the coming of the great and dreadful day of the LORD (2:1, 2, 11, 31).

Zephaniah prophesied,

The great day of the LORD is near—
near and coming quickly.
Listen! The cry on the day of the LORD will be bitter,
the shouting of the warrior there.
That day will be a day of wrath,
a day of distress and anguish, a day of trouble and ruin,
a day of darkness and gloom,
a day of clouds and blackness (1:14, 15).

Malachi was still speaking of this day in the next to the last verse of the Old Testament: "See, I will send you the prophet Elijah before that great and dreadful day of the LORD comes" (4:5).

It is evident from the references to the darkening of the sun, moon, and stars that this is what Jesus was referring to in Matthew 24:29–31. "Immediately after the distress of those days

'the sun will be darkened,
and the moon will not give its light;
the stars will fall from the sky,
and the heavenly bodies will be shaken.'

At that time the sign of the Son of Man will appear in the sky, and all the nations of the earth will mourn. They will see the Son of Man coming on the clouds of the sky, with power and great glory. And he will send his angels with a loud trumpet call, and they will gather his elect from the four winds, from one end of the heavens to the other." Peter wrote of this day, "But the day of the Lord will come like a thief. The heavens will disappear with a roar; the elements will be destroyed by fire, and the earth and everything in it will be laid bare" (2 Peter 3:10). In the liturgy of the church this is expressed by the *Dies Irae*, which means the "day of [God's] wrath."

NO RAY OF BRIGHTNESS

The statement of this doctrine in Amos is not only the first such statement in Scripture, it is also a classic statement. It can be carefully examined for what it teaches about the characteristics of this coming day of judgment.

The first characteristic is the obvious one: *darkness*. Amos says that it will be a day of "darkness, not light" (v. 18). In view of the many biblical references that say that the light of the sun, moon, and stars will be blotted out, it is quite possible that this involves a literal darkness. Indeed, in the New Testament hell is described as a place of darkness (Matt. 8:12, *passim*). But to limit the word to this literal meaning would, I think, miss the most important thing about it. In the

Bible, light and darkness are strong images. Light is good because it is associated with God. God is said to dwell in the midst of unapproachable light (Ps. 104:2). Jesus is said to be light itself: "I am the light of the world" (John 8:12; 9:5). Things thrive in the light. By contrast, darkness is bad. Evil grows in the dark. So when Amos says that the Day of the Lord is going to be a day of darkness he does not necessarily mean—though he may mean—that the sun is going to be blotted out and the earth is going to get dark. He especially means that God's blessing will be withdrawn and men and women will be without the Light of life.

Think about this characteristic carefully. When people are in the dark they are without God. So the day of God's judgment is going to be a day in which those who have not come to God through faith in the Lord Jesus Christ will be separated from Him. There are those who would say, "So what! I am separated from God now; I am doing all right! Why should I worry about being separated from God hereafter?" The answer is that while mentally and willfully you are separated from God, in very practical terms you are not nearly as separated from God as you will be. Actually, the presence of God surrounds you. God makes this a world in which you can earn a living, put a roof over your head, feed yourself, and enjoy life. God is responsible for that. If God were not with you now to some degree, life would be more miserable than you can possibly imagine. But imagine a time when you are completely separated from God, from whom all good comes (James 1:17)! Name anything you consider good. Then imagine being without it. Friendship? No friendship; that is from God. Love? No love; that is from God. Sex? That is God's gift. Health? Peace of mind? Self-worth? Laughter? All those things are from God. You must imagine yourself without food or clothing, just existing—apart from God. When

you begin to think in those terms "darkness" becomes a serious matter.

This is not a relic of the past, something that has to do with Israel but has nothing to do with us. This is God's Word to our generation also. Will you live without God now? Then, in a greater sense you will live without God forever. It is a choice you can make. But weigh the consequences! Jesus said, "What good is it for a man to gain the whole world [now], yet forfeit his soul?" (Mark 8:36).

The second characteristic of the Day of the Lord is *isolation*. While we have light we see one another and feel we are with one another, even though space separates us physically. We smile. Smiles are returned. In the dark, we cannot see. There are no smiles, and we feel isolated.

This is an image of what it will be like to be in eternity without God. Satan separates things. If you go in the devil's way, you will be increasingly isolated from God and other people. In *The Great Divorce* C. S. Lewis pictures hell as a city from which most of the people have withdrawn. They have moved away to the suburbs, and then away from those suburbs to other suburbs. It is because they cannot stand one another. In Lewis's book hell is increasing isolation in which people spend their time thinking about past hurts and how much they hate one another. They have nobody to talk to, nobody to converse with, nobody to understand them, nobody to sympathize with. That is what it means to be in the dark spiritually. It is to be alone without Christ.

By contrast, heaven is a place where all are increasingly drawn together. God draws people to Himself. That is why glimpses of heaven provided for us in the Bible usually show millions of people gathered around the throne of God, singing His praises: "To him who sits on the throne and to the Lamb be praise and honor and glory and power, for ever and ever!" (Rev. 5:13). Those millions will not only want to know God better, they will also want to know one another.

The third characteristic of the day of God's judgment is that it is *inescapable.* This is what Amos suggests in verse 19, in his picture of a man trying to escape a fierce lion. In the context of his prophecy, the lion is the Lion of Judah. He is the God-lion. So Amos is picturing a person who is trying to run away from God. The man runs as fast as he can, heart beating wildly, sweating profusely from his life-or-death exertion. Suddenly, as he flees down the path, he meets a bear. It is the God-bear. Trembling with fright he veers off and dashes the remaining distance to his house. Staggering inside he slams and bars the door. He is totally undone, but he mistakenly thinks that he is safe. To catch his breath he rests his hand on the wall at which point a poisonous snake, which has been lurking inside, bites him and he dies. This is not fate. One might escape fate. This is God in the day of His wrath on the ungodly. God is inescapable. No wonder Amos says, "Prepare to meet your God, O Israel" (4:12).

This is one reason why the day of God's judgment is called a "day." It is not that this event is to be begun and concluded within one twenty-four-hour period. As I read the Bible, I think that there will be a series of judgments covering what may be a considerable portion of time.[1] The Bible speaks of a "day" because God's judgment is as fixed in the calendar of events and is therefore as inescapable as any day, say the tenth of July, 1985, or the first of October, 2001.

The final characteristic of the Day of the Lord is *utter hopelessness.* Amos conveys this by asking, "Will not the day of the LORD be darkness, not light—pitch-dark, without a ray of brightness?" (v. 20). In the darkest days of the Vietnam war, when things seemed to be falling apart, it was not uncommon for government spokesmen to attempt to reassure the American people by saying

that although things were indeed dark at least we were now beginning to see the first glimmer of light at the end of the tunnel. Actually there was no light, as we now know. But the promise of some small ray of brightness was meant to be an encouragement and a reason to press on. There will be no glimmers of light in that day, says Amos. The Day of the Lord will be blacker than an ebony cat at midnight. It will be total disaster. The state of the lost will be one of utter hopelessness, as it always is for those who set themselves against God.

FLEE FROM THE WRATH TO COME

There is only one bright point in this portrait of the coming great darkness: the Day of the Lord has not come yet. As Amos writes, that day is imminent for Israel. He sees its approach so vividly that many commentators have viewed his book as being utterly pessimistic. This is not quite accurate. Certainly Amos sees the great, gathering darkness. He knows the people will never repent sufficiently as a nation to avoid the disaster. Nevertheless, there are some who may repent. There may be a remnant, and God may be merciful to them (5:15). Therefore, even in the midst of this bleak picture, Amos does not hesitate to appeal for the people's good response: "Away with the noise of your songs! I will not listen to the music of your harps. But let justice roll on like a river, righteousness like a never-failing stream!" (5:23, 24).

The day of God's judgment on the nation of Israel is now past, but our "day," the day of the final judgment, is still pending. It too is inescapable. Still there is hope for those who will turn to Christ and by Him be made into those who will worship God in spirit and truth, as Jesus said (John 4:24).

If judgment is inevitable, as Amos (and the entire Bible) says it is, then the only logical thing is to flee to the place where it has already been poured out, that is,

[1]See Boice, *The Last and Future World,* Chapter 8, pp. 114–23.

to the cross of Calvary. Only there may a guilty sinner find shelter. Augustus Toplady knew this secret and expressed it in one of the best-loved hymns in the English language, "Rock of Ages." Toplady lived in England in the 1700s and wrote this hymn in the first year of the American Revolution, 1776. He was in a field in England when suddenly a storm swept down out of the sky. He was far from a village and had no shelter, but he saw a large rock ahead of him and thought that, if he leaned against it, he might escape some of the storm's violence. When he got to the rock he saw that it had been split open. There was a crack into which he could fit. He went in and was sheltered from the storm. While waiting there, he thought of God's coming judgment and of the fact that Jesus, the Rock of Ages, was broken by God so that sinners like ourselves, who hide in Him, might be safe. Struck by this thought, he found a playing card that had been lying at his feet and wrote, "Rock of Ages, cleft for me, let me hide myself in thee."

Are you hiding in that Rock? There is no other shelter. It is only there where you can safely meet God.

24

At Ease in Zion

(Amos 6:1–14)

*Woe to you who are complacent in Zion, and to you who feel secure on Mount Samaria,
you notable men of the foremost nation, to whom the people of Israel come!*

The title for this study comes from the King James translation of Amos 6:1, which says, "Woe to them who are at ease in Zion." The New International Version says, "Woe to you who are complacent in Zion," but in either case the point is obvious. There is an ease that should not exist among God's people. If you are in that condition, this study is for you particularly.

In itself being at ease is not bad. In fact, there are verses in the Bible that invite us to rest or promise rest at the end of life's labors. Jesus said, "Come to me, all you who are weary and burdened, and I will give you rest. Take my yoke upon you and learn from me, for I am gentle and humble in heart, and you will find rest for your souls" (Matt. 11:28, 29). The Book of Hebrews speaks of Sabbath-rest: "There remains, then, a Sabbath-rest for the people of God; for anyone who enters God's rest also rests from his own work, just as God did from his. Let us, therefore, make every effort to enter that rest, so that no one will fall by following their example of disobedience" (4:9–11). In Revelation a voice from heaven says, "Blessed are the dead who die in the Lord from now on," and the Spirit answers, "They will rest from their labor, for their deeds will follow them" (14:13). Since we are told in Isaiah that "the wicked are like the tossing sea, which cannot rest" (57:20), there is clearly a desirable rest associated with godliness

that we should seek—quietness here and a cessation from labor in the life to come.

On the other hand, there is also a wrong kind of rest about which Amos is talking. It is the rest of indifference. We see the distinction in a military setting. Imagine a group of soldiers on a hot march. They have finished the day's work, and as they march into camp the command goes out: "At ease!" Then: "Dismissed!" There is nothing wrong with that rest. It is well earned. But this is a far different thing from the ease that characterized the military forces of the United States at Pearl Harbor, Hawaii, on December 7, 1941. For many that ease proved fatal.

As we study the sixth chapter of Amos we should ask ourselves if we are at ease in this bad sense. One of the previous pastors of Tenth Presbyterian Church, which I now serve, once characterized American evangelicals as "fat sheep." He meant that they had grown fat on good biblical teaching and were inclined to be lazy and inactive. One of my elders complains that many who sit under my ministry do so for "R and R," rest and relaxation. If this is true, it is a sad state for most Christians. To be sure, there are times when we need to "come apart and rest awhile"—when we have been battered by our spiritual warfare and need to regain our breath and footing. But that is no great need for most of us. If you are a Christian, there is work to be done. This is no time for ease. If you are not yet a Christian, the case is even more desperate. You are in mortal danger, and the work before you is that greatest of all works: believing on Jesus (John 6:29).

I want to ask three questions of this text. First, who are these who are complacent in Zion? Second, what is wrong with their complacency? Third, if something is wrong, what can be done about it?

SLUMBERING SOULS

During the first year of Charles Haddon Spurgeon's ministry in the new Metropolitan Tabernacle in London, this prince of Baptist preachers developed a sermon on Amos 6:1 entitled "Scourge for Slumbering Souls." He imagined them to be asleep in Zion, and he set out to wake them up. He called them by name: the presumptuous, the procrastinators, the self-indulgent, the careless, the indifferent. Spurgeon tried to make each aware of his danger.

First are the *presumptuous*, described in verse 1. They trust in "Zion" and feel secure on "Mount Samaria." This presumption is based, on the one hand, on a theological conviction and, on the other hand, on a military advantage. Let me explain. Zion is another name for Jerusalem. So when Amos speaks of being complacent in Zion he is speaking of the people of the southern kingdom who believed themselves safe simply because they were God's people and lived in Jerusalem. God's temple was in Jerusalem. So was the throne of David. These people believed that nothing could ever happen to Jerusalem, because God would preserve it at all costs. Of course, the prophets spoke against this. Jeremiah was emphatic in saying that this was a misplaced confidence. God would not preserve the city when the hearts of the people were far from Him. Still, the people would say, "God is faithful to His promises and will never let Jerusalem fall." This really meant, "We will be safe no matter what we do; we are exempt from judgment." Our equivalent would be, "We are safe because we are evangelicals."

The situation in Samaria was somewhat different. Samaria was the capital of the northern kingdom, just as Jerusalem was the capital of Judah, but it did not have any special promises of God to cling to. Instead, the Samaritans trusted in their splendid military defenses. This is why Amos speaks of *Mount* Samaria. When I visited Samaria I was struck by its natural military advantages. It is high on a hill. The hill has steep sides. The ancient town was protected by thick walls that could hardly be approached even with a battering ram due to their high elevation. The only approach was by a winding road that made its way up one side of the hill and entered the city through a set of multiple fortifications.

The people of Samaria felt secure because of these defenses, just as the people of Jerusalem felt secure because of their city's special association with the name of God. Both were foolish to think that they could trust these things while ignoring God.

Spurgeon saw the presumption of Zion and Samaria as that of trusting good works. He wrote, "He that trusts in his own works leans upon a broken reed. As well attempt to cross the storm-tossed ocean upon a child's paper boat, or mount to the heaven of God in the philosopher's balloon,—as well attempt to put out the fire of a blazing prairie by carrying in your hand a little water scooped from the neighbouring stream, as hope by any means to get rid of thine own iniquities by doing better, or of thy past sins by future holiness. I tell thee, man, thy prayers, thine alms-giving, thy fastings, thy repentings, thy church-goings, thy chapel-goings, are all as nothing in the eye of him who demands perfect obedience, and will never accept anything short of perfect righteousness from man. Away, away, away with these gaudy rags! they will be unravelled ere long; thou mayest toil at the loom night and day, but thy work shall be rent in pieces and not a shred shall be left, for thou art spinning nothing but a spider's web which Justice shall tear in pieces, and like Adam, whose fig-leaves could never cover him, thou shalt cry before God, 'I knew that I was naked, and I hid myself.' Woe, then, to those that are at ease in Zion."[1]

God challenged those who trusted in Jerusalem and Samaria to look at the cities of Calneh, Hamath, and Gath (Amos 6:2, 3)—each of which had once possessed equally strong fortifications. These cities were destroyed. God asks, "Why should I preserve you if I did not preserve them?" He might ask the presumptuous of our day, "Why should I preserve you for the sake of your supposed goodness, when so many who were better than you are in hell?"

The second who is at ease in Zion is the *procrastinator*. He is described in verse 3: "You put off the evil day and bring near a reign of terror." This person says, "I suppose that if the day of judgment is going to come, it will come. But there is nothing that can be done about it and, besides, it's far off. I'll deal with such things later." The sad truth is that such people do *not* deal with spiritual matters later. They do as they have done today. Barring a miracle, the miracle of God's grace in the new birth, they will do the day after tomorrow as they will do tomorrow and so on until that last and dreadful day, when they perish in their sins. They are like the Roman governor Felix to whom Paul preached. Felix was moved by Paul's discourse, but he was not ready to change and so put off that one decision through which God would have saved his soul. He said, "That's enough for now! You may leave. When I find it convenient, I will send for you" (Acts 24:25).There is no record that he ever did. Presumably Felix died without

Christ and without hope, as so many procrastinators do today. If you have been putting things off, now is the time to turn to Jesus.

And do not forget that judgment may not be as far off as you think! The Lord told of a certain rich man who spent his time amassing wealth. He had so many crops he hardly knew what to do with them. So he said, "I will tear down my barns and build bigger ones, and there I will store all my grain and my goods. And I'll say to myself, 'You have plenty of good things laid up for many years. Take life easy; eat, drink and be merry.'"

God said to him, "You fool! This very night your life will be demanded from you. Then who will get what you have prepared for yourself?" (Luke 12:18–20).

The story of the rich fool leads next to those who are at ease spiritually: the *self-indulgent*. Such are described in verse 4: "You lie on beds inlaid with ivory and lounge on your couches. You dine on choice lambs and fattened calves." The fault described in these verses is not mere wealth. It is no more a sin to lie down on an ivory (or brass) bed than a canvas cot, or eat lamb (if you can afford it) rather than grits. Money in itself is not evil. It can be used in God's service like anything else. Still we who have means cannot get off the hook as easily as that, for the point of these verses is that wealth tends to make us self-indulgent—"After all, I earned it, and I have a right to spend it on myself if I want to"—and indifferent to others. As a general rule we can say that the more we have the less generous we become. More cash, more dash! More substance, more indulgence!

We demonstrate this truth as a nation. The United States is the richest nation in the world. But in terms of the percentage of our Gross National Product (GNP) given for foreign aid the United States ranks fifth from the bottom among

---

[1]Charles Haddon Spurgeon, "Scourge for Slumbering Souls" in *The Metropolitan Tabernacle Pulpit*, Vol. 7, 1861 (Pasadena, Tex.: Pilgrim Publications, 1973), p. 554.

the major western nations—behind Sweden, the Netherlands, Norway, Denmark, France, Belgium, Canada, New Zealand, Britain, Germany, and Japan. In this list only Finland, Austria, Switzerland and Italy are stingier than we are.[2]

It is true that the United States did display great national generosity at the end of World War II. At the height of the Marshall Plan (begun in 1947 to rebuild war-ravished Europe) America gave almost three percent of its GNP annually. But as the United States prospered in the post-war years, giving plummeted radically until by 1975 that former three percent had become a mere 0.24 percent. In those twenty-eight years (between 1947 and 1975) our GNP doubled. We were twice as rich by 1975 as at the end of the war. But we gave only 1/11 as much of our substance. Moreover, what we did with even that reduced amount is startling. In 1975 we gave $3.67 billion in foreign aid. But more than half of that was for military assistance! Only $1.5 billion was for economic development. And while we are speaking of the military, we should note that the United States spends $246 million each day for current military purposes—more than the entire annual budget of the United Nations World Food Program. In sixteen hours the United States spends more on arms than the World Health Organization and the Food and Agricultural Organization spend in an entire year.[3]

Let me make my own position clear. I am not advocating a reduction in military spending. In a world like ours strong defense is necessary for peace, and even a weakened United States (such as we now are) is a strong deterrent to aggression. Our strength is the strength of other millions. However, I am saying that our military spending is far out of proportion to charitable giving, and that more, much

more would be accomplished by an increase in the latter than in the former. In any case, we are not generous, as we claim to be, and the richer we become the more self-indulgence grows. Even Samaria could not have equaled our own self-indulgence.

The last of those who are at ease in Zion are portrayed in verses 5 and 6: the *careless* and *indifferent*. Careless "strums away" on his harp, like David, and improvises on musical instruments. He "drinks wine" by the bowlful and uses the "finest lotions." Indifferent "does not grieve over the ruin of Joseph." What is wrong with this first group? Certainly it is not their music, instruments, drink, or lotions. David was the great musician of Israel and is praised for it. The problem is not here. It is rather that by giving themselves wholly to these fine but far from necessary things, such people are oblivious to the truly necessary elements of life. They do not have thoughts for their soul. So they will drift into hell strumming and humming the worthless songs of our culture. Their easy-going manner, knowledge of the best wines, and beautiful skin will not save them.

What is wrong with the indifferent? Their sin is that they do not grieve for Joseph. Joseph is another one of those many names of the patriarchs used for Israel as a whole; it means the descendants of Joseph. The people do not care about the declining state of those around them.

The Pride of Jacob

At the beginning of this study we asked three questions: Who are the ones complacent in Zion? What is wrong with them? And if something is wrong, what can be done about it? In answering the first question we have already begun to see answers to the second, but the answer Amos gives is different and more

---

[2]Chart of "Estimated Official Development Assistance from Industrialized Countries as a Percentage of GNP in 1975" (World Bank figures). Cited by Sider, *Rich Christians*, pp. 50, 51.

[3]Sider, *Rich Christians*, pp. 50, 52.

profound than anything we have said thus far. He says that the main thing wrong with the presumptuous, procrastinating, self-indulgent, careless, and indifferent people of his day (and ours) is *pride*. These would be astounded to be told that they are proud. But they are, and this is the root cause of their failings.

We passed over this theme in detailing the nature of those who are at ease in Zion, but it was at the beginning of the chapter. There Amos pronounced woe, not merely on those who are complacent, but also, as he spells it out, on those who were the "notable men of the foremost nation." The phrase is ironic. The leaders were not "notable," save in their vices. The nation was not "foremost," except that it would be the "first" to go into exile (v. 7). This is the way these leaders thought about themselves. They were presumptuous, lazy, self-indulgent, careless, and indifferent, but they were proud to be that way! They really thought they were somebody. And if it was the case that they were enjoying life more than others, it was not (so they believed) because they had taken advantage of these other people or pursued personal success rather than God and His righteousness. It was because they were better than other people. They prospered because they deserved it and others did not.

How dangerous such a devilish outlook is! We now read, "The Sovereign LORD has sworn by himself—the LORD God Almighty declares:

'I abhor the pride of Jacob
    and detest his fortresses;
I will deliver up the city
    and everything in it'" (v. 8).

Suppose you are a Christian who is at ease in Zion. What follows from the pride that has made you complacent? The first thing is that you become *insensitive* to the needs of others. You are at ease; others are not. You are rich; others are poor. Your needs are met; others lack many of life's necessities. If you would, you could help many out of your resources. But you are not willing to do that because you think *you* deserve everything you have. They deserve nothing.

The second thing that happens is that you become *irresponsible*, not only in regard to the needy but also where your own family, neighbors, church, city, or government is concerned. There is work to be done, much work. Work never ceases. But you have opted out because it is much easier to enjoy your abundance, isolated from the very real problems around you, than to sacrifice your ease for the good of others. I live in a city where there is much to be done: evangelism, social work, visiting, counseling—practically any good thing in any area of the city's life. There are tens of thousands of Christians. But I would suppose that in most cases thousands of these never do anything exceptionally good. They are not even responsible citizens, let alone compassionate ambassadors for Jesus Christ. When problems are not dealt with, when responsible and able people withdraw, evil enters in and affects everyone, good and bad alike. Moreover, it accumulates with the passing of time. The irresponsibility is not only to this present generation but to our children and their children.

Third, the situation is dangerous, and you become *oblivious* to the danger. An old expression says, "Idle hands do the devil's work." It is in periods of idleness that we get into trouble. That happened to one person who was literally at ease in Zion: King David. It was in the time of the year when the armies went out to war. David should have been out with the troops, but he sent Joab while he remained in Jerusalem—at ease. We are told that one day he was walking around on the roof of his palace and saw a woman bathing on a roof nearby. She was beautiful. Her name was Bathsheba. David sent for her and began an adulterous relationship, she being another man's wife.

Thus began the worst period in the long life of King David.

Are you a Christian who falls into this category? Are you at ease in Zion? Have you said to yourself, "I've done my bit for God and the church. It's time to quit now. There are younger people who can do the work. Let them do it. I don't have to do anything"? If you are saying that, you are on the road to great trouble. Let me say that I do not intend to disparage your past service. It may have been great. It may be greater than I or anyone else now living will ever do. But no matter how great it was, the attitude I have just described is still dangerous. It comes from pride—"I've done everything that could ever be expected of me; I can rest on my laurels"—and it issues in an insensitive spirit, an irresponsible attitude and an oblivious stance precisely where danger most threatens.

Wake up from such lethargy! Look about you! See the work that most needs to be done and get on with it! It is in such work that you will be most like the Lord Jesus Christ, your master, who "humbled himself and became obedient to death—even death on a cross!" (Phil. 2:8). It is only people like that whom God honors.

Earlier I said that I was applying these truths to Christians. But suppose you are not a Christian. Suppose you have rejected the One who died for your salvation. What shall we say of you? If the plight of the Christian is dangerous, what of your danger? If the Christian is irresponsible, are not you even more so? If he is insensitive, you are doubly insensitive, for you are insensitive not only to the needs of other people but also to your own. Jesus was talking about you when He said, "What good is it for a man to gain the whole world, yet forfeit his soul?" (Mark 8:36). He meant that a person who has accumulated things but neglected his relationship to God is a fool because he has made a bad bargain. Wake up and turn to Jesus! To be at ease in Zion when your eternal destiny is not settled is the most foolish of all life's follies, and the end is the greatest of tragedies.

WHAT CAN BE DONE?

My last question is simply: If something is wrong, as it is, what can be done about it? As in the case of question 2, I have already begun to answer it.

First, you can awaken to your danger. This is the point of the entire Book of Amos after all, a point that becomes clear even in the verses that end this sixth chapter. The verses speak of judgment, and their purpose is to wake people up. They begin to ask questions again, as Amos does throughout and did quite pointedly in chapter 3. Here he asks,

Do horses run on the rocky crags?
   Does one plow there with oxen? (v. 12).

He is saying, "You do not operate irrationally when you go out riding or when you set out to plow the fields to plant grain. You're not foolish then. Why be foolish now? Wake up to the fact that sin brings judgment and that prosperity is not your attainment but is rather the blessing of the Lord."

Second, you can turn from sin, perhaps even from some of those riches that have a hold on you. Even more, you *must* turn from sin, for God commands it. It is not the preacher who calls for justice. It is God. It is not the preacher who calls for the doing of righteousness on the earth. It is God. Is there sin in your life? If so, it is holding you back. It is making you complacent. Turn away from it. God will help you. Know that you cannot sin and serve God simultaneously.

Third, you can get busy. There is much to be done, and if you are engaged in this work you will at least be short of time for sinning. Read the Bible. Help a friend. Start a class. By all means, do something of spiritual good for someone.

Finally, you can imitate others who are already laboring. As I made the previous point you may have been thinking, "Yes, I would love to do one of those things, but I just don't know how." You may be right. But there are people who do know how and are working at doing what they know to do. Get next to them and learn from them. Here is a deacon. He has labored in the church for many years. He has visited hundreds, even thousands of people in their homes and has prayed with them often. Ask if you can go with him the next time he visits. He will be glad to have you, and you will profit more from that association than from a year in seminary. Here is a Sunday school teacher. She has taught for many years.

Get next to her, perhaps as a helper at first. Find out how she teaches, what she does for preparation, how she gets involved with her pupils personally. Imitate those things at her direction. You will learn more from her than in a graduate school of education. Here is an elder. Get to know him. Find out what he does. The apostle Paul was an elder and he said, "Follow my example, as I follow the example of Christ" (1 Cor. 11:1).

This study has no end—at least no end that I am providing. It is open-ended, because you must provide it by your personal response to Jesus Christ.

25

Five Visions

(Amos 7:1–9; 8:1–9:10)

This is what he showed me: The Lord was standing by a wall that had been built true to plumb, with a plumb line in his hand. And the LORD asked me, "What do you see, Amos?"

"A plumb line," I replied.

Then the Lord said, "Look, I am setting a plumb line among my people Israel; I will spare them no longer. "The high places of Isaac will be destroyed and the sanctuaries of Israel will be ruined; with my sword I will rise against the house of Jeroboam."

It is hard to tell how many sermons have been put together to form the Book of Amos. It is possible that nothing in Amos was preached exactly as we have it. Still we can see where various sermons might begin or end. Chapters 1 and 2 are an obvious unit. Amos could have begun with such a message on first entering Israel from Judah to preach at Bethel. Chapters 3 through 6 could go together; they could also be shortened forms of several sermons. A new section seems to begin with chapter 7.

The thing that holds the last part of the book together, beginning with chapter 7, is a description of five visions having to do with judgment. Three of these are found in chapter 7: swarms of locusts (vv. 1–3), a fire (vv. 4–6) and a plumb line (vv. 7–9). One is in chapter 8 (vv. 1, 2), and a final one, a vision of the Lord standing by the altar, is found in chapter 9 (vv. 1–4). It is a fitting end to the prophecy, for, having warned in the opening section that judgment was coming and having explained the reasons for it as the book goes on, Amos now displays the symbols of the judgment and makes his last appeal for the spiritually alive to flee from it. The inevitability of judgment comes through strongly here, for it is based on the unchanging character of God. We think it would be nice if we could change Him—if we could get Him to be less holy, less upright, more indulgent. But we cannot change Him. God is who He is. Consequently, we must come to terms with Him rather than He with us. These visions teach us to do that while there is yet time.

GOD'S PLUMB LINE

It has been argued by some that there is not a shred of hope in Amos. They discount the last verses (9:11–15) as being attached by an editor and view everything else as a message of utter judgment. That view is faulty, as we have already seen. It also fails to fit the meaning of the first three visions. These three visions belong together because they show a progression from what God says He is not going to do to what He will do. They show that He will not destroy Israel utterly, that is, the righteous along with the unrighteous, but that He will rigorously measure all by His own perfect standard.

The first vision reminds us of Joel, because it is a vision of locusts, and an actual locust invasion was the occasion of Joel's prophecy. Amos says that he saw God preparing the locust swarm. It was to come after the king's harvest but at the time of the second, more important one. The first harvest was apparently a form of taxation. It came early in the growing season. The second came at the end of the season and was the one at which food was gathered in for the winter. A destruction of this crop was serious, because if you missed the earlier one there was always the second to fall back on. But if you missed the second harvest, there would be nothing to eat. By speaking of this detail Amos strengthens a picture of what would in any case be a terrible and devastating judgment.

Amos tells us that he pleaded with the Lord against this judgment: "Sovereign LORD, forgive! How can Jacob survive? He is so small" (v. 2). The basis for Amos' appeal is that the locusts would destroy the kingdom completely, and God says that the locust plague—perhaps symbolic of an actual, totally destructive invasion—would not take place.

The second vision is of fire, the fire of judgment. This is more clearly symbolic, for it is described as drying up the great deep and devouring the land (v. 4), which literal fire would not do. It symbolizes a judgment on Israel that would leave nothing in its wake. Amos objects as he did the first time: "Sovereign LORD, I beg you, stop! How can Jacob survive? He is so small!" (v. 5). God replies that this totally destructive judgment will not take place either.

It is quite possible, as we look back on the history of Israel in these closing years of its existence, that the locusts and fire refer to actual invasions from the east that were turned back. Certainly there were several of these. If that is the case, then God is saying that He has often turned back the judgment that was due Israel (and is often due us) for sin. What we experience in life as the result of God's judgments is always far less than we ac-

tually deserve. This does not mean that God is unjust. Every sin will eventually be punished, either in Christ or in the person of the sinner himself. But it does mean that God is merciful and that He customarily withholds judgment, giving only warnings of it for long periods, in order that the wicked might have time to repent. This is a theme that we have seen several times previously and which we can easily apply to our own country. Have we been going through times of difficulty? Are there shortages, natural disasters, inflation? These things are warnings from God, and God's people especially should be in the vanguard of those who repent of their sins, humble themselves, seek the Lord and pray so that He will repent of even greater disasters and heal our land.

The third vision is of the Lord standing by a wall that had been built true to plumb, with a plumb line in His hand. A plumb line is a string with a weight on the end. When the string is held up the weight is pulled directly down by gravity, and the result is a true vertical. When God is pictured as standing by the wall with a plumb line in His hand this is a way of saying that He is about to check Israel to see if the nation is as upright as it claims to be. The vision says that the wall, which represents Israel, had been built true to plumb. That is, it had started out correctly. God had graciously called a people to Himself and had given them the law to govern their religious and political lives. In those early days they were what they should be. They could have passed the test. But will they pass it now? We know the answer if we have understood the book. There is not a chance that they will pass it. They have deviated from God's norm, inclined to disobedience, and then tumbled into sin entirely.

There are two particular candidates for rejection (v. 9). One is the corrupt national religion—"the high places . . . and the sanctuaries of Israel." The other is the government—"the house of Jeroboam." Both are measured by the plumb line of God and are found wanting.

Motyer writes, *"The high places and the sanctuaries . . . were places where grace was abused and law was neglected. Grace was abused first of all in its nature. The grace of God in the Mosaic tradition was God's freely given love reaching out to draw sinners to himself. It was spiritual throughout: in its origin in God and in its benefits among men. But at the shrines the grace sought was the benefit of worldly prosperity through fertility in the land, in the stock and in the family. Grace was abused, secondly, in its appropriation, for in Scripture grace is bestowed in answer to prayer, but in the sanctuaries the blessing of God was sought by means of ritual fornication—the human fertility act being used as a visual aid to prompt the god to perform his parallel function for the world. Is it any wonder that this abuse of grace fell before the plumb-line? Furthermore, as we have seen, there was nothing more to the shrines than this, no pressure for a reformed life, no voice of the law of God calling to obedience. The shrines therefore were judged by the plumb-line and were found inadequate: they abused grace and forgot law.*

"The second candidate for rejection was the house of Jeroboam. . . . This politically able king—the first to be named after the founding king of the schismatic northern kingdom and the last king to achieve anything like affluence and stability for his kingdom—receives scant attention in the narrative of the book of Kings, but it is recorded that he did what was evil in the sight of the Lord; he did not depart from all the sins of Jeroboam the son of Nebat, which he made Israel to sin (2 Kings 14:24). Now the sin of Jeroboam the son of Nebat—dealing with the matter broadly and not at all in detail—was basically the sin of disobedience to the law

of the Lord. His kingdom was given to him upon moral conditions: *If you will hearken to all that I command you, and will walk in my ways, and do what is right in my eyes by keeping my statutes and my commandments . . . I will be with you, and will build you a sure house . . .* (1 Kings 11:38). But Jeroboam did no such thing. Indeed his first major act was to disobey Yahweh in the matter of the shrines at Bethel and Dan and in the setting up of golden calves. Jeroboam, therefore, is the man who rejected the law of the Lord and proceeded to corrupt the grace of the Lord also."[1]

It is because of these truths that the incident regarding Amaziah the priest (considered earlier) is brought in. In this incident the corruption of the state religion and government and their collusion are dramatized, and the judgment on both, revealed to Amos in the vision of the plumb line, is given a particular expression where the priest is concerned. "Therefore this is what the LORD says: 'Your wife will become a prostitute in the city, and your sons and daughters will fall by the sword. Your land will be measured and divided up, and you yourself will die in a pagan country. And Israel will certainly go into exile, away from their native land'" (v. 17).

IS THIS AN IMPROVEMENT?

We said earlier, when we introduced the three visions of chapter 7, that they show a progression from what God says He is not going to do to what He will do. That is, they show that He will not destroy Israel utterly, the righteous along with the unrighteous, but that He will rigorously measure all by His own perfect standard. On the surface this seems to be an improvement, and perhaps even Amos felt so because he did not protest this vision as he had the first two. What objection could he have to God's testing of His people? In such a testing the Judge

---

[1]Motyer, *The Day of the Lion*, pp. 165, 166.

of all the earth will certainly do right.

But is it an improvement? It is if a person can measure up to God's standard, if his or her life is as upright as the divine plumb line. But if that is not the case, it is no improvement at all. The one whose life is not upright will be condemned by God's standard and judgment will come, as the visions that follow in chapters 8 and 9 make clear.

The difficulty here is that we do not think as God thinks and therefore constantly measure ourselves by other human standards rather than by God's standard of perfection. Imagine a class of children who are about to receive an art lesson from one of their teachers. The first step in their lesson is to draw a straight line on the left side of their sheet of paper. But before the teacher can tell them how she wants them to do it the principal stops by and calls her out of the room. She is gone about ten minutes. While she is gone the children continue with what she has told them to do. They all draw lines. Doing that would not take long, of course. So they finish and then wonder what they should do next. They decide to compare their lines to see who drew the straightest one. Johnny says to Philip, who is sitting next to him, "My line is straighter than your line."

"No, it isn't," Philip says.

They get a group of girls to come over and settle the argument, and they eventually agree that Philip's line is straightest. "But," says Mary, "my line is straighter than either of your lines."

"Is it?" asks Philip. They all look at Mary's paper and, sure enough, her line is the straightest of all. This gets the children going, and pretty soon they have made comparisons all the way around and can tell in what order all the papers should come. Robert has the worst line; he was never very good at art anyway. The girls have the best. Mary's is the best of all. But at this point the teacher comes back to the room and says that she did not want a freely drawn line but one

drawn with a ruler. She then goes around to each child's desk and draws the ruler line on each paper, next to the hand-drawn one. Now every hand-drawn line, even Mary's, looks very crooked indeed.

This is the effect of having our lives evaluated by God's plumb line. Before God steps in, the lines we have been drawing by the making of many small ethical decisions seem fairly straight. When we compare them with other people they seem even better because we naturally tend to compare them with those who do worse than we do. We rate ourselves highly. But then God steps in, and we all look crooked.

That is the trouble with appealing to God's justice. Many think that all they want from God is justice. They say, "God, it isn't right for You to judge us with Your locusts and fire. Some of us are better than others, and we demand that You take those differences into account."

So God says, "All right, we'll see who really measures up to being good." He sends His plumb line: Jesus Christ. He says, "This is what's good. Who measures up to that?" No one does, of course. We are condemned. Learn this great lesson: an appeal to justice will save no one. All will be condemned by God's justice. But if you will forget your pride, abandon such arrogance and instead ask, not for justice, but for mercy, you will find that the same Christ by whom our corruption is revealed is also the Christ who died on Calvary that our sin might be covered and we might receive a new life.

RIPE FOR JUDGMENT

Each year at harvest time the people of Israel kept the feast of booths at which token offerings of the abundance of the land were brought thankfully to God. The feast was joyful because the blessing of the harvest, in which the fruit of the land had become ripe, was a promise of future years' prosperity. It is likely that this festival lay behind the fourth of

Amos' visions: a basket of ripe fruit (8:1, 2). Ripe fruit! What could be more luscious or more delightful? Yet God says that the basket is the nation of Israel and that they are indeed ripe—for judgment. "The time is ripe for my people Israel; I will spare them no longer."

Unlike the earlier visions, this point is made in a double way in regard to the basket of ripe fruit. The ripeness is one way of forecasting judgment. The other is a pun on the Hebrew words for "summer fruit" (*qayis*) and "end" (*qēs*). These sound alike. So when Amos replies to the Lord that he sees a basket of ripe *qayis*, God replied, "*Qēs!*" An end is come upon Israel.

This is something that Oswald Spengler, the German historian, would revel in. In his well-known and widely acclaimed attempt to write a universal history of humanity, *The Decline of the West*,[2] Spengler makes use of biological or nature cycles to trace how cultures are born, grow strong, deteriorate, and die. He used this pattern to explode the myth of universal and inevitable progress in history and to predict the eventual decline of western civilization—hence, the title of his work. Spengler would enjoy the image of ripe fruit, as I said. He would say that this is exactly the point to which, like Israel, western civilization has come. The problem with Spengler's thinking is that his prediction of the west's decline is based on a kind of naturalism foreign to the Bible's world view. Spengler would call birth, growth, decline, and death natural and inevitable. By contrast, the Bible traces decline and death to sin and maintains that it is not at all natural or inevitable but is brought on rather by the hard and impenitent hearts of a perverse and sinful people.

Would Amaziah, Jeroboam, or any other leader in Israel plead for justice at this point? If so, Amos will bring in the plumb line from vision 3. What about their treatment of the poor? What about their marketing practices? What about the justice meted out in their courts? In each of these areas they are found wanting:

> Hear this, you who trample the needy
> and do away with the poor of the land,

saying

> "When will the New Moon be over
> that we may sell grain,
> and the Sabbath be ended
> that we may market wheat?"—
> skimping the measure,
> boosting the price
> and cheating with dishonest scales,
> buying the poor with silver
> and the needy for a pair of sandals,
> selling even the sweepings with the wheat.

The LORD has sworn by the Pride of Jacob: "I will never forget anything they have done" (8:4–7).

I fear for America when I read that, for if Israel's sins were great, are not ours even greater? Verse 5 describes much of our business practices when it speaks of "skimping the measure, boosting the price and cheating with dishonest scales." I do not know about the last phrase ("cheating with dishonest scales"), though there are probably some who do that. But the first two ("skimping the measure" and "boosting the price") are a classic description of an inflationary economy: less for more. Ask the housewives about the clothing we buy. The material is less substantial, the hems barely turned under, the seams barely held together. Decorations fall off. Yet the price is higher. Cars cost more and fall apart sooner. City services, such as public transportation, cost more, yet the quality is less. And whom does it hurt? Not the well-to-do. They simply vote themselves higher salaries and pay the higher costs. It is the poor who suffer, those who are old and on fixed incomes.

---

[2]Oswald Spengler, *The Decline of the West*, 2 vols., trans. by Charles Francis Atkinson (New York: Alfred A. Knopf, 1926, 1928).

Don't we "trample the needy and do away with the poor of the land"?

And how about the first part of verse 5? It describes how the merchants of Israel could hardly wait until the feast days and the sabbaths were over so they could start selling again. Their fault was one of attitude. But we have them beat cold. We have learned that we do not even have to wait until the feasts and sabbaths are over. We use every day to do business, Sundays included. What do you suppose God thinks of that? He does not like it, and He will not forget what we have done. "I will never forget anything they have done," He says (v. 7).

I think that is frightening too. You and I forget things, especially the wrong we have done. In some ways it is good we do, because we would be unable to function in this life if we remembered all our faults all the time. We have to forget some of the past to get on with life. But God does not forget. He remembers everything, and one day we must answer for the wrongs we have done.

At the end of the chapter God's judgment on the kingdom of Israel is spelled out again. It is in three parts: 1) a general description of death, destruction, and mourning throughout the land, reminiscent of the description of the Day of the Lord in chapter 5; 2) a subsequent time of famine so far as hearing the words of God is concerned; and 3) a prediction of the death of even the young men and fair women. The second section is most interesting:

"The days are coming," declares the Sovereign LORD,
"when I will send a famine through the land—
not a famine of food or a thirst for water,
but a famine of hearing the words of the LORD.
Men will stagger from sea to sea
and wander from north to east,
searching for the word of the LORD,
but they will not find it" (vv. 11, 12).

We know that this happened in Israel,

as the age of the two kingdoms closed and the four hundred silent years before the coming of the Lord Jesus Christ set in. In those centuries no prophets appeared; the word of God ceased. It was a dreadful thing. Fortunately, we are not in that state today. We have no new revelation, but the revelation we do have—given by God in the Bible for the church throughout its entire history until the coming again of Jesus Christ—is widely proclaimed. The problem in our day is not a famine of the words of God but that so many do not value this, the greatest treasure anyone can ever possess.

Today in America (and in many other parts of the world) a person can turn on a radio at almost any time of the day or night and hear faithful gospel preaching. It is not always profound. It is sometimes colored with cultural peculiarities. But it is usually sound, and much of it is very good. In America a person can go to practically any hamlet, town, or city and there find a body of believers who meet regularly to worship God. We have Christian books, Christian schools, Christian films, Christian seminars. The problem is not the lack of these things. It is the attitude of millions who simply have no time for God's Scriptures.

Do we have time for God's Word? Do we study it as God's great gift to us in this age of His grace? Our attitude should be that of John Wesley, who wrote: "I am a creature of a day, passing through life as an arrow through the air. I am a spirit come from God, and returning to God. Just hovering over the great gulf; till, a few moments hence, I am no more seen; I drop into an unchangeable eternity! I want to know one thing—the way to heaven; how to land safe on that happy shore. God himself has condescended to teach the way: For this very end he came from heaven. He hath written it down in a book. O give me that book! At any price, give me the book of God! I have it: Here is knowledge enough for me. . . . I sit down alone. Only God is here. In his presence I open, I read his book; for this end, to find the way to heaven. Is there a doubt concerning the meaning of what I read? Does anything appear dark or intricate? I lift up my heart to the Father of Lights:—'Lord, is it not in thy word, "If any man lack wisdom, let him ask of God"? Thou "givest liberally, and upbraidest not." Thou hast said, "If any be willing to do thy will, he shall know." I am willing to do, let me know, thy will.' I then search after and consider parallel passages of Scripture, 'comparing spiritual things with spiritual.' I meditate thereon with all the attention and earnestness of which my mind is capable. If any doubt still remains, I consult those who are experienced in the things of God; and then the writings whereby, being dead, they yet speak. And what I thus learn, that I teach."[3]

James I. Packer says even more precisely, "Let us, then, take our Bibles afresh and resolve by God's grace henceforth to make full use of them. Let us read them with reverence and humility, seeking the illumination of the Holy Spirit. Let us meditate on them till our sight is clear and our souls are fed. Let us live in obedience to God's will as we find it revealed to us in Scripture; and the Bible will prove itself both a lamp to our feet and a light upon our path."[4]

LORD OF THE ALTAR

The last of Amos's five visions occurs in chapter 9. It is the most unsettling of all. It is a vision of the Lord standing by an altar, speaking words of judgment. So far as the other words in Amos go, these are the most comprehensive and most devastating. God describes Himself as the Sovereign Lord, who builds up and tears down. He says that the Israelites are to be judged as the pagans, so far as He is concerned. They are no different from the people of Cush (v. 7). They are to be judged utterly. No one will escape. They will be like grain shaken in a sieve, but "not a kernel will fall to the ground" (v. 9). Everyone will die. No matter where they run to hide, from there the hand of God will take them. He has set His eyes on them "for evil and not for good" (v. 4).

These words are so terrible that one tends to pass over the image of God standing by the altar, which introduces them. But when carefully considered the image is even more terrible than the words. What is the point of the altar? The altar is the place where sacrifices are made for sin, where God through the sacrifice is reconciled to the repentant worshiper. It is a place of mercy, an emblem of God's great love. But what do we have in this vision? This is not a scene of mercy. On the contrary, it is a scene of judgment as the Christ of judgment stands on the altar to strike even the church. In the day of this judgment grace is ended, for the Lord of grace has become the Judge of those who have spurned salvation.

It is still the day of grace for us, but that day will end, and the time will come when we will see Christ by the altar. How will you meet Him in that day? He will be your Judge or Savior, and you will meet Him either as one of His redeemed people or as one of the condemned. If you are not in Christ, you are condemned already (John 3:18). Flee to Him now, while there is yet hope.

---

[3]John Wesley, *The Works* (Grand Rapids: Zondervan, from the authorized edition of 1872), vol. 5, pp. 3, 4.

[4]James I. Packer, *Beyond the Battle for the Bible* (Westchester, Ill.: Cornerstone Books, 1980), p. 104.

26

Days of Fruit and Wine

(Amos 9:11–15)

"In that day I will restore David's fallen tent. I will repair its broken places, restore its ruins, and build it as it used to be, so that they may possess the remnant of Edom and all the nations that bear my name," declares the Lord, *who will do these things. "The days are coming," declares the* Lord, *"when the reaper will be overtaken by the plowman and the planter by the one treading grapes. New wine will drip from the mountains and flow from all the hills. I will bring back my exiled people Israel; they will rebuild the ruined cities and live in them. They will plant vineyards and drink their wine; they will make gardens and eat their fruit. I will plant Israel in their own land, never again to be uprooted from the land I have given them," says the* Lord *your God.*

At least four times in the early chapters of Amos the phrase "in (or on) that day" occurs of God's judgment, the theme of the book (2:16; 8:3, 9, 13). This phrase appears again now but in a totally unexpected way. It refers, not to the coming day of judgment, but to a new day of God's blessing.

This should interest many people, because dreams of a Golden Age have often intrigued philosophers, statesmen, poets, and people in general. Plato wrote of such an age in his *Republic.* The Roman poet Virgil popularized an ideal age in his *Fourth Eclogue.* In more recent times Thomas More, Samuel Butler, and Edward Bellamy wrote of a utopia. Others, such as Henry David Thoreau, Robert Owen, and Leo Tolstoi, not only wrote about it but actually tried to create one. In our century communists speak of utopia as a classless state. Capitalists think of such an age in terms of material prosperity brought on by capitalism. The difficulty with each of these visions is that men and women seem unable to

achieve it. They dream of what a Golden Age should be. They draft plans for how their dreams might be achieved. But they always fail. History teaches that such plans are inevitably followed by disillusionment. In fact, the lesson of history might well be that if such an age is ever to be established, it must be God who establishes it.

This is exactly what the Bible teaches, and the verses that end Amos are an example. This has been a book about judgment, so unrelenting in its disclosure of the people's sin and God's rising wrath that many commentators view words of hope of future blessing as out of place.[1] Yet this is a prophetic pattern, and it is not quite the case that hope has been entirely lacking previously, as we have seen in the earlier exposition. The prophecy is of judgment. But Amos, like so many other Old Testament writers, seems unable to let the matter rest there. Judgment will come. He is certain of that. But beyond judgment will be a day of blessing in which the house of David will be

---

[1]See for example, Mays, *Amos: A Commentary.* "This promise of salvation is hardly a saying of Amos" (p. 165).

restored, security will be established, and great material and physical blessing will come to the land.

BLESSING FOR ISRAEL

These verses say several important things about the coming Golden Age. First, it will be a time of *blessing for Israel* particularly. Students of the Bible take such prophecies in different and sometimes mutually exclusive senses. But if they are to be taken literally, as we should take them unless there is a specific and overriding reason for taking them figuratively, then they obviously refer to a time of national blessing for Israel. God says that He "will restore David's fallen tent . . . repair its broken places, restore its ruins, and build it as it used to be, so that they may possess the remnant of Edom and all the nations that bear my name" (vv. 11, 12).

Second, this is to be a time of great *material prosperity*. "The days are coming . . . when the reaper will be overtaken by the plowman and the planter by the one treading grapes. New wine will drip from the mountains and flow from all the hills. I will bring back my exiled people Israel; they will rebuild the ruined cities and live in them. They will plant vineyards and drink their wine; they will make gardens and eat their fruit" (vv. 13, 14). The blessing of these days may be supernatural. Certain sentences of this description sound supernatural—the reaper overtaking the plowman, for example. The blessing may be natural, this being merely poetic language for a time of abundance. Whatever the case, the blessing is material. It is not right to view these promises as essentially spiritual in nature.

Third, the passage teaches that the blessings to come, unlike the many past blessings, will be *permanent*. That is, they will not be followed by a falling away on Israel's part and a consequent judgment or series of judgments by God. The blessings will continue forever or at least by

a transformation of that time into the time of eternity. This is what the last verse teaches: "I will plant Israel in their own land, never again to be uprooted from the land I have given them" (v. 15).

I said that verses like these have been taken in different senses by Bible scholars, and I want to return to this problem now because it bears on the doctrine of the last things, which these verses introduce. One interpretation—which differs from my own—is that these prophecies have already been fulfilled for Israel in the regathering of the people following the Babylonian captivity; thus, we need not apply them to any future age. I do not think this is right, as I hope to make clear. But it is not an interpretation to be taken lightly. Several years ago I published some material on prophecy in which I referred to the promises of land made to Abraham in Genesis 15:18–21 ("On that day the LORD made a covenant with Abram and said, 'To your descendants I give this land, from the river of Egypt to the great river, the Euphrates— the land of the Kenites, Kenizzites, Kadmonites, Hittites, Perizzites, Rephaites, Amorites, Canaanites, Girgashites and Jebusites'"). I argued that one of the reasons why I believe in a literal Golden Age, a millennium, is that this promise of God to Abraham has never yet been fully fulfilled. The Jews have possessed some of that land, but not all of it. After I had published this opinion one gentleman from central Pennsylvania wrote me to say that the promise to Abraham had been fulfilled and that 1 Kings 4:21–25 shows this to be the case: "Solomon ruled over all the kingdoms from the River to the land of the Philistines, as far as the border of Egypt. . . . He ruled over all the kingdoms west of the River, from Tiphsah to Gaza, and had peace on all sides." Those verses refer to a wide expanse of land and might well be taken as a fulfillment of God's original promise of a land to Abraham.

But is it the case that the blessing under

Solomon fully fulfills the earlier promise? In my opinion, it is not. It is true that under Solomon the Jews controlled land from the borders of Egypt to the Euphrates. But even that vast area is less than the territory described as the land of the Kenites, Kenizzites, Kadmonites, Hittites, Perizzites, Rephaites, Amorites, Canaanites, Girgashites, and Jebusites. The Hittites, for example, occupied the central area of what is today modern Turkey. Moreover, even though Solomon controlled the land between the Euphrates and Egypt, he did not actually possess it. He was merely a powerful king who held these other lands in tribute. These were not the Jews' lands.

There is this difficulty too. Amos, whose words we are studying, wrote after the days of great national blessing under Solomon. Yet he is not looking backward to those past days. He is looking forward to a day of future prosperity which, so we must understand, will surpass the former blessing. That day came either in the reestablishment of the Jews in Palestine under Nehemiah, Ezra, and their successors (which was hardly a time of abundant blessing), or it is yet to come. In my view, the only possible position is the last one.

The second objection is that the prophecies were not fulfilled in regard to Israel and should not be expected to be fulfilled there for the reason that they are fulfilled spiritually in and for the church. The argument goes like this. The people of God in the Old Testament era were Jews. In the present era the church is the community of God's people. This is an improvement since the church enjoys fully what was only previously enjoyed in anticipation, and the church must not be superceded once again by Judaism. Example: In the days of Judah and Israel God was worshiped at a literal temple in Jerusalem. That temple was torn down, and God has promised to erect another. But the temple that replaced it was not a literal temple of stone. Rather it was a spiritual temple of living human beings united into the spiritual body of the living Christ. To go back to a literal temple again, after the fulfillment, would be unnecessary and improper.

This makes good sense from the point of view, which is right so far as it goes, that the types of Israel's worship are fulfilled in Christ and the church. But I cannot help thinking that this is not the same issue as God's use of Israel as a nation in the future. Nor can I forget that in Romans 9–11 Paul, who certainly understood the church and knew that many Old Testament prophecies had been fulfilled in it, nevertheless spoke forcefully of a future role for Israel.

ROMANS 11

Romans 11 is the most important chapter. Paul is dealing with a personal as well as a theological problem in this chapter in that he was a Jew and had grown up thinking, as all Jews did, that the blessing of God would come to the various nations of the world through Judaism. The fact that the Messiah was a Jew confirmed this. Even after Paul had been converted he still expected the Jews to believe first and then carry the salvation message to other races. This did not happen. It is true that as Paul went about his missionary work certain Jews believed: Timothy, Aquilla and Priscilla, and others. But, for the most part, Jews did not believe, and as the gospel expanded into the Roman world it seemed that the church of Jesus Christ was becoming increasingly gentile. Paul found himself asking, "Does this mean that God has turned His back on Israel? Has He cast off the Jews? If He has, what of the promises of future and eternal blessing? Or is this a wrong way of thinking? Does God have a future age of blessing in mind that will unfold after the age of the Gentiles is complete?"

Romans 11 is Paul's thoughtful answer to those questions. It falls into several parts. First, Paul says that although it is true that most Jews (in his day) had rejected Christ, it is not true that God has cast off His people. He has not utterly rejected them for the simple reason that there are Jewish believers. Paul himself was one.

Second, the situation in Paul's day was no different from what it had always been. It was never the case that each and every Jew was saved. No Jew was ever saved just by being a Jew, just as no one is automatically saved today just by being born into a church family. It was always only a remnant that was faithful. Those of Elijah's day are an example. Not all were saved then, for when God encouraged His downcast prophet He said, "I have reserved for myself seven thousand who have not bowed down the knee to Baal" (Rom. 11:4). Elijah had complained that he was the only believer left ("I am the only one left, and they are trying to kill me"). God answered that this was not so; there were actually seven thousand. But even at that it was still just seven thousand. Not every Jew was faithful. Paul argues that what was true then is also true now: "So too, at the present time there is a remnant chosen by grace" (Rom. 11:5).

Still, there are some differences between the past and present, as even Paul must admit. If nothing else, this is an age in which God is doing something important and remarkable among the Gentiles. That is true, says Paul. But even this is not without reference to Israel. God allowed Israel to fall as a nation, but their fall is not beyond recovery. On the contrary, the preaching of the gospel to the Gentiles is meant "to make Israel envious . . . [to] arouse [them] to envy and save some of them" (vv. 11, 14; cf. Rom. 10:19). This is his third point.

Fourth, Paul argues from Israel's case to that of the Gentiles to warn those who are now blessed to be careful lest they also fall away. "If some of the branches have been broken off, and you, though a wild olive shoot, have been grafted in

among the others and now share in the nourishing sap from the olive root, do not boast over those branches. If you do, consider this: You do not support the root, but the root supports you. You will say then, 'Branches were broken off so that I could be grafted in.' Granted. But they were broken off because of unbelief, and you stand by faith. Do not be arrogant, but be afraid. For if God did not spare the natural branches, he will not spare you either" (vv. 17–21). Moreover, just as the gentile branches can be broken off, so can the natural branches that have been broken off be grafted back in. "After all, if you were cut out of an olive tree that is wild by nature, and contrary to nature were grafted into a cultivated olive tree, how much more readily will these, the natural branches, be grafted into their own olive tree!" (v. 24).

Will that happen? Yes, says Paul in his fifth and last point. "Israel has experienced a hardening in part until the full number of the Gentiles has come in" (v. 25). But the time will come when the elect of the Gentiles will be gathered in, and then God will begin to work with Israel as a nation again. "So all Israel will be saved, as it is written:

'The deliverer will come from Zion;
   he will turn godlessness away from
   Jacob.
And this is my covenant with them
   when I take away their sins'" (vv. 26, 27).

In view of this passage, which explicitly looks beyond the time of God's blessings on the church, it is certainly right to take a passage such as Amos 9:11–15 as referring to a still future age of Jewish blessing.

THINGS TO COME

What are we to anticipate in this age of blessing? To answer this question we need to look at many texts in Scripture, order them as best we can and then say, "This *seems to be* what the Scriptures teach." But we must be careful in our interpretation and speak without dogmatism. I think there are the following five events.

First, there are many passages that say that Israel will be regathered into its own land. Our text in Amos is one important example, but there are many more. There are prophecies of a scattering of Israel, fulfilled in the dispersals of the northern and southern kingdoms in 721 and 586 B.C. respectively, followed by prophecies of a regathering. Jeremiah wrote, "The days are coming . . . when men will no longer say, 'As surely as the LORD lives, who brought the Israelites up out of Egypt,' but they will say. 'As surely as the LORD lives, who brought the Israelites up out of the land of the north and out of all the countries where he had banished them'" (Jer. 16:14, 15). Similar prophecies are found in Isaiah 11:11, 12; 60:21; Ezekiel 36:24–28, and other writers. As we have already seen in this volume, this is a central theme of Hosea, for although God will scatter the people, naming them "Scattered" (*Jezreel*), "Not-Loved" (*Lo-Ruhamah*) and "Not-My-People" (*Lo-Ammi*), the time would come when He would call them back again and rename them: "Planted" (*Jezreel*), "Loved" (*Ruhamah*) and "My People" (*Ammi*). "The Israelites will be like the sand on the seashore, which cannot be measured or counted. In the place where it was said to them, 'You are not my people,' they will be called 'sons of the living God'" (Hos. 1:10).

This first step in God's plan for the ultimate blessing of Israel may be unfolding before our eyes. We cannot say for sure whether the events of our own time are a fulfillment of these prophecies, yet they may be. Certainly it is noteworthy that the modern state of Israel was founded in 1948 and that since then many Jews have returned to Israel. From 1882 to the present the Jewish presence in Palestine has grown from an estimated 24,000 persons out of a total population of 624,000 to over two and a half million.

The second event in the sequence of Israel's future is the repossession of Old Jerusalem, particularly that part of Old Jerusalem that includes the temple area. This has taken place recently. In June, 1967, as a result of the Six-Day War, Jewish troops moved into the temple area. The commanding general, Moshe Dayan, who marched to the Wailing Wall, the last remnant of the ancient temple, declared, "We have returned to our holiest of holy places, never to leave her again."

The event I would list third in this sequence is a bit more controversial: the anticipated rebuilding of the Jewish temple. I see two areas of controversy. First, it is controversial in Israel, the Zionists being on one side and the more liberal Jewish thinkers on the other. Second, there is disagreement about this aspect of biblical interpretation by biblical scholars, as I indicated earlier.

For instance, at a 1971 Conference on Biblical Prophecy held in Jerusalem, Edmund P. Clowney, former president of Westminster Theological Seminary, took the view that the new temple will be composed of living men with Jesus Christ Himself as the cornerstone. He declared, "We dare not promise to a people with the covenant name of Israel, second-class citizenship in the kingdom of heaven by way of the restoration of an earthly economy with a temple of stone. To do so is to obscure the gospel."[2] On the other hand, at the same conference Charles Lee Feinberg, dean and Professor of Semitics and Old Testament at Talbot Theological Seminary, argued from a literal interpretation of Ezekiel 40–48 that "the temple will be rebuilt."[3]

What are we to say in the face of such disagreement? We must at least be cautious in our interpretations. Neverthe-

---

[2]Edmund P. Clowney, "The Final Temple," *Prophecy in the Making*, ed. Carl F. H. Henry (Carol Stream, Ill.: Creation House, 1971), p. 85.

[3]Charles Lee Feinberg, "The Rebuilding of the Temple," *Prophecy in the Making*, p. 109.

less, while not denying the reality of the new spiritual temple which is the church of Jesus Christ, it seems to me that there are far too many references in Scripture to the existence of a temple at the time of Christ's return to dismiss at least the probability of its rebuilding. Ezekiel seems to be speaking of such a temple in the chapters cited by Feinberg. Daniel implies its existence in his prophecy, that Antichrist (whom he calls the prince) will cause the sacrifices being conducted in the temple area to cease (Dan. 9:27). The same event is referred to by Jesus in Matthew 24:15, by Paul in 2 Thessalonians 2:3, 4, and by John in Revelation 11:1, 2. These references make certain that the prophecy of Daniel was not considered to be fulfilled in the former partial desecration of the temple by Antiochus Epiphanes approximately 170 years before the birth of Christ. The repeated references to the temple in the New Testament as well as in the Old make the future existence of a literal temple likely.

The most potent objection to the view that the temple will be rebuilt is that it seems inconceivable that those who believe in the perfect sacrifice of Jesus Christ would ever construct a temple in which animal sacrifices would be resumed. But this objection fades away if the Jews will be regathered in Israel first not as believers in Jesus Christ but as unbelievers. Under these circumstances it is conceivable that the temple could be rebuilt and the old Mosaic order reinstated.

Moreover, there is already talk of this happening. Shortly after the recapture of Old Jerusalem during the Six-Day War a reporter asked the well-known Israeli historian Israel Eldad, "Do your people intend to rebuild the Temple?"

Eldad replied, "From the time that King David first conquered Jerusalem until Solomon built the Temple, just one generation passed. So will it be with us."

"What about the Dome of the Rock which now stands on the temple site?" the reporter continued. (The Dome of the Rock is the Mosque of Omar, which is sacred to Islam.)

"It is, of course, an open question," Eldad answered. "Who knows, maybe there will be an earthquake."[4]

I received a letter in the same vein from a young American who had been traveling in Israel. He wrote, "The last and most important message I want to convey to you is the unmistakable feeling among the Jews of Jerusalem that the temple will be rebuilt within twenty or thirty years from now, if not sooner. From the Israeli soldier to the orthodox Jew riding the bus to the Wailing Wall the feeling is there. All one need do is ask, as I have done, although I grant you no one knows the exact details of reconstruction. If the temple indeed is rebuilt in our lifetime, now that the Jews have returned after almost two thousand years, what is to suggest that the stage will not be set for the appearance of the Antichrist of Matthew 24:15?"

The fourth event in this sequence will be the appearance of two great witnesses to God in Israel during the years of Antichrist's tribulation. Their work is described in Revelation 11. According to this chapter, the two witnesses will perform a remarkable work of preaching, centered in Jerusalem. They will perform great miracles by which they themselves will be protected. Then, after three and a half years, they will finally be overcome by Antichrist and be killed, but three and a half days later they will be raised up by God and received into heaven.

The last of these events, the fifth in this sequence, is related to the preaching of these two witnesses: a time of great national revival in Israel. In other words, events will happen exactly as Paul declared in Romans when he wrote, "So all Israel will be saved" (Rom. 11:26). Many

---

[4]Hal Lindsey with C. C. Carlson, *The Late Great Planet Earth* (Grand Rapids: Zondervan, 1970), p. 57.

will think this a far-out possibility, considering the traditional opposition of Jews to Christianity. But I am not sure it is as far out as many persons would imagine, in view of the new interest in Jesus by many Jewish thinkers.

Sholem Asch, the well-known Polish Jewish author, was reported as saying in the context of an interview published in the *Christian Herald*, "No other religious leader . . . has ever become so personal a part of people as The Nazarene. When you understand Jesus, you understand that he came to save you, to come into your personality. It isn't just a case of a misty, uncertain relationship between a worshipper and an unseen God; that is abstract: Jesus is personal!"

Contantine Brunner, the Jewish philosopher, has written, "What is this? Is it only the Jew who is unable to see and hear? Are the Jews stricken with blindness and deafness as regards Christ, so that to them only he has nothing to say? Is he to be of no importance to us Jews? Understand then what we shall do: We shall bring him back to us. Christ is not dead for us—for us he has not yet lived; and he will not slay us, he will make us live again. His profound and holy words, and all that is true and heart-appealing in the New Testament, must from now on be heard in our synagogues and taught to our children, in order that the wrong we had committed may be made good, the curse turned into a blessing, and that he at last may find us who has always been seeking after us."

Before his death Professor Albert Einstein was asked, "Do you accept the historical existence of Jesus?"

He answered, "Unquestionably! No one can read the Gospels without feeling the actual presence of Jesus. His personality pulsates in every word. No myth is filled with such life."

Finally, in a brilliant paragraph, Hans Joachim Schoeps, the Jewish theologian,

has written, "The Messianism of Israel aims at that which is to come, the eschatology of the Gentile church at the return of him who has come. Both elective covenants confront the ebb and flow of the finite world in the shared expectation that the decisive event is still to come—the goal of the ways of God that he travels with mankind in Israel and in the Church. The church of Jesus Christ has preserved no portrait of its lord and savior. If Jesus were to come again tomorrow, no Christian would know his face. But it might well be that he who is coming at the end of days, he who is awaited by the synagogue as by the church, is one, with one and the same face."[5]

No one would say on the basis of these quotations that the Jews of today are ready as a whole to accept Jesus as the Son of God and their Savior. Nevertheless, such words are relatively new in the mouths of Jewish thinkers and indicate that the day may not be so far off when Israel will be ready to receive the one who was formerly rejected but who will return to fulfill His promises toward them. Even now their words indicate a new openness to the person of Jesus and a new expectation of a Messiah who is to come.

OUR GREAT SALVATION

What does this mean for those who are studying prophecy? It means several things. First, since the regathering of Israel in Palestine and the reconstitution of their traditional religion are a prerequisite to the events of the last days and since this seems to be happening, this alone suggests that the end may be near. I have outlined a sequence of five events that concern developments within Israel in the days immediately preceding the Lord's final return to the earth at Armageddon: the regathering of the Jews in Palestine, the repossession of Old Jerusalem, the rebuilding of the temple,

[5]Quoted by Arthur W. Kac, *The Rebirth of the State of Israel—Is It of God or of Man?* (London: Marshall, Morgan & Scott, 1958), pp. 227–31.

the appearance of the two witnesses of Revelation, and a final widespread national revival. Two of these events may have already occurred. Who can say how quickly the next three may come?

Second, we can learn from Israel. One of the lessons that God has used Israel to teach is that obedience is followed by blessing, and disobedience by judgment. This applies to Israel, but it also applies to individuals, the church, and nations. Will our nation seek God and walk in His ways? If so, God will bless our nation. If not, we will be judged. Will those who are Christians humble themselves and pray and seek God's face and turn from their wicked ways? If so, God will bless them and prosper the church. If not, there will be chastisement. The holy God demands holiness in those who follow Him.

Finally, there is the lesson of grace. God is gracious in His dealings with His people. He is gracious with Israel. He is gracious with the church. The question for us is: Will we respond to God's grace or turn from it? No wonder that when Paul gets to the end of that long chapter in Romans, which we have looked at in detail (ch. 11), the overwhelming wonder of the grace of God possesses him and he cries out in what is one of the Bible's greatest doxologies:

> Oh, the depth of the riches of the wisdom and knowledge of God!
> How unsearchable his judgments, and his paths beyond tracing out!
> "Who has known the mind of the Lord?
> Or who has been his counselor?"
> "Who has ever given to God,
> that God should repay him?"
> For from him and through him and to him are all things.
> To him be the glory forever! Amen.

This is our God. We may not completely understand the past, and we certainly do not understand the future. But we see enough to marvel at the grace of our God and respond to Him[6]

---

[6]Substantial portions of this chapter are borrowed (with changes) from chapter 6 of Boice, *The Last and Future World*, now out of print.

OBADIAH

27

Major Message From a Minor Prophet

(Obadiah 1–9)

The vision of Obadiah. This is what the Sovereign LORD says about Edom—We have heard a message from the LORD: An envoy was sent to the nations to say, "Rise, and let us go against her for battle"—"See, I will make you small among the nations; you will be utterly despised. The pride of your heart has deceived you, you who live in the clefts of the rocks and make your home on the heights, you who say to yourself, 'Who can bring me down to the ground?' Though you soar like the eagle and make your nest among the stars, from there I will bring you down," declares the LORD.

Of the twelve books of the Minor Prophets the most "minor" of all is Obadiah. Minor does not mean unimportant, of course; it refers only to length. But by this standard, the standard of length, Obadiah is noteworthy, for it is by far the shortest book not only of the twelve Minor Prophets but of the whole Old Testament. It has one chapter, and that contains only twenty-one verses. Moreover, we know very little about it. Although the Old Testament mentions at least twelve individuals called Obadiah, none is to be identified with the prophet. There is also uncertainty regarding when the book was written. It refers to a sin of Edom at the time of the sacking of Jerusalem, but this could have happened as early as 850 or as late as 312 B.C.

The book is "minor" in another way as well: in terms of most people's knowledge of it. Who knows what is in Obadiah? Very few, even among conscientious Bible students. Yet the book has a major message for our and every other age.

EDOM

The theme of the book is a denunciation of Edom. Consequently, it is important to know something about the history of this ancient kingdom. So far as geography goes, Edom (also known in the Bible as Seir, Hor, and Esau) was the territory bordering Judah to the east and south. That is, it was to the east of the Jordan River and extended southward from the borders of Moab to the Gulf of Aqaba. On the eastern side Edom was bordered by the desert. It was approximately 20 to 30 miles wide and about 100 miles long.

The northern and eastern areas of this territory contained parts fit for cultivation, but these were not what gave importance to the land. The real importance of Edom was due to two factors. First, it was situated along the great trade routes between Syria and Egypt and could profit from this trade. Trade brought business, and the inhabitants grew rich on tolls extracted from the many caravans. The second factor was Edom's natural strength and security. The central area is characterized by red sandstone cliffs that rise to heights of more than 5,000 feet above sea level. These are easily fortified. As a result of having made their home within this natural fortress, the people of Edom were free to wage war and levy tribute on others while themselves being relatively free of outside interference.

Edom's major towns were Teman in the south, Bozrah in the north, and Sela (the capital) hidden away in the most inaccessible part of the sandstone highlands. Sela later became Petra, of which more must be said later.

The earliest history of Edom is lost to us today, although at an early date the region was settled by Horites who came from the neighborhood of Lake Van in northern Syria. This was very early, because by the time of Abraham there was already a kingdom tucked away in the mountains of this country. The Bible refers to it in the account of Abraham's victory over the four kings who had attacked the area of Sodom and Gomorrah and carried off Abraham's nephew Lot. In the midst of this account we read that the four kings under Kedorlaomer "defeated the Rephaites in Ashteroth Karnaim, the Zuzites in Ham, the Emites in Shaveh Kiriathaim, and *the Horites in the hill country of Seir*" (Gen. 14:5, 6).

Somewhat later in biblical history, Edom appears in the story of Abraham's grandsons, Jacob and Esau. When Jacob was returning to the land of promise after many years with Laban at Haran, Esau came out to meet him from Edom where, in the meantime, he had apparently gone with his people. The Bible refers to this by saying, "Jacob sent messengers ahead of him to his brother Esau in the land of Seir, the country of Edom" (Gen. 32:3); it adds that after their meeting Esau returned there (Gen. 33:16). Still later, Edom appears in the story of the Exodus of the people of Israel from Egypt. When the people had come out of Egypt into the Sinai and wanted to pass on to the Promised Land through Edom, the Edomites refused to give them passage even though

Moses promised to harm nothing and even pay for whatever water the people and their herds should drink (Num. 20:14–21).

David conquered the Edomites in a great battle recorded in 2 Samuel 8:13, 14, and from that time on through the reign of Solomon the Edomites were subject to the descendants of Jacob. One writer notes: "Until this time Edom must have been thought of as Israel's 'elder brother' in being stronger, older, and more developed. By this battle 'the elder' was 'supplanted' by 'the younger' in clear historical analogy to the Jacob-Esau parallel in Genesis. From this point on one can trace the bitter rivalry which is documented in the prophecy of Obadiah."[1]

The end of Edom is shrouded in mystery. We know only that the nation lost its independence in the fifth century B.C. and was controlled by the Nabataeans from about 312 B.C. In this period Edom was called Idumaea, the place from which Herod the Great, an Idumaean, came. From the time of the Mohammadan conquests the region has been virtually unoccupied save for Bedouins and, in recent history, by military outposts of the modern state of Jordan. It has indeed been brought to nothing, as Obadiah foretold.

The Pride of Edom

The fall of Edom was not to go without explanation, of course, and it is for this that Obadiah is written. It is an explanation of the fall, which at the time of writing was yet future. What is the explanation? The fall of Edom was to be God's judgment on it because of its overriding and offensive sin of pride. The first nine verses contain this judgment.[2]

In these verses the chief concern is the

---

[1]John D. W. Watts, *Obadiah: A Critical Exegetical Commentary* (Grand Rapids: Eerdmans, 1969), p. 15.

[2]These verses are paralleled to a remarkable degree in Jeremiah 49:7–22, which raises the question of whether Jeremiah is borrowing from Obadiah, Obadiah from Jeremiah, or both from another source. While the matter is complicated, the prevailing opinion among scholars is that Jeremiah (the longer and more polished book) has borrowed from Obadiah's pungent denunciations, which Jeremiah apparently also does with certain sections of Isaiah and Amos. If this is the case, however, it affects the dating of Obadiah which must in consequence be placed before the fall of Jerusalem in 587 B.C. There is a further discussion of this matter in the next chapter.

sin mentioned so forcefully in verse 3. Obadiah quotes the Lord as exclaiming, "The pride of your heart has deceived you." It is for this that judgment came upon the nation.

We have a problem at this point, of course. Most people today do not consider pride all that bad, certainly not something for which (in our judgment) God would destroy an entire nation. But this says more about our light views of sin than it does about God's workings. What does the Bible say? According to the Bible, pride is the sin of sins and the most damning. Frank Gaebelein writes of the problem: "How difficult it is to awaken even Christian people to an understanding of the real nature of pride! As G. Campbell Morgan suggests, one may stand before a congregation and hold their breathless interest by a recountal of dramatic stories of lives ruined by drink and other carnal sins. But try to expound a text such as this from Obadiah, 'The pride of thine heart hath deceived thee,' and there is a marked difference in attention and response. The reason is the fact that the true nature of pride is so little understood.

"Look at it this way. Here are two statements, each of which might fall from the lips of some well-meaning church member. Referring to another person, someone says, 'He is a good man but proud.' Such a remark hardly strikes our ears as inappropriate or shocking. We are all too willing to admit that goodness and pride may be companions within the same life. But consider this remark, 'He is a good man but a thief.' Immediately our moral sensibilities are outraged. 'Hold on!' we say. 'What do you mean? A man cannot at the same time be good and a thief.' Yet in the sight of God pride is fully as bad as stealing, if not worse."[3]

The full measure of pride is seen when we recall that this was the sin of Satan, the father of all sin. It was pride that caused him to say, "I will ascend above the tops of the clouds; I will make myself like the Most High" (Isa. 14:14). Nothing lies so much at the heart of the problems of the human race as this prideful desire to take over God's place or, which amounts nearly to the same thing, to pretend that we can do without Him.

IMPREGNABLE DEFENSES

The root of pride is saying that we can do without God, but there are many ways in which this expresses itself. On the personal level we imagine that we can do without God in our family life, our business, or in regard to our health, or in a dozen other areas. On the national level pride often expresses itself in characteristic boasts of Edom.

What was it about which Edom was proud? The first answer is: her defenses. Due to her unique geographical situation, Edom was almost impregnable. For years the extraordinary nature of her defenses was unknown to biblical scholars due to the fact that the real stronghold of Edom at Petra was lost to the western world. Widely known in ancient times and greatly admired, it was lost to western knowledge for nearly one thousand years until rediscovered by the Swiss explorer Johann Ludwig Burkhardt in 1812. Burkhardt had heard rumors of the city and wanted to see it. So, knowing that the Arabs of the region would normally never allow him to enter the city, he informed them that he had vowed to offer a goat to Aaron, the ancient high priest of Israel, upon the traditional site of Aaron's tomb. This was located on a mountain that rose above the city. Since the Arab guides could make no objection to so holy a vow, Burkhardt was permitted to enter.

The sight that burst on the wondering eyes of Burkhardt is remarkable. The city is entered through a narrow winding gorge or canyon, called a *siq*. This is about a mile long and is in no place really wide. On the average it is about fifteen feet

---

[3]Frank E. Gaebelein, *Four Minor Prophets* (Chicago: Moody Press, 1970), pp. 48, 49.

from towering wall to towering wall. A conduit for a small stream runs along its length, and as one makes his way through this breath-taking canyon, as the author himself did in 1960, he notes remnants of ancient pavement, a carved aquaduct, and the beginning of many thousands of ornately carved caves in the walls. The caves served as homes for those who once lived there. Toward the end of the passage the traveler suddenly comes on the first of the magnificent buildings that have been carved into the face of the rock. It is the temple of Al-Khazneh, which towers upward for one hundred and thirty feet above the canyon floor.

Rounding another bend the traveler is in Petra itself. It is a level valley of slightly less than one square mile surrounded by many mountains. In it are the ruins of the several successive civilizations that have occupied the spot, the last and most impressive being Roman. There are homes, temples, and treasuries. In the mountains there are additional safe areas for defense.

How impregnable it all seems! Experts say that because of the configurations of the *siq* through which Petra is entered, it would be possible for a dozen men to hold it against an army. Again, even if the *siq* were breached, it would be possible for the inhabitants to carry on a successful defense from the mountains. From a human perspective it is hard to imagine a safer spot than Edom and its capital city of Petra. It is understandable that the inhabitants might well say, as Obadiah reports the citizens of Edom as saying, "Who can bring me down to the ground?" (v. 3). Yet God said that Edom would be brought down. "'Though you soar like the eagle and make your nest among the stars, from there I will bring you down,' declares the LORD" (v. 4).

Moreover, the destruction to be brought about by the Lord would be total and not merely the kind of destruction that even an enemy might bring. This is the meaning of verse 5, which says,

"If thieves came to you, if robbers in the night—Oh, what a disaster awaits you— would they not steal only as much as they wanted? If grape pickers came to you, would they not leave a few grapes?" Even if thieves sneaked into Petra and plundered it, obviously something would be left. No matter how vigilant and systematic they were, they could not carry away everything. At harvest time even the grape pickers leave some grapes. Not so with God's judgment. In that judgment everything was to be taken. Petra was to be left in the condition in which we find it today.

Was God being particularly harsh with Edom? No, this is His way with all nations. God exalts a nation. Those in power see it as a cause for personal pride. They boast that they are better than others and can even do without God. Then God brings the nation down. This has been the case with all the great kingdoms of the world. Historians tell us that the world has seen twenty-one great civilizations. But each has passed away in time to make room for the next. Once there was Egypt, but ancient Egypt was destroyed and that which is now Egypt is no world power. Once there was Babylon, but it too passed away. So with Greece and Rome. So it will be with the great powers of our own day: the Soviet Union and the United States.

Is the United States destined for destruction? We cannot say. She may recover her godly heritage. She may last until the Lord returns. But we should be warned by God's judgment on Edom. Do we boast that we are strong? That we have the largest army, the most missiles, the more effective navy? Do we boast that our technology is superior to that of the rest of the world? If so, we must watch out! God says that He can bring even our nation down.

STRONG ALLIES

The second item about which Edom was proud was her allies. The Lord mentions this in verse 7. This verse reveals a people who think they are secure, not only because of their superb natural defenses, but because of a virtual traffic in allies revealing a vast network of alliances. Because the people of Edom did not sufficiently understand the hearts of men and women, they did not foresee that these imagined allies would eventually prove untrue and betray them to their enemies.

It is the same today. We are in a situation in the United States where in recent years it has become favorable to trust not so much in the power of our military might but in our thriving relationships with other countries. Ours has been called "an age of diplomacy" or a time of "detent." If armaments cannot bring peace, so the argument runs, perhaps diplomacy will. Well, there is nothing wrong with attempting to establish good relationships with neighboring nations, and it is certainly better to have many diplomatic relations (no matter how strained) than none at all. But we cannot trust in these! That is Obadiah's point. Other nations will deceive us. The only thing in which a nation is ever truly secure is a humble and obedient relationship to God.

Is it wise to have alliances? Yes, but we must not trust in alliances. Are we to have an army? Yes, that too. But we are not to trust in the army. We are to trust in God only and show it by attempting to establish righteousness and justice in our land.

Exceptional Wisdom

There is one more item that, in the twisted thinking of the Edomites, became a factor in their consummate pride. It was wisdom, mentioned in verse 8. According to this verse, the people were as much as saying, "No matter what comes, we can handle it; we know how to get around in this world; we're smarter than anyone."

From the human perspective this was not just empty arrogance, for the Edomites really were noted for their wisdom. For example, Eliphaz, the foremost of Job's friends and the chief representative in that book of human wisdom, was a Temanite; that is, he was from Edom. Another of Job's friends was a Shuhite, a name that is still given to a mountain in Edom. Edom is also referred to in the phrase "the men of the East," whose wisdom in some texts is linked to that of Egypt as the highest of the ancient world. Thus, in 1 Kings 4:30, we read, "Solomon's wisdom was greater than the wisdom of all the men of the East, and greater than all the wisdom of Egypt." Similarly, Jeremiah 49:7, employing the words of Obadiah, asks, "Is there no longer wisdom in Teman? Has counsel perished from the prudent? Has their wisdom decayed?" In this verse, as E. B. Pusey, one of the most valuable commentators on the Minor Prophets, notes, "He speaks as though Edom were a known abode of human wisdom, so that it was strange that it was found there no more. He speaks of the Edomites as prudent, discriminating, full of judgment, and wonders that counsel should have perished from them. They had it eminently then, before it perished. They thought themselves wise; they were thought so; but God took it away at their utmost need."[4]

Today on television and in the newspapers we hear and read much about the ability of this country and its leaders to handle the political and other problems of this world. The thought is that we are able. We are adequate for whatever circumstances history may bring. But we are not able. We cannot solve this world's problems. What we need is that personal and national humility that prays, "O righteous Father, I cannot cope with the situation, nor can we as a nation. Help us! Teach us repentance! Lead us in the way we should go!"

[4]Pusey, *The Minor Prophets*, vol. 1, p. 359.

IF MY PEOPLE . . .

Neither our nor any other nation is ever going to be 100% Christian, and there will never be any universal righteousness until the Lord Himself returns to establish it. Nevertheless, God will exalt a nation to the degree that it acknowledges its dependence on Him and seeks righteousness.

Here is where the duty of the Christian community within a nation, however large or small that community may be, comes in. It is the duty set before it in 2 Chronicles 7:14. "If my people, who are called by my name, will humble themselves and pray and seek my face and turn from their wicked ways, then will I hear from heaven and will forgive their sin and will heal their land." This sets forth a course of action that is the precise opposite of that found in the text from Obadiah. In Obadiah a nation is found to be exalting itself in pride, and God says that the nation will be brought down. In 2 Chronicles 7:14 a people who are called by God's name are to humble themselves, as a result of which God promises to forgive their sin and heal their land. God's people are also sinful. But if they will confess their sin and seek Him, He will bring healing to the land because of this remnant.

There are four things God's people must do. First, we must humble ourselves. The reason for this is obvious. If pride is the original sin and the source of all other sins, as it is, and if humility is the opposite of pride, as we know it to be, then the cure will begin not at the periphery but at the very core of the problem. We must begin with humility, which means that we must begin with the confession that we are not adequate for the problems that confront us and must seek help from God. Moreover, it is believing people who must do this. We too are prideful, perhaps at times even more so than the unbelieving world. We cannot expect those who do not know the Lord to humble themselves if we will

not do it. Repentance must begin with the household of God, as the Bible tells us.

Second, we are instructed to pray. It seems strange that those who are God's people must be encouraged to do this, for we should be praying always (1 Thess. 5:17). Still, we must be encouraged, for prayer is work and as a result we often let this precious privilege slip from us. To pray means spending time with God. It means searching our hearts before Him.

Third, we are to seek God's face. What does this mean? It might be thought merely another way of saying that we are to pray. But if that is the case, the verse is redundant. In the context it is far more likely that the verse is speaking of seeking God's will for us personally. It means looking to see the way His face is pointed and that on which His eyes are set. This is quite practical. It means that if we are serious about the healing and preservation of our land and about our place as His agents in bringing about a measure of that healing, then there will be specific work for us to do. There will be hungry persons to feed, thirsty people to whom to give a glass of cold water, strangers to welcome and house, naked ones to clothe and prisoners to visit. There will be many to tell of the grace of God toward us in Jesus Christ.

Finally, we are to turn from our wicked ways to serve Him. It is significant that this comes last. If it came first, if we were first told to turn from our wicked ways, undoubtedly the vast majority (even of God's people) would reply in genuine surprise, "What wicked ways? We are not wicked; we are actually pillars of righteousness in our communities." However, after having humbled ourselves and having prayed and sought God's will for our lives, the situation is entirely different. Now we are able to measure unrighteousness and faltering service by His plan for us, and in that light we see what sin is and turn from it.

This is what exalts a nation—the response to God of those who know God. As a result, they humble themselves, pray, seek His face, and turn from their wickedness.

How many responsive and obedient believers must do this? There are times when the voice of a thousand is required for only one to be heard. At other times, as now, the voice of one can count as a thousand. God told Abraham that He would spare the corrupt cities of Sodom and Gomorrah if only ten righteous persons could be found there. Would He not spare our land if even a portion of those many millions who consider themselves Christians would call on Him? If we would do that practically—humbling ourselves, praying, seeking God's will, turning from specific sin—God would doubtless answer from heaven with such blessing that we would experience a genuine healing in our land. Unlike Edom, which God promised to bring down, God would exalt our nation as a channel of blessing for other peoples.

28

Your Brother's Keeper

(Obadiah 10–14)

Because of the violence against your brother Jacob, you will be covered with shame; you will be destroyed forever. On the day you stood aloof while strangers carried off his wealth and foreigners entered his gates and cast lots for Jerusalem, you were like one of them. You should not look down on your brother in the day of his misfortune, nor rejoice over the people of Judah in the day of their destruction, nor boast so much in the day of their trouble. You should not march through the gates of my people in the day of their disaster, nor look down on them in their calamity in the day of their disaster, nor seize their wealth in the day of their disaster. You should not wait at the crossroads to cut down their fugitives, nor hand over their survivors in the day of their trouble.

I am often moved by the stories coming out of the Prison Fellowship ministry launched by Charles Colson, but this one overwhelmed me. Colson had been conducting a seminar in the Indiana State Prison where just weeks before a man had been electrocuted. After he had finished, one of the volunteers who had entered the prison with him lingered to talk with a man from death row. The condemned prisoner was James Brewer who, Colson knew, had recently become a believer. A plane was waiting to take Colson back to Indianapolis, where in two hours he was to have a meeting with the governor, so Colson pressed the volunteer to hurry. "We've got to go," he called out.

"Just a minute, please," the volunteer answered.

"No," said Colson, "time's up; we've got to get going."

The volunteer replied, "Please, please, this is very important. You see, I am Judge Clement. I sentenced this man to die. But now he is born again. He is my brother, and we want a minute to pray together."

Colson tells how he stood frozen in place, looking on that scene. Here were two men—one black, one white, one powerless, one powerful, one condemned to die, the other the judge who had pronounced that sentence. Yet here they stood grasping a Bible together, united as one Christian brother with another. Is there anything greater than that? Is any force in the world more powerful?

The Sin of Edom

I begin this way as a contrast to the theme of Obadiah 10–14. These verses present a specific sin of Edom, which was an aggravated *lack* of brotherhood, and show how it grew out of Edom's pride.

It is a characteristic of the Hebrew prophets that when they speak against a person or nation, foretelling an imminent judgment by God, they do so in a judicial framework. That is, they make their accusation, then go about it to prove its validity. This is what Obadiah is doing in these first two sections of his prophecy. He makes his accusation in verses 1–9. Then in verses 10–14 he shows why it is valid and why the judgment of God must come.

At first glance these sections seem to

be talking about different things. In the opening part the keynote is pride, as I have indicated. According to Obadiah, the pride of Edom deceived the people into trusting in their natural defenses, their numerous allies and their acknowledged wisdom, rather than in God. Obadiah says that their wisdom will fail, their allies will prove treacherous and their defenses will be overcome. This is quite general and may easily be applied to any nation at any time in history. (America too will fall if it trusts in external props rather than in the living God of history.) In the second section of the book this emphasis changes and we suddenly find Obadiah dealing with what was obviously a specific incident in history. At one point or another—it is hard to say when—Jerusalem was overrun by enemies, and the people of Edom, who should have mourned at the misfortune of their brothers, actually did the opposite. They rejoiced at Judah's loss and participated in the looting.

As I say, these seem to be two entirely different matters. But they are not, and it is easy to see that they are not, as soon as this matter of accusation and proof is taken into consideration. The accusation is that the people of Edom had sinned greatly in their pride. How are we to know that this was so? We cannot see the heart. How are we to demonstrate that the Edomites were prideful? The answer is in this next section, for Obadiah is saying that the proof of the pride of Edom is in the way they treated Israel. Pride leads to an unjustified sense of personal superiority, and when we feel this way about ourselves we naturally look down on others and mistreat them. Thus, Edom's mistreatment of the people of Jerusalem was proof of her pride and the specific grounds for God's judicial intervention.

SIN AGAINST A BROTHER

The particular horror of Edom's actions is that they were performed against those who were related to them in a special way. Edom had descended from Esau, one of the twin sons of Isaac, the son of Abraham. The Jewish nation had descended from Jacob, the other twin son. So the two nations were brother nations and mistreatment of one by the other was particularly heinous because of this relationship. At one point in Deuteronomy the Jews were told, "Do not abhor an Edomite, for he is your brother" (Deut. 23:7). This obligation also worked the other way around, but the Edomites had broken this sacred relationship. The prophecy says, "Because of the violence *against your brother Jacob,* you will be covered with shame; you will be destroyed forever" (v. 10).

I wish there was a good English word to describe this sin, but unfortunately there does not seem to be. The best we can do is an awkward English word containing fifteen letters: *unbrotherliness.* Many sins have strong words. "Gluttony" is a word that has impact. "Murder" is strong. So are "adultery," "slander," "deceit," "self-indulgence." Even a word like "covetousness" is strong. But "unbrotherliness"? Unbrotherliness lacks impact with us. So to be told that this is the ultimate proof of pride and the historical grounds for God's utter destruction of a nation seems ludicrous.

This was not absurd in ancient times, however, and the fact that it seems so to us only shows how far our own culture has fallen from a proper, God-given regard for family relations. We may not have a high regard for brothers or sisters, husbands or wives, parents or children, but God does have this high regard for family relations, and the Bible everywhere speaks of them. For example, even in so practical a matter as making financial provisions for one's relatives the Bible says, "If anyone does not provide for his relatives, and especially for his immediate family, he has denied the faith and is worse than an unbeliever" (1 Tim. 5:8). Those are strong words, but they are not too strong. God has put us in families, and God holds these relationships sacred.

What does unbrotherliness mean? It means acting toward my brother, or any other family member, in a way I should not act. My brother is one I should love, no matter what he does. My brother is one I should encourage, even if he tends to discourage me. My brother is one I should defend, however great his enemies. If I do not do those things, I am being unbrotherly. To laugh at my brother when he makes a mistake is unbrotherly. To take delight in his failures is unbrotherly. To rejoice in his misfortune is unbrotherliness of the worst sort.

As we stated earlier, it is not easy to date the specific offense against brotherliness in Edom's case, though it would be helpful in understanding the book if we could do so. According to Obadiah, on the occasion of an overthrow of Jerusalem by her enemies, the Edomites first stood by and then later participated in Judah's misfortune both by raiding the city and by catching some of the escaping people and turning them over to their enemies (vv. 11–14).

History tells us that Jerusalem was invaded on four occasions. We can eliminate two of these as not involving Edom (the capture of Jerusalem by Shishak, 2 Chron. 12; the defeat of Amaziah by Jehoash, 2 Chron. 25), but there are still two invasions where the misbehavior of Edom may be placed: 1) the sack of Jerusalem by the Philistines and Arabs during the reign of Jehoram, about 850 B.C., and 2) the overthrow of Jerusalem by the Babylonians in 587 B.C. How are we to decide between the two? At first glance one thinks of the final overthrow of Jerusalem, especially since Ezekiel tells of a specific offense of Edom against Jerusalem at this time (Ezek. 35; cf. 2 Kings 25:1–7; Ps. 137:7). Ezekiel writes, "This is what the Sovereign LORD says: I am against you, Mount Seir, and I will stretch

out my hand against you and make you a desolate waste. I will turn your towns into ruins and you will be desolate. Then you will know that I am the LORD. Because you harbored an ancient hostility and delivered the Israelites over to the sword at the time of their calamity, the time their punishment reached its climax . . ." (vv. 3–5). This sounds very much like Obadiah 14: "You should not wait at the crossroads to cut down their fugitives, nor hand over their survivors in the day of their trouble."

The chief difficulty with this view is Jeremiah's apparent dependence on Obadiah, referred to in the last chapter. If Jeremiah does refer to Obadiah, then Obadiah was written before Jeremiah and therefore also before the fall of Jerusalem to Babylon at the later of the two dates.

The other incident is more vague. In 2 Chronicles 21:16, 17 we are told of an invasion of Jerusalem by the Philistines and Arabs: "The LORD aroused against Jehoram the hostility of the Philistines and of the Arabs who lived near the Cushites. They attacked Judah, invaded it and carried off all the goods found in the king's palace, together with his sons and wives. Not a son was left to him except Ahaziah, the youngest." This passage has no mention of the Edomites, but a few verses before this, in verses 8–10, we are told of a rebellion of Edom against Jehoram and of Jehoram's unsuccessful attempt to bring the people of Edom back under his control. Although we are not told so specifically, it is possible that the Edomites collaborated with the Philistines and Arabs when the latter took Jerusalem.

Here is a historical problem that is just not possible fully to resolve at this time, though in view of the apparent use of Obadiah by Jeremiah the earlier date should probably be preferred. Scholars are rather equally divided.[1] The interesting thing, however, is that if the in-

---

[1]Frank E. Gaebelein has a discussion of these possibilities in which he lists the scholars to be found on each side (*Four Minor Prophets*, p. 13). The division is not between liberal and conservative scholarship.

cident referred to by Obadiah *is* the earlier of the two (around 850 B.C.), then the offense was certainly repeated later at the time of the Babylonian invasion and the two incidents together give a lasting pattern of unbrotherly behavior on the part of the Edomites. Apparently, the bad blood between Esau and Jacob was hard to erase, and each act of misbehavior on the part of Edom only made the next one easier and more intense.

THE GROWTH OF SIN

This is worth emphasizing, for a debilitating growth of sin is the virtual history of Edom. We have seen its origins in the friction between Esau and Jacob (Gen. 25:19–34; 27:1–46; 33:1–17). We saw it on a national level at the time of Israel's exodus from Egypt (Num. 20: 14–21). In Obadiah we have already seen it in the progression from pride to the specific sins of indifference and ruthless conduct. As Pusey says, "Pride was the root of Edom's sin, then envy; then followed exultation at his brother's fall, hard-heartedness and bloodshed."[2]

Few great sins ever happen overnight. David committed adultery with Bathsheba and then murdered her husband, but this was not something that happened easily and quickly for David. He sinned first by staying home in Jerusalem instead of going to battle. He should have been in the fields with his troops. Big sins are always built upon little sins. The sin of unbrotherliness has small beginnings, but it grows. A battle between two men will lead to a battle between two families. If the situation is right, the battle between two families can lead to a battle between two cities, and the battle between cities can lead to a battle between nations.

We have this growth of sin in Obadiah first in a progression from the general sin of pride to the specific sin of unbrotherliness. Second, we have it in the growth of unbrotherliness itself. In Obadiah 11–

14 we find an intensification of this offense from mild beginnings to some horrible effects. The prophet mentions seven things.

First, there is the sin of *standing aloof* when our brother stumbles. The text says, "On the day you stood aloof while strangers carried off his wealth and foreigners entered his gates and cast lots for Jerusalem, you were like one of them" (v. 11). It is interesting that this failure on the part of Edom stands first in the list of sin's progression, for it takes us back to the first form of unbrotherly conduct in the Bible. The world's first brothers, Cain and Abel, were divided by God's acceptance of Abel's offering and His displeasure at Cain's. Cain was angry and therefore lured his brother into the fields where no one could see them and killed him. When God came demanding, "Where is your brother Abel?", Cain tried to stand aloof. He said, "Am I my brother's keeper?" (Gen. 4:9). This is what Edom was doing. Jerusalem was threatened by enemies, and the people of Edom said, "This is no business of ours. We're not their keepers. Whatever happens, happens; if they fall, it's only what serves them right. We're going to mind our business; we expect other people to mind theirs."

You say, "But weren't they right? Certainly we're not our brothers' keepers." Yes, you are! You have a responsibility to other men and women and a special responsibility to those within your immediate family and the family of God, which is the church. God holds you accountable! Where you can help, you must help. Where you can encourage, you mu. encourage. Where you can defend, you must defend.

This first offense, bad as it is, soon led to a second one. We are told, "You should not *look down on* your brother in the day of his misfortune" (v. 12) and again, "You should not . . . *look down on* them in their calamity in the day of their disaster" (v. 13). This may have two possible

[2]Pusey, *The Minor Prophets*, vol. 1, p. 354.

meanings, as seen in the slightly different translations of the New International Version and the older Authorized Version. The New International Version translates the verb: "look down on," that is, "despise." If this is the meaning, the Edomites are blamed for considering themselves stronger and wiser than the Jews, a fault that goes back to the pride mentioned in the first section (v. 3).

On the other hand, the Authorized Version translates the verb: "look on," that is, "look into," "explore" or "show special curiosity" in regard to another person's misfortune. If this is the meaning, there is progression from the aloof stance mentioned in verse 11 to an improper curiosity about their brother's tragedy. It is true that the people of Edom stood aloof from Judah at the time of her fall, but while that is bad in itself there is a certain sense in which they did not stand aloof enough. They stood aloof so far as help was concerned, but they were there in order to find out the gory details of their rival city's fall.

I know Christians who act like that. They never help anyone, but they are not averse to finding out the wicked details of some other Christian's failings. Have you heard of someone who has fallen into some sin, and have you been tempted for curiosity's sake to see what the trouble is? According to Obadiah, this is something you should not do. Do not be too curious about other Christians' problems. Above all, do not be curious about their sins. They are servants of the Lord. Before the Lord they stand or fall. (I do not mean that if another Christian is overtaken in a sin, the sin is to be ignored. The principle for dealing with sin is in the first verse of Gal. 6: "If someone is caught in a sin, you who are spiritual should restore him gently. But watch yourself, or you also may be tempted." Our obligation is to restore—if we hear about it.)

The third stage in this unfortunate growth of unbrotherliness is in the second half of verse 12: "You should not

. . . *rejoice over* the people of Judah in the day of their destruction." This progression is easy to understand, for whenever there is hostility between two brothers, or nations, or churches, whatever it may be, and the one sees the other in misfortune the natural thing is to be happy about it. You say, "Do Christians do that today?" Certainly, they do! Christians talk about other Christians and can even be happy that the other one has sinned. Somehow it makes them appear better.

The fourth stage is *boasting*, also in verse 12. "You should not . . . boast so much in the day of their trouble." This grows from pride and is closely related to rejoicing over another's misfortune. We rejoice because we consider ourselves better. If we saw ourselves on the same level as others, we would mourn with them and turn to God in humble thanksgiving that we have been spared, though our sins are also many.

Up to this point, all steps in this abhorrent growth of unbrotherliness have been attitudes, or at least actions of a negative sort. The Edomites stood aloof in the day of Jerusalem's trouble. This led them to look down on their brothers, rejoice in their misfortune, and ultimately boast that they were stronger, wiser, and superior to those who had fallen. This particular sin cannot be confined to attitudes, however. What we think inevitably issues in actions, and this is exactly what we find in the fifth, sixth, and seventh items mentioned by the prophet. What are these items? The fifth is that the Edomites "*march*[ed] *through* the gates of my people in the day of their disaster" (v. 13). The sixth is that they "*seize*[ed] *their wealth*" (v. 13). The last, a compound description involving three related actions, is that they "*wait*[ed] *at the crossroads* to *cut down* their fugitives [and] *hand over* their survivors in the day of their trouble" (v. 14).

This last verse says that the Edomites actually caught Jews who were escaping from Jerusalem, rounded them up and then delivered them back into the hands of their enemies. This is the ultimate growth of their sin. It sounds terrible, and it is. But this is something of which Christians are sometimes also guilty— not in a literal sense (they do not have the opportunity)—but in serving the cause of Satan through their treatment of Christians who have sinned or erred in some doctrine. I may be wrong in this, but I believe that there are some Christians who spend more time serving the enemy by delivering fellow believers into the hands of unbelievers than they do serving God. Our duty to other believers is to build them up (Eph. 5:12) and restore them if they have sinned (Gal. 6:1).

GROWING WITH GOD

With verse 14 Obadiah has completed his case against Edom. As Gaebelein says, "Obadiah has concluded his examination of Edom's damning sin. Unsparingly he has dissected it. Step by step he has shown its development. With inexorable logic he has demonstrated the causes of that 'perpetual hatred' with which Ezekiel was later to charge" the country (Ezek. 35:5).[3] There is nothing left for Obadiah to do but speak of that coming day of the Lord that will be judgment for Edom as well as deliverance for those the Edomites have mistreated.

But there is this to add. It is true that the sin of Edom, long indulged, worked itself into the very character of the people and therefore inevitably flowed on in history. But that same flow of history also brought one who lived by an entirely different standard.

There was a day in history when two kings confronted one another for the first time. One was an earthly king. He sat that day at the pinnacle of power. His name was Herod Antipas. Herod was a son of Herod the Great, who was an Edomite or (as the New Testament has

it) an Idumean. Herod the Great had slaughtered the babes of Bethlehem in his desire to exterminate Christ. His successor, Antipas, with whom we are concerned, was no better. He had beheaded John the Baptist and had been called "that fox" by Jesus (Luke 13:32). Antipas had everything he wanted. His income, expressed in American money, would be in excess of 6 million dollars a year. All the pleasures of life were his. If anyone stood in his way . . . well, the life of that person meant as little to him as the lives of the innocents of Bethlehem had meant to his father. The motto of his reign was: "What will it profit *me?*"

The other king was Jesus. He was the King of Kings, one who, according to the flesh, was the natural heir to David's throne and who, according to His divine nature, was the supreme King over all the kings of this earth. But He did not look like a king. He stood in humble clothing. He had been rejected. Within hours He was to die a felon's death. If Jesus had wished, He could have called forth legions of angels who would have vindicated His cause instantly and have swept the usurper Herod from the throne. But Jesus did not want the throne in that way. He did not want the throne until you and I could share it with Him. To make that possible He would die.

Herod said, "What does it profit *me?*"

Jesus said, "What can I do that will be the greatest possible benefit to My brethren?" God vindicated Jesus! Jesus went to the cross. He died. But His death was followed by a resurrection, and today He lives to enable those who believe on Him to behave as He did and bring a true, supernatural brotherhood to this world. For his part, Herod went on with his revelry but soon was banished to Lyons, France, where he died in misery.[4]

This is the choice before you: to go Herod's way or Jesus' way. You cannot

---

[3]Gaebelein, *Four Minor Prophets*, p. 31.

[4]I am indebted for this comparison to a small tract written years ago by Joseph Hoffman Cohn for the American Board of Missions to the Jews, entitled "The Man from Petra," No. 65 in the series "What Every Christian Should Know About the Jews" (revised 1961, no original date of publication).

do both. If you drift, the way will be Herod's. You will live for self: you will end up thinking yourself better than others and mistreating them. If your life is to be different from that—and your end as well—you must follow Jesus.

29

Deliverance in Zion

(Obadiah 15–21)

"The day of the Lord *is near for all nations. As you have done, it will be done to you; your deeds will return upon your own head. Just as you drank on my holy hill, so all the nations will drink continually; they will drink and drink and be as if they had never been. But on Mount Zion will be deliverance; it will be holy, and the house of Jacob will possess its inheritance. The house of Jacob will be a fire and the house of Joseph a flame; the house of Esau will be stubble, and they will set it on fire and consume it. There will be no survivors from the house of Esau." The* Lord *has spoken.*

History is filled with the reversal of people's fortunes. When Jacob returned to the Promised Land after living on the other side of the desert with Laban, his brother Esau came from Edom to meet him. Esau had four hundred armed men, an army. Jacob had his motley collection of shepherds and livestock. The two embraced each other and then parted, Esau returning to Edom where his prosperity evidently continued to increase. In the Genesis account it takes an entire chapter to list Esau's mighty descendants: "These were the kings who reigned in Edom before any Israelite king reigned. . . . These were the chiefs descended from Esau, by name, according to their clans and regions" (Gen. 36:31, 40). Esau gave birth to kings. But of Jacob we read: "Jacob lived in the land where his father had stayed, the land of Canaan" (Gen. 37:1).

Jacob was a stranger in Canaan, as his fathers had been before him. He himself was a shepherd. While he lived like this, and even afterward, when his descendants went down to Egypt and became slaves to the Egyptians, Esau and his descendants prospered—and boasted of their superiority to Jacob's children.

How history changes things! Today, in fulfillment of the prophecies of God concerning Edom, Edom is a wasteland, its people gone: "I will make Mount Seir a desolate waste and cut off from it all who come and go. . . . I will make you desolate forever; your towns will not be inhabited" (Ezek. 35:7, 9). For her part, Israel is again back in the land of promise.

JUDGMENT ON EDOM

When we talk about the present nation of Israel we must be very careful, however. For Israel has not returned to Palestine in belief—she is a very secular nation—and her regathering in this century is not necessarily the fulfillment of biblical prophecies. Still, it is hard to doubt that this may be a part of that fulfillment. Edom has been scattered, just as Obadiah and other prophets foretold. Has Israel not been regathered in an opposite but exactly parallel fashion?

These questions arise as we study the third and last section of Obadiah's prophecy. The first section (vv. 1–9) concerned the pride of Edom. Edomites boasted that they were secure in their mountain fortresses. They were invincible. If their defenses should fail, which they thought was impossible, they still had their numerous allies and that superior wisdom that had always stood them in good stead. They did not need God. They certainly did not need other men and women, particularly their despised brothers and sisters in Jerusalem.

This sin of pride, great in itself, led to an additional sin of a more overt nature, the subject of the second section of Obadiah's prophecy (vv. 10–14). Edom's scorn of the Jews led to mistreatment of them, for when Jerusalem was overrun by enemies, the Edomites began by looking on in glee and then actually participated in looting and in the eventual capture and betrayal of the unfortunate escapees. In Obadiah's handling of these sins, the unbrotherly treatment of the people of Jerusalem by the Edomites was proof of their greater sin of pride and thus the historical reason for God's ultimate judgment of them in the flow of history.

This brings us to Obadiah's third section (vv. 15–21). Having made his accusation and having proved its validity, the prophet now declares God's judgment: "The day of the LORD is near for all nations. As you have done, it will be done to you; your deeds will return upon your own head. Just as you drank on my holy hill, so all the nations will drink continually; they will drink and drink and be as if they had never been" (v. 15).

This is not the first time we have come across "the day of the LORD" in the Minor Prophets. The phrase does not occur in Hosea, though a message of judgment is present. But the concept is prominent both in Joel and Amos. In Joel the Day of the Lord is linked to the invasion of the land by locusts, which was the occasion of the prophecy. Joel writes:

Blow the trumpet in Zion;
    sound the alarm on my holy hill.
Let all who live in the land tremble,
    for the day of the LORD is coming.
It is close at hand—
    a day of darkness and gloom,

a day of clouds and blackness.
Like dawn spreading across the
    mountains
    a large and mighty army comes,
such as never was of old
    nor ever will be in ages to come (2:1,
    2).

Joel's central image for the Day of the Lord is darkness—"darkness and gloom . . . clouds and blackness"—which he obviously gets from the blocking out of the sun by the invading locust swarm. However, Amos uses the same imagery even though he is not thinking of locusts:

Woe to you who long
    for the day of the LORD!
Why do you long for the day of the LORD?
That day will be darkness, not light. . . .
Will not the day of the LORD be darkness,
    not light—
    pitch-dark, without a ray of brightness? (5:18, 20).

Amos said that this day would mean judgment for Israel, even though the people thought it would be a day of their vindication. The people of the northern kingdom apparently longed for this day, thinking it would mean deliverance for them and judgment for their enemies. Amos turns the tables, maintaining that they along with the heathen nations will be judged.

This is the concept we encounter (for the third time) in Obadiah. But just as Joel and Amos each have their own characteristic way of talking about this day and make their own emphases, so does Obadiah make his distinct contribution. Obadiah pictures the drunken orgy of conquest that took place the day Jerusalem was overrun. In that day the Edomites also entered Jerusalem and "drank on [God's] holy hill," along with others. Edom, Obadiah says with poetic justice, along with the other nations, is going to drink again. But this time the cup will not hold wine. It will be the cup of the wrath of God (cf. Jer. 25:15, 17).

As you have done,
    it will be done to you;

your deeds will return upon your own
head.
Just as you drank on my holy hill,
 so all the nations will drink continually;
they will drink and drink
 and be as if they had never been (vv.
 15, 16).

There are two features of Obadiah's
prophecy of judgment that are particularly interesting. First, even though this
is a prophecy directed almost exclusively
against Edom, the prophet declares that
"the day of the LORD is near *for all nations.*" This is not just a casual comment,
for although he has spoken only of Edom
up to this point, he now talks about a
variety of peoples and places: "people
from the Negev [and] the foothills"
(v. 19), "the Philistines" (v. 19), "Ephraim
. . . Samaria . . . Benjamin . . . Gilead"
(v. 19), "Zarephath" and "Sepharad"
(v. 20). We have the feeling that Obadiah
could have expanded this list indefi-
nitely; and if this is the case, then he
could have included our own or any other
nation as well. He might have said, "The
day of the LORD is near for the United
States of America" or "The day of the
LORD is near for the Soviet Union." It is
a tragedy of nations that their people
somehow think themselves exempt from
the judgments that have overtaken others. If they cannot learn from the Bible,
they should at least learn from history.
Nations fall. All are judged. Moreover,
what is true for nations is true for us
personally. The day comes when God
will judge everyone. The Bible says, "Man
is destined to die once, and after that to
face judgment" (Heb. 9:27).

The second interesting feature of this
statement about judgment is Obadiah's
belief that it is near: "The day of the LORD
is *near* for all nations." This raises a question is most minds. At the very latest
Obadiah was prophesying about 500
years before the birth of Christ, and perhaps 850 years before. That means that
his words were spoken or written between two and three thousand years ago.

Since the Day of the Lord has not come,
in what sense is it right for Obadiah to
have declared this judgment "near"? Is
this not stretching language beyond any
reasonable limits? Does it not mean that
Obadiah was mistaken?

There are some who say this, of course.
They say the same thing about the Lord's
promise to come again (John 14:3). But
there are several things we should think
about before we reach this conclusion.

First, although the Day of the Lord has
been delayed for most nations, the Day
of the Lord was not long delayed for
Edom. Edom was judged. Moreover, if
a late date is chosen for Obadiah (perhaps following the fall of Jerusalem to
Babylon in 587 B.C.), the destruction came
not long afterward.

Still, this does not solve the whole
problem. Obadiah speaks not merely of
the judgment of Edom but of a judgment
that "is near for *all nations.*" How can
that statement be true? At this point we
need to understand that the Bible's view
of nearness is more what we would intend by the word "imminence." That is,
the judgment is near in the sense that it
can occur at any moment. Imminent
means "threatening to occur immediately, impending." An imminent event
does not necessarily occur immediately,
but it could. Therefore one must be ready
for it.

An illustration may help. Imagine that
a preacher is talking to a large congregation and that, as he begins, he places
his Bible on the pulpit so that it is hanging out over the edge. This Bible is very
precariously balanced. Although the
preacher is not aware of it himself, the
congregation notices what has happened
and is anxiously wondering when the
Bible will fall. No one knows when it will
fall. It might sit there throughout the sermon. But, on the other hand, the preacher
might jar the pulpit or even knock the
Bible off deliberately. The situation is
critical. When the preacher is speaking
quietly and is not touching the pulpit,

the congregation relaxes somewhat. When he gets louder and begins to thump the pulpit, they become worried.

This is the sense in which God's judgment is near, not only to nations but to every one of us. There are times when things are quiet and we do not anticipate the judgment so much. At other times we hear of wars and rumors of wars, the sea of the nations is troubled, and we wonder if God's final intervention in history may not be just around the corner. We become anxious. But notice: judgment is no less near in quiet times than in stormy ones. At any moment God may set the wheels of His final reckoning in order. That is why we must prepare for the Day of the Lord and be ready through faith in Jesus our Savior. Jesus Himself said, "Keep watch, because you do not know on what day your Lord will come" (Matt. 24:42).

BLESSING FOR ISRAEL

Judgment on Edom is the first half of this example of the reversal of national fortunes in history, but there is a second half too. It is the lifting up of Israel from its downcast state—overrun, cut down, handed over to its enemies—to a place of blessing and power once again. Obadiah says,

But on Mount Zion will be deliverance;
  it will be holy,
and the house of Jacob
  will possess its inheritance (v. 17).

After telling how Israel will be used as a flame to punish Esau ("they will set it on fire and consume it," v. 18) and showing how the peoples of the region will be redistributed as Israel expands into the "mountains of Esau," the "land of the Philistines," "Gilead," "Zarephath," "Sepharad" and "the Negev" (vv. 19, 20), Obadiah concludes:

Deliverers will go up on Mount Zion
  to govern the mountains of Esau.
And the kingdom will be the LORD'S
  (v. 21).

This is a great section of the Word of God for Israel. As surely as God says He is going to bring judgment on Edom (which He has done), so does He say He is going to give deliverance to His own people, bless them and enable them to possess these territories.

This must be taken literally. It must refer to a period of blessing of God on Israel as yet not seen. Some do not take the words this way. Either they say that the prophecies have been fulfilled by the humble regathering of the nation in Judah after the Babylonian exile, or they apply these promises of blessing to the church and view them as being fulfilled spiritually in these days. As I have pointed out in dealing with similar prophecies, I do not see how either of these views is possible. Above all, I do not see how the promises can be spiritualized. The only possible way to interpret the first two-thirds of Obadiah is to take the work literally. It deals with a literal nation, a literal period in history, and literal sins. Even the third part foretells a period of literal judgment on Edom, as we have seen. How is it that all of a sudden, between verses 16 and 17, we have to shift gears and say that the last few verses of Obadiah must be spiritualized? I do not see how this is possible.[1]

Having said this, however, it is also worth noting that the substance of Obadiah's promises are also promises for those who are members of Christ's spiritual body, the church. There are three main emphases, all in verse 17. First, Obadiah promises that the Day of the Lord will mean deliverance for God's people. Deliverance from what? In the

---

[1] I have discussed this matter at greater length in dealing with the earlier prophets in this volume, particularly in discussing the final oracles of Amos. See "Days of Fruit and Wine" (Amos 9: 11–15), pp. 179–186.

case of Israel this is clearly a deliverance from earthly enemies such as Edom, the Philistines, Arabs, and Babylonians. In our case it is deliverance from sin's power. Are we not delivered from sin already? Yes, in a sense. This is what redemption means—deliverance from the bondage of sin by the Lord Jesus Christ, because He loved us. Still, like creation, which has also participated in Christ's work, "we . . . groan inwardly as we wait eagerly for our adoption as sons, the redemption of our bodies" (Rom. 8:23). We are waiting for the great work of God in our salvation to be complete.

Second, Obadiah speaks of a day when Mount Zion "will be holy." We are not holy, and "without holiness no one will see the Lord" (Heb. 12:14). What shall we do? There is nothing we can do. But God will do what needs to be done. He will make us holy, little by little now and perfectly later when we are taken out of this life into eternity.

That Obadiah speaks of a day when Mount Zion will be holy shows that he is thinking here of a great future day. Frank Gaebelein notes, "These are weighty words, because they show exactly why human efforts alone will never bring in the kingdom. For an essential element of that promised reign of worldwide peace and righteousness is holiness. And holiness is the one thing no man apart from Christ possesses. Let us not be deluded, no, not even by the idealism of our time. Christless peace conferences will never abolish war. No United Nations will bring in the kingdom without the King. The one essential element of holiness will be lacking. Had Obadiah written nothing but these five words, his prophecy would be immortal."[2]

Third, Obadiah promises that in that future Day of the Lord, which is judgment for Edom and the nations, "the house of Jacob will possess its inherit-

ance." The inheritance of Israel is land. So this is a promise that Israel will again settle in the land once given to Abraham, partially possessed and then lost during the time of Israel's scattering. This is why the last verses of Obadiah speak of so many places from which the Jews are to be regathered.

But as we said earlier in reference to the other promises, this has a spiritual application for us too. It is a promise that we too will possess our possessions. As Gaebelein says, "No people on earth have greater potential possessions than Christian believers. . . . To them God has promised the supply of every need according to his riches in glory by Christ Jesus and for them he makes everything work together for good. Moreover, Christians have in the Bible the full revelation of God. They have dwelling in their hearts the Holy Spirit to guide them into all truth. But how few of us even begin to enter into this heritage! . . . When it comes to some of the choicest treasures of our faith, we simply do not possess our possessions. We repeat the Twenty-third Psalm, for instance, and say to ourselves that it is marvelous to think of the Lord's being our shepherd. But difficulty and trouble come, and we worry. What we have been doing with God's truth is merely to admire it. We have not possessed it to the extent of putting it to full use by unwavering trust."[3]

THE MAN FROM PETRA

In the sixty-third chapter of Isaiah there is a dramatic scene in which a blood-stained divine warrior comes marching up the valley of the Kidron toward Jerusalem, and the cry goes out:

> Who is this coming from Edom,
>   from Bozrah, with his garments stained crimson?
> Who is this, robed in splendor,
>   striding forward in the greatness of his strength?

[2]Gaebelein, *Four Minor Prophets*, p. 39.
[3]Ibid., pp. 41, 41.

The warrior answers,

> "It is I, speaking in righteousness,
>   mighty to save."

The prophet, watching from the walls of the city, still has this question:

> Why are your garments red?
>   like those of one treading the
>   winepress?

The traveler answers,

> "I have trodden the winepress alone;
>   from the nations no one was with me.
> I trampled them in my anger
>   and trod them down in my wrath;
> their blood spattered my garments,
>   and I stained all my clothing.
> For the day of vengeance was in my heart,
>   and the year of my redemption has
>   come" (vv. 1–4).

Who is this warrior? He is none other than the Lord Jesus Christ, returning to Jerusalem in the day of His wrath after having subdued the nations as Obadiah foretold. He is the great "I am," speaking in righteousness (Isa. 63:1). He is the Judge and Savior (v. 4).

The time is coming when God is going to sort things out and punish unrighteousness. If we were to look at this past period in the history of Edom and Israel, we might conclude that Edom will escape and Israel will always suffer. Here is Edom: a nation of sinners, but in power, impregnable in Petra. Here is Israel: chosen of God, but disciplined because of sin—her city overthrown, her people scattered. A person might look at this and say, "Well, that's the end of Israel! Off they go to Babylon! They're never going to come back from that captivity. Who ever heard of a captive nation rising and repossessing their land? It has never happened before; it is certainly not going to happen in this case." Yet God brings Edom down, and He exalts His people.

In this world the ungodly often seem to flourish; the godly are stricken. But God says that in the ultimate working of His plan the ungodly are going to be punished—the Day of the Lord will come upon them—while those who are His people will be lifted up and blessed in Jesus Christ.

If the Day of the Lord has not yet come, it is in order that God might show grace to more people. In the apostle Peter's day skeptics were saying that because things seemed to continue as they have been from the beginning, therefore there is no judgment. But Peter answered, "The Lord is not slow in keeping his promise, as some understand slowness. He is patient with you, not wanting anyone to perish, but everyone to come to repentance" (2 Peter 3:9). God is delaying the ultimate working out of His judgment on many nations until those whom He will call to faith in the Lord Jesus Christ do come. This is the day of His grace.

If you are not a believer in Christ, God tells you to believe in Him now. Run to Mount Zion for salvation! Run to Jesus! If you are a believer, then do as Israel will do and possess your great possessions.

JONAH

30

The Prophet Who Ran Away

(Jonah 1:1–3)

The word of the LORD came to Jonah son of Amittai: "Go to the great city of Nineveh and preach against it, because its wickedness has come up before me."

But Jonah ran away from the LORD and headed for Tarshish. He went down to Joppa, where he found a ship bound for that port. After paying the fare, he went aboard and sailed for Tarshish to flee from the LORD.

Many years ago in Chicago two homosexuals by the names of Leopold and Loeb were brought to trial for the murder of a young lad. Their lawyer was the well-known agnostic defense attorney Clarence Darrow, the man famous for his arguments at the Scopes' trial regarding the teaching of evolution in the public schools of Tennessee. The Chicago trial was a long one, but at last it drew to a close and Darrow found himself summing up the evidence. The testimony of one witness had been particularly damaging. So Darrow referred to it, saying, "Why, a person could as easily believe this man's testimony as he could believe that the whale swallowed Jonah."

There were some people on the jury who believed that the whale had indeed swallowed Jonah. Moreover, they believed that Leopold and Loeb were guilty and convicted them. But the statement, "A person can as easily believe that as believe that the whale swallowed Jonah," became a rallying cry for many who wished to deny the truthfulness of this narrative.

SIGN OF JONAH

We live somewhat later in history and have knowledge about fish that was not available to those living in Darrow's day.

Christians are less inclined to insist that the fish was a whale; neither the Old Testament Hebrew nor the New Testament Greek says "whale." The references are only to "a great fish." Nevertheless, those who adhere to the total trustworthiness of the Bible, now as then, rightly insist that Jonah was literally swallowed and was thus preserved alive for three days by the fish's action. To those who believe in the literal bodily resurrection of Jesus Christ, such an event is not at all impossible.

Moreover, there is a direct connection between the two. When unbelieving scribes and Pharisees asked Jesus for a sign that might substantiate His extraordinary claims, Jesus replied, "A wicked and adulterous generation asks for a miraculous sign! But none will be given it except the sign of the prophet Jonah. For as Jonah was three days and three nights in the belly of a huge fish, so the Son of Man will be three days and three nights in the heart of the earth" (Matt. 12:39, 40). Jesus referred to the experience of Jonah as a historical illustration of His own literal resurrection, thus reinforcing the truthfulness of this narrative.

To believe this is not popular, of course. It will not gain the world's attention. If Christian people, particularly a Christian

211

minister, deny such things—if I should say, "Now, of course, a whale cannot swallow a man, and therefore we know that we should not take the story of Jonah literally"—some people at least would pay attention. They would say, "Dr. Boice is denying the Bible. He does not believe in Jonah." This would be news. But if I maintain, as I do, that this story is factual and, furthermore, that the words of Christ also indicate that this is true, people shrug their shoulders and say, "Well, what do you expect a preacher to believe?" To regard Jonah as factual is not calculated to gain either respect or attention. Yet the book is true, and it is only when we regard it as true that it speaks to us forcefully.

There are a number of reasons why many will not believe the historical nature of Jonah's experience. They are summarized by Frank E. Gaebelein in *Four Minor Prophets:* 1) the abundance of the supernatural; 2) the unprecedented nature of Jonah's mission to Nineveh; 3) the reference to Nineveh in the past tense, "was"; 4) the supposed grossly exaggerated size of Nineveh; 5) supposed inaccuracies; and 6) the fact that the book contains late words supposedly incompatible with vocabulary used during the time Jonah was living.

But there are answers to each of these points, as Gaebelein shows.[1] First, the problem with miracles begs the question of God's omnipotence; for if God is able to raise up Jesus, He is certainly able to preserve Jonah and do the other supernatural acts attributed to Him. Second, other prophets also went to foreign nations—Elijah to Zarephath (1 Kings 17:8–24; Luke 4:26), Elisha to Damascus (2 Kings 8:7–15). Third, the use of "was" is merely a convention of narrative writing. Fourth, the reported size of Nineveh may well include the adjacent populations, what we would call suburbs. Fifth, the so-called inaccuracies are unproven.

Sixth, so-called late words occur in Old Testament books from both early and late periods.

MERCY AND SOVEREIGNTY

There are other reasons beyond the miraculous to study this book. An obvious one is for what it teaches of the mercy of God. What is the story about if not God's mercy? There is the mercy of God to Nineveh, which made Jonah angry. There is the mercy of God to Jonah himself, for Jonah certainly did not deserve it. There is even the mercy of God to the pagan sailors mentioned in Jonah 1. All were recipients of God's mercy. If we understand the book at this point, we will find ourselves identifying with those who perhaps, from our natural point of view, are unworthy of such mercy. These will be people like the woman next door who lets her dog run through your flower bed, or like the couple down the street who are "swingers." They will be Jews or blacks, rich or poor, those of some other ethnic background, or someone who has wronged you by slander or a hostile act. These are the ones we should love for Christ's sake. As Gaebelein writes: "In a day when prejudice and hate inflame men's emotions and pervert their judgment, Jonah speaks with compelling force about limiting our love and sympathies only to some of our fellow human beings and excluding others from our pity and compassion."[2]

Jonah should also be studied for what it teaches about God's sovereignty, the point on which the book is most informative and most profound. Understanding God's sovereignty is a problem for some Christians, though there are some features of sovereignty that are not a problem. Most of us do not have problems with God's sovereign rule in natural law. Gravity is one illustration. God exercises His rule through gravity, and we do not have difficulty at this point. In fact, we

[1]Gaebelein, *Four Minor Prophets,* pp. 60, 61.
[2]Ibid., p. 125.

are even somewhat reassured that objects conform to such laws.

The point at which we do have problems is when the sovereign will of God comes into opposition with a contrary human will. For example, there is the Christian who is married to another Christian but who, for whatever reason, is seeking a divorce. The Scriptures are plain. The couple are to remain together. But one of them declares, "I know what the Bible says, but I don't care. I have had it! I am going to get a divorce anyway." What happens here?

Again, we may imagine a person who begins to get far from the Lord and who therefore gives up his or her times of Bible reading, fellowship with Christian friends, church attendance, and giving to support the Lord's work. Each of these duties is clearly prescribed in the pages of God's Word, but the Christian neglects them, sometimes with great energy and determination. What happens at that point? God could crush the human will and thereby accomplish His own purpose with a ruthless hand. There are times when He has done this, as in the contest between Moses and Pharaoh. But generally He does not. What happens in such cases? Does God give up? Does He change His mind? Or does He accomplish His purposes in some other way, perhaps indirectly? The answer is in the Book of Jonah.

A GREAT COMMISSION

Interestingly enough, the book starts with a lesson on sovereignty—a commission to Jonah, and with Jonah's refusal to heed it. That is, it begins with a formal expression of God's sovereign will and a man's determined opposition to it. We read, "The word of the LORD came to Jonah son of Amittai: 'Go to the great city of Nineveh and preach against it, because its wickedness has come up before me.' But Jonah ran away from the LORD and headed for Tarshish" (1:1–3).

The location of Tarshish is disputed.

It has been identified with one of the cities of Phoenicia, which is unlikely. It has also been identified with ancient Carthage. Most probably, Tarshish was on the far coast of Spain, beyond Gibraltar. If this is right, it means that Jonah was determined to go as far as possible in the opposite direction from which God was sending him. Nineveh was east. Tarshish was west. We can visualize the geography if we imagine Jonah coming out of his house in Palestine, looking left down the long road that led around the great Arabian desert to the valleys of the Tigris and Euphrates Rivers, and then turning on his heel and going down the road to his right.

Why did he do it? We can imagine some reasons. We can imagine, first, that Jonah was overcome by thoughts of the mission's *difficulties*, which are expressed very well in the commission. God told Jonah that Nineveh was a very "great city," and indeed it was. In addition to what the book itself tells us—that the city was so large that it took three days to cross it and that it had 120,000 infants or small children (4:11)—we also know that it was the capital of the great Assyrian empire, that it had walls a hundred feet high and so broad that three chariots could run abreast around them. Within the walls were gardens and even fields for cattle. For one man to arrive all alone with a message from an unknown God against such a city was ludicrous in the extreme. What could one man do? Who would listen? Where were the armies that could break down such walls or storm such garrisons? The men of Nineveh would ridicule the strange Jewish prophet. "Certainly," as Hugh Martin, one of the most comprehensive commentators on this book, has written, "Jonah could not but foresee that some such reception in 'that great city' was about the most friendly he could anticipate. To be despised and simply laughed at, as a fanatic and fool, must have appeared to him inevitable, if indeed his fate should not be worse."[3] If Jonah had been overcome with the thought of the difficulties of such a mission and because of them had fled to Tarshish, we could well understand him. Yet not a word in the story indicates that it was the difficulties that upset this rebellious prophet.

Perhaps it was *danger*? The second word in God's description of the city is "wickedness." If Jonah had taken note of that wickedness and had refused to obey for that reason, this too would be understandable. Indeed, the more we learn of Nineveh the more dangerous the mission seems. We think of the prophecy of Nahum. Nahum's entire prophecy was against the wickedness of Nineveh, and the descriptions of it are vivid.

"Woe to the city of blood,
    full of lies,
    full of plunder,
    never without victims!
The crack of whips,
    the clatter of wheels,
    galloping horses
    and jolting chariots!
Charging cavalry,
    flashing swords
    and glittering spears!
Many casualties,
    piles of dead,
    bodies without number,
    people stumbling over the corpses—
all because of the wanton lust of a harlot,
    alluring, the mistress of sorceries,
who enslaved nations by her prostitution
    and peoples by her witchcraft" (3:1–4).

What was one poor preacher to do against such wickedness? Indeed, would people like this not simply kill him and add his body to the already high heap of carcasses? Thoughts like these could have made Jonah afraid; and if he had been afraid, we would not blame him. But again, not a word in the story indicates that it was danger that turned Jonah in the opposite direction.

What was the reason then? In the fourth chapter of the book, after God has already brought about the revival and has spared the Ninevites from judgment, Jonah explains the reason, arguing that it was precisely because of this outcome that he had disobeyed originally. He knew that God was gracious and that God was not sending him to Nineveh only to announce a pending judgment. He was sending him so Nineveh might repent. Jonah's own words are: "O LORD, is this not what I said when I was still at home? That is why I was so quick to flee to Tarshish. I knew that you are a gracious and compassionate God, slow to anger and abounding in love, a God who relents from sending calamity" (4:2).

As we read these words carefully we realize the reason why Jonah did not want to go to Nineveh. Those who lived there were enemies of his people, the Jews, and he was afraid that if he did go to them with his message of judgment, they would believe it and repent, and God would bless them. He did not want them blessed! God could bless Israel. But Jonah would be damned (literally) before he would see God's blessing shed on these enemies. He fled to Tarshish. We can understand the geography and Jonah's motives if we can imagine the word of the Lord coming to a Jew who lived in New York during World War II, telling him to go to Berlin to preach to Nazi Germany, and instead of this, he goes to San Francisco and takes a boat for Hong Kong.

Are we in the spiritual ancestry of Jonah? We have never been sent to Nineveh. We may never have had to run away to Tarshish. But the commission that has been given to us is no less demanding than Jonah's, if we are Christians. Is it not true that our attempts to avoid it are often no less determined than Jonah's when he tried to run away?

[3]Hugh Martin, *The Prophet Jonah: His Character and Mission to Ninevah,* original edition, 1866 (London: Banner of Truth Trust, 1958), p. 40.

Most Christians come into contact with the world in at least three places: in their neighborhoods, at work (unless they work for a totally Christian organization), and in their spare-time activities—clubs, hobbies, sports, and adult education courses. The people they meet in these places all have great needs. They need Christ, first of all, if they are not Christians. But they also need friendship, understanding, achievement. In some cases, there are even physical needs brought on by sickness, poverty, or some other physical deprivation. Christians are often strangely insensitive to these needs and often make excuses to avoid the personal sacrifices necessary to carry out the work of Christ. They say—we have all heard the excuses and, I am afraid, often make them ourselves—"I am too busy," "I have too many problems of my own," "Charity begins at home," or even "I am not called."

Jonah's commission consisted of two main words. He was to "go," and he was to "preach"—precisely what we have been told to do in the Great Commission. We are to go into all the world. And we are to preach (or teach) all that we have been taught by Jesus. Matthew's form of the Great Commission says, "Therefore go and make disciples of all nations, baptizing them in the name of the Father and of the Son and of the Holy Spirit, and teaching them to obey everything I have commanded you. And surely I will be with you always, to the very end of the age" (Matt. 28:19, 20). We are to go; but we remain inactive. We are to preach; but our tongues are often strangely silent.

Strangely silent! Strange that we should be silent when there is such a wonderful story to tell! John R. W. Stott illustrates in his book *Our Guilty Silence* what we often do.[4] He describes how he was on an overnight train from London to Pembrokeshire in South Wales and how a young land agent, who shared the sleeper, repeatedly took the name of the Lord Jesus Christ in vain. He had the upper bunk. In the morning, while getting ready to wash, he accidentally dropped his shaving equipment and swore about it. At this point Stott remained silent, making all the usual excuses—"It's none of your business"; "You've no responsibility for him"; "He'll only laugh at you." It was only after an inner struggle of some fifteen minutes that Stott eventually spoke of Christ and managed to leave the man an evangelistic booklet. We all have these difficulties. Only not all of us eventually overcome them and actually share the gospel.

WINGS OF THE DAWN

Verse 3 tells of Jonah's attempt to get away from God and gives the consequences of that attempt. It is surprising that Jonah did not think of these consequences before he ran or consider how impossible it is to escape from God.

Jonah lived relatively late in Old Testament history, certainly long after the psalms were written. He therefore had ample opportunity to know those great words in Psalm 139: "Where can I go from your Spirit? Where can I flee from your presence? If I go up to the heavens, you are there; if I make my bed in the depths, you are there. If I rise on the wings of the dawn, if I settle on the far side of the sea, even there your hand will guide me, your right hand will hold me fast" (vv. 7–10).

Did Jonah know these words? Probably. Then why did he not remember them as he set out in the ship for Tarshish?

As I read that psalm I find myself wondering if the name of the ship on which Jonah set out might not have been *The Wings of the Dawn*. The story does not give the name. But that would have been a good name for a ship; and if the ship mentioned in Jonah were so named, how well suited it would have been to Jonah's

[4]John R. W. Stott, *Our Guilty Silence* (Chicago: InterVarsity Press, 1967), pp. 9, 10.

situation! Did he notice the name, if this is what it was? Did he notice the rats getting off as he stepped on? If I understand sin and disobedience at all, I suspect that Jonah noticed none of these things, so set was he on disobedience. No more do we when we take our "wings of the dawn"—whether they be preoccupations with a job, an attitude, a cherished sin, or some other form of disobedience—to sail away from God.

GOD'S SOVEREIGNTY

At this point we find our first great lesson regarding God's sovereignty. Built into Jonah's first attempts to get away from God are two results that will follow anyone who tries to disobey Him.

First, Jonah's course was downhill. He would not have described it that way. He would have said that he was improving his life, just as we do when we choose our own course instead of God's. But it was downhill nevertheless. This is suggested in verse 3, where we are told that Jonah went "down" to Joppa. It is always that way when a person runs from the presence of the Lord. The way of the Lord is up! Consequently, any way that is away from Him is down. The way may look beautiful when we start. The seas may look peaceful and the ship attractive, but the way is still down.

There was another result. In his excellent preaching on Jonah, Donald Grey Barnhouse often called attention to it by highlighting the phrase about Jonah "paying the fare." He noted that Jonah did not get to where he was going, since he was thrown overboard, and that he obviously did not get a refund on his ticket. So he paid the full fare and did not get to the end of his journey. Barnhouse said, "It is always that way. When you run away from the Lord you never get to where you are going, and you always pay your own fare. On the other hand, when you go the Lord's way you always get to where you are going, and he pays the fare." That is worth repeat-

ing: *When you run away from the Lord you never get to where you are going, and you always pay your own fare. But when you go the Lord's way you always get to where you are going, and He pays the fare.*

Jonah illustrates one half of that statement. The story of Moses' mother, Jochebed, illustrates the other half. Jochebed conceived Moses during a time of great persecution by the Egyptians, a time in which Hebrew male infants were being thrown into the Nile river to die. When the child was born, Jochebed and her husband, Amram, tried to hide him as long as possible, suspecting, I believe, that this was the one who had been promised by God to be the deliverer of the people. But at last the baby's cries grew too loud, and another plan was necessary. The mother made a little boat of bulrushes, covering it with tar. She placed Moses in it and set it in the reeds by the riverbank. Then she stationed Miriam, Moses' sister, at a distance to see what would become of him. Though she wanted her baby more than anything else in the world, Jochebed entrusted the matter to God, allowing Him to do as He wished with the child.

The daughter of Pharaoh came down to the river, saw the ark in the water, and sent her maids to fetch it. When it was opened, she saw the baby. He was crying. This so touched the woman's heart that she determined to save him and raise him in the palace. But what was she to do? The child needed a wet nurse. Where could she find one?

At this point, Miriam, who had been watching from a distance, came forward and asked if she could be of assistance. "Shall I go and get one of the Hebrew women to nurse the baby for you?" Miriam asked.

"Yes," said the princess. Jochebed was brought.

Jochebed was about to receive back the child she most dearly wanted. She would have done anything to have kept him. She would have scrubbed floors in the palace! In fact, if the daughter of the Pharaoh had said, "I am going to give you this child to raise, but I want you to know that I have seen through your stratagem. I know that this young girl was not up on that hill watching by accident. She must be the sister of this baby and, therefore, you must be the mother. You can have your child. But as a sign of your disobedience to the Pharaoh, I am going to cut off your right hand"— if she had said that, Moses' mother would probably have held out both hands, if only she could have had the child back. But that is not what happened. Instead, Pharaoh's daughter gave the child back, declaring, "Take this baby and nurse him for me, and I will *pay you*" (Exod. 2:9, italics mine).

"I will pay you." That is the point for which I tell the story. Jonah went his own way, paid his own fare and got nothing. Jochebed went God's way. Consequently, God paid the fare, and she got everything. I repeat it once more: When you run away from the Lord you never get to where you are going, and you always pay your own fare. But when you go the Lord's way you always get to where you are going, and He pays the fare.

BUT THE LORD

In one sense Jonah's story is over at this point; that is, the story of his choice, his disobedience, is over. God has given His command. Jonah has disobeyed. Now Jonah must sit back and suffer the consequences as God intervenes supernaturally to alter the story. This is made clear by the contrast between the first two words of verse 3 ("But Jonah") and the first three words of verse 4 ("Then the LORD"). It is true that Jonah had rejected God. He had voiced his little "but," as we sometimes do. He is allowed to do it. God's sovereignty does not rule it out. But now God is to act, and His actions will be more substantial than Jonah's.

What did God do? He did three *great* things. First, He sent a *great storm*. The text indicates that it was a storm of unusual ferocity, so fierce that even experienced sailors were frightened. Each time I read about it I think of that other storm that also frightened experienced men on the Sea of Galilee. The men were Christ's disciples, and Christ was with them, though asleep in the boat. For awhile they rowed. But they were in danger of sinking and were afraid. So they awoke Jesus and cried, "Lord, save us!"

Jesus replied, "Why are you so afraid?" Then He arose and rebuked the winds and the sea, and there was a great calm. The disciples asked, "What kind of man is this? Even the winds and the waves obey him!" (Matt. 8:23–27).

Note the contrast. The Lord who can calm the troubled waters of your life is the same Lord who can stir them up to great frenzy. What He does depends on whether He is with you in the boat or, a better way of putting it, whether or not you are with Him. If Jesus is in your boat—if you are going His way and are trusting Him—then, when the storms come, you can cry out, "Master, help me!" and He will calm the violence. But if you are running from Him—if He is not in your boat and you are disobeying Him—then He will stir the waves up.

Second, the Lord prepared a *great fish*. Farther on in the story God also prepared a small worm to eat the root and so destroy the plant that shaded Jonah. On the one hand, God used one of the largest creatures on earth to do His bidding. On the other hand, He used one of the smallest. Apparently it makes no difference to God. He will use whatever it takes to get the disobedient one back into the place of blessing. Are you running away from God? If so, He may use the cankerworm to spoil your harvest. He may use the whirlwind to destroy your barns and buildings. If necessary, He will touch your person. He will use whatever it takes, because He is faithful to Himself, to you, and to His purposes.

Finally, God saved a *great city*. This

last act, like the others, is an act of mercy. The city did not deserve saving. Yet He saved it, thereby preserving it from destruction for a time.

A CONTINUOUS PERFORMANCE

God's perseverance will be discussed in later chapters, but it is important to look at one aspect of it in this present connection. The apostle Paul wrote: "Being confident of this, that he who began a good work in you will carry it on to completion until the day of Christ Jesus" (Phil. 1:6).

Quite often we look at that verse merely as a statement of the "eternal security" of the Christian, which is all right. God will certainly continue His work with us, regardless of what happens, and will preserve us for heaven. But this verse also means—we must not miss it—that God is so determined to perfect His good work in us that He will continue to do so with whatever it takes, regardless of the obedience or disobedience of the Christian. Will you go in His way? Then He will bless your life and encourage you. Will you run, as Jonah ran? Then He will trouble your life. If necessary, He will even break it into little pieces, if by so doing He enables you to walk in His way once again. If you disobey, you will find your initial disobedience easy. But after that the way will grow hard. If you obey Him, you will find the way paved with blessing.

31

The God Who Will Not Let Go

(Jonah 1:4–16)

Then the Lord *sent a great wind on the sea, and such a violent storm arose that the ship threatened to break up. All the sailors were afraid and each cried out to his own god. And they threw the cargo into the sea to lighten the ship.*

But Jonah had gone below deck, where he lay down and fell into a deep sleep. The captain went to him and said, "How can you sleep? Get up and call on your god! Maybe he will take notice of us, and we will not perish."

Then the sailors said to each other, "Come, let us cast lots to find out who is responsible for this calamity." They cast lots and the lot fell on Jonah.

So they asked him, "Tell us, who is responsible for making all this trouble for us? What do you do? Where do you come from? What is your country? From what people are you?"

He answered, "I am a Hebrew and I worship the Lord, *the God of heaven, who made the sea and the land."*

This terrified them and they asked, "What have you done?" (They knew he was running away from the Lord, *because he had already told them so.)*

The sea was getting rougher and rougher. So they asked him, 'What should we do to you to make the sea calm down for us?"

"Pick me up and throw me into the sea," he replied, "and it will become calm. I know that it is my fault that this great storm has come upon you."

Instead, the men did their best to row back to land. But they could not, for the sea grew even wilder than before. Then they cried to the Lord, *"O* Lord, *please do not let us die for taking this man's life. Do not hold us accountable for killing an innocent man, for you, O* Lord, *have done as you pleased." Then they took Jonah and threw him overboard, and the raging sea grew calm. At this the men greatly feared the* Lord, *and they offered a sacrifice to the* Lord *and made vows to him.*

The lessons of the first three verses of Jonah are great, for they concern the impossibility of running away from God and the consequences of such an attempt. The consequences are that the path we take is downhill, that we never get to where we are going, and that we always pay our own bills. At this point of the story, however, God Himself intervened in a supernatural way, so that the lessons of the remainder of the chapter are as great as those at the beginning.

We learn that disobedience always involves others in peril. We learn how God acts when His will is opposed.

Special Intervention

The way God operates when His will is opposed leads again to the issue of God's sovereignty and carries us a step farther in our understanding of it. First, we saw that God's sovereignty expresses itself in what we might call a natural spiritual order. According to this principle, no path of disobedience is ever blessed. Now we also learn that God will intervene in special ways to insure the accomplishment of His purposes.

This special intervention occurs twice in the first chapter. The first is in the way God dealt with Jonah when he ran away. The second is in God's dealing with the sailors.

Jonah had sinned. According to some theologies, in which almost everything depends on man's obedience to God and very little on God's elective purposes with man, this should have been the end of the matter. If Jonah had sinned, God should simply have said, "Jonah, you have done it now. You have disobeyed Me, and as a result of that you have forfeited the right to be called My child. I am casting you off." That kind of response makes sense according to a man-centered theology. But it is not the way God operates. To put it in theological language, God had elected Jonah to a special task and had determined that the task be accomplished. God took His election of Jonah so seriously that He would actually sink the ship on which the disobedient prophet was sailing, if necessary, rather than allow him to get on to his own destination. The story says, "Then the LORD sent a great wind on the sea, and such a violent storm arose that the ship threatened to break up" (v. 4).

One verse earlier we read the words "but Jonah." That verse tells us of Jonah's act of disobedience. We might say that those two words, "but Jonah," represent human depravity expressing itself through the old nature. In verse 4, in place of the words "but Jonah," we have the words "then the LORD." "Then the LORD" is an expression of the sovereign grace of God persevering with His people.

There is no question about our being allowed to resist God or disobey Him. We all do it. We do it easily. Though a pagan, Virgil wrote correctly, *"Facilis decensus Averno"* ("The descent to hell is easy"). When we disobey God, He does not rearrange the stars of heaven to say, "Stop, do not go farther." He lets us go. At first He does not put great obstacles in our path. If we choose to stop reading our Bibles, He does not send a special prophet to get us reading them again. If we stop praying, He does not send a disaster into our lives to make us turn to Him. Not at first! He simply allows us to go downhill and to pay for our own foolish choices. However, when we persist in our disobedience, He gets rougher. He begins gently, just as we gently disobey. But in the end He sends a tempest.

The outcome of the great storm was that by means of it God accomplished His purposes with Jonah. He accomplished His purposes with the people of Nineveh. He even accomplished His purposes in an ironic and preparatory way with the unbelieving sailors, for the story suggests that they came to believe on Him.

THE SAILORS

The disobedience of one of God's servants always involves others in peril, even innocent people. For Achan's sin, all Israel was defeated at Ai. For the sin of David in numbering the people, 70,000 died of pestilence. Similarly, because of Jonah's sin, innocent sailors were on the verge of drowning. They knew how to sail a ship, but this storm was beyond them. We are told that they were "afraid" of it and that "each cried out to his own god. And they threw the cargo into the sea to lighten the ship" (v. 5).

The sailors were like today's world leaders who, though they are not godly men, nevertheless do as well to cope with our problems as they know how. I admire the sailors. As I read the story, I find them to be hard-working, courageous men who knew their business well. These men had been in storms before. They knew what to do. They knew that in great storms the solution was to lighten the ship by casting the cargo overboard, which they did. Nevertheless, the storm was so great it frightened them, even though they had done all they could to save the situation. When they could do nothing more, they called on their gods.

Is this not a picture of today's world, a picture of government and politics? The trouble with our leaders is not that they are incompetent men. It is rather that the problems they are attempting to tackle are just too big for them. I am glad I do not have to deal with the world's sagging economy. I am glad I do not have to struggle to eliminate misunderstanding between nations in order to advance world peace. These enormous problems are beyond any human ability, regardless of how talented the statesmen are. So we see such men trying everything possible and then, when all else fails, calling on God.

We must not be smug at this point and overly blame the sailors, for we remember that the trouble that came on them had come because of Jonah. This means that, in some situations at least, problems come to the world because of God's judgment on His own children.

The brilliant French writer Jacques Ellul has a paragraph in which he shows how inseparably the lives of Christians and non-Christians are linked. He writes, "The safety of all depends on what each does. But each has his own thing to do. They are in the same storm, subject to the same peril, and they want the same outcome. They are in a unique enterprise, and this ship typifies our situation. What do these sailors do? First, they do all they humanly can; while Jonah sleeps, they try all human methods to save the vessel, to keep the enterprise going (v. 5). What experience, nautical science, reason, and common sense teach them to do, they do. In this sense they do their duty. The sailors are in charge of the world, and in normal conditions they discharge their task correctly. We can ask no more of them. The tragic thing

here, however, is that if conditions cease to be normal, it is not the fault of the sailors, the pagans; it is the fault of the Christian who has sailed with them. It is because of him that the situation is such that the knowledge and tradition of the sailors can do no more. We have to realize once again that this is how it usually is with the world; the storm is unleashed because of the unfaithfulness of the church and Christians. This being so, if the tempest is God's will to constrain his church, a will by which the whole human enterprise is endangered, one can easily see why man's technical devices are of no avail."[1]

While the storm was raging, Jonah, who represents the church, was asleep deep within the hold of the ship. How many of God's people are asleep today? How many are impervious while the tempest rages?

You Can't Sleep Forever

When Jonah had gone down into the hold of the ship to sleep, seemingly in drugged indifference to the calling of God, he must have thought himself alone and safe, at least for the time being. But suddenly his sleep was interrupted by the captain. This man was a pagan, like the sailors. He did not know the true God. His ideas of religion were undoubtedly filled with superstitions. Nevertheless, he believed enough in united prevailing prayer to want all on board to pray together. Since he did not know Jonah or what god he worshiped, it was just possible that Jonah worshiped a god who could do something if the other gods failed.

His words were abrupt, for he was disturbed that Jonah could sleep when the ship was in peril. "How can you sleep? Get up and call on your god! Maybe he will take notice of us, and we will not perish" (v. 6). Even a Christian is not allowed to ignore reality forever.

---

[1]Jacques Ellul, *The Judgment of Jonah* (Grand Rapids: Eerdmans, 1971), p. 41.

Meanwhile, up on the deck of the ship, the sailors had been discussing the storm and had concluded that it was not at all like other storms they had witnessed. They had been able to handle other storms. But this storm was ferocious, supernatural. Verse 4 ("the LORD sent a great wind on the sea") says literally that the Lord "hurled" the tempest. The sailors had concluded that the storm was a judgment against one of their number who had done something horrible. So they decided to cast lots to discover the culprit. It was at this moment that Jonah arrived from below deck.

Nothing in life ever really happens by chance. So when the lot was cast, the lot inevitably singled out Jonah.

People may think that such things are determined by chance. They speak of "Lady Luck" or work out "mathematical" odds. But God tells us that He controls what happens. A verse in Proverbs says: "The lot is cast into the lap, but its every decision is from the LORD" (Prov. 16:33). In this case the lot was something like a pair of dice, made from the anklebone of a sheep; the lap was the flat surface made when a man, who in those days normally wore a long garment, would squat down and spread his knees. The dice were cast into the lap, but God determined the outcome. Donald Grey Barnhouse often paraphrased this verse by saying that "man throws the dice; but it is God who makes the spots come up."

MANY QUESTIONS

As soon as Jonah was singled out by lot, a flurry of questions came from the troubled sailors. This would have happened in any case, but it was especially true in Jonah's in that no one really knew him. We catch some of the flavor of this from the writing: "So they asked him, 'Tell us, who is responsible for making all this trouble for us? What do you do? Where do you come from? What is your country? From what people are you?'" (v. 8). Undoubtedly there were more questions even than these. Every man would have had one. But at last they were all out, and Jonah had his turn to speak.

Notice the irony. Jonah had run away from God and was in this difficult position because he would not preach to pagans. But here he was, in spite of himself, about to do precisely that. It is even possible that there were men of Nineveh among these sailors. God was about to show that His purposes will always be accomplished, even (if He so wills it) by one who is obstinately disobedient.

It is amusing to me that, in spite of his determination to disobey God and the rupture of fellowship between himself and God which that must have caused, Jonah gave a very good testimony. Perhaps he had been a preacher too long and the habit of it was with him. Or perhaps, like Peter at the campfire of the high priest, he was just unable to lie convincingly. Logically, he might have been able to tell just the bare facts and let it go at that. Verse 10 says that he rehearsed his story, culminating in his running away. But Jonah could not stop at that point, it seems. So even in his state of disobedience and in the trauma of the moment, Jonah told of his background and indicated that he was a servant of the Creator and covenant-keeping God, Jehovah. Moreover, he was brilliantly relevant as he said it. "I am a Hebrew and I worship the LORD, the God of heaven, who made the sea [they needed a god who made the sea just then] and the land [the very place where each of them most wanted to be]" (v. 9).

Gaebelein writes of this testimony, "In addition to acknowledging himself a Hebrew, [Jonah] gave a witness then and there for his Lord. He may have been endeavoring to resign his commission, but he could not change his heart, which remained that of a true prophet. So he pointed these mariners to the only Lord God."[2]

---

[2]Gaebelein, *Four Minor Prophets*, p. 78.

An interesting phrase appears here, for, having been told of Jonah's testimony, we are immediately informed that the sailors were "terrified." We have already been told once that the men were afraid; they were afraid of the storm. We will be told once more that as a result of God's act in calming it they "greatly feared [that is, reverenced] the LORD" (v. 16). But why, we might ask, were the men exceedingly afraid at this point, more afraid apparently than they were of the storm itself?

The reason was that they knew about Jonah's God. These were men who had traveled from port to port around the Mediterranean Sea, hearing many stories of other people and their gods. Are we to think they had never heard of the Hebrew people or of the Hebrew God, Jehovah? Of course, they had heard of Him! He was the God who had brought down the plagues on Egypt so that His people might be led out. He was the God who had parted the waters of the Red Sea to allow the Israelites to escape into the desert and who had then closed the waters on the pursuing Egyptian forces. He had led the Hebrews in the wilderness for forty years, protecting them by a cloud that spread out over their encampment during the daytime to give them shade but which turned into a pillar of fire by night to give them light and heat. He had provided manna to eat and water to drink. He had parted the waters of the Jordan River to enable them to cross over into Canaan. He had leveled the walls of Jericho. He had caused the sun to stand still at Gibeon so that Joshua would have time to achieve a full victory over the fleeing Amorites. This was a great God, this God of the Hebrews; and it was this God, not a weak god, who was pursuing them for the sake of Jonah.

No wonder the men were terrified! "What have you done?" they asked. "What should we do to you to make the sea calm down for us?" was their next question (v. 11).

TWO MORE QUESTIONS

It is too bad that Jonah did not learn as much from the questions the sailors asked him as they had from his testimony, or he would not have answered their questions as he did.

The sailors had asked, "What have you done?" This was a rebuke. If Jonah had answered properly, it would have led to his repentance. There was no answer but the full confession of sin. Martin deals well with this question. "Suppose yourself in Jonah's place, and hear the question put to you—to you, a man of God, by heathen men, 'Why hast thou done this?' Did your God provoke you to flee from him? Did he deal so hardly and unkindly with you that you had no alternative but flight? Were you tired of your God? Had you found him out—as no more worthy of your trust and obedience? Had you got to the end of all the duty that you owed to him—or of all the protection and support that he could afford to you? [Why didn't you listen to him?]

"Produce your strong reasons. Has God been a wilderness to you? Have you found a better friend? Have you found a worthier portion? Have you found a sweeter employment than meditation in his word and calling on his name? . . .

"Have you found him unfaithful to his promise? Have you discovered that he discourages his people? Will you say that the more you have known him, the less you have thought of him? It looks like it, O backslider. It looks like it, if you can remember days when you loved him more, and served him better than now."[3] If Jonah had been able to think clearly along these lines, he would have acknowledged that nothing God had done or could ever do could deserve his disobedience, and he might have repented.

---

[3]Martin, *The Prophet Jonah*, pp. 167, 168.

But Jonah was like many of God's people when they sin. Instead of thinking clearly, he hardened his heart, kept his back turned to God, and plunged on into even greater alienation.

The state of Jonah's heart is revealed in his answer to the second question: "What should we do to you to make the sea calm down for us?" Notice that it was not the sailors who thought up the idea of throwing Jonah overboard. That was Jonah's idea. They said, "Tell us what to do to get out of this; we'll do anything you say."

And what did Jonah say? He might have called on them to repent of their sin and turn to Jehovah in order to become His followers. Jonah was in the midst of sin himself, so this answer was hardly open to him. Again, he might have tried to bluff his way out of the situation. He might have said, "I don't know what to do. God hasn't shown me. Here, give me an oar. I'll help you out." Jonah could not say this either, for he knew what the consequences of such indifference would be. The storm would have gotten worse, and eventually everyone on board would have drowned. He could have said, "It is obvious what we must do. God wants me to go to Nineveh, and we will not be safe until I do. Turn the boat around. Let's go back. Then the storm will stop." I think that if Jonah had followed this course, not only would the storm have stopped, but they would have had the best wind back to Joppa imaginable. This is not what Jonah said either.

Jonah's actual answer is a sad one. So determined was he to resist the Lord's will that he actually said, "Pick me up and throw me into the sea, . . . and it will become calm. I know that it is my fault that this great storm has come upon you" (v. 12). Jonah meant, "I would rather die than do God's will."

Can a Christian become so hardened that he prefers death to what God wants him to do? I wish we could say No to that question, but unfortunately the an-swer is Yes. A Christian can become hardened. This is the course of sin. What begins easily with just a step to the west instead of to the east soon accelerates into a maelstrom of self-destruction.

An apparent illustration of this is the life of the late Bishop James Pike, who rose to national fame through his controversial opinions and frequent denials of church doctrines. At the beginning his denials were not very extreme. He denied the Virgin Birth (or at least questioned it) and presumably had a less-than-orthodox view of the Scriptures. But these wrong steps soon led to others. His ecclesiastical rise—he was the Episcopal bishop who in 1958, together with the Stated Clerk of the United Prebyterian Church, Eugene Carson Blake, launched the proposal for a gigantic merger of protestant denominations later known as the Consultation on Church Union—was accompanied by an increasing decline of his commitment to other important doctrines. Even his own relatively liberal church was embarrassed, and there were several charges of heresy, though a heresy trial was avoided. There were also personal tragedies. Pike developed a drinking problem that led to his joining Alcoholics Anonymous. He had three marriages, the first being annulled and the second ending in divorce after producing four children. One son committed suicide. Pike drifted into the occult and claimed to have made contact with his deceased son through a Philadelphia medium named Arthur Ford. Finally, he left the church and died at last in 1969 in the Judean desert while researching a book on the historical Jesus; he had told friends it would be the most sensational of his writings yet.

Pike's story is particularly tragic, both for his own sake and for those who were involved in his fate. But it is a pattern played out on a less dramatic level in the lives of many disobedient Christians. Disregard of God's Word or of others' fates (as Jonah of the fate of Nineveh) soon leads to a disregard of one's own. We must be warned and must follow another path. Instead of brazening it out, we must learn to say with David, "Search me, O God, and know my heart; test me and know my anxious thoughts. See if there is any offensive way in me, and lead me in the way everlasting" (Ps. 139:23, 24).

TRUE CONVERSIONS

Someone has said that non-Christians never look better than when they are compared with some Christians, and that is certainly true if the Christians are disobedient ones. It is true in this story. Jonah, in his disobedience, is quite willing that all the inhabitants of Nineveh perish; for his message is one of impending judgment, and his fear is that it might be suspended if he should preach to them and they should repent. But the sailors, themselves pagans like the people of Nineveh, are unwilling that Jonah (just one man) should perish even though he has brought them into a position of great danger. Jonah has said that he should be thrown overboard. The sailors have every right to heed him. But they are unwilling to see him die if it can be prevented. They do their best to save him. The Hebrew text says literally, "Nevertheless, the men *digged* to bring it to the land" (v. 13).

Even pagans have their limits, however. So at last, when it was evident that they could not win against the waves, they asked Jehovah to hold them guiltless for Jonah's death and then threw the rebellious prophet overboard. At once the sea ceased its raging, and the men were left in silent wonder on the gently rolling deck.

What happens next is the climax of chapter 1, in spite of the fact that the final verse tells of Jonah being swallowed by the great fish. That verse should really begin chapter 2, and the verse that should end chapter 1 is verse 16. "At this the men greatly feared the LORD, and they

offered a sacrifice to the LORD and made vows to him." This seems to mean, quite simply, that the sailors were converted through their experience with Jonah. It means that in an ironic way God was already accomplishing His purposes in spite of His prophet's stubborn rebellion.

The fact that the sailors were saved is evident in practically every word used. To begin with, this is the third time that the men are said to have *feared* something or somebody. The first was the storm (v. 5). The second was the disclosure that Jonah was a Hebrew who worshiped Jehovah (v. 10). This time they are said to have feared (that is, respected) Jehovah Himself. There is a progression.

Moreover, they were worshiping *Jehovah*. Earlier, when we were told of their prayers, we read: "All the sailors were afraid and each cried out to his own god," that is, to idols. Now, after Jonah has been thrown overboard and the wind has stopped, we are told that they prayed to Jehovah, Jonah's God. And how did they worship? Well, they performed a sacrifice—this was the Jewish means of approach to God—and they made vows.

If the sailors had made their vows before their deliverance, I would not be so impressed. Theirs may have been only a foxhole conversion. We may imagine a situation in which a soldier is crouching in a foxhole looking down a hill against which an enemy is advancing. Naturally he is afraid for his life. He begins to pray: "O God, if there is a God, don't let me get killed! I don't want to die! Save me! If You save me, I will do anything You want! I'll even . . . yes, I'll even become a missionary!" Suddenly the soldiers turn off in another direction. The battle shifts, and he is saved. Does he remember his conversion? Not at all. He turns to his buddy and says, "Boy, we sure had a close call that time. Let's celebrate when we get our next leave. I know where we can drink and gamble and sin our fill." That is a foxhole conversion, but that is not what happened to the sailors. They made their vows *after* they had been delivered. Consequently, I believe that they were converted and that they must have vowed to serve Jehovah all their days.

IRONY AND GREAT GRACE

This is a great irony. We remember that Jonah was running from God because he did not want God to save the heathen in Nineveh. But the first great event in the story was the conversion of the heathen sailors, who were in many respects just like the pagans of Nineveh. And Jonah was not there to see it!

This carries us farther in the lessons of this book about God's sovereignty. What God is going to do, He will do. If He has determined to save Mary Jones, God will save Mary Jones. If He has determined to save John Smith, God will save John Smith. Moreover, those whom He saves will never perish, neither will anyone pluck them out of Christ's hand (John 10:28). But notice, God can do this through the obedience of His children, as He does later with Nineveh through Jonah, in which case they share in the blessing. Or He can do it through His children's disobedience, as here, in which case they miss the blessing. Either way, God blesses those whom He will bless. But the one case involves happiness for His people while the other involves misery. Which will it be in your case? Will you resist Him? Will you refuse His Great Commission? Or will you obey Him in this and in all matters?

Perhaps you are not yet a Christian. If not, then learn from God's grace to the sailors. You have not yet perished in your godless state because God, who made the sea around you and the dry land on which you walk, preserves you. Do not remain indifferent to Him. Turn to Him. Approach Him on the basis of the perfect sacrifice for sin made once by His own Son, Jesus Christ, and follow Him throughout your days.

32

Prayer From the Depths

(Jonah 1:17–2:10)

But the Lord provided a great fish to swallow Jonah, and Jonah was inside the fish three days and three nights.
From inside the fish Jonah prayed to the Lord his God. He said:
"In my distress I called to the Lord, and he answered me. From the depths of the grave I called for help, and you listened to my cry. You hurled me into the deep, into the very heart of the seas, and the currents swirled about me; all your waves and breakers swept over me. I said, 'I have been banished from your sight; yet I will look again toward your holy temple.' . . . Those who cling to worthless idols forfeit the grace that could be theirs. But I, with a song of thanksgiving, will sacrifice to you. What I have vowed I will make good. Salvation comes from the Lord."

When Jonah was turning his back on God, it did not bother him at all that God was thus abandoned by him. But suddenly, when Jonah was thrown overboard to his death, he found himself in the position of apparently being abandoned by God, and he did not like this at all. In the water and then in the great fish, he learned what hell was like, and it was there at the nadir of his misery that he repented and turned to God again.

Jonah was not really abandoned by God, but he felt that he was. It was in this last extremity that the hand of the Lord was, from our perspective, most evident. Ellul states clearly: "We should remember the significance of water in the Old Testament and then in the church. Water denotes swallowing up and death. Yet it is also closely linked with the presence of the Spirit of God. This is part of the general principle that in God's revelation no sign is ever purely negative because God's own action is never negative. Most signs are ambivalent, and that which denotes death also has within

it the promise of life. At the beginning of the creation story the waters symbolize the void, nothingness, the abyss. But we cannot stop there: the Spirit of God moves over the face of the waters."[1]

What Ellul says of the water is also true of the fish with which this section begins. On the one hand, it was a symbol of total abandonment, of hell. Jonah even spoke of it in those terms. "From the depths of the grave [literally Sheol] I called for help, and you listened to my cry" (2:2). But on the other hand, it was (unknown to Jonah) the means God would use to deliver him from the deep.

The Great Fish

It is almost a pity that the fish mentioned in Jonah has attracted so much attention, for in doing this it has detracted from the other very valuable lessons of this book. What has happened has been described by Thomas John Carlisle, who wrote, "I was so obsessed with what was going on inside the whale that I missed seeing the drama inside

---

[1]Ellul, *The Judgment of Jonah*, p. 41.

Jonah."[2] Nevertheless, in being sensitive to the one danger we do not want to fall into the other danger of neglecting the miraculous nature of the story entirely.

So what of the great fish? Was it a whale? Did it really swallow Jonah? Can a person actually believe in such a story? Or is it so ludicrous as to make all refutation unnecessary?

On one level, a discussion of this problem is hardly necessary. Those who believe in the God of the Bible will have little difficulty believing that such a miracle is possible. If the God of the Bible can raise up Jesus Christ from the dead, He can certainly cause a great monster of the deep to be alongside the ship when His prophet is thrown overboard and can cause it to swallow him. On the other side, for those who disbelieve in miracles, the evidence, whatever it may be, is meaningless. If miracles do not happen, then this story about Jonah did not happen. It will not even help to point out that, strictly speaking, the swallowing of Jonah is not even a miracle, for to such minds the story will clearly be seen as a myth, not a fact.

On another level, however, a discussion of the miracle does have value. For instance, it shows that Christians who believe in such things are at least not totally unaware of the difficulties that may be involved. Or again, it may also show skeptics that the situation is not so unbelievable as they, perhaps without much thought or evidence, conceived that it was.

BRITANNICA RESEARCH SERVICE

It should be interesting to many skeptics that the Library Research Service of the *Encyclopedia Britannica* regularly distributes information supportive of the biblical narrative. This service is available to anyone who purchases a set of the *Encyclopedia*. Anyone researching a subject and not finding that the *Encyclopedia* has covered it adequately, may write and ask for information on his subject, and a mimeographed report (generally pre-prepared) will be sent to him.

If a person requests information on the possibility of a whale having swallowed Jonah, a four-page report will be mailed, the bulk of which consists of information taken from an article on the "Sign of the Prophet Jonah and Its Modern Confirmations," which was published in the *Princeton Theological Review* in 1927. It is followed by a bibliography in which some of the articles are supportive of the incident and some are not. The article itself concludes: "The story of Jonah occurs in Hebrew literature and tradition as an historical record. It can hardly be disputed that the tests applied to it are in fairness bound to be the most careful, accurate, and dispassionate that science and history can supply. Physiological tests entirely disprove the alleged impossibility of the story. It is shown by study of the structure of the sperm whale and its habits that it is perfectly possible for a man to be swallowed alive and after an interval vomited up again, also for him to remain alive for two or three days within the whale. Historical tests show that a similar event has happened in later times in at least one case, and that it is quite possible for an authentic record to have survived over even a much longer period than 700 years."[3]

The article leading up to this conclusion is in two parts. The first part distinguishes, as all honest writing on the subject has done, between those whales or other great fish that could conceivably swallow a man and those that could not. A generation ago one heard that a whale could not swallow Jonah simply because the throat of the whale is too small. "A whale has difficulty swallowing an orange," was the viewpoint. This objection

[2]Thomas John Carlisle, *You! Jonah!* (Grand Rapids: Eerdmans, 1968), p. 21.
[3]A. J. Wilson, "Sign of the Prophet Jonah and Its Modern Confirmations," *Princeton Theological Review*, Oct., 1927, pp. 630–42.

arose from a failure to distinguish between the Greenland whale, which does have a very small throat and which was the whale best known to seamen of an earlier generation, and the sperm whale or cachalot, which has an enormous mouth, throat, and stomach. An average specimen of the sperm whale might have a mouth 20 feet long, 15 feet high, and 9 feet wide; that is, the mouth would be larger than most rooms in an average-sized house.

It is known that the sperm whale feeds largely on squid, which are often much larger than a man. Whalers have sometimes found whole squid of this size in a dead whale's stomach.

As to whether a man could survive in a whale's stomach, the *Britannica* article maintains that he certainly could, though in circumstances of very great discomfort. There would be air to breathe, of a sort. It is needed to keep the animal afloat. But there would be great heat, about 104–108°F. Unpleasant contact with the animal's gastric juices might easily affect the skin, but the juices would not digest living matter; otherwise they would digest the walls of the creature's own stomach.

But has there ever been a case of a man actually having been swallowed by a whale and then regurgitated or saved by some means? This is the matter dealt with in the second half of the journal article, and apparently there are such cases. One case concerns a voyage of the whaling ship *Star of the East*, which in February, 1891, spotted a large sperm whale in the vicinity of the Falkland Islands. Two boats were launched, and in a short while one of the harpooners was able to spear the fish. Those in the second boat attempted to attach a second harpoon, but the boat capsized in the process and one man was drowned. A second sailor, James Bartley, disappeared and could not be found. In time the whale was killed and drawn to the side of the ship where it was made fast and the blubber removed. The next day the stomach was hoisted on deck. When it was opened, the missing sailor was found inside. He was unconscious but alive. Eventually he was revived by sea water and after a time resumed his duties on board the whaling vessel.

It is also possible, as the article shows, that the fish in Jonah's case may not even have been a whale. The Hebrew text merely says *dag*, which may be any kind of great fish. It may have been a species of shark, a Rhineodon or "Sea Dog," for instance; if this is so, then there are other accounts of men being swallowed that are also relevant. The Sea Dog, while a member of the shark family, does not have the terrible teeth generally associated with sharks and grows to a size comparable to that of many whales. In his widely read book, *Kon-Tiki*, Thor Heyerdahl describes such a shark that followed his raft for a time in the mid-Pacific.

JONAH AND NINEVEH

In addition to the data on whales, there are a number of links between the prophet Jonah and Nineveh that are also supportive of the Old Testament story. A few of these are cited by Gaebelein. First, there is a seal belonging to the reign of Amasis II of Egypt (570–526 B.C.) which shows with remarkable clarity a man emerging from a sea monster. This seal is cited by an archaeologist named Knight in a volume entitled *Nile and the Jordan*, published in 1921. The figure has been identified as Jonah. A second interesting bit of information is the name of the mound in the upper Tigris valley under which the remains of ancient Nineveh were discovered. The site of Nineveh had long been lost. But the mound had been called "Neby Yunas" ("The Prophet Jonah") for centuries.

Gaebelein points out that the association of Jonah and his story with ancient Nineveh may have been preserved due to the worship of the fish-god Dagon that went on there. In any other city Jonah's experiences would have had little effect on the response to the preaching. But if Jonah had been swallowed by a great fish and had then been thrown up on the coast of Phoenicia, perhaps in sight of witnesses who may have conveyed this tale to those in Nineveh, it is easy to see how a population that worshiped a fish-god may have received him as a divine messenger and have remembered and preserved the tale long afterward. Whatever the case, the association of Jonah with Nineveh seems to be an old one.

A TURNING POINT

To concentrate so much on what happened inside the great fish that we miss noting what happened inside Jonah is to make a great mistake, however, as I have indicated. So we must now turn to Jonah's prayer to God from inside the monster. As we read it we discover that the prayer reveals the truly great miracle. It shows that though Jonah had been brought to the depths of misery within the fish, he nevertheless found the mercy of God in his misery. He discovered that though he had forsaken God, God had not forsaken him, though it seemed that He had. In brief, Jonah found salvation even before the fish vomited him up on the land.

With the exception of verse 10, the second chapter is a record of this prayer. Since the book is only four chapters long it is obvious that the prayer is important. "From inside the fish Jonah prayed to the LORD his God. He said: 'In my distress I called to the LORD, and he answered me. From the depths of the grave I called for help, and you listened to my cry. You hurled me into the deep, into the very heart of the seas, and the currents swirled about me; all your waves and breakers swept over me. I said, "I have been banished from your sight; yet I will look again toward your holy temple." The engulfing waters threatened me, the deep surrounded me; seaweed was wrapped around my head. To the roots of the

mountains I sank down; the earth beneath barred me in forever. But you brought my life up from the pit, O LORD my God. When my life was ebbing away, I remembered you, LORD, and my prayer rose to you, to your holy temple. Those who cling to worthless idols forfeit the grace that could be theirs. But I, with a song of thanksgiving, will sacrifice to you. What I have vowed I will make good. Salvation comes from the LORD'" (2:1–9).

FOUR PRINCIPLES

Jonah's prayer has four characteristics of all true prayer. These characteristics should be in our own prayers at all times, particularly when we get into trouble because of disobedience and need to repent and get ourselves back on the right path.

The first is *honesty*. The prayer is starkly honest. So often Christians are dishonest in their prayers. They come to the Lord trying to overlook some circumstance that He has caused, ignore some sin that He has highlighted, or obtain some request that He has already clearly rejected.

What we do may be illustrated by a story frequently told by Donald Grey Barnhouse. On one occasion his daughter had come to him with a request that he had denied. "Well, then, what do you want me to do?" she asked. He told her what he wanted and then went on with his work. She remained standing in front of him.

At length Mrs. Barnhouse called to the daughter from another room. "Where are you? What are you doing?" she asked.

The daughter replied, "I am waiting for Daddy to tell me what he wants me to do."

At this point Barnhouse raised his head and said to her, "Whatever you are doing, you are not waiting to find out what I want you to do. I have told you what I want you to do, but you do not like it. You are actually waiting to see if you can get me to change my mind."

Any perceptive Christian can see himself in that story, for many of our prayers are attempts to get God to let us do something He has already clearly forbidden. If we go on to reject His will and thus reap the fruits of our disobedience, we frequently try to explain away the results.

Christians ought to be the greatest realists in the world. But they are not, especially when they are disobeying God or running away from Him. Instead of being honest about their trouble, as Jonah was, they find themselves trying to explain their miseries away. They say, "Well, I suppose things like this just happen." Or, "It's hard, but I can handle it; maybe if I just keep going things will get better." Jonah did not do this. Instead, in verses 3–6 he acknowledged his trouble—he had been cast into the deep, the floods had covered him, to all appearances he was cast out of God's sight, he had gone down to the bottoms of the mountains of the earth and, barring a miracle, the earth was about him forever.

Jonah not only acknowledged his misery; he acknowledged that it was God who had caused it. "You hurled me into the deep," he said. Not circumstances! Not the sailors! It was "your [God's] waves and breakers." We might argue that the sailors did have a role and that it was Jonah himself who had suggested that he be thrown overboard. But these are minor technicalities, and Jonah is done with technicalities. They do not matter. He was in desperate straits, and God was the One who was causing them.

In one sense, this increased the terror of his situation. The situation was bad enough. He was far from land with no path of escape. But add the fact that God had caused it! God had addressed Himself to Jonah in the character of a judge. He had summoned him to trial, witnessed against him, cast a verdict of guilty, and then sentenced him to death, proceeding at once to the implementation of the sentence—this was a terror

almost beyond words! Hugh Martin, who notes this, observes, "Oh! if he found courage or composure amidst circumstances like these to address his soul in prayer, and that, too, believing prayer, to the Lord, how great a marvel or miracle of grace must that prayer be!"[4]

On the other hand, there is also a sense in which the acknowledgment of God's presence, even in judgment, is a comfort. For it is better to fall into the hands of God, even in judgment, than to be apart from Him.

David is a case in point. We read at the end of 2 Samuel that David sinned in causing the people of Israel to be numbered and that God, through the prophet Gad, gave David three choices, one of which was to be God's judgment. David could choose seven years of famine, three months of defeat before his enemies or three days of pestilence. David chose the latter because, he said, "Let us fall into the hands of the LORD, for his mercy is great; but do not let me fall into the hands of men" (2 Sam. 24:14). It was a wise decision; for though the judgment came, we read that when the plague reached Jerusalem the Lord was grieved by the calamity and said to the angel who destroyed the people, "Enough! Withdraw your hand" (v. 16). God is a God of judgment, but His judgment is tempered by the mercy that is so prominent a theme in Jonah.

PENANCE

Jonah's prayer is also characterized by *penance.* "Penance" is an old-fashioned word, but it is a good one. It means "confession," "self-abasement," or "mortification showing sorrow for and repentance of sin." Clearly, this is a step beyond mere honesty, for it is possible to be honest about one's situation, acknowledge that God has caused it, and yet be unrepentant about it. We can acknowledge that God caused it but still get angry.

[4]Martin, *The Prophet Jonah*, p. 193.

In one such instance a Christian girl married a man who was not a Christian, ignoring the advice of her pastor and friends. Then she knew great misery as the marriage turned sour and ended in divorce. She knew that the situation was her own fault and that the breakup of the marriage was only an inevitable outworking of God's laws in her own particular situation, but she resented God for it. Instead of repenting of the sin, she drifted away from Christian friends and activites. Only much later, by the grace of God, did she return to Him.

We know that Jonah's was true penance in two ways. First, he acknowledged that everything that had happened to him, while caused by God, was nevertheless his own fault. He deserved it. This is the meaning of verse 8, one of the great verses of the book: "Those who cling to worthless idols forfeit the grace that could be theirs." An idol is anything that takes the place of God. So Jonah is saying that whenever a believer puts something else in the place of God and thereby turns from Him, he inevitably also turns from God's mercy. God is not less merciful, but the believer has rejected that mercy and therefore deserves all that comes on him.

Jonah's prayer also showed penance in that Jonah did not ask God for anything. If he had, we might suspect that his repentance had a hidden motive. Perhaps he was repenting just so he could get out of the fish and back on dry land. In reality he asked for nothing. He was genuinely sorry for his disobedience.

THANKSGIVING

The third characteristic of Jonah's prayer was *thanksgiving*. "Thanksgiving?" we might ask. "Why thanksgiving? What could Jonah, swallowed by a fish, in the midst of the ocean awaiting death, possibly be thankful about?" If we continue to ask the question in terms of a physical deliverance, there is no answer; Jonah's attitude continues to be puzzling. But if we ask the question in spiritual terms and think of a spiritual deliverance, the answer is easy. True, Jonah had no hope of deliverance from the fish. But he had found the grace of God again—his own word is "salvation" (v. 9)—and for this he was profoundly thankful.

Jonah was not thankful that God had delivered him from the fish because God had not yet delivered him. He was not thankful that God was going to deliver him, because he had no idea that God was going to do it. What he was thankful for was that God had turned him from rebellion and had caused him to call on the name of the Lord once again. He was thankful for salvation. He was thankful for the abiding grace of God.

Ellul discusses the prayer in these words: "Jonah has not been answered if we take the answer to be rescue from the belly of the fish, salvation from hell. But he has been answered if we take the answer to be adoption under the care of the God who takes on the totality of our sufferings, dramas and situations. He is answered because grace does not fail in any way, and even if there is no visible, actual and personal sign, Jonah can state that the answer takes place because grace has been granted to him from all eternity. Jonah rediscovers this grace of God at the very moment his situation is hopeless and to all appearances nothing more is to be expected. His refusal and flight were clearly outside grace. Events have taken place without any indication of a favorable intervention, only signs of judgment. But suddenly, when he has accepted his condemnation, when he has acknowledged before God that he was guilty and that God was just, he sees that at no point did God cease to show him grace. . . .

"Nothing proves this to Jonah. No fact confirms his insight. He does not have even the first beginning of deliverance. But simply in the very fact that he has been able to repent, to condemn himself, to recognize the sentence of the just judge, he has reason enough to say: 'Thou hast delivered me.' It is here indeed that the great decision is taken."[5]

It is also here that the great miracles are performed. It is not when history is redirected by some supernatural, spectacular event, not when bodies are brought to life or heavenly bodies are stopped in their normal motion that the great miracles occur. It is when a person comes to acknowledge his or her sin and confess it before God and when, as a consequence, God restores the broken Creator-creature relationship.

SACRIFICES AND VOWS

There is one final characteristic of Jonah's prayer that should not escape notice, for, in terms of his rebellion, it is the most significant of all. *Jonah is now ready to take his place alongside the ungodly.* Earlier he had said, "I am a Jew, and I do not want to preach to the heathen." Now he was willing to take a place beside them as one who needed God's mercy.

A person may ask, "But where do you find that in the story?" You find it in a parallel between verse 9 of this chapter and verse 16 of chapter 1. Verse 9 says, "I, with a song of thanksgiving, will *sacrifice* to you. What I have *vowed* I will make good." The earlier verse says, speaking of the sailors, "At this the men greatly feared the LORD, and they offered a *sacrifice* to the LORD and made *vows* to him." The sailors, who were heathens, learned to approach God as He must be approached—through the blood of an innocent victim sacrificed for sin and through a personal commitment expressed in a vow. Jonah, the prophet of the Lord, also approached through the sacrifice (promising to do in the future what he obviously could not do in the belly of the great fish, if that should be possible) and made a vow.

It is hard to miss the point. Jonah, despite his earlier protestations, came to God, not as a Jew who deserved special privileges or concessions, but as a sinful human being who was one with all other sinful human beings and who needed God's grace.

It is thus with us all. If you come to God claiming privileges, boasting of your own special achievements and therefore expecting God to accept you or acknowledge you on the basis of your own merit, you have no hope of salvation. The Scriptures explicitly say that God will not pay court to human merit: "For it is by grace you have been saved, through faith—and this not from yourselves, it is the gift of God—not by works, so that no one can boast" (Eph. 2:8, 9). On the other hand, if you come to God, admitting that you deserve nothing from Him but His just wrath and condemnation, if you place your faith in His Son, the Lord Jesus Christ, who willingly became your sacrifice, and if you promise to serve Him and be His faithful disciple till your life's end, then He saves you and brings you into a deep experience of the grace of God.

Charles W. Colson, known nationally because of his involvement in the Watergate scandal, is one who found this kind of grace. By his own confession, Colson had been driven by pride. But he came to see this one night in the living room of a good friend, Thomas Phillips, president of the Raytheon Company, who had just become a Christian. As they talked, Phillips shared the story of his conversion and then read from the chapter in *Mere Christianity* in which C. S. Lewis speaks of pride being "the chief cause of misery in every nation and every family since the world began." This struck Colson forcefully, and he acknowledged (privately) that it was true of him. A few minutes later, after he had left the Phillips' home and was seated in his car, a tremendous sense of release came over him and he prayed, crying, "God, I don't

---

[5]Ellul, *The Judgment of Jonah*, pp. 48, 49.

know how to find you, but I'm going to try! I'm not much the way I am now, but somehow I want to give myself to you. Take me."[6] At that point Colson had not yet understood the importance of the death of Jesus Christ, and he had certainly not surrendered his life to Him. But the prayer was honest and repentant. Colson was coming to God as a sinner, and the God who receives sinners (and only sinners) heard him and rapidly led him to a knowledge of Christ and the assurance of salvation.

No one has ever truly repented till he or she has acknowledged that there is nothing in any person that can possibly commend him or her to God. And no one has ever been saved who has not come to God on the basis of the sacrifice that He alone has provided.

The last phrase of the prayer makes this plain: "Salvation comes from the LORD" (v. 9). Salvation is possible only because God makes it possible. It is of Him.

JESUS SAVIOR

"Salvation comes from the LORD." This thought was a blessing to Jonah; but if it was a comfort to him, it should be even more of a comfort to us who live this side of the cross of Jesus Christ. For this is what "Jesus" means. When the angel explained the meaning of the name to Joseph he said, "You are to give him the name Jesus, because he will save his people from their sins" (Matt. 1:21). The wording is slightly different, of course; but the meaning is precisely the same: "Salvation comes from the LORD."

Thus far in our study of Jonah we have stressed that the story of the rebellious prophet is our story. But we should not miss the point that in another sense it is also the story of our Lord, who went down to hell for us bearing our sin and then was raised from the dead to bring many sons with Him into glory. In other words, Jonah is a story of salvation, and this is always God's story. Have you seen that truth? A marginal note in the New Scofield Reference Bible indicates that the sentence "Salvation is of the LORD" (v. 9, KJV) is "the theme of the Bible," and indeed it is. We have run from God, all of us. But none need perish. God has Himself provided the way into eternal life through the death of His Son.

---

[6]Charles W. Colson, *Born Again* (Old Tappan, N.J.: Chosen Books/Fleming H. Revell, 1976), pp. 108–17.

33

The Greatest Revival in History

(Jonah 3:1–10)

Then the word of the LORD came to Jonah a second time: "Go to the great city of Nineveh and proclaim to it the message I give you."

Jonah obeyed the word of the LORD and went to Nineveh. Now Nineveh was a very large city; it took three days to go all through it. Jonah started into the city, going a day's journey, and he proclaimed: "Forty more days and Nineveh will be destroyed." The Ninevites believed God. They declared a fast, and all of them, from the greatest to the least, put on sackcloth.

When the news reached the king of Nineveh, he rose from his throne, took off his royal robes, covered himself with sackcloth and sat down in the dust.

The third chapter of Jonah contains the high point of this remarkable story, for, however remarkable the preceding action has been and however great the miracles, the most remarkable action and the greatest miracles are in the results of Jonah's preaching. The result was the greatest and most thorough revival that has ever taken place. Writes Gaebelein, "Heretofore the emphasis has been upon the prophet's preparation; tremendous as the miracle of Jonah's preservation in the sea monster has been, it is more a preface than a conclusion. Now the veil is drawn aside, and something of the strange purpose of the Almighty in dealing with his prophet is revealed. If the miracle of the fish is great, that of this chapter is greater. For here is the record of nothing less than the greatest mass conversion in history. Though generalities must always be used with caution, we may say that never again has the world seen anything quite like the result of Jonah's preaching in Nineveh."[1]

The first noteworthy fact about this revival is that it began with God's call to just one man: Jonah. And even that was after he had apparently disqualified himself from future service.

THE SECOND TIME

We cannot really imagine what it would be like if we were in the place of God, nor should we. But if we were God and if we were confronted with the situation as we have found it at the end of chapter 2, I imagine that at this point we would say that we had had just about enough of Jonah. We would recall that Jonah was a man whom we had chosen to be a prophet and to whom we had imparted a special measure of understanding in spiritual things. We would remember that we had already given him a full and blessed ministry in Israel and that we had then called him to do a tremendous work in Nineveh. Jonah should have been delighted. But instead of being delighted he had refused this call. Finally, he had become so set in his determination that he had declared that he would rather die than return to the place of blessing. He had requested to be thrown overboard.

[1]Gaebelein, *Four Minor Prophets*, p. 95.

We would recall that even then we had been gracious to him. Instead of allowing him to die we had saved him. We had brought him to a place of repentance. Then we had spoken to the fish, and it had returned Jonah to the land.

How gracious we had been! No one could expect more. So if we were God and if we should reason at this point that we had saved Jonah but that he had nevertheless disqualified himself from ever being a prophet again, who could blame us? If we were to say, "Go home now, Jonah. I am glad you have repented of your disobedience, but you are no longer useful to me," we would be just and reasonable in so doing. But this is not God's way. Thus, instead of reading of God's rejection of Jonah, we find these words: "Then the word of the LORD came to Jonah a second time: 'Go to the great city of Nineveh and proclaim to it the message I give you'" (vv. 1, 2). The important point is that God came to Jonah the second time and that the commission was the same as on the first occasion.

Does God always do that? Does God stoop to use those who have rejected His calling, turned a deaf ear to His word, and pursued a course of determined disobedience? Yes, He is like that. Yes, He does use such messengers. If He did not, none of us could serve Him.

We find the principle of the Lord coming to an individual a second time quite often in Scripture. Take the case of Abraham. The word of the Lord came to Abraham when he was a devil worshiper living in Mesopotamia, like all his family. The fact that they were a family of idol and, therefore, devil worshipers is stated in several Old Testament passages (Josh. 24:2, 3, 14; Isa. 51:1, 2). The story of Rachel's having hidden the idols of her father (Gen. 31) shows that Abraham's relatives still owned and cherished idols at least three generations after God had called him out of Mesopotamia. But God called him out of Ur of the Chaldees and sent him around the northern edge of the great Arabian desert to Palestine, which God was giving him. Stephen recalls this word in his speech, saying, "The God of glory appeared to our father Abraham while he was still in Mesopotamia, before he lived in Haran. 'Leave your country and your people,' God said, 'and go to the land I will show you'" (Acts 7:2, 3). We might think that such a revelation and promise would have caused Abraham to travel all the way to the land God was giving. But when we read the account (Gen. 11; 12), we find that he did not. Abraham left Ur, it is true. But he stopped at Haran, still hundreds of miles from Palestine. He would have stayed there had God not come to him a second time. God said on this occasion: "Leave your country, your people and your father's household and go to the land I will show you; I will make you into a great nation and I will bless you; I will make your name great, and you will be a blessing" (Gen. 12:1, 2).

The same is true of Moses who became, under God, one of the great leaders of history. We are not told much detail of the early life of Moses, only that he was raised by his mother with the blessing of the daughter of Pharaoh for the first months or years of life and that he was afterward raised in the palace of Pharaoh. Still, we know that God had revealed Himself to Moses during this period. In the same speech of Stephen that mentions Abraham we read that when Moses killed the Egyptian he did so supposing that "his own people would realize that God was using him to rescue them" (Acts 7:25). This was Moses' way of bringing about a deliverance, but it was not God's. Consequently, Moses had to flee from Egypt to Midian, where he lived for the next forty years. We might say that Moses had ruined his chances and destroyed his future ministry. Yet after he had lived in Midian for this long period of time and when he was eighty years old, God appeared to him in a burning bush, saying, "So now, go. I am sending you to Pharaoh to bring my people the Israelites out of Egypt" (Exod. 3:10). God had appeared to Moses a second time.

We find the same thing in the case of the apostle Peter. Peter had boasted that no matter what should happen he would not desert the Lord. "I am ready to go with you to prison and to death," Peter said (Luke 22:33). Jesus revealed that Peter would deny Him three times before morning. And Peter did (Luke 22:54–62)! What shall be done with Peter now? Shall he be cast off? Shall he be disqualified from future service? The Lord appears to Peter to recommission him to service, asking on three separate occasions (corresponding to Peter's three denials), "Simon son of John, do you truly love me?" (John 21:15–17). When Peter answers on each occasion, "Yes, Lord, you know that I love you," Jesus responds, "Feed my sheep." The Lord came to Peter a second time.

A number of years ago a young girl in Philadelphia felt the call of God to Christian service. But she married a non-Christian, who soon left her to go his own way. The experience brought the girl back to desiring God's will. But what was she to do? Should she divorce her husband? The Scriptures taught that she should not follow this course. According to 1 Corinthians 7, she was to be open to any possible reconciliation. She decided to leave the matter in God's hands. Having confessed her sin to God, she let her separated husband know that she was open to reconciliation if he desired it. When he declined, she let the matter rest. Within a few months her husband was killed in a car accident, and God directed her to apply to Wycliffe Bible Translators for missionary work. The word of the Lord clearly came to her a second time.

The Lord comes a second time to all who are His true children. Have we never, like Abraham, stopped at our Harans?

Of course, we have. We are sent on errands, but some sin or preoccupation detains us. Have we never, like Moses, taken matters into our own hands and formulated our own plans? Of course, we have. Like Peter, we have even denied our Lord on occasions when we should have spoken for Him. We have disobeyed Him. We have run away from Him. Some of us, like Jonah, have run very far indeed. Does God cast us off? Does He disown us? No! He disciplines us, it is true. But, having done that and having brought us to the place of repentance, He returns the second time to recommission us to service. Moreover, He comes a third, a fourth, a hundredth, a thousandth time, if necessary, as it often is. None of us would be where we are now in our Christian lives if God had not dealt thus with us. Oh, the greatness of the unmerited grace of God! We deserve nothing. Yet we receive everything, even when we foolishly turn from it.

William Banks speaks of how grace comes to people today: "We are moved to speak of Jonah's God as the God of the Second Chance. But honest sober reflection compels the saint to speak of Him as the God of the 999th chance! Such gracious mercy as was extended to Jonah here, and to David, and to the thief dying upon the cross, and to Peter—surely it has been granted to all believers through the precious blood of Jesus Christ."[2]

Two More Lessons

Two additional lessons appear in this passage. First, when the word of the Lord came to Jonah the second time, it came with the same commission he had received the first time.

We often think, when we are on the verge of running away from God, that if we run away and if the Lord should nevertheless speak to us again, He might take note of the fact that we have run away and therefore change the command. He does not. When we think or

---

[2]William Banks, *Jonah, The Reluctant Prophet* (Chicago: Moody Press, 1966), p. 72.

act in this disobedient way, we are acting like children who do not like what they are being told to do and who therefore throw a tantrum, thinking that this might get the parents to change their minds. An indulgent or foolish parent might fall for this manipulation, but a wise parent will not. Nor does God! Consequently, after He has dealt with the tantrum, sometimes by means of a spanking, God returns to us with the same commission as before. Why try to resist it? Learn that if you try to run away from God, sooner or later He is going to catch up with you and that, when He does, you will have to face the very thing you are running away from. Experience His grace now instead of judgment.

The second lesson is found in the one change in the second expression of the commission. The first commission had two key verbs in it: "go" and "preach." In this commission the first verb is the same. But the second phrase, "preach against it," is changed to "proclaim to it the message I give you." When we remember that the greatest revival in history followed Jonah's doing precisely that, we may reason that the spiritual life of our own time would be quite different if only those words were followed by the thousands of clergymen who fill our pulpits each Sunday. They preach. No one doubts that. But is their sermon the message God has given them? Is their preaching that which He has bid them proclaim? Today God's ministers are called to proclaim the message of the Bible, embodying all the counsel of God. But many consider this unsophisticated or old-fashioned and so substitute the supposed wisdom of men. Their words lack power, and they bring judgment on their own heads.

OBEDIENT AT LAST

The first time the word of the Lord came to Jonah telling him to go to Nineveh, Jonah ran away. This time, having learned the consequences of running away, he obeyed. The contrast is with the similar command recorded in chapter 1. In that chapter, after God had told Jonah, "Go to the great city of Nineveh and preach against it," we see the prophet's disobedience: "*But* Jonah." Here, after the identical commission, we read, "Jonah obeyed the word of the LORD and went to Nineveh" (v. 3). This is something we should covet for every true Christian. Too often we try to outguess or outmaneuver God. We try to "out-but" Him. Our response should be obedience. Did God say it? Then let us do it. Let it be said of us, "John Smith, Mary Jones (or whatever your name may be) obeyed the word of the Lord."

What will the result be? In the first chapter, after Jonah had voiced his "but" to God, he found that God opposed him. God sent the storm. On this occasion, Jonah obeyed and "the Ninevites believed God. They declared a fast, and all of them, from the greatest to the least, put on sackcloth" (v. 5). Jonah's obedience was followed by the outpouring of God's power.

The difference was that Jonah was now walking according to "the word of the LORD." In the first instance, he was trying to get away from God's word. In the second instance, the Word was with him. The author of Hebrews says rightly: "The word of God is living and active. Sharper than any double-edged sword, it penetrates even to dividing soul and spirit, joints and marrow; it judges the thoughts and attitudes of the heart" (Heb. 4:12). It is through His word alone that God brings blessing and opens the closed and rebellious hearts of men.

A GREAT REVIVAL

When Jonah entered Nineveh he began to proclaim his message: "Forty more days and Nineveh will be destroyed" (3:4). This does not seem to be a very impressive message. In the English Bible it is only eight words, and in Hebrew it is even shorter: five (*Hod arbahim yom wenineweh nehpaketh*). The words are a simple prophecy of judgment. Yet they were greatly blessed, because they were truly God's words and not the words of a mere man. According to the following verses, they were used of God to bring about a genuine and pervasive revival in the city.

We can almost see Jonah as he entered a day's journey into the city and began to cry out his message. What would his reception be? Would the Ninevites laugh? Would they turn against Jonah and persecute him? As he cried out people stopped to listen. The hum of commerce died down and a holy hush stole over the collecting multitudes. Soon there were weeping and other signs of a genuine repentance of sin. At last the message of Jonah entered even the palace, and the king, divesting himself of his magnificent robes, took the place of a mourner alongside his repenting subjects. We read, "When the news reached the king of Nineveh, he rose from his throne, took off his royal robes, covered himself with sackcloth and sat down in the dust. Then he issued a proclamation in Nineveh:

"'By the decree of the king and his nobles: Do not let any man or beast, herd or flock, taste anything; do not let them eat or drink. But let man and beast be covered with sackcloth. Let everyone call urgently on God. Let them give up their evil ways and their violence. Who knows? God may yet relent and with compassion turn from his fierce anger so that we will not perish'" (vv. 6–9).

What did the people believe? Whom did they believe? We are not told that the people believed Jonah, in spite of his deliverance and the fact that the Lord Jesus Christ later declared that Jonah was himself a "sign" to the Ninevites (Luke 11:30). We are told that the people "believed God." Faith should never rest in the messenger, but in God who gives the message. This is one mark of all true revival and true preaching.

Scholars have sometimes objected to this on grounds that the information furnished about the city is not accurate. It has been pointed out that though the city was indeed large—the circumference of the inner walls was about seven and three-fourth miles—it is hardly possible, even with extremely crowded streets, that it would have taken Jonah three days to cross it. But the answer to this is that the description probably refers to what we would call the fullest extent of the city including the suburbs. It may even refer to a fuller, geographical area including farms and outlying fortifications. A parallel comes from the cities of the Middle Ages. In Europe during the Middle Ages people lived near walled cities in order to be able to retreat into them when danger threatened. In times of peace, when no danger threatened, people spilled beyond the walls to farm and pursue other occupations. This was true of hundreds and thousands of cities, even little ones. It would be true of a large capital city such as Nineveh.

It is breath-taking to come to the true high point of the story in the account of God's repentance from bringing judgment: "When God saw what they did and how they turned from their evil ways, he had compassion and did not bring upon them the destruction he had threatened" (v. 10).

The Repentance of God

That this and other verses in the Bible speak of God changing His mind (literally, "repenting") has been a problem for some students of Scripture. But it should not be, once the phrase is understood.

To begin with, this is clearly a case of employing human language to describe that which is ultimately beyond human language. God is always beyond our understanding. Consequently, we should not be surprised when phrases like this tend to confuse us. We should balance them with other statements—like that of Balaam, who said, "God is not a man, that he should lie, nor a son of man, that he should change his mind. Does he speak and then not act? Does he promise and not fulfill?" (Num. 23:19). If we must choose between apparent contradictions, we must side with the truth that God is not changeable and that He does not deal falsely in the revelation of Himself to us.

Second, we must realize that in this case there is not even a true contradiction, for the city that God had promised to destroy, the wicked city of Nineveh, ceased to exist after Jonah's preaching. True, it came back, as Nineveh slipped into sin again years later. We find Nahum writing of a judgment that did eventually come. But for now the city ceased to exist as sinful Nineveh and therefore came to enjoy God's blessing. Here Martin writes perceptively: "It was wicked, violent, unrighteous, atheistical, proud, and luxurious Nineveh which God had threatened to destroy. A city sitting in sackcloth and ashes, humbled in the depths of self-abasement, and appealing as lowly suppliants to his commiseration—a Nineveh like that—*that* Nineveh, he had never threatened. *That* Nineveh he visited not with ruin. He had never said he would. The Nineveh which God threatened to destroy passed away; it became totally another city—far more so, in virtue of this change in moral state, than if it had been translated from its olden geographical position, and wholly transformed in its architectural appearance. Surely its great moral change had made it more truly another place—a kind of new creature, old things having passed away, and all things become new—than any alteration in its physical aspect could have done. It really, in God's estimation, is not the Nineveh he threatened at all. The terrific threatening does not apply now. 'God saw their works'—their fruits meet for repentance, namely, that they turned from their evil way—and God 'repented of the evil that he said that he would do unto them, and he did it not.'"[3]

Ultimately, however, the problem posed by the repentance of God is solved, not by observing the repentance of men and women, but by noticing that God repents of the evil He would do by taking the punishment for that evil on Himself. When the Hebrew speaks of God repenting, most often the word is *nacham*. It refers to an inner suffering needing to be consoled. Did God suffer? Not at the time of Jonah and the Ninevites. But He did so later in the person of His Son, the Lord Jesus Christ. In Jesus, God took the world's evil on Himself precisely so that He might repent of the need to visit the outworking of that evil on men. Ellul sees this clearly. "In reality God's repenting in the face of man's repentance is Jesus Christ. Each time there is any question of this repenting in Scripture we thus have a new prophecy of Jesus Christ who puts into effect both the justice of God and also the love of God without doing despite to either the one or the other."[4]

Here the message of Jonah hits quite close to home. Like Jonah and the Ninevites, each of us today needs to repent of sin and turn to the righteous and merciful God of the universe. But our repentance from sin, assuming we do repent, is made possible only because God Himself first repented of the evil by taking our judgment on Himself. Jesus bore our judgment. Consequently, our turning from sin must be at the same time a turning to Jesus through whom alone we have forgiveness.

STEPS TO REVIVAL

The repentance of the Ninevites suggests the steps we should follow if we have not come to that kind of repentance. It suggests "four distinct steps" to a revival of true godliness and religion, as Gaebelein indicates in his perceptive study.

First, there must be a *faithful preaching* and a *faithful hearing* of the Word of God.

[3]Martin, *The Prophet Jonah*, pp. 290–91.
[4]Ellul, *The Judgment of Jonah*, p. 100.

Jonah preached what God had given him to preach, and it was highly effective. It was not a lengthy message, but that did not matter. It was not an intellectual message, but that did not matter either. Perhaps it was not even an eloquent message, but neither did that matter. All that was necessary was that it was God's message, preached and heard in the power of God's Holy Spirit.

Charles Haddon Spurgeon, one of the greatest preachers who ever lived, was saved by such a message. He was a boy at the time, and he had gone to a Primitive Methodist Chapel whose pulpit was filled on that particular morning by a man who had no education and could barely read or write. He preached on the text, "Look unto Me, and be ye saved." He stuck to it, for he had little else to say. "My dear friends, this is a very simple text indeed. It says, 'Look.' Now lookin' don't take a deal of pain. It ain't liftin' your foot or your finger; it is just, 'Look.' Well, a man needn't go to college to learn to look. You may be the biggest fool, and yet you can look. A man needn't be worth a thousand a year to be able to look. Anyone can look; even a child can look. But then the text says, 'Look unto *Me.*' Ay, many of ye are lookin' to yourselves, but it's no use lookin' there. You'll never find any comfort in yourselves. . . . Look to *Christ.* The text says, 'Look unto *Me.*'" After about ten minutes of such preaching the speaker had quite exhausted what he had to say. But he noticed the young Spurgeon sitting under the balcony and, fixing his eyes on him, went on, "Young man, you look very miserable. And you always will be miserable—miserable in life, and miserable in death—if you don't obey my text; but if you obey now, this moment, you will be saved. Young man, look to Jesus Christ. Look! Look! Look!" It was not a polished sermon. But it was a true sermon based on God's Word, and God blessed it. Spurgeon did look and was converted.[5]

We need this preaching today. There is no greater need in America or in any other part of the world than to hear the clear preaching of the timeless truths of the Word of God. If we would have blessing in our personal lives, it must come by response to the teachings of this Book. If we would have blessing in our churches and in our land, the same response is necessary. So flock to any faithful preaching of God's Word, and fill your mind with it. If you are in a position to share it with others, do so clearly and without apology. Do not mind that unbelievers scoff. Do not mind that liberal scholars pronounce it untrue. God will send blessing.

Second, there must be *belief in God.* Notice that the Ninevites did more than just hear Jonah's message. As soon as they heard, they responded by believing God. This is the way it has always been and must be. People are not led to faith through visions. Give a person a vision of God, and he will declare it interesting. It will not lead him to faith. "Faith comes from hearing the message, and the message is heard through the word of Christ" (Rom. 10:17).

Third, having heard the word of God and having believed God, the city then took *action* on its faith by proclaiming a fast and putting on the clothes of mourning. There is no true belief without some corresponding action. In the Book of Hebrews, in that great chapter on faith (chap. 11), we are told that Abel believed God and *offered* a proper sacrifice; Enoch *pleased* God by walking close to Him; Noah *built an ark;* Abraham *obeyed* and *went* from his own home to a new land that God would show him; Isaac *blessed Jacob* according to God's instructions; Jacob *blessed* the sons of Joseph; Joseph *gave instructions* for his body to be brought back to Canaan at the time of the Exodus; Moses *refused* to be known

[5]Spurgeon tells this story in his *Autobiography, Volume I: The Early Years, 1834–1859* (Carlisle, Pa.: The Banner of Truth Trust, 1973), pp. 87, 88.

as the son of Pharaoh's daughter but *chose* rather to be mistreated with the people of God than to enjoy the pleasures of sin for a time. In each case belief resulted in specific action by which the person's trust in God was demonstrated.

In the 19th century there was an acrobat (Jean Francois Gravelet) who was known by the stage name Blondin because of his fair coloring. Blondin gained a reputation for himself in Europe before coming to America, and once here he gained even greater fame by walking across Niagara Falls on a tightrope. Thereafter he was associated in everyone's mind with the Falls. He did numerous stunts on his crossings. On one occasion he pushed a wheelbarrow across. On another he paused to eat an omelet. Once or twice he carried his manager on his back. On one of these latter occasions, after he had reached the edge again, he is said to have turned to a man in the crowd and to have asked him, "Do you believe I could do that with you?"

"Of course," answered the man. "I've just seen you do it."

"Well, then, hop on," invited the acrobat. "I'll carry you across."

"Not on your life!" replied the spectator.

There was clearly a form of belief in the man's first response, but it did not result in action. What is called for spiritually is a belief that will fully commit itself to Jesus, thereby allowing Him to carry the believing one over the troubled waters of this life.

Tom Skinner, one of the most effective black evangelists in America, demonstrated the reality of his new belief in Christ by immediately informing the members of his New York City street gang of his conversion, even though he knew that it would be interpreted as a sign of weakness and that some would welcome the opportunity to turn on him.

Finally, as part of this action, there must be a *turning from specific sin*. The Ninevites turned from the sin that was most characteristic of them: violence. We read in verse 8: "Let them give up their evil ways and their violence." We too must turn from our specific sins, whether sexual indulgence, pride, selfishness, lack of love for our Christian brothers and sisters, laziness, materialism—whatever it may be. We must not repent in vague terms. We must repent specifically, if we would be blessed by God and come to know Him fully.

God More Merciful Than His Prophet

(Jonah 4:1–11)

But Jonah was greatly displeased and became angry. He prayed to the LORD, "O LORD, is this not what I said when I was still at home? That is why I was so quick to flee to Tarshish. I knew that you are a gracious and compassionate God, slow to anger and abounding in love, a God who relents from sending calamity. Now, O LORD, take away my life, for it is better for me to die than to live."

But the LORD replied, "Have you any right to be angry?"

Jonah went out and sat down at a place east of the city. There he made himself a shelter, sat in its shade and waited to see what would happen to the city. Then the LORD God provided a vine and made it grow up over Jonah to give shade for his head to ease his discomfort, and Jonah was very happy about the vine. But at dawn the next day God provided a worm, which chewed the vine so that it withered. When the sun rose, God provided a scorching east wind, and the sun blazed on Jonah's head so that he grew faint. He wanted to die, and said, "It would be better for me to die than to live."

But God said to Jonah, "Do you have a right to be angry about the vine?"

"I do," he said, "I am angry enough to die."

But the LORD said, "You have been concerned about this vine, though you did not tend it or make it grow. It sprang up overnight and died overnight. But Nineveh has more than a hundred and twenty thousand people who cannot tell their right hand from their left, and many cattle as well. Should I not be concerned about that great city?"

I doubt if there ever has been a story of God's dealings with men that should give more cause for rejoicing than the story of Jonah. Jonah's story is a story of God's mercy. First, there had been mercy for Jonah, who had been given a great commission. Even though he rebelled at the idea of preaching to the pagans of Nineveh, God persevered with him to turn him from his folly and brought him at last to that great capital city of Assyria. God's mercy to Jonah involved the storm, the great fish, the repentance of Jonah within the fish, and then God's recommissioning of him after he had been cast up on the shore. We read at that point that "the word of the LORD came to Jonah a second time" (3:1).

Parallel to the story of God's dealing with Jonah is God's dealing with the sailors who were manning the ship taking him to Tarshish. This too shows God's mercy. The sailors were pagans at the beginning of the story. We are told that in the midst of the storm "each cried out to his own god" (1:5). By the end, after they had heard Jonah's testimony and had witnessed the calming of the sea after the rebellious prophet had been thrown overboard, we find them worshiping Jehovah, offering sacrifices, and making vows.

Finally, and greatest of all, there is the account of God's mercy to Nineveh. Nineveh was not godly. On the contrary, it was a particularly wicked city. But God

243

used the preaching of Jonah to bring a revival to Nineveh, probably the greatest revival in history. We read that "the Ninevites believed God. They declared a fast, and all of them, from the greatest to the least, put on sackcloth" (3:5). This repentance was so great that even the king was affected. God postponed the judgment that Jonah had prophesied.

If there had ever been a cause for rejoicing, certainly those three evidences of God's mercy—first to His prophet, then to the sailors, and eventually to Nineveh—should provide it, and we should expect Jonah himself to be literally leaping with joy and thanksgiving. Instead, when we come to the fourth and final chapter, we find Jonah in the worst "blue funk" imaginable. In fact, he was angry about what had happened, violently angry. He was angry with God.

We find a series of additional lessons in this chapter as God deals with Jonah at the depth of his attitudes. In these final encounters the book more or less comes full circle. At the beginning it was the story of just two personalities: Jonah and God. After Jonah had run away, the sailors came into the story and then eventually all the people of Nineveh. Now, at the end, we are again back to God and His rebellious prophet. It is always that way. God gives us work to do; the work involves other people. But in the end, when it gets right down to basics, it is always a question of each of us as an individual and God. It is a question of whether or not we have obeyed him.

JONAH'S DISPLEASURE

Jonah's anger at God's mercy to the people of Nineveh is disclosed in the first three verses of chapter 4, so we turn to them for an analysis of Jonah's mood. The verses say, "But Jonah was greatly displeased and became angry. He prayed to the LORD, 'O LORD, is this not what I said when I was still at home? That is why I was so quick to flee to Tarshish. I knew that you are a gracious and com-passionate God, slow to anger and abounding in love, a God who relents from sending calamity. Now, O LORD, take away my life, for it is better for me to die than to live'" (4:1–3).

Obviously, Jonah is angry. He had obeyed God, doing what God wanted; but God had not done what Jonah wanted. Jonah had told the Ninevites that judgment was coming in forty days, but it had not come. He felt betrayed. He felt that God had let him down by not destroying the city as he, Jonah, had predicted. Moreover, in all this he had not the slightest interest in the people of Nineveh. He should have been happy at their deliverance. Instead, he was displeased that God had not wiped them from the face of the earth. If God had destroyed the city, he would have returned home delighted.

In Jonah's anger at God we notice three significant things. First, he tried to *justify himself* both in his own eyes and in the eyes of God. That is, he tried to justify his former disobedience. He said, in effect, "This is why I refused to go to Nineveh when You first called me; what is more, I was right in refusing."

One Friday night when I was in seminary, I was invited by a former headmaster of the Stony Brook School on Long Island to come to the school that weekend to preach for the morning chapel service. Normally I would have been delighted with such an invitation. But this was a Friday night of exam week, and I had an important test on Monday morning. In those days I did not have a collection of sermons I could fall back on. So I knew that if I accepted this invitation I would have to spend most of Saturday preparing my sermon. Then I would have to drive up to the school on Saturday evening, and on Sunday afternoon and evening I would have to drive back. I knew that I would come to the examination on Monday morning with no time having been spent in study. I explained this to my former headmaster, but he was unimpressed. He said that if I put the Lord's work first, the Lord would take care of the exam. I remember thinking that He probably would *not* take care of it, at least not to my satisfaction. I took the assignment anyway, and, sure enough, I did not get the *A* on the exam that I had been expecting; I got a *B* −. At that point I found myself on the verge of saying, "You see, God, I shouldn't have done what You requested because it turned out exactly as I predicted." Fortunately, God gave me wisdom to know that in this case the difference between one grade and another was next to nothing but that the preaching was important.

The point of my illustration is that we all do what Jonah did. Things do not turn out as we wish, so we seek to justify our disobedience. We need to learn that we are not sufficient to pass on the appropriateness or inappropriateness of the outcome, nor are we responsible for it. We are responsible only for performing the whole will of God.

The second thing Jonah did in his anger is somewhat harder to explain, though it is easy to notice. Jonah tried to *turn God against God*. Or to put the same thing in other language, he tried to quote God's word back to Him in his warped desire to show that he, Jonah, was right and that God was wrong. This is what he was doing in verse 2. Jonah was probably thinking of Exodus 34:6, 7 as he argued. The verses in Exodus say, "And he [the Lord] passed in front of Moses, proclaiming, 'The LORD, the LORD, the compassionate and gracious God, slow to anger, abounding in love and faithfulness, maintaining love to thousands, and forgiving wickedness, rebellion and sin.'"

"Now," said Jonah, "is that or is that not what You have said? And if it is what You have said, why did you send me to Nineveh with a message that You never intended to fulfill? Is it not true that I, Jonah, am the consistent one and that You are wrong?"

We should find this frightening. It is frightening in itself and also because of its parallels. What is the most infamous of all attempts to turn the word of God against God? It is Satan's use of Scripture in his temptation of Christ. Jesus had replied to Satan's first temptation to turn stones into bread by quoting from Deuteronomy 8:3: "It is written: 'Man does not live on bread alone, but on every word that comes from the mouth of God'" (Matt. 4:4). Satan retaliated by quoting some Scripture of his own. He took Jesus to a pinnacle of the temple and challenged Him to throw Himself down, saying, "It is written: 'He will command his angels concerning you, and they will lift you up in their hands, so that you will not strike your foot against a stone'" (Matt. 4:6). It was a quotation of Psalm 91:11, 12, but he used it wrongly, as Jesus next pointed out. Jesus replied that it is not possible to use one verse of Scripture to overthrow another, and the Bible clearly says, "Do not put the Lord your God to the test" (Matt. 4:7; Deut. 6:16).

Satan was using the Bible, the Word of God, to justify evil and show that the course God had set for Jesus was not right. This is what Jonah was doing. So at no point is the diabolical nature of his rebellion more evident than here. In seeking to justify himself and prove God wrong by Scripture, Jonah took a place as Satan's spiritual progeny.

Ellul applies this to our own tendencies to self-justification. "This is a grave warning; it is not enough to lean on a biblical text to be right; it is not enough to adduce biblical arguments, whether theological or pietistic, to be in tune with God. All this may denote opposition to God. It may even be a way of disobeying him. The using of God's word to tempt God is a danger which threatens all Christians. Every time the Christian thinks he has God's Word in store to be used as needed, he commits this sin, which is that of Satan himself against Christ. This is the attitude of the historian who dissects Scripture to set it against

Scripture, of the theologian who uses a text to construct his doctrine or philosophy, or of the simple Christian who opens his Bible to find himself justified there, or to find arguments against non-Christians or against Christians who do not hold the same views, arguments which show how far superior my position is to that of others. It is not for nothing the Bible shows us that this attitude of Jonah is that of Satan. . . . This should stir us to great caution in the reading and use of the Bible. It is not a neutral book which one can read and then take arguments from it. It is an explosive power which must be handled with care."[1]

This does not mean that we should leave the Bible alone and not study it, of course. We avoid the danger Ellul speaks of by faithfully applying this formula: When we find ourselves reading the Bible to find verses and passages that justify our own behavior, we are wrong and are in danger; when we read the Bible and find verses that expose our sin and thereby draw us increasingly closer to God, who will forgive our sin and cleanse us from all unrighteousness, then we are on the right track and will find blessing.

Ellul writes: "What revelation teaches us about ourselves is all to the effect that we are not righteous, that we have no means of justifying ourselves, that we have no possibility of disputing with God, that we have no right to condemn others and be in the right against them, and that in this extreme distress only a gracious act of God which is external to us (though it becomes internal) can save us. This is what Scripture teaches us, and if we stick to this, reading the Bible is useful and healthy and brings forth fruit in us."[2]

Jonah did one more thing in his anger, and at that point it was almost comic: *he asked for death again.* "Now, O LORD take away my life, for it is better to me

to die than to live" (v. 3). It is hard to understand the prophet's apparent death wish. When he had run from God and God had caught up to him in the storm, he thought it would be better to die than obey. He asked the sailors to throw him overboard. Now, having obeyed, he is still unhappy and says once more that he would rather die and get it all over with. It is a warning that it is possible to obey God but to do so with such a degree of unwillingness and anger that, so far as we are concerned, the obedience is no better than disobedience.

WHAT IS WRONG, JONAH?

At this point of the story we rightly ask ourselves, "But what is wrong with Jonah?" He should have been happy; he is unhappy. He had been instrumental in the gift of spiritual life to thousands; he prefers death. He claimed to be cognizant of God's grace and mercy, which he himself had experienced; he resents God for it and says that he would have preferred wrath for Nineveh.

One thing wrong with Jonah is that he is not reconciled to the will of God even yet. He had been opposed to God's will at the beginning and had run away because of his opposition. God had pursued him and had brought him to the point of obedience. He had even experienced the marvels of a rediscovery of God's grace while in the belly of the great fish and had repented of his sin with one of the most moving and genuine prayers in all Scripture. Perhaps only David's great psalm of repentance can be said to rival it (Ps. 51). Yet, in spite of this, Jonah's attitudes had not really changed. He was still unwilling to see the people of Nineveh saved, and he resented the God of mercy for having saved them.

We often act the same, even when we are apparently obeying God. We are doing what we think we should be doing, living the kind of life we think a Christian

---

[1]Ellul, *The Judgment of Jonah,* p. 74.
[2]Ibid., p. 75.

should live. But secretly we are unhappy and angry with God for making the requirement. For this reason many Christians look and act miserable much of the time.

Second, Jonah had forgotten God's mercy to him. We object, "But how could Jonah of all people forget God's mercy? And forget it so quickly?" Jonah should have perished miserably inside the great fish. He had renounced God. It would have been only proper if God had renounced him. Yet God had showed him great mercy, first in bringing him to repentance and then in saving him and recommissioning him to preach in Nineveh.

Jonah had certainly experienced mercy at the hand of God. But there was the long journey across the desert, and man's memory is short. Jonah had forgotten God's mercy and was therefore ill-prepared to appreciate it when God showed the same mercy to others. We must remember this when we find ourselves wondering, somewhat regretfully, why God does not judge someone else for his sin. When we do that—as we all do—we are forgetting that we were once where that other person is now and that we would not be where we are now were it not for God's great mercy to us.

The third reason why Jonah was angry was that he did not know God as well as he thought he did. Undoubtedly he was proud of his knowledge of God. He was a Jew, first of all, and Jews had received an accurate revelation of God which the pagans did not possess; they had the Law and the record of God's dealings in history. Moreover, Jonah was a prophet—not just any Jew, but rather one who had studied the Law and who had been commissioned by God and given special revelations by Him. If anybody knew God, it was Jonah! But did he? He knew something of God, it is true. But he did not know God well enough to grieve over sin as God grieves over sin, or to rejoice at the repentance of the

sinner. Instead, he was like the older son of Christ's parable, who sulked while the father celebrated and felt cheated by the prodigal's return.

In our day we sometimes find ourselves wishing that the Lord Jesus Christ would return, usher in the final judgment and escort His own into heaven, and we are grieved when unbelievers scorn our belief in the Second Coming. We wish Jesus would come. We cannot understand His delay. This is because we do not understand God well enough. Peter knew people who thought like this, and he wrote an explanation to them, saying, "In the last days scoffers will come, scoffing and following their own evil desires. They will say, 'Where is this "coming" he promised? Ever since our fathers died, everything goes on as it has since the beginning of creation.' . . . But . . . , dear friends: With the Lord a day is like a thousand years, and a thousand years are like a day. The Lord is not slow in keeping his promise, as some understand slowness. He is patient with you, not wanting anyone to perish, but everyone to come to repentance" (2 Peter 3:3, 4, 8, 9).

Peter explained the delay of God's judgment by God's mercy, saying that Jesus has not yet returned in order that all whom God desires to call to faith in Him might be born, have the gospel preached to them and believe. Aren't you glad that Jesus did not return before you were born and believed in Him? Well, then, rejoice that His delay makes possible the salvation of countless others. God is a God of judgment. But He is also a God of mercy. We need to know Him as that.

THREE QUESTIONS

Jonah had not learned this, however. So God began to teach him more about His mercy, doing so by means of three significant questions that conclude the book.

God likes to ask questions because they

are effective in helping us see the state of our hearts. God asked questions of Adam and Eve: "Where are you? . . . Who told you that you were naked? Have you eaten from the tree that I commanded you not to eat from? . . . What is this you have done?" (Gen. 3:9, 11, 13). He questioned Cain after he had murdered his brother: "Where is your brother Abel? . . . What have you done?" (Gen. 4:9, 10). Saul was asked the same thing after he had foolishly intruded into the priest's office by offering sacrifices: "What have you done?" (1 Sam. 13:11). After David had sinned in committing adultery with Bathsheba and having her husband killed, Nathan came to ask him, "Why did you despise the word of the LORD by doing what is evil in his eyes?" (2 Sam. 12:9). God asked Isaiah, "Whom shall I send? And who will go for us?" (Isa. 6:8). Jesus asked Judas, "Are you betraying the Son of Man with a kiss?" (Luke 22:48).

It is the same in the Book of Jonah. God asks, "Have you any right to be angry? . . . Do you have a right to be angry about the vine? . . . Should I not be concerned about that great city?" (vv. 4, 9, 11).

What does God's first question to His sulking prophet mean? Quite simply it is a challenge to Jonah to judge whether the angry prophet or the great and holy God of the universe is right. It is as though God had said, "We are looking at the identical situation in two different ways, Jonah. I am pleased with it. You are angry. Which of us has the proper perspective?" Whenever God asks that type of question, we must recognize that, whatever our thoughts or feelings may be, it is always God who is correct and not we. "Let God be true, and every man a liar" (Rom. 3:4).

Jonah did not think like that. He did not confess his error. Instead, he became even angrier and left the city. On its outskirts he constructed a little shelter for himself, and then waited to see if God might not destroy the city after all. Suddenly God's promise to destroy Nineveh seemed very important to him.

Here he made three errors, as Ellul points out. First, he *quit*. He abandoned his mission to Nineveh even though he had no right or instruction by God to do it. Since God had sent Jonah to Nineveh to preach to the people and since, as a result of Jonah's preaching, they had repented and turned to Jehovah, Jonah should have stayed and taught them more perfectly, becoming a Calvin to Nineveh as the great protestant reformer was blessed to the city of Geneva. But Jonah was not willing to do this for the city. In the same way, many Christians today abandon the work God has given them because God does not carry through according to their expectations or their timetable. Students abandon their work when it begins to prove difficult. Parents give up on their children. Many abandon their jobs. Ministers quit the ministry. We have no right to do that.

Second, Jonah built *a little shelter for himself*, a private retreat, which again he had no right to do. Were there no shelters in Nineveh? No homes? No places where the prophet of Israel, who had been the vehicle of such great spiritual blessing, would be welcome? Of course, there were. But Jonah was not interested in these shelters. He still secretly despised the people and hoped that God would judge them. To put it starkly, Jonah launched a little separatist movement in which he established his own independent church or denomination—all because he disliked the people of Nineveh. Ellul says, "He creates his own domain in the shade where he will be at peace according to his own measure, just as Christians try to make a church according to their own measure—it is not the body of Christ—and a divine kingdom according to their own measure, full of intentions which are good and effective and well constructed, but which are only a fresh demonstration of their autonomy in relation to God."[3]

Jonah's third error was to become a *spectator*. He sat in the shadow of his shelter "to see what would happen to the city" (v. 5). He was not called to be a spectator, any more than Christians are called to be spectators of the world's ills and misfortunes today. He was called to identify with those people and help them as best he could by the grace of God.

SOMETHING FOR JONAH

Jonah had still not come around to God's way of thinking, but God had not given up on him. God had a second question. But before He asked it, He did something to prepare Jonah's heart for the message. First, He caused an unusually fast-growing vine to spring up next to Jonah's rude shelter. We are told that it became a shadow for him, that is, a protection from the blazing desert sun. We read, "Jonah was very happy about the vine" (v. 6).

This is remarkable—that Jonah was "very happy." It is the first time in the story that Jonah has been happy about anything. The first thing we read about in the story was God's commission to him to preach in Nineveh; he had not liked that. Then there was the storm; he had not liked that. He did not like the great fish, even though it had been the means of saving him from certain death. Apparently, he had not been happy even with the second commission. He had not been happy with the repentance of Nineveh. Nothing pleased him. But here at last "Jonah was very happy." Why? The answer is obvious. Jonah was pleased because at last, after all the compassion of God for other people, God was finally doing something for Jonah. Selfish? Of course, it was. And petty too! For the vine was a trifle compared with the conversion of the entire city of Nineveh.

Having caused the vine to spring up, God then did something else. He caused a worm to attack the vine so that the plant withered. And after that He caused a vehement east wind to blow from the desert that brought Jonah to the point of fainting from the terrible heat. Now Jonah became angrier than ever, and again he expressed a wish to die.

At this point God asked His second question. His first question had been, "Have you any right to be angry?" It was a question as to who was right, God or Jonah. This time God asked, "Do you have a right to be angry about the vine?" By this question God exposed Jonah's pettiness, for his anger had brought him from the grandeur of being angry at God—one who is at least a worthy opponent—to being angry at such a petty thing as a vine or worm.

The same thing happens when we become angry. We begin by being angry at big things, but quickly we become angry at petty things. First we are angry with God. Next we express our anger at circumstances, then minor circumstances. Finally, our shoelace breaks one morning, and we find ourselves swearing. God was showing this to Jonah, saying, in effect, "Look where your anger has taken you, Jonah. Is this right? Is this the way you want to live? Do you want to spend the rest of your life swearing at petty annoyances?"

At last God asked His final question, and it is with this question that the book closes. God said, "You have been concerned about this vine, though you did not tend it or make it grow. It sprang up overnight and died overnight. But Nineveh has more than a hundred and twenty thousand people who cannot tell their right hand from their left, and many cattle as well. Should I not be concerned about that great city?" (vv. 10, 11).

Jonah had been sorry for the vine. So God does not talk to him about the adult population of the city, who undoubtedly deserved the judgment Jonah was so anxious to have fall on them. God talks about the cattle, who were innocent, and the

---

[3]Ibid., p. 79.

smallest children, designated as those who could not yet discern between their right hand and their left. Was God not right to show mercy for their sake, if not for the adult population? Does not even Jonah's compassion for the vine vindicate God's judgment?

WIDENESS IN GOD'S MERCY

The book ends with a question, a question that has no written answer. This is not a mistake. It ends on a question in order that each one who reads it might ask himself or herself the same question: Is God not right? Is He not great for showing mercy?

The lessons of this book are many. There are lessons that concern Jonah himself. He is a type of practically everything: a type of Christ (who was buried but who rose again), a type of Israel, a type of all believers (for we all run away from God at times and need to be disciplined). There are lessons that concern Nineveh and the true meaning of repentance. There are lessons relating to the doctrine of God's sovereignty over men and nature.

But greater than all these lessons is the lesson of the greatness of the mercy of God. How great is God's mercy? We have a hymn that says, "There's a wideness in God's mercy, like the wideness of the sea." But even that is not wide enough. The real measure of the wideness of the mercy of God is that of the outstretched arms of the Lord Jesus Christ as He hung on the cross to die for our salvation. That is the wideness of God's mercy. That is the measure of the length to which the love of God will go.

How can we, who have known that mercy and benefited from it, be less than merciful to others? How can we do less than love them and carry the gospel to them with all the strength at our disposal?

Subject Index

Scripture Index

257